RISK AND CAPITAL ADEQUACY IN COMMERCIAL BANKS, ed. by Sherman J. Maisel. Chicago, 1981. 436p (A National Bureau of Economic Research monograph) index 81-3324. 42.00 ISBN 0-226-50281-3. CIP

The 1970s saw significant change in financial markets and the portfolio management of banks. Increased volatility of interest rates and increased competition for funds have led to more frequent losses and the increased risk of insolvency of financial institutions. This volume seeks to provide objective measures of the risks taken by a bank's management. It explores the measurement of risk associated with banks' portfolios and banks' need for a sufficient equity base to avoid insolvency. The book is divided into two approximately equal parts. The first, primarily written by Sherman Maisel, covers theories of portfolio and capital adequacy. The second part is a series of empirical studies by various experts on the measurement of risk and capital adequacy. Specific studies cover such topics as the impact of changes in interest rates on banks' profits and capital, the calculation of present values of uncertain cash flows, and the implications of the analysis for the regulation of financial institutions. This book is essential for libraries supporting graduate programs in business and/or economics. It would also be a desirable acquisition for libraries serving strong undergraduate business programs or specialized programs in finance or banking.

Risk and Capital Adequacy in Commercial Banks

A National Bureau
of Economic Research
Monograph

Risk and Capital Adequacy in Commercial Banks

Edited by **Sherman J. Maisel**

The University of Chicago Press

Chicago and London

SHERMAN J. MAISEL is professor in the School of Business Administration at the University of California, Berkeley.

The University of Chicago Press, Chicago 60637
The University of Chicago Press, Ltd., London
© 1981 by The National Bureau of Economic
Research
All rights reserved. Published 1981
Printed in the United States of America
85 84 83 82 81   5 4 3 2 1

Library of Congress Cataloging in Publication Data
Main entry under title:

Risk and capital adequacy in commercial banks.

(A National Bureau of Economic Research monograph).
Bibliography: p.
Includes indexes.
1. Bank capital—United States—Addresses, essays,
lectures. 2. Banks and banking—United States—
State supervision—Addresses, essays, lectures.
3. Risk—Addresses, essays, lectures. I. Maisel,
Sherman J., 1918–   II. Series: National
Bureau of Economic Research monograph.
HG1616.C34R57   332.1′2   81-3324
ISBN 0-226-50281-3   AACR2

Relation of the Directors to the
Work and Publications of the
National Bureau of Economic Research

1. The object of the National Bureau of Economic Research is to ascertain and to present to the public important economic facts and their interpretation in a scientific and impartial manner. The Board of Directors is charged with the reponsibility of ensuring that the work of the National Bureau is carried on in strict conformity with this object.

2. The President of the National Bureau shall submit to the Board of Directors, or to its Executive Committee, for their formal adoption all specific proposals for research to be instituted.

3. No research report shall be published by the National Bureau until the President has sent each member of the Board a notice that a manuscript is recommended for publication and that in the President's opinion it is suitable for publication in accordance with the principles of the National Bureau. Such notification will include an abstract or summary of the manuscript's content and a response form for use by those Directors who desire a copy of the manuscript for review. Each manuscript shall contain a summary drawing attention to the nature and treatment of the problem studied, the character of the data and their utilization in the report, and the main conclusions reached.

4. For each manuscript so submitted, a special committee of the Directors (including Directors Emeriti) shall be appointed by majority agreement of the President and Vice Presidents (or by the Executive Committee in case of inability to decide on the part of the President and Vice Presidents), consisting of three Directors selected as nearly as may be one from each general division of the Board. The names of the special manuscript committee shall be stated to each Director when notice of the proposed publication is submitted to him. It shall be the duty of each member of the special manuscript committee to read the manuscript. If each member of the manuscript committee signifies his approval within thirty days of the transmittal of the manuscript, the report may be published. If at the end of that period any member of the manuscript committee withholds his approval, the President shall then notify each member of the Board, requesting approval or disapproval of publication, and thirty days additional shall be granted for this purpose. The manuscript shall then not be published unless at least a majority of the entire Board who shall have voted on the proposal within the time fixed for the receipt of votes shall have approved.

5. No manuscript may be published, though approved by each member of the special manuscript committee, until forty-five days have elapsed from the transmittal of the report in manuscript form. The interval is allowed for the receipt of any memorandum of dissent or reservation, together with a brief statement of his reasons, that any member may wish to express; and such memorandum of dissent or reservation shall be published with the manuscript if he so desires. Publication does not, however, imply that each member of the Board has read the manuscript, or that either members of the Board in general or the special committee have passed on its validity in every detail.

6. Publications of the National Bureau issued for informational purposes concerning the work of the Bureau and its staff, or issued to inform the public of activities of Bureau staff, and volumes issued as a result of various conferences involving the National Bureau shall contain a specific disclaimer noting that such publication has not passed through the normal review procedures required in this resolution. The Executive Committee of the Board is charged with review of all such publications from time to time to ensure that they do not take on the character of formal research reports of the National Bureau, requiring formal Board approval.

7. Unless otherwise determined by the Board or exempted by the terms of paragraph 6, a copy of this resolution shall be printed in each National Bureau publication.
(Resolution adopted October 25, 1926, as revised through September 30, 1974)

Contents

Acknowledgments

This volume results from numerous discussions among the principal participants of this project—David Lane, Sherman Maisel, David Pyle, Barr Rosenberg, William Sharpe, and the late Paul Cootner—on the methods of applying modern theories of finance to problems of measuring risk in financial institutions. Each of us had spent considerable time and effort working on related problems. The National Bureau of Economic Research, with its long history of research on financial institutions and risk measurement, furnished a receptive environment in which to develop our ideas. The project was aided and support for research was provided by a grant to the National Bureau of Economic Research from the National Science Foundation (no. APR76-02511). The views contained in this volume do not necessarily reflect those of the National Science Foundation.

We were later joined in our efforts by Roger Craine, Larry Golen, Laurie Goodman, Robert Jacobson, J. Huston McCulloch, Jay Morrison, Stephen Nadauld, Philip Perry, and James Pierce, in discussions, in research, and in writing this volume. Significant contributions were made by a dedicated group of research assistants, including Melvin Jameson, Robert Marks, Henry Moore, and Thomas Mroz. Claire Gilchrist did an excellent job in typing many manuscripts and shepherding this volume through many preliminary versions.

We received significant aid in data, computer time, and criticism from the staffs of the Board of Governors of the Federal Reserve System; the Federal Reserve Banks of San Francisco and New York; the Comptroller of the Currency; and the Federal Deposit Insurance Corporation. Laurence Rosenberg, program officer at the National Science Foundation, was particularly helpful with sage advice at various times during the project.

We are indebted to our Advisory Committee, each of whom contributed time, effort, and useful ideas:

Dr. George T. Conklin, Jr., chairman of the board, Guardian Life Insurance Company of America, New York City

Dr. Robert Einzig, vice-president, Planning, Transamerica, San Francisco

Mr. John Heimann, Comptroller of the Currency, Washington, D.C.

Mr. Albert J. Hettinger, Jr., partner, Lazard Freres and Co., New York City

Dr. Donald Kaplan, director, Office of Economic Research Federal Home Loan Bank Board, Washington, D.C.

Dr. Henry Kaufman, partner, Salomon Brothers, New York City

Mr. Harry Keefe, president, Keefe, Bruyette and Woods, New York City

Dr. William Longbrake, director of research, Federal Deposit Insurance Corporation, Washington, D.C.

Dr. James J. O'Leary, vice-chairman, United States Trust Company of New York, New York City

Governor Charles Partee, Board of Governors of the Federal Reserve System, Washington, D.C.

Mr. Leland Prussia, vice-chairman, Bank of America, San Francisco

Mr. Carl Reichart, president, Wells Fargo Bank, San Francisco.

Mr. Charles S. Sanford, Jr., executive vice-president, Bankers Trust Company, New York City

Dr. Kenneth M. Wright, vice-president and chief economist, American Life Insurance Association, Washington, D.C.

While the project was a collaborative one, primary credit and responsibility for the work in each chapter rests with those whose names are attached to it.

1   Introduction

During the 1970s, financial markets became more volatile, more competitive, and riskier. The Depository Institutions Deregulation Act of 1980 marked a major forward step toward still greater competition. In the minds of financial managers, it greatly increased the amount of uncertainty about the future and made it harder to choose wisely among operating policies. The act was merely one more factor adding to the complexity of decisions required from both managers and regulators. Risks of failure multiplied. The march of events appeared to demand rapid improvement in the techniques of analysis if latent difficulties were to be found and removed and new ones avoided.

The studies in this volume apply modern financial analysis to problems facing banks, especially the analysis derived from the theories of portfolio risk. They utilize recent developments from other spheres in order to improve decision-making by banks and the public. Particular emphasis is placed on measurements of risk and capital adequacy.[1] With more objective evaluations and a better understanding of potential trade-offs, unnecessary risks can be avoided, other risks can be reduced, and bank capital will not be wasted.

Other issues analyzed in this volume concern the degree to which the regulatory system can be improved and controls reduced. If the price-market system is given a greater role in determining the types and amounts of loans and investments that banks can make and the liabilities they can offer, efficiency can be improved. Opportunities exist to directly reduce examination and regulatory costs. Still more important are potential steps to improve bank decisions by allowing them to follow more closely market logic and developments rather than government rules and regulations.

1. Later chapters define in specific detail the technical terms found in the Introduction.

1

Portfolio theory shows that the risk that an institution will fail depends on the relationship between its economic net worth and the volatility of its portfolio returns which depend on its assets, liabilities, commitments, and operating costs. Difficulties arise because many future movements in asset returns as well as in the costs of liabilities cannot be accurately predicted. They depend on future events, such as inflation, monetary policy, the level of interest rates, and changes in the gross national product (GNP).

Financial markets appear to be efficient in using available information to predict the expected levels of returns and of asset values. However, because of happenings that are unexpected and unplanned for, such a prediction is only one element in a broad distribution of possible outcomes. The eventual results and accompanying gains or losses depend on events outside the control of the individual institution.

The most frequent cause of losses and insolvency of financial institutions is their failure to plan adequately for events that may occur but are not expected. Banks become insolvent when, wittingly or unwittingly, they concentrate too many of their loans, investments, or activities in areas where unanticipated events are likely to cause losses that move together and may be substantial. Possibilities of high profits blind them to their portfolio risks.

This volume analyzes four major approaches that firms can take to find and reduce risks.

1. Most vital is the need to diversify assets and liabilities so that the impact of unexpected events will not be overwhelming. In several cases of large losses, banks appear to have underestimated the probability of wide interest swings. Increases in interest rates cause heavy losses in the value of portfolios that contain loans, securities, and liabilities with an average maturity that is long. But a similar lack of diversification may occur by concentrating loans within a single industry, in a particular location, in foreign markets, or by making off-balance-sheet commitments.

2. The risks from nondiversification or from unforeseen events can be measured by estimating the probability distributions of possible outcomes around those that are predicted. The larger the share of such distribution that lies far below expected outcomes, the greater the danger. Knowledge of such perils can be used by an institution to reduce the total level of its risks of losses to an acceptable level.

3. As an alternative, capital can be increased so that it is sufficient to absorb any losses likely to occur with a specific probability (see chap. 8). In fact, one definition of adequate capital is the amount required to assure that the probabilities of future insolvency are reduced below a predetermined level.

4. From the public point of view, the danger that depositors or those who lend to an institution will lose their funds when an institution fails can be eliminated by insurance. A third party can guarantee the depositors

against loss. Such insurance is provided to many depositors by the Federal Deposit Insurance Corporation (FDIC) and similar federal agencies for the savings and loan and credit union industries. Our analysis asks how these organizations can be certain that the rates they charge are "fair"; that is, that premiums cover exactly the risks of loss they assume from an institution. Of special interest is the degree to which insurers can minimize their regulatory requirements while still protecting themselves against the assumption by individual firms of undue risks at the insurer's expense.

1.1   Risks and Regulations

During the 1970s, banks assumed many more risks than they had assumed in previous decades. The increased danger becomes evident when we examine changes in bank portfolios and consider the number of large banks that failed or required assistance from the FDIC. Between 1935 and 1970, no large bank became insolvent. The largest bank to fail had assets of $40 million. After 1970, the size of banks requiring assistance grew. More than twenty banks with assets of over $50 million failed. The bail-out of First Pennsylvania Bank, with over $8.4 billion in assets, by the FDIC in April 1980 raised the total assets of banks requiring assistance to over $20 billion.

During the 1970s, attacks on the government's role in the banking industry multiplied. Greater attention was given to the possible deleterious effect of government regulations. One result of this steady pressure against government regulation of financial institutions was the Deregulation Act of 1980. It brought about fears of additional failures, especially among thrift institutions.

1.1.1   Added Risks

Several of the studies for this volume show that the degree of risk assumed by banks went up rapidly. Chapters 4, 5, and 16 all present such evidence. The ratio of loans to deposits grew even as the ratio of capital to assets fell. The percentage of risky assets climbed. Traditional measures of liquidity showed declines as liability management led to the borrowing of large sums at market interest rates for extremely short periods. By the end of 1979, the largest bank holding companies reported managed liabilities (money purchased in the short-term market) equal to more than 80 percent of earning assets. The ability to retain such funds can shift rapidly. As an example, Franklin National Bank, one of the largest to close, was forced over the brink into bankruptcy when over $2 billion of such money—60 percent of its liabilities—fled in less than four months.

Book equity capital as a percentage of total assets also fell. From a ratio of 8.1 percent in 1960, it had fallen by 1970 to 6.6 percent, and it stood at 5.7 percent in 1979 (Federal Financial Institutions Examination Council

1980). The ratio of capital to assets dropped faster and further among large banks. In 1979, the five largest bank holding companies had a ratio below 3.75 percent.

These data on capital are those reported in the traditional accounting statements of the banks. These statements fail to reflect actual changes in values. Examination of balance sheets, confirmed by the changes in value shown by movements in the price of bank stocks, reveals a much larger drop in net worth. Chapters 3 and 5 discuss measurements of bank capital. The published reports do not include the values of intangibles or losses in asset values. An independent estimate of movements in net worth can be obtained by dividing the market value of a bank's equity by the amount reported on its books. A consistent record of these market-to-book ratios is available for ninety-eight large bank holding companies on the COMPUSTAT tapes (see chap. 5).

For the three years 1971–73, these data show that the average market value of bank equity was 25 percent above that reported. The stock market apparently judged that intangible assets—such as the value of deposits, location, and information—had value beyond that shown on the books. In contrast, for the three years 1977–79, the market valued the average bank at only two-thirds of its book value. Asset values fell as a result of rising interest rates. Since these losses were not recorded, most banks showed assets at well above their true values. Book values were also overstated because they failed to account for other problems, such as a higher ratio of poor loans and the threat of more competition accompanying deregulation.

Another source of increases in risk is found in the growing proportion of bank assets held abroad and the greater share of bank earnings arising from foreign operations. In 1970, 6.5 percent of the assets of United States banks were foreign. By 1979 this ratio had risen to over 17.2 percent. The five largest bank holding companies reported that in 1979 more than half their net income came from foreign operations. In addition to increased foreign risks, most large banking companies expanded into a number of nonbanking activities, many of which carried greater dangers of losses.

1.1.2   Rules and Regulations

During the 1970s, dissatisfaction with the methods of examining and regulating financial institutions mounted. It was claimed that the existing regulatory system was partly to blame for the poor record of the economy in saving and capital investment. Financial institutions play a major role in capital formation and distribution. They assert that their efficiency, proper choice of investments, and decision-making have been seriously hampered by the arbitrary regulations over investments, expansion, and required capital imposed on them by regulators ignorant of the facts and using inadequate theories and understanding of how institutions control risks (Vojta 1973).

Existing regulations and the bank examination system attempt to control capital, liquidity, diversification, and risks while promoting sound management. However, controls are based on tradition, industry norms, and subjective evaluations. How to measure risks and what constitutes adequate capital have not been formulated in objective terms. It is unclear whether the decline in the ratio of capital to assets was due to market forces or to weaknesses in the regulatory system. In critical cases, problem banks have ignored regulatory constraints because suggestions for change could not be formulated in an enforceable manner.

Yet the need for some regulation is widely recognized. Without regulation, an undue percentage of financial institutions are likely to take excessive risks. Because of the large amount of leverage, the difficulty of depositors' policing risk levels, the high cost of information, and the number of small, uninformed depositors, an institution can profit by raising its risk ratio. Moral hazards are also high; it is hard to protect against conflicts of interest and self-dealing.

The regulations also aim at halting excessive instability in the money supply. In the past such instability led to severe contractions in jobs, production, and general economic activity. General agreement exists that decided advantages accrue to the public welfare if depositors, borrowers, and check recipients can be assured that individual financial institutions are sound (Merton 1979; Edwards and Scott 1979). Such assurance can be given in various ways, such as by requiring deposit insurance, by restricting risks assumed by the institutions to low levels, or by requiring capital adequate to absorb potential losses.

Different techniques are available to assure a proper degree of solvency and soundness. The problem is to make certain that the techniques adopted involve minimum interference in efficient operations of individual firms and financial markets as a whole. Efficient operations require improved estimates of the risks of loss and insolvency that firms assume as a result of their particular operations. There must also be better estimates of the amount of capital available to absorb these potential losses.

The introduction of federal deposit insurance was a major reform. It reduced fear among depositors, ended bank runs, and strengthened the stability of the economy. It also potentially increases competition and choice among borrowers and lenders by making entry easier. Depositors do not have to seek size to ensure the safety of their claims.

However, the existing system contains several actual and potential flaws. Because insurance premiums are fixed and flat at all levels of risk or capital adequacy, bank managers and stockholders can profit by increasing their risks at the expense of the FDIC and uninsured depositors. As a result, to curtail excessive risks, detailed regulations and examinations are necessary. Many observers believe it would be more efficient to protect the public by greater use of the market and through insurance properly priced to reflect risks rather than through regulations (Scott and Mayer 1971; Barnett 1976*b*).

Another potential danger is the ambiguous position of uninsured depositors. Those in large banks have been insured de facto, while those in small banks have suffered losses. Moreover, since protection is not a matter of law, in critical periods all banks may become suspect. Unless changes are made, the future may witness major runs, together with all the problems the deposit insurance is supposed to avoid. Even if such a point is not reached, fear may bring about concentration of funds in only a few large banks, causing critical problems for the smaller banks.

It is also claimed that the system penalizes the well-managed bank. Poor managers are protected by the umbrella of the FDIC. Only in extreme situations will the stockholders and management be forced into bankruptcy. In most cases the FDIC helps bail them out of bad decisions. Many banks have been carried for long periods by the forbearance of the FDIC. When the economy was shaken in 1973, 1974, and 1980, a number of banks, including several large ones, turned out to have assumed excessive risks. The examination process did not protect the public against poor or unscrupulous management.

1.2   The Risk of Insolvency

At the beginning of any period, a bank has a certain distribution of assets, liabilities, commitments, and operating procedures. In economic terms, it has capital and reserves equal to the difference between the market value of its assets and its liabilities. It expects to earn a certain income during the course of the year and to make payments against its liabilities. At the start of the period, its income and the amounts that will be due to others can only be estimated. Their expected values and the probability that unpredicted events will cause shortfalls from these values depend on how the firm selects its assets, on its operations, and on movements in the economy. By the end of the period, unanticipated events are likely to lead to results far different from those projected.

The risk that a bank will become insolvent depends on the level of expected income and payments from it, the probable variance of this income, and its initial capital. The bank will become insolvent if events cause its income to be so negative as to more than offset its initial capital plus any contributions less any dividends paid during the year. The amount of risk depends both on the probability of insolvency caused by negative movements in income compared with initial capital and reserves and on the amount required to make depositors, lenders, and investors whole if insolvency occurs.

Income during the year is total economic income. It is not simply net earnings as reported on the books. To net book earnings must be added capital gains or losses in asset values. The two together make up economic income or total return. Risk measurement requires consideration of the firm's economic income and economic balance sheet.

1.2.1   Changes in Values

The value of a firm at any time equals the discounted expected future cash flows from both its assets and its liabilities. This value, and therefore the firm's income, will vary from initial expectations for a variety of reasons. We can conveniently divide potential changes into those affecting the value of existing assets and liabilities, which we call wealth effects, and those occurring as a result of operations during the year, spoken of as operating or income effects.

Wealth effects are changes that result from alterations in the rates of discount applied to currently scheduled cash flows. At the beginning of a year, a bank's assets and liabilities have an expected cash flow that accords with the particular portfolio selected. This cash flow will depend on promised interest payments, operating costs, expected defaults, expectations of delayed payments, and the time profile of expected amortization and principal payments.

The economic worth of a bank depends on the rate at which the cash flow is discounted to obtain its present value. Each class of positive or negative flows is discounted at a separate rate. The particular rate applicable to each class of asset or liability depends upon:

1. The costs and expected defaults of each activity. Thus the rate of interest charged on consumer loans is far higher than that on loans to brokers because handling costs and losses are greater. Such differences are adjusted for in calculating present values.

2. The flows from some activities are less predictable than others. The uncertainty risk must be paid for by a larger discount factor.

3. Normally, discount rates are higher the further into the future is the timing of the expected flow. Such differences among periods can be measured by discount factors provided by the term structure of interest rates on default-free assets.

Between any two evaluations, the discount rates applicable to each activity can shift because of a change in the values of any of these three factors—margins between gross and net interest, uncertainty or risk premiums, and the term structure of interest rates. If discount rates rise, the wealth or present value of a portfolio falls.

Operating or income effects on the bank's value result from changes in the portfolio made during the course of a period's operations and from changes in the scheduled cash flows from the assets or liabilities or from other types of operations, such as foreign exchange trading. New or refinanced loans or investments will have different expected returns and risks than will those in the original portfolio. Depending on what is happening in the market, loan payments may be speeded up or delayed. Commitments may be taken down unexpectedly. Deposits may flow out or in. The firm may drastically alter its overhead or its type of activities. Some operating results can be anticipated, but many will be unexpected.

Some of the risks in this category are those of liquidity management, including that from disintermediation and commitments, and critical shifts in operations. If interest rates rise, the firm may experience an unexpected takedown of commitments, a failure to repay loans, a shrinking of sources of lower-cost funds. It may have to liquidate some assets, incurring transactions costs. Any of these factors can lead to a sharp change in income and total returns.

1.2.2 Net Worth

The value of a bank can shift between two periods because operations change income and outgo and also reshuffle future expected cash flows. At the same time, movements in the discount factors alter the present value of these future flows. Bank records and balance sheets often fail to record such actual changes in the values of assets and liabilities. If interest rates rise and the present value of a government bond drops from $10,000 to $9,000, the books continue to show it valued at its initial cost. In such cases, footnotes to balance sheets may show both book and market values of securities.

The shifting discounts also alter values of loans and other assets, as well as those of deposits and other liabilities and of intangibles not shown on the books. The effect of these shifts in discount rates and expected cash flows must be accounted for in calculating the bank's actual capital available to offset risks in case total returns become negative. Risks are reduced by actual net worth, not the net worth shown on the books.

1.3 The Rescue of the First Pennsylvania Bank

Chapter 5 presents a brief study of the rescue of the First Pennsylvania Corporation by an assistance package from the FDIC, aided by a group of large banks.[2] This case appears to document both the theoretical and the empirical analysis contained in this volume. Insolvency among large banks develops primarily when they assume nondiversified risks too large in comparison with their economic net worth. In this case, as in most cases, interest rate risks are most significant. I include the facts and conclusions from this case in this introduction because they illustrate so

---

2. The data and conclusions are drawn from the corporation's annual reports, not from examination or other data.

well the major points of our work. Only rarely is it possible to find, as we did in this instance, after results had been published, an example that embodies so completely all the dangers the study warned against.

The record reveals an organization that, as a result of the specific policy choices it made, began taking high risks in the early 1970s. The bank's earnings as a result of these policies were poor, but not disastrous. But, as the decade progressed, this policy of high risk-taking was not altered even as dangers grew in the economy. The amount of portfolio risk assumed by the bank continued to expand rapidly. Between December 1978 and December 1979, a time when most observers were warning against emerging dangers from possible large fluctuations in interest rates and in the economy, the bank actively increased the risk in its portfolio.

On 28 April 1980, the FDIC announced a special assistance program. It would lend $325,000,000—with no interest rate for the first year and below-market rates for the next four years—to First Pennsylvania Bank. According to the FDIC, the loan was made to prevent the bank from closing, following a finding that its continued operation was essential to provide adequate banking service in the community.

First Pennsylvania National Bank is a successor to the first private bank established in the United States in 1782. At the end of 1979, it was the twenty-third largest bank in the United States, with over $8.4 billion in assets.

1.3.1   Increasing Risks

Tables 5.5, 5.6, and 5.7 detail the steady increase in the risks assumed by First Pennsylvania Corporation between 1967 and 1979. At the start of the period, book equity equaled 8.7 percent of net earning assets. At the end, the ratio was 4.2 percent. Using stock market values for equities, the ratio was 16.6 percent in 1967 and fell to 1.6 percent by 1979.

Neither the constant fall in the ratio of net worth to assets nor regulatory pressure stopped the bank from assuming ever larger portfolio risks. The share of earning assets financed by managed (interest-sensitive) liabilities was 26 percent in 1967. It rose steadily to 74.9 percent in 1979. The bank increased its earning assets by over 400 percent during this period, while its demand and savings deposits rose about 40 percent. Less than 10 percent of its rapid growth was funded by these more stable deposits. Risks were augmented by active trading in securities and mortgages. As interest rates rose during the decade, net operating earnings before loan losses of the bank declined. At the same time, earnings became more variable.

Similar risk-taking appeared in the corporation's loan portfolio. The bank was at the upper extreme of risks among banks, as evidenced by the share of loans in its portfolio and the high gross earnings from the portfolio. Until 1973, the stock market welcomed the increased risk and high leverage; the corporation's common stock sold at unusually high multiples for its earnings and book equity. But by 1974 the risks caught up. An upward shift occurred in the level of loan losses. An especially large increase in loan loss provisions was made for 1975 and 1976, while net charge-offs expanded greatly in 1976. At the same time, higher interest rates on its liabilities plus poor performance and failures to pay some loans by borrowers led to a fall in operating earnings.

Chapters 4 and 5 show that operating and loan losses are not likely to cause insolvency unless a bank also has a low initial capital and the losses are augmented by losses from high interest rate risks. First Pennsylvania seems to confirm these results.

Our analysis shows that a prior period's net earnings after loan losses are the best predictor of the next period's expected earnings. But unexpected events will cause earnings to rise above or fall below expectations. A drop in earnings will be fatal to a firm only if the unanticipated results cause earnings negative enough to wipe out all capital and reserves as well as claims against prior taxes.

Before 1980, the largest earning declines for First Pennsylvania occurred in 1976 and 1979. In 1976, predicted net earnings (using actual loan charge-offs) were expected to be 0.55 percent of earning assets. Instead, the bank experienced negative earnings of 0.04 percent before taxes but after loan losses. Such a shortfall of 0.59 percent should be considered probable, given past variations. In 1979 the drop was from predictable earnings of 0.55 percent to an actual rate of 0.10 percent. If loan loss provisions are used instead of actual loan charge-offs, the size of unexpected changes is about the same, but the timing varies somewhat. Despite these unpredicted declines, the bank reported book earnings after tax credits of $18 million in 1975 and $16 million in 1979.

The first six months of 1980 again witnessed a shortfall from expectations. But predictable earnings after loan losses, based on the 1979 results, were only 0.10 percent of earning assets. Instead of a small earnings, the company reported losses at an annual rate of 0.80 percent. This drop of 0.90 below expectations was nearly twice that of any decline the bank had experienced in the previous decade. (The loss is probably overstated, since the bank almost certainly took the opportunity of its unusual situation to write off more loans than usual.) Even so, the data in chapter 4 show that a fall of 0.90 percent is probable under adverse economic conditions. Managers and regulators should recognize the potential volatility of earnings and plan to absorb such unpredictable swings through maintaining adequate capital. In fact, the book capital shown by the bank at the start of 1980 was over $350 million—far more than ample to absorb the reported operating loss of $30 million, but as we shall see the reported total was misleading.

1.3.2   Interest Rate Risk

The analysis in this volume indicates that the greatest danger to financial institutions arises from interest rate risks, principally borrowing short and lending long. Again, the First Pennsylvania case tends to confirm this analysis. Interest rate risk depends on the net difference in the maturity (more correctly, duration) of a bank's assets and liabilities. The longer the average maturity of the assets, the larger will be the fall in their value if interest rates rise. Effects of higher interest rates show up partly through a decline in net operating income, as payments on liabilities rise faster than income from assets. More important, however, are drops in capital values owing to the market's projection of future rates.

Table 5.7 shows a rise in the share of securities in the bank's assets between 1975 and 1979. At the same time, the average maturity of the investment portfolio nearly doubled. The bank obviously sought higher interest rate risks, probably on the assumption that it could beat the market. In 1979 the average maturity of securities held by the bank was over ten years—a period at least twice as long as the maturity of the average bank's security portfolio.

The total maturity of all assets is determined by the composition of the loan portfolio and the amount of short-term assets in addition to holdings of securities. The maturity (duration) of the assets other than securities is difficult to estimate. It depends on the maturity for which loans are written, on the frequency and the amount by which interest rates can be varied, and on the probability that borrowers will be able to meet contractual terms. Even though other assets in First Pennsylvania were worth four times as much as the investments in securities, it appears probable that the interest rate risk for all the other assets combined was less than that for the securities alone. As a rough guess, despite their much larger size, their total change in value owing to movements in interest rates may have been only 25 to 100 percent of that experienced by the investment portfolio. According to this guesstimate, the effect of a 1 percent change in interest rates on the bank's wealth would be from 1.25 to 2.0 times the effect from the portfolio of securities alone.

1.3.3   Net Worth

At the start of 1980, the book value of the bank's equity was reported as $350 million. However, a footnote to the balance sheet showed that the market value of its securities was $191 million below the amount at which they were carried on the books. If we use ratios of 1.25 and 2.00 to account for similar effects on the remainder of the portfolio, we can estimate that the published balance sheet overstated tangible assets by from $238 to $382 million. Intangibles probably would add somewhat to net worth, though how much is uncertain.

According to these calculations, actual net worth was somewhere between a negative number and $160 million. The percentage available to cover risks of losses was between a negative ratio and 2 percent of earning assets. On 31 December 1979 the stock market valued the bank's equity at $136 million.

1.3.4   Changes in the First Quarter of 1980

At the end of the first quarter of 1980, First Pennsylvania reported a loss in net earnings, after a provision for loan losses and taxes, of $5 million. In addition, it reported net losses from sales of securities of $1.4 million. Neither of these sums would amount to much if the bank had actually had the $350 million of net worth shown on its balance sheet.

However, during this period interest rates on United States government securities rose between 20 and 30 percent. Risk premiums increased, and mortgage prepayments slowed. These forces caused a further drop in the net worth of First Pennsylvania's securities portfolio of up to $150 million. The widened gap between the market and the book value of the securities portfolio alone should have been sufficient to wipe out any net worth the bank might have had at the beginning of the year.

The reaction of uninsured depositors and lenders to these developments seems slower than might have been expected. Perhaps they failed to recognize the increased danger that they would not be repaid in full. Perhaps they reasoned—correctly—that the FDIC would bail them out. In any case, starting in March, a steady withdrawal of funds held in the bank by uninsured depositors got under way. With it came a spate of rumors that the bank was in trouble. The outflow accelerated. By 23 April the bank was borrowing over $600 million from the Federal Reserve. Rather than declaring the bank insolvent, the FDIC mounted a rescue operation to allow the bank to remain in operation.

In this example, the bank assumed substantial portfolio risks out of proportion to its economic capital. Although the interest rate movements that occurred were large, they were not improbable in view of interest rate history. Given a situation of inadequate capital, economic events— not unexpectedly—brought about a need for the FDIC rescue.

1.4   What Can Be Learned?

This volume presents theories that explain how risks arise and how they are measured. The theories are based on simplifying assumptions. When institutions and markets are examined, coincidence between facts and many of the assumptions is good. Still, care must be exercised in applying the results. Adjustments may lag. Significant variables may be omitted. Information and transaction costs may be high. Existing regulations are important in shaping what happens. However, despite these problems, the approach and the empirical data of this volume do serve to increase greatly our knowledge of the measurement of capital adequacy. The techniques developed are capable of further development and refinement.

One may hope that improved applications of modern theories and better analysis of risk and capital can serve multiple purposes. Of primary importance is better decision-making within banks. Capital is scarce and should be used where needed. Although banks have specialized for centuries in the analysis of risk, current developments constantly raise new questions. The concept of what a bank is and does continually changes.

Our large banks are no longer local institutions specializing in loans to business. The scope of their activities has expanded in all dimensions. Thus markets are regional, national, and international. With bank holding companies and Edge Act corporations, their geographical and industrial range expands. Competition increases from other institutions and from other markets. Liabilities are no longer accepted passively or merely as a result of marketing programs. They are actively bought and managed. Interest rates fluctuate through far wider ranges. Old established corporations such as Penn Central or W. T. Grant become insolvent. New industries such as real estate investment trusts appear like a wave of the future but lead, instead, to serious losses for the banks. Large brokerage firms fail. Foreign governments collapse under economic strain or revolution.

Traditional concepts of both credit and liquidity risks require reexamination. The role of capital and its measurement become more critical as the amount available in banks falls. Many bankers welcome the idea of leaving behind the security of diminished competition within a wall of government regulations. Others are comfortable in what they are doing. They fear change even though it may be inevitable.

The analysis in this volume builds a better base for understanding what is happening and where it may lead. It attempts to throw light on why risks occur; how the danger to banks can be reduced; and how managers and owners can better measure the risks they are accepting so that they can be properly weighed against potential gains.

Just as important as better firm decisions is knowledge of how to improve our regulatory system. While some regulation is necessary, critical questions arise as to how much and of what type. Our current system is complex and expensive. The major costs are not those found in the budgets of the regulatory agencies, but rather the costs to the economy as a whole.

There are clear indications that existing regulations reduce productivity and raise the costs of borrowing and lending. Many feel that regulations are a dead hand that constrains the efficient operations both of banks and our total financial system.

Some costs seem obvious. Competition is reduced. The wastes of nonprice competition proliferate. The distribution of income from intermediation is not in accordance with market forces. The hidden costs may be even more important. How far are day-to-day decisions of bankers warped by a failure of regulations and the examination process to stay abreast of current developments? Is there any reason to believe that regulations can keep up? The general philosophy of our economy holds that gains and losses are necessary to keep managements alert and abreast of events. Lacking the discipline or information of the market, regulators will always lag behind in knowledge of what is happening. Such lags can be costly. They can also lead to evasion or to elaborate efforts by banks to reshape operations around the constraints of the regulations.

If one grants that regulatory agencies serve a necessary function, then we must strive to improve their operations. How can recent theoretical developments aid their decision-making? Are we at a point where the amount of detailed controls can be reduced? Even if there is no major alteration in techniques, a better understanding of risk and capital can reduce the fear of disaster, which is the primary justification for many existing regulatory features. Those who support existing restrictions rarely compare costs and benefits.

A major difficulty with existing regulations is that they are primarily subjective. In important cases, the regulations do not work. They depend upon banks' agreeing with the judgment of the regulators. Because decisions are subjective, they are extremely difficult to enforce in court. Even with increased powers from the right to issue cease and desist orders, banks that choose to be obdurate can hold off corrective actions until it is too late.

One of the purposes of these studies is to introduce more objective standards. They show that risk can be measured and, within limits, priced. Systems can be established with clearer rules, understandable to all. While advantageous, it is not necessary that measurements be exact. The reduction of uncertainty and an increased ability to base judgments on a firmer foundation can lead to decided improvements.

1.4.1   The Need to Prepare for the Unpredictable

Traditional management and examination processes properly emphasize risks from lack of liquidity, credit, and diversification. They examine capital, growth, and management. Studies for early warning systems designed to identify banks likely to fail, as well as the studies made for this book, confirm that these are critical variables. What has usually not been as clear is the magnitude of specific dangers and the cost of corrective actions.

There seems to be too much emphasis on retrospective concepts. Dangers to banks are less likely to arise from known types of dangers. While some bankers may be ignorant or stupid, clearly the vast majority are not. Regulations should be shaped so as to optimize the behavior of the great bulk of the industry, not to make the many suffer for the mistakes of the few.

On the whole, anticipated risks carry market premiums. Banks can choose higher-risk investments and expect to be paid for their choice. Over a period, however, they will not make large or unusual gains from selecting known high-risk investments. The market as a whole can bear risks well and therefore pays premiums primarily for nondiversifiable risks. Profits will not increase simply because more risks are taken. At the opposite extreme, faulty choice of activities or inept management may bring about losses. Revenues from poorly selected operations will fall below expenses. Such losses show up as low overall earnings, as a decrease in actual capital, and as a low level of expected net worth. If they are not corrected, insolvency will follow.

Major dangers to banks are more likely to arise from unanticipated changes. Movements of interest rates, of reserves, of output, and of international events cause vast swings around expected returns. It is the knowledge that these swings will occur and will at times be large that forms the key to avoiding bankruptcy. The emphasis on examinations and expected defaults in categories of loans is useful for pricing and in planning for small portfolios, but too often the danger of macroevents has been neglected. As in the case of the First Pennsylvania, too high a risk from unpredictable movements has been accepted.

To measure the dangers of unpredictable events, we need to estimate the probable distribution of returns about their expected value. Later chapters discuss the difficulties of such measurements. They also present examples of how such estimates can be made, as well as giving orders of magnitude for various risks.

The danger of insolvency for portfolios with specific volatilities can be reduced to a given level by the inclusion of adequate capital. The discussion that follows shows the relationship between volatility, net worth, and risks. It demonstrates how these relationships can be measured. One particular measure is the insurance premium, fair to both the insurer and the insured, needed to cover portfolios containing specific levels of volatility and capital.

A key point that emerges is that the probability distributions for unpredictable events can be estimated. When a bank selects its assets, liabilities, commitments, and operations, it determines both the level of expected returns and the chances that losses will occur. It cannot know with certainty what results will be achieved, but it can minimize its probability of bankruptcy by making sure that the risks it assumes do not exceed the capacity of its economic capital to absorb possible losses.

1.5   The Structure of This Volume

This book is divided into two parts that are distinct in content and exposition. Part 1, consisting of chapters 2 through 7, summarizes the bulk of the study of capital adequacy. These chapters explain the theory and measurement of capital adequacy. They show how the risks of insolvency can be calculated, and they discuss measures of portfolio variances and net worth. They give some general background on capital in the regulatory process and suggest how the deposit insurance process might improve its use of market information.

Part 1 generalizes and draws upon the detailed studies contained in part 2 as well as upon a number of other studies conducted as part of the overall project. It discusses results in a less technical manner, to make knowledge of capital adequacy available to a wider readership.

Part 2 consists of some of the special studies performed for the project. They were sponsored by the National Bureau of Economic Research and funded by the National Science Foundation. These studies contain material at different levels of technical difficulty. They are included because they break important new ground in the development of the theory of capital adequacy and the measurement of portfolio risks in financial institutions.

I   The Theory and Measurement of Risk and Capital Adequacy

2 Insolvency and Capital Adequacy

2.1 Introduction

In most industries, the amount of capital deemed adequate for a firm is found to vary widely depending upon the type of firm and the attitudes of its owners and creditors toward risk. Among banks, in contrast, capital adequacy can be defined more rigorously. The amount of capital needed hinges upon what risks of insolvency are considered suitable for the economy. Such hazards, in turn, depend upon the combination of assets, liabilities, and capital in a bank's portfolio. Determining capital adequacy requires evaluating the risks of insolvency that result from particular portfolio choices. The amount of risk in a set of assets and liabilities, as well as the true or economic value of capital, must be measured.

The contrast between banks and other firms is inherent in the nature of their functions. Most firms deal with a limited number of suppliers of funds who tend to be sophisticated and, in addition, can impose restrictions on the firm's borrowing and operations to protect their funds. Banks, on the other hand, deal with numerous depositors and creditors. Most customers have no choice except to hold the bank's liabilities as long as they need deposit services. To perform their primary function, banks must offer deposit contracts that contain a minimum hazard of default. The efficiency of deposit contracts declines as their default risk rises (Merton 1979).

Default risks cause a loss in efficiency because they increase information and transaction costs and threaten the reliability of the payments system. The costs when a default-free deposit is accepted are minimal. In contrast, if risk of default exists, time and effort must be spent in assessing the probabilities of default and of the losses that would result.

This chapter was prepared by Laurie Goodman of the staff of the Federal Reserve Bank of New York before she joined the Reserve Bank.

This chapter defines and explains the forces that cause capital to be adequate or inadequate in banks. These depend upon the amount of a bank's capital compared with the risks it assumes when it selects its portfolio of activities. The discussion shows that risks arise because of the probability that a bank will have a negative real income large enough to wipe out all its capital and make it insolvent. For each period, a bank expects to earn a particular amount of real income that includes its net earnings plus changes in the net value of its assets and liabilities. Because the future will differ from expectations, however, only a small likelihood exists that this exact income will result.

When a bank selects its portfolio of assets, liabilities, and other commitments, it chooses both the level of income expected at the end of the period and the shape of the distribution of possible outcomes around this expected amount. The distributions depend upon how the income of the portfolio of activities will vary with economic events that have some possibility of occurring. This chapter discusses the forces that determine both the level of the expected returns and the shapes of the distributions around such expectations. In addition it outlines some of the factors that must be examined in determining the true (economic) capital of an institution.

2.1.1   Adequate Capital

Capital is adequate either when it reduces the chances of future insolvency of an institution to some predetermined minimum level or, alternatively, when the premium paid by the bank to an insurer is "fair"; that is, when it fully covers the risks borne by the insurer. Such risks, in turn, depend upon the risk in the portfolio selected by the bank, on its capital, and on the terms of the insurance with respect to when insolvency will be determined and what losses will be paid. The first paper in part 2, by W. F. Sharpe, discusses some of the technical problems in measuring adequate capital.

A correct measure of the risks of insolvency is extremely important to a bank's managers, shareholders, and uninsured creditors, as well as to the insuring authorities. At the time of insolvency, there is a major restructuring of the rights of the claimants against the firm. In insolvency, the economic value of the firm is considerably reduced because of bankruptcy and related costs. Such costs can be large because of high legal fees and heavy transaction and liquidation charges.

Losses in value arise because prospective buyers of the firm or its assets have inadequate information as to the value of the assets compared with that available to its managers. Loans whose value depends upon prior knowledge of the borrower often can be sold only at discounts. Other assets such as local municipal bonds also have narrow markets and therefore potentially large transaction costs for a sale. If the bank actually goes out of existence, other losses from loss of information based on past relationships occur to borrowers, to employees, and even to depositors, who will have to build up new connections.

2.1.2   Risks in Portfolios

Portfolio theory supplies the necessary tools for measuring the risks of insolvency. A bank selects a portfolio consisting of a variety of individual activities with respect to assets, liabilities, commitments, non-balance-sheet operations, and net worth (capital and reserves). Activities include such aggregates as consumer loans, government bonds with a particular maturity, lending and borrowing of federal funds, foreign exchange trading, and similar operations. The functions that combine into an aggregate activity depend upon both empirical and analytical concepts.

The risk of insolvency is a function of the current economic value of the bank's capital—that is, the present value of the expected cash flows from the firm's portfolio—and the probabilities that either the expected cash flow or the discount rate at which the flow is valued will alter. The existing capital and activities and the expected changes in them give an expected end-of-period net worth. However, expectations are unlikely to be realized exactly. Because of economic events, total income (including changes in capital values) will exceed or fall short of expected levels (Markowitz 1971; Sharpe 1964; Lintner 1965b; Mossin 1966; Merton 1974, 1977a).

Measuring the risk of a portfolio requires calculation of its expected end-of-period net worth and of the probable distribution of possible net worth values around this level. The bank will become insolvent if events cause its income to be so negative as to more than offset its initial capital plus any contributions less any dividends paid during the period. Risk depends on both the probability of insolvency and the expected losses in case of such failure.

2.1.3   Insolvency

For purposes of measuring adequate capital, a bank may be considered *insolvent* either when its liquidity is so low that it cannot pay its debts (i.e., a negative cash flow cannot be met); or when the market value of its assets reduced by the costs of bankruptcy is less than the value of its liabilities to its customers, computed under the assumption that all such obligations will be met fully.

It is difficult to determine whether a firm meeting its cash demands is insolvent. Examining current book values is not an adequate test. Large investment or loan losses reflecting higher market interest rates may not show up on the books. As the Sharpe study shows, there may also be unrecorded implicit claims against the FDIC insurance fund.

On the other hand, one cannot simply correct the book values by marking loans and investments to market and writing off losses. The balance sheet fails to show significant intangible assets. The accrued information in an ongoing firm as well as its oligopoly position may be worth a good deal. These types of assets are traded and bring considerable returns in the market. Also, balance sheets frequently do not show future commitments such as those to make commercial and industrial loans, those to lend to financial institutions, those to make real estate loans, standby letters of credit, and foreign exchange contracts. The unwinding of these commitments may bring about gains and losses. These too must be evaluated in determining whether the firm is actually solvent.

The actual determination of insolvency is not simple. An accurate determination requires calculation of the present value of the firm based on discounting all future cash flows. There must also be an estimate of whether in future periods the firm will be able to meet projected cash demands. When they are discounted to determine present values, the future cash flows must be corrected for their risks and uncertainty. If the firm's liabilities plus bankruptcy costs exceed its assets, it is insolvent. However, under existing procedures, this may not lead to an actual declaration of insolvency. Regulators are likely to delay bankruptcy procedures beyond insolvency's economic occurrence. In a desire to be fair to the stockholders and borrowers, and to avoid political recriminations, regulators close banks only with the greatest reluctance.

2.1.4   Book versus Economic Capital

In determining a bank's insolvency it is sensible for regulators to differentiate between its economic or actual ongoing value and the amount it would be worth in liquidation. At times, however, such a policy leads to overemphasis on book and underemphasis on actual market values. There is a failure to recognize that market values reflect expected earnings while book values overstate or understate real net worth.

When interest rates rise and market values fall, no capital loss need be shown if the security is held to maturity. But this is purely an accounting convention. A real loss has occurred. The loss is reflected in the lower income earned during a holding period compared with the return on a similar investment at market prices. When regulators base decisions on book rather than economic capital, they are not using significant information available about expected earnings.

Too frequently, individuals assume that high interest rates will fall to some lower or past average rate. They are betting against the collective view of the market. Such implicit forecasts can be dangerous. If a majority of experts believed rates would fall, this would be reflected in market rates. Many institutions lost large sums in the mid-1960s by assuming that rates would return to lower levels. While they could avoid showing book losses by not engaging in capital transactions, such action did not protect them against losses through reduced income.

2.1.5 A Delay in Determining Insolvency

Because judging the value of expected future cash flows is so difficult, a great deal of discretion as to when to declare a bank insolvent has been left to the regulatory authorities. Legally, under title 12 of the United States Code, section 191, the Comptroller of the Currency may put a national bank into receivership whenever he or she becomes "satisfied of the insolvency" of that bank. Generally, state banking authorities have the same power for banks under their jurisdiction. Nowhere in the law is *insolvency* defined, and the Federal Bankruptcy Act does not apply to banks.

Courts have criticized this clause as giving too much power to the Comptroller of the Currency, but they have generally upheld it. Their rationale is that (*a*) it is a specific grant of power from Congress, and the wording of 12 USCA §191 is unambiguous, and that (*b*) the Comptroller will be able to act more quickly than a court. Legal precedent indicates that the shareholders and creditors together cannot challenge the Comptroller's decision. The bank may directly challenge the decision only on the grounds of error of law, fraud, or mistake. The court system has never reversed the Comptroller's actions.

It is important to realize that it may not always be optimal in a cost-efficient sense for the Comptroller of the Currency to declare a bank insolvent even when it is. If there are no real bankruptcy costs, it is clear that insolvency should be forced at the point where the bank cannot, in the long run, meet its obligations. If there are real bankruptcy costs, some system of transfers between shareholders, uninsured depositors, and the regulatory agencies may be possible so that the costs can be avoided, leaving everyone better off. This type of transfer may be prohibitively costly to negotiate. Moreover, if a declaration is delayed when a bank is insolvent, the uninsured depositors may take their money out, leaving the entire loss to the FDIC. If bankruptcy is not forced, the shareholders also have an incentive to reorganize their assets so as to maximize the value of their capital at the expense of the FDIC. While such costs would usually be larger to the FDIC than incurring the initial bankruptcy costs, no simple relationship exists. It depends upon the transactions costs of negotiations, bankruptcy costs, and monitoring costs.

2.2 A Model of the Risks of Insolvency

The probability that a bank will become insolvent in any period depends upon the volatility of the value of its assets, liabilities, and operating costs, on its ability to retain deposits or credit, and on the amount of capital it starts with plus what it retains or obtains from its owners. Banks choose particular assets and liabilities. As a result, the institution's expected value depends on how its portfolio will react to future events, and on the likelihood that a particular combination of events will occur (Dothan and Williams 1980). Values will alter with changes in interest rates, the gross national product, the money supply, and similar factors.

2.2.1   The Distribution of Returns

Figure 2.1 diagrams a model of the risk of insolvency. The bank's assets have a present value of A_0 and liabilities of L_0. Its net worth is $A_0 - L_0 = C_0$. This capital value, C_0, is shown in the diagram. At the end of a period, depending on its current choices and forecast events, the bank is expected to have a new expected value, shown as $\tilde{C}_1$. (Values or returns whose outcome depend upon future events are shown with a tilde [~].)

The difference between C_0 and $\tilde{C}_1$ is the expected return, $\tilde{R}_z$, adjusted to account for expected dividends or capital contributions. Between the present and the next evaluation, however, events are likely to cause unanticipated changes in the value of the bank's activities. The total expected return as well as the probable distribution of the actual return around the expected value depends on the choice of activities and on such factors as projected income, payments on liabilities, operating costs, loan losses, and changes in interest rates.

In figure 2.1 the curve illustrated is the distribution function of $\tilde{R}_z$ centered on the expected end-of-period net worth. To the left of the zero point in the diagram, net worth is negative, and the bank is insolvent. The solid area under the curve indicates the probability of insolvency. To determine risk requires measuring the bank's initial net worth (C_0); the expected return in the period $(\tilde{R}_z)$; and the probability distribution or variance of the expected return [var $(\tilde{R}_z)$] (assuming a roughly normal distribution).

The probability of insolvency will depend on the amount of capital, C_0, and on the choice of assets and liabilities, as well as on dividend policy. These together determine both the expected return in the period $\tilde{R}_z$ and its probability distribution. McCulloch shows in his study examples of how such distribution functions can be estimated for particular activities. He also discusses in detail the importance for such estimates of the assumptions about the underlying process that determines the probable distribution of activities, the time between the estimates, and the correla-

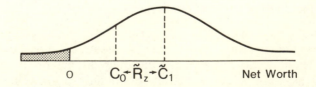

$$C_0 \cdot \tilde{R}_z \cdot \tilde{C}_1$$

0   Net Worth

Fig. 2.1   Model of expectation and variance of net worth.

tion among movements of the individual assets and liabilities. McCulloch also demonstrates the wide dispersion of potential risks that result from different choices of portfolios, including initial capital.

2.3   The Chances of Insolvency

A bank at any time chooses a particular distribution of assets, liabilities, commitments, and operating procedures. It has capital and reserves equal to the difference between the market value of its assets and its liabilities, which, in turn, depend upon how the market forecasts and values expected movements in the economy. By the end of the period, unanticipated events are likely to lead to results far different from those projected. The paper by Craine and Pierce (chap. 12) analyzes some of the factors involved, particularly in anticipations of interest rates.

It must be noted that the amount of hazard arising from a portfolio choice depends both on the probability of insolvency caused by negative movements in income compared with initial capital and reserves, and on the amount required to make depositors, lenders, and insurers whole if insolvency occurs. Total income is not net earnings as reported on the books. To net book earnings must be added capital gains or losses in asset values. The two together make up economic income or total return. Risk measurement requires consideration of the firm's economic income and its economic balance sheet.

2.3.1   Past and Future Conditions

For purposes of analysis, it may be useful to differentiate banks vulnerable to risks that arise from weaknesses evident in the current environment from those that incur risks because they have assembled portfolios vulnerable to possible untoward events (Flannery and Guttentag 1979).

When evaluated, some banks are found to be risky because of past results or management decisions. Losses in book capital may be evident. The trend of earnings may be down. The ability to obtain funds to pay off depositors or lenders may be low. The management's ability to make proper operating choices may be questionable.

On the basis of past performance, other banks may appear far less hazardous. Their earnings trend may be strong. They may have a low record of loan losses. But they may be extremely vulnerable to possible future movements in the economic environment. Changes in interest rates may cause a drastic fall in the value of their assets. Sudden increases in takedowns against existing commitments may occur. There may be failures to repay loans and a sharp decrease in lower-cost sources of funds. Losses may arise from an overconcentration in regional, foreign, or specific industry loans. The firm may have to liquidate some assets, thereby incurring high transactions costs. The history of First Pennsylvania Corporation shows an accumulation of losses from many events of this nature.

In their study of the bank examination process, Flannery and Guttentag (1979) note that most of the emphasis in existing procedures aims at finding banks that are problems because they have not adjusted well to the existing environment. They note that only a minimal effort has been made to measure risks of events that are possible but not forecast. Most discussions and texts on bank management and lending also neglect estimates of risks from unexpected events.

In contrast, this study emphasizes the need to consider the wide range of possible future events in measuring capital adequacy. Risks arise because the expected values of assets change and because alterations in cash flows require either raising funds at costs higher than returns on the existing portfolio or else liquidating assets at values below their book.

2.3.2   Movements in Portfolio Values

Markowitz (1971) has shown that probable changes in or the "risk" of a combination (or "portfolio") of assets and liabilities is a function of the risks of the individual elements, their importance in the combination, and the relationships among them. The capital asset pricing model (CAPM), based on the work of Sharpe (1964), Lintner (1965b), and Mossin (1966), offers an explicit expression for a bank's value.

The present value of a bank depends on expected cash flows, on risk-free interest rates, on the return on the market portfolio, and on the market price of risk. The book or face value of each activity can be translated into economic value by a three-step process:

1. The promised gross return must be equated to an expected net flow by correcting for operating expenses and nonperformance, including a provision for loss.

2. Net flows are transformed to certainty equivalents (risk-free returns) depending on the variance and covariance of the expected returns with the market and on the rate of exchange between returns and risk.

3. Each certainty equivalent return can be discounted to present values by the risk-free rate of interest for each future income period. The discount rates vary with the time to maturity of the risk-free flow from the asset.

Changes in any of these items will cause the total return to differ from that originally expected. Predictions of risk require estimating possible changes in operating expenses and losses, to obtain an estimate of net yields; the market's discount for risk; and the risk-free interest rate.

For example, a mortgage may carry a face interest rate of 11 percent. The estimated risk-free return will be the 11 percent less allowances for each of these factors. Compared with government bonds, mortgages will have larger expenses and losses. The mortgage returns must be further discounted because they vary more than returns on risk-free securities. Finally, the value of their expected yield is reduced because risk-free long-term yields are higher and vary more than do short-term ones. On the average, these three forces may reduce the expected rate of return on a mortgage with a face yield of 11 percent by 250 basis points, or to 8.5 percent. The factors causing these reductions of promised returns compared with actual returns vary over time. Experience shows that, as a result, the average rate at which expected future mortgage cash flows are discounted will vary so that the 250 basis point reduction is merely the center of a range between 150 and 350 basis points. The expected return of an 11 percent mortgage over time has ranged from 7.50 percent to 9.5 percent around the average expected return of 8.5 percent.

In any period, the yield from an activity is its net cash flow plus the change in its capital value between the start and the end of the period. Changes in capital values, in turn, depend on how the discount factors move. Thus, in recent years, actual returns on mortgages have been as low as −3 percent, while in others they have been as high as 13 percent. The risk of an activity depends on the expected variance of such returns. [var (r)].

In examining the hazards to a bank, it is necessary to estimate the risks of the individual assets and liabilities it picks. However, these risks do not simply cumulate. To estimate the total hazard and adequacy of capital, the action of the overall portfolio must also be analyzed.

2.4   Changes in the Returns of Individual Assets

This section describes a simple mathematical model for measuring the expected returns and volatilities of individual assets and liabilities. For purposes of analysis, they can be grouped into a limited number of activities i (K activities, with assets numbered $1 \ldots J$ and liabilities $J + 1 \ldots K$). The expected return and variance for the bank depend upon the weights of the individual activities in the portfolio, their expected returns, and their variances and covariances. Because of the importance of interest rate risk, assets and liabilities, in addition to being grouped by type, must also be grouped by their expected cash flow in each year. As an example, McCulloch shows in his paper (chap. 10) differing risks for three separate securities, each with the same maturity but with different forms of cash flows.

2.4.1   The Value of an Activity

The value (positive or negative) of an activity equals its discounted risk-free equivalent cash flow. First, expected cash flows must be estimated. These are promised returns less corrections for normal expenses, delays, or defaults. The paper by Maisel and Jacobson (chap. 9), for example, shows gross book returns of 10.5 percent on consumer loans and 8.5 percent on commercial loans in the early 1970s. The respective net returns were 5.5 percent and 5.7 percent. Expected cash flows are projections of such net returns. Second, to find present values, these cash flows must be transformed into certainty equivalences ($\tilde{F}_{it}$) of risk-free cash flows that must be discounted at the risk-free interest rate ($\tilde{r}_{ft}$). Even though gross and net returns differ, the present value of commercial and consumer loans might be equal when they are corrected to certainty equivalences. The papers by Morrison and Pyle (chap. 13) and by Nadauld (chap. 14) develop in detail models and forecasting procedures for both $\tilde{r}_{ft}$, the risk-free interest rate, and $\tilde{F}_{it}$, certainty equivalent cash flows (cf. also Lanstein and Sharpe 1978; Boquist, Racette, and Schlarbaum 1975).

2.4.2   Certain Equivalent Cash Flows

As noted, to find the certainty equivalence of the cash flow from each of the bank's i activities requires estimating the gross, net, and certainty equivalent flows. The expected net cash flow from each activity will be volatile. The greater the variance of its returns, the less desirable will be the asset. This negative factor or risk must be paid for. In comparison with one that is risk-free, a risky asset must accrue net income beyond the risk-free return. The existence of both expected losses and expenses plus possible variances account for the larger promised gross returns on non-risk-free assets. The amount of such needed additional income increases the rate at which the flow from the asset is discounted. When the expected actual cash flows have been corrected to certainty equivalences, their market values in future years are labeled as $\tilde{F}_{i1} \dots \tilde{F}_{iT}$ for the years $1 \dots T$.

2.4.3   Discounting by the Risk-Free Rate

When these certainty equivalent market values have been estimated for an activity i, its present value c is found by discounting by the marketwide discount factors $\tilde{q}_i \dots \tilde{q}_T$ that are expected to prevail in each particular future year and the present values summed. Thus:

$$(1) \qquad c_i = \tilde{q}_i \tilde{F}_{i1} + \tilde{q}_2 \tilde{F}_{i2} + \dots + \tilde{q}_T \tilde{F}_{iT},$$

where $\tilde{q}_t = 1/(1 + \tilde{r}f_t)$ and $\tilde{r}f_t$ is the risk-free rate of return between periods O and t. For example, the expected return on an activity in the first period $\tilde{r}_{i1}$ equals the discounted expected cash flow $\tilde{q}_1 \tilde{F}_{i1}$.

2.4.4   Changes in Discounts, Cash Flows, and Certainty Equivalences

The returns in a period can differ from expectations in at least three ways. Events in the economy and in the firm will alter discount rates, shift expected cash flows, and change the market value of risks. The actual return for any holding period will be:

(2) $$\tilde{r}_{it} = m_{it} + \tilde{c}_{i,t+1} - c_{it},$$

where m_{it} is the cash flow actually received in the period and the total return includes this cash flow plus the changes in value of the activity during the period. The risk in an activity [$\text{var}(\tilde{r}_{it})$] depends upon the way this total return may vary with events.

Changes in value depend upon movements in future risk-free interest rates and the expected cash flows during the period. To simplify presentations, it is common to assume that the cash flow received during the period is reinvested. Thus the value of an activity at the end of the first period will be:

(3) $$c^*_i = q^*_1 F_{i1}{}^* + \tilde{q}^*_2 \tilde{F}_{i2}{}^* + \ldots + \tilde{q}^*_T \tilde{F}_{iT}{}^*,$$

with the asterisks denoting values at the end of the period.

The actual holding period return then on activity i will be:

$$r_i = \frac{c^*_i}{c_i} - 1.$$

This holding period return is the weighted average of the changes in the return for each of the future periods over which there is an expected cash flow. As noted, it depends upon interest earned or paid during the period, the change of the discount rates applicable to each future period, and the changes in the certainty equivalent cash flows.

2.5 Changes in the Bank's Value

The expected change in a bank's value and its risk or probability distribution [$\text{var}(\tilde{R}_z)$] is a function of the activities the bank picks for its portfolio, of the interrelationships or covariances among the individual activities, and of the distribution of probable future states for the economy and the bank, the so-called events.

Each class of activities i has a share (X_i) in the total portfolio (V_0) of the bank. X_i depends upon the total portfolio and is calculated from $X_i = V_i / \sum_{i=1}^{K} V_i$, where V_i is the positive or negative market value of activity i.

2.5.1   The Covariance Matrix

As just noted, to handle risks most efficiently, one should consider the cash flow from each class of activities in each period. We thus think in terms of a vector Y_z that contains the relative share of the expected annual cash flows from each activity in the bank. This is simply the share of each activity's future payments in the bank's present value.[1]

---

1. Note Y_{it} is the proportion of activity i's present value attributed to the payments expected in year t. Then the vector Y_z is: $[X_1 Y_{11}, X_1 Y_{12} \ldots X_1 Y_{1T}, X_2 Y_{21} \ldots X_2 Y_{2T}, \ldots, X_K Y_{K1} \ldots X_K Y_{KT}, 0 \ldots 0]$.

We define a covariance matrix

$$D = \text{cov}(r_{it}, r_{j\tau}).$$

Most of this volume is concerned with the theory and empirical estimations of particular covariance (D) matrixes of returns. The theory is general and explains the movements of returns related to all possible events. In the empirical work, we have primarily attempted to estimate the risks for banks of different activities related to unexpected movements in interest rates, commitments, deposits, defaults, and operating expenses.

The total expected variance in the bank's return given the covariance matrix is

$$(4) \qquad \text{var}(\bar{R}_z) = Y_z D Y_z'.$$

In thinking about the factors causing a bank's expected variance and risk, a useful background is the extensive literature based on portfolio theory and the capital asset pricing model (CAPM). The study by Rosenberg and Perry (chap. 16) explains and analyzes the relationships in this model.

It is common usage in this literature to analyze these risks under three headings. Market risks (also called systematic risks) are those movements of the firm's returns that are correlated with movements of returns for the market portfolio—a combination of all securities, each in proportion to market value outstanding. Some of the bank's activities such as defaults, shifts in operating expenses, and changes in the overall price of risk are likely to react to the same events that cause movements in the value of the market portfolio. Depending on the particular set of activities the bank has chosen, the reaction of the bank's returns to these events may be greater or smaller than those of the market as a whole.

In addition, however, because it may react in a unique manner to such factors as interest rates, foreign exchanges, localized depressions, or overexpansion in the real estate market, the bank's returns may move quite differently from those of the market. Such nonmarket returns may be further subdivided into factors likely to cause banks as a group to move more or less together—called extramarket covariance—and specific risk unique to the individual bank.

2.5.2 Market Risk or Beta

These concepts can be illustrated by showing the relationship between the bank and the market given the generalized covariance matrix of returns. Let Y_m represent the vector of activities in the market portfolio equivalent to Y_z for the bank. Then the variance of the market portfolio is

$$(5) \qquad \text{var}(\bar{R}_m) = Y_m D Y_m'$$

and the covariance of the bank's expected returns with the market is

(6) $$\text{cov}(\tilde{R}_z, \tilde{R}_m) = Y_z DY_m'.$$

Beta, or the sensitivity of the bank's return to movements in the market portfolio, is

(7) $$B_z = \frac{Y_z DY_m'}{Y_m DY_m'}.$$

This is the covariance of the bank's returns with the market divided by the variance of the market's returns. This responsiveness of the bank's returns to the market depends upon the relationship between the movements in the bank's activities and the movements in the returns on the market portfolio. The responsiveness is a weighted average of the responsiveness of the individual activities engaged in by the bank.

2.5.3   Nonmarket Risks

The nonmarket risk is designated $\text{var}(R_\epsilon)$. It is uncorrelated with the market component of risk. The two together equal the total risk or variance of the bank. Thus

(8) $$\text{var}(\tilde{R}_z) = \text{var}(B_z \tilde{R}_m) + \text{var}(\tilde{R}_\epsilon)$$

or

(8a) $$\text{var}(\tilde{R}_z) = B_z^2 \text{ var } \tilde{R}_m + \text{var}(\tilde{R}_\epsilon).$$

The total risk of a bank can be analyzed in terms of its market and nonmarket risk. Moreover, the larger the bank's responsiveness to the market (B_z), the greater will be the impact on it of changes that affect the value of securities as a whole. Conversely, the larger the share of nonmarket risks, the less will its returns respond to movements that affect the market.

This share is important because the CAPM indicates that in an efficient market investors will pay for and receive higher returns than the market average only for assets that bear increased systematic market risks. The nonmarket risks of securities can be completely diversified away if the individual investor selects a diversified portfolio. From the investor's point of view, nonsystematic risks require only such a strategy of proper diversification. However, the bank manager or the FDIC or other regulators are in a different situation. The risk of insolvency depends upon the bank's total risk $\text{var}(\tilde{R}_z)$ related to its level of capital. A failure to diversify properly increases the risks, but not the bank's value to investors. In fact, the investor may avoid the bank if he finds it difficult to offset the undesired risk.

As part of the study for this volume, Goodman and Sharpe (1978) analyzed the market and nonmarket risk in an index of bank stocks in New York and outside New York. They found that the amount of risk and the relationship to the market (beta) varied a great deal over time. Risks in the 1930s, 1960s, and 1970s were two to three times as high as in the 1940s and 1950s.

In the earlier and later periods the betas were close to one. During the middle years they were much lower, falling under 0.5. Over the past twenty years, market risk for these indexes averaged about 40 percent of the total risk. Of course these indexes, because they contain ten to fifteen stocks, benefit from diversification, even if only among bank stocks, and therefore have a reduced total risk and a higher percentage of market compared with nonmarket risk than would an individual bank. The effect of specific residual risk, although not of extramarket covariance, is reduced when a group of banks is considered.

The ratio of nonmarket to total risk for individual banks is much higher. Thus, table 16.2 of the Rosenberg and Perry paper (chap. 16) shows the mean and range of these factors in 1977 for individual banks. The average market beta is about 1.0, but the range for 101 banks is from 0.17 to 1.93. The nonmarket risk (in this case based on logarithmic returns) for individual banks shows a range from 0.025 to 0.125 around a mean of 0.071.

2.6 The Major Causes of Fluctuations in Values

A variety of risks face banks at all times. Skilled risk management enables the bank to absorb the shock of unexpected events that would otherwise cause insolvency. Management of the bank's portfolio depends upon the proper classification of assets and liabilities in accordance with their possible reactions to unexpected events. The portfolio must be classified so that all activities whose values are likely to react in a similar manner are grouped together. While the returns for a given loan depend on its proper underwriting, the risk and returns to a bank depend more on the relationship among activities than on individual loans. To manage risks, one must recognize the basic sources from which dangers spring. It is then necessary to estimate how much risk arises from each activity. Finally, the amount of variance in a bank's portfolio depends on the weight of each type of activity in the total.

A well-diversified portfolio of loans, even with high individual nonmarket risks, should return neither more nor less than a normal (corrected for market risk) profit. Its face interest rates should cover normal returns plus expected operating costs and losses. Insolvency develops when firms fail to recognize this fact. By reaching for what seem like high promised returns, they either fail to diversify or accept too great a market risk. Typically, they neglect past events that they consider abnormal. An emphasis on individual loans misses the true dangers that arise from events affecting whole classes of assets and liabilities. Furthermore, because investors can diversify, nonmarket risks do not carry interest yields commensurate with their face yields. The measurement of risks should emphasize the need to examine broad classes of risks, not individual loans. An improved classification system can call attention to the most critical areas and allow a better expenditure of effort.

2.6.1   Types of Risk

Greatest is the risk of interest rate movements. When interest rates rise, banks must pay more for current liabilities. More significant, increases in the long end of the term structure raise discount factors for future promises to pay. How much this will lower capital values depends on the duration of the portfolio (the weighted average of the time periods of future cash flows, where weights are the present value of the future cash flows). Risk premiums may also increase, lowering capital values still further. The expected cash flow may become less favorable as assets are extended and liabilities lost or shortened.

If the interest rate risk is high, substantial adverse changes may cause insolvency. The degree of danger depends on the scheduled dates of cash flows from assets and liabilities and on the probable magnitude of shifts in the interest rate structure. It is the bank's net exposure, taking into account assets, liabilities, and capital, that determines its total interest rate risk (Macaulay 1938; Samuelson 1943; Hicks 1946; Grove 1974).

The papers by McCulloch, Craine and Pierce, Morrison and Pyle, Nadauld, and Lane and Golen (chaps. 10, 12, 13, 14 and 15) analyze in detail the theory underlying interest rate risks. They also measure the degree of risk in particular activities. They show how risks can be lowered by reducing the duration of the portfolio either by choosing assets with a lower duration or by increasing the maturity of the liabilities. The risks they find include changes in portfolios through outflows, delays in repayments, and speeding up of takedowns against commitments, as well as the effect of interest movements on capital values and total income.

Many discussions in the banking literature concentrate on loan loss or credit risk—the risk that borrowers will default or perform poorly. Variations in the default rate of typical banks around industry averages have not been large. However, occasionally an individual bank may depart considerably from the average. This potential must be estimated. Poor underwriting of individual loans can lead to above-normal losses, but errors of this kind are typically caught in time. Banks with above-average losses in one period tend to have a reduced probability of a second year of unanticipated losses. They regress back to the mean.

As the Maisel and Jacobson paper (chap. 9) shows, banks whose loans carry high interest rates seem, as theory says they should, to charge enough to offset any added risk. One cannot assume that a well-diversified portfolio of loans whose individual risks appear high is either more or less profitable or risky than a similarly diversified portfolio of loans whose individual risks appear low. In a fairly competitive market, loans carry interest rates related to their true risks. A class of loans may stay out of line for several years, and a bank may underestimate individual risks in attempting to compete, but such errors are not fatal. Studies of bank examinations seem to show that both lenders and examiners are able to recognize past mistakes.

Another risk is that operating margins may deteriorate. Margins depends on receipts from assets, on costs of funds, and on operating expenses. Banks may err in their liquidity management. When rates on current liabilities shift, movements may also occur in the amount and source of funds. A rise in market rates may be accompanied by unexpected surges in takedowns of commitments. In considering operating risks, attention must be paid to items not shown on the balance sheet. In addition to commitments, foreign exchange contracts, letters of credit, and trust operations may be important. One fortunate fact with respect to operating risks is that, on the whole, a sudden deterioration is unlikely. Most situations cast shadows well in advance. Dangers arise primarily from failure to correct past trends.

Among banks as a whole, the greatest risks and most common causes of failure are fraud, either internal or external, and insider abuse. Owners and managers alter the portfolio to enhance their personal investments or those of family and friends. There can also be defalcations by members of the staff; or the bank can be defrauded as a result of undue trust or inadequate investigation of borrowers.

The risk from fraud and insider abuse varies with the size of the bank. Most failures of small banks are due to fraud. As the size of the bank grows, the probability that a defalcation can be large enough to cause insolvency decreases. It does not disappear, however, as is evidenced by the demise of the United States National Bank of San Diego.

The most significant risk for most banks is a failure to diversify. This risk may arise from a concentration of long-term maturities and, therefore, excessive interest rate risks. It may also stem from a concentration of loans in specific industries or locations—small banks in single neighborhoods or towns; large banks assuming too many foreign risks; or banks lending to a related group of investors or companies. A similar lack of diversification may arise from excessive short-term borrowing or a concentration in other types of managed liabilities.

This list makes it clear that, while the basic rules and regulations prohibiting lending more than 10 percent of capital to a single borrower is a step toward diversification, it is far from sufficient. Nondiversification develops when a group of loans or investments are likely to react in the same way to outside forces. While concentration of loans to a single borrower can be important, other factors can also dominate non-diversification. If movements in the returns from the individual loans and investments are completely correlated, diversifying into innumerable separate loans or securities does not reduce risk at all. The effectiveness of diversification depends upon selecting loans or activities where the correlation among the activities is either negative or slight.

Holding a number of assets and liabilities with identical patterns of expected cash flows, but half positive and half negative, gives almost complete protection against interest rate risk. On the other hand, because each one's return will move almost identically with interest rates, no matter how well diversified is a portfolio of twenty-year municipal bonds there will be virtually no reduction of such risk. Similarly, the number of loans to different real estate investment trusts or to different companies and government agencies in country X or region Y might give very little reduction of risk if the borrowers are similarly affected by economic or political events. Measuring diversification requires a proper model of actual risks. One cannot simply count loans or borrowers; one must classify the portfolio into those activities whose returns are closely correlated.

2.7 Capital

In assessing the total risk of the portfolio, capital plays a critical role. As shown in figure 2.1, available capital can offset other losses. The greater the initial capital and the more is added from earnings or new investment, the less is the danger of insolvency. That equity capital requires no fixed outlays means that the average duration of a portfolio grows with its ratio of capital to other liabilities. As the paper by McCulloch shows, the relationship between risk and capital is nonlinear. Given a certain risk in a portfolio, the danger of insolvency falls rapidly as capital is increased, but after a point additional capital has only a minor effect.

The cost of capital or the value of leverage in a bank is difficult to measure. There may well be differences between the cost of capital to the public or to the economy and the cost to the stockholders or managers. Differences arise because of possible subsidies through the chartering and insurance system, because of tax advantages to the firm but costs to the government, and because of imperfections in financial markets, especially for small banks.

The previous discussion noted that *capital* refers to the market value of a bank's capital. It reflects the fact that the market values of both assets and liabilities will differ from book values, and that numerous intangible assets and liabilities may not appear on the books. Capital may be thought of as the difference between the asset side of the economic balance sheet, where all tangible and intangible assets are valued at market or economic values, and the economic value of deposits, borrowed funds, and implied as well as actual commitments.

2.7.1 The Economic Value of Liabilities

Sharpe notes that the "economic value" of the insured deposits will be less than the nominal value if there is any possibility of default. Assume a depositor puts $100 into a checking account. The bank promises to pay the depositor $100 if the bank is still in business when the customer returns. Suppose the bank will be able to pay off the depositor in full with a probability of 0.9, and with a probability of 0.1 will not be able to pay the depositor anything. The economic value of the deposit is $90. The depositor in effect has a claim of $90 on the bank and a claim for $10 on the FDIC. Thus the true value of the bank's promise to pay deposits on demand is less than the nominal deposit amount, since the bank may not be able to pay all claims. The depositor may be thought of as having a claim on the bank for the actual value of the promise to pay and a claim on the FDIC for the difference between the nominal value of the deposits and the "economic" or actual value of the promise to pay.

Uninsured depositors are in fact partially insured because the FDIC usually arranges mergers with other banks instead of simply paying off the insured depositors. Barnett (1976*a*) has noted that

> out of $4 billion in deposits at failed banks through 1975, approximately $267 million was lost or is expected to be lost. Of this amount unprotected depositors stood to lose about $13 million, the corporation absorbing the remainder . . . the high recovery rate for depositors is attributable at least in part to the fact that $9 out of every $10 in deposits were in bank failures which were handled by purchase assumption transactions in which the FDIC provided assistance enabling another bank to assume the failed bank's liabilities. This arrangement provides, in effect, 100 percent insurance to uninsured depositors and general creditors as well as to FDIC insured depositors.

Hence uninsured depositors, like depositors, may be viewed as having a claim on the bank for the actual value of the bank's promise, that is, less than the nominal value of the deposits. They also have a claim on the FDIC for an amount somewhat less than the difference between the nominal value of the deposits and the present default-free value of the bank's promise.

Borrowed money consists primarily of federal funds, securities sold under repurchase agreements, certificates of deposit, commercial paper, borrowings from foreign banks, and borrowings from the Federal Reserve Board. The value of borrowed funds on the economic balance sheet is the actual value of the promise to repay the amount borrowed plus interest that has accrued. Although federal funds are not insured, the actual value of the promise to repay principal plus interest would be very close to the nominal value. Since federal funds are overnight or very short-term borrowings, and since the regulatory agencies are not known for their swiftness, there is generally time to get the money out once it becomes known the bank is weak and before it is declared insolvent. For banks in a rather weak capital position, but not actually insolvent, federal funds are not available. Certificates of deposit (CDs) are insured up to $100,000. For the insured CDs, the FDIC liability is the difference between the nominal value of promise and its actual value. The economic value of large negotiable CDs may be evaluated by their secondary market value. Borrowings from the Federal Reserve would be listed on the economic balance sheet for somewhat less than their nominal value, but not nearly as little as might be anticipated, since the Federal Reserve often demands secured creditor status with respect to their loans.

2.7.2   The Economic Value of Assets

Assets refers to tangible and intangible assets. Securities usually have an easily discernible market value. The market value of loans may be difficult to find, as there is no active secondary market. However, they may be looked upon as roughly equivalent to bonds with the same promised stream of payments and the same degree of riskiness. Footnotes to bank balance sheets show the difference between the market and book values of their securities. Similar factors cause gaps between book and economic values of loans, but they fail to appear anywhere in reports.

Intangible assets and liabilities are of numerous types. The present discounted value of monopoly rents generated from demand, time, and savings deposits would be listed on the asset side of the economic balance sheet. These rents would consist of the difference between the cost of servicing demand deposits and the alternative cost of funds with a similar term to maturity. This would be part of the intangible asset category. The Maisel and Jacobson paper (chap. 9) contains information on such values.

The present discounted value of bank-customer relationship includes two factors. First a company may make regular loan payments, where it otherwise would not, to maintain a good relationship with its bank and make funds more readily available in the future. Second, the bank may have information about a borrower from past lending relationships that cannot be sold. Thus the loan may be worth more to the bank as an ongoing concern than it would to a bank without access to the information.

Credit lines, standby letters of credit, and other future commitments including loans and securities sold under repurchase agreements will be included in the value of the intangibles. The entry under intangibles will be the difference between the amount the customer paid to gain access to the credit line or standby letter of credit and the expected cost to the bank. If, for example, the line of credit is on relatively unfavorable terms to the bank, that is, if the expected marginal cost of funds is greater than the expected return, this will be entered as a negative number under the value of future commitments and make the value of intangibles smaller. In this example, if the credit line is not legally binding and is on extremely unfavorable terms, the bank can refuse to make the credit available, thereby terminating the bank-customer relationship. It must decide which course of action is cheaper.

The value of the charter is the economic rents that can be derived because entry is limited. This cannot be totally distinguished from monopoly rents from deposits owing to legal interest rate ceilings, since even with legal restrictions the level of services would presumably bid away excess rents. The distinction between rents extracted from the position of the bank as the monopoly supplier of loans and the rents extracted owing to the bank-customer relationship is very murky. When trying to value intangibles one must be careful not to double count.

The *value of management* refers to the fact that managers of some banks can earn more than the normal rate of return for their shareholders because they have very specialized skills. The relevant intangible value is the present value of future management-derived profits. This raises the issue why the managers do not demand their "rents" in the form of additional compensation. One possibility may be that management as a whole and not a single manager is responsible for the rents. There may be very high transaction costs in organizing the managers into a bargaining unit and figuring out how the rents should be distributed.

2.7.3   The Market Value of Capital

The market value of capital can be illustrated by a few examples. Consider the change in the balance sheet if the assets become riskier but the value of the assets remains unchanged. This is what Sharpe in his paper (chap. 8) refers to as a value-preserving spread. The economic value of the deposits and borrowed funds goes down, since the bank is less apt to pay off the depositors, even as the added risk raises equity values.

A bank increases the riskiness and potential return of its assets. As a result, the bank will be able to pay off $100 of depositors' money only 80 percent of the time rather than 90 percent. The other 20 percent of the time the bank will be able to pay off nothing. The economic value of deposits has fallen to $80. The value of the FDIC liability has gone up to $20. However, the asset side of the economic balance sheet remains constant. Assets still sell for their expected value of $100 even though their risk or variance has increased. Higher promised interest rates make up for the greater risk. On the opposite side of the balance sheet, however, the value of capital rises. This occurs because the institution's stockholders will reap rewards if the risky assets pay out better than expected. If returns fall below expectations, they will share the losses with the FDIC. They have an improved position.

If the assets become more valuable, both the value of the deposits and the value of capital will go up. With less chance of default, the actual value of the promise to pay depositors and the holders of borrowed funds is higher. The rest of the gain will go to the stockholders.

Liquidating value will in general be lower than the economic or "ongoing concern value." At best, part of the intangibles will be lost. Often, assets such as loans cannot be sold at "market value" because the market for buying a given bank's loans is thin. If only a few banks are bidding, they will be willing to trade off a smaller probability of a larger profit for a larger probability of winning. If it were costless for individuals and other businesses to buy secondary loans, they could always be sold at market. This is apparently not the case. Attempting to liquidate quickly will lower liquidating value even further.

2.8   Controlling Capital Adequacy

This chapter has shown that capital is adequate when a bank controls the risk in its portfolio and maintains a level of capital sufficient to reduce possible losses and insolvency to an acceptable minimum. Insolvency can be avoided either by increasing the amount of capital or by reducing the level of portfolio risk. Experience shows that, left to themselves, some banks will pick a relationship between capital and risk that will bring about insolvency. Bankruptcy may occur because of either inadvertence or greed. Some managers may not have sufficient knowledge of the risks they are assuming, while others may take extraordinary risks to increase their profits.

Selection of a risk/capital ratio that threatens insolvency is possible if either the market or the insurer fails to require adequate levels of capital. The market, left to itself, is likely to fail in this sphere because of the difficulty and the expense a large number of depositors face in policing each institution. Attempts by the market to control a bank's risks have been inefficient and historically have not worked well. Such inefficiencies and losses in the general welfare were greatly reduced by the introduction of deposit insurance. However, since the advent of the FDIC, individuals and firms have left almost all of the policing to the insuring agency, a task it shares with other regulators. The FDIC has assumed most of the risks that depositors and creditors of banks would normally have to bear.

Either the market or the insurer can use various techniques to make certain that capital is sufficient. One method is regulation. The risks of insolvency can be reduced to any desired level by restricting the types and amounts of assets and liabilities held by a bank. Banks holding only short-term government notes would be virtually risk-free. But removing or greatly restricting banks' function of lending to businesses and individuals would eliminate some of the most valuable services they perform.

In a similar way, banks could be restricted to lending primarily their own capital. With a high enough level of capital, risks could be reduced to any acceptable level. But, again, inefficiencies would be large. The public would lose the great advantages of intermediation through deposits or other risk-free assets.

A better procedure is to determine what maximum level of risk is desirable from the point of view of the bank, the public, and the insurer. Such levels of risk can then be approximated by establishing procedures to measure and control the dangers of insolvency in individual banks. Such measurements and establishment of limits require an understanding of how risks arise and how they combine in portfolios.

The chapters that follow explain how bankers and insurers or regulators can measure both the risks in activities and in portfolios and the level of economic capital. They also show examples of actual measurements. If similar measures are refined, they can serve to improve bank operations while making the process of insuring and regulating more efficient.

3 The Measurement of Capital Adequacy

In measuring capital adequacy and estimating the risk of insolvency, the first step is to establish the value of the economic balance sheet of a bank—that is, the present value of the expected cash flows from a firm's existing portfolio of assets and liabilities. Next the expected balance sheet of the bank at the end of a period must be projected. Finally, to measure risk one must assess the volatility or distribution function of this expected value. Many of the papers in this volume show techniques for estimating the probability of such changes. Some assume that future values will move in accordance with past distributions of movements of the values of similar assets, liabilities, or portfolios. Others make future distributions conditional on forecasts of events both within the bank and in the macroeconomy.

3.1 Applications of Modern Theories of Finance

In recent years, modern theories of finance have made major advances in improving the knowledge required to measure capital and portfolio risks. The papers in this volume are both contributions to and applications of these theories. The key factor in recent developments has been the application of rigorous mathematical analysis to simplified models of financial markets. When their assumptions apply, these theories demonstrate that the task of measuring risk and capital adequacy can be accomplished with a limited number of formulas and a manageable amount of information.

Most of the existing theories have been applied to large active markets, such as those for common stocks, bonds, or commodities. Applications to a specific problem, such as measuring bank capital, require additional theoretical developments. They also require empirical studies to see what type of information is available for this use, how the theories can be applied, and how closely the markets conform to the theoretical assumptions.

Controversies persist with respect to the empirical verification of the theories. The studies that follow recognize many such problems. Although they are only a start toward a desired solution, they do indicate that the newer theoretical concepts can improve our techniques of analyzing bank capital needs. While not yet at a stage for complete solutions, the techniques can be applied in specific cases. The studies serve to increase knowledge of critical issues and of where to look for solutions.

The models from modern finance emphasize the likelihood that markets are efficient and utilize all available information. Financial markets act as tremendous machines or computers that are constantly driving rates of return into congruence with the underlying risks they contain. Modern theories contrast with much traditional analysis of financial institutions that has tended to emphasize special features of each market and institution. In this later literature, banks are pictured as specialized firms with monopoly powers. Government regulations are critical. Information is poor and expensive. Emphasis is on the analysis of specific markets and actions rather than on more general equilibrium solutions.

One of the purposes of our study was to see whether the modern models can be applied to the banking system. Even though the market does not agree in many respects with the assumptions of the theories, the results indicate that such prospects are good. It is true that not all monopoly profits are competed away. The market as a computer works more slowly and erratically than is generally assumed. Forecasts are poor, and many banks make far from optimum choices. They pick bad portfolios. Information and transaction costs are significant.

Because individual cases do diverge from theory, close analysis of each institution is necessary and worthwhile. By using knowledge derived from modern theories, individual bankers can make better decisions, and more logical and efficient regulations can be formulated.

3.2   The Steps in Measuring Capital Adequacy

The determination of risks in a bank and the adequacy of its capital can be handled through a procedure with five separate but closely related steps: (1) dividing into activities; (2) estimating net worth; (3) estimating expected values; (4) estimating distribution functions of expected returns; and (5) relating capital and risks.

3.2.1   Activities

The initial need is for a logical division of assets, liabilities, and other operations into pertinent activities. The purpose of combining functions into a limited number of activities is to make use of existing information concerning differences in earnings and risks in analyzing the bank's current situation. A logical breakdown into activities increases the ability to use market and other knowledge to improve the estimates of current net worth and of portfolio risks. The number of activities studied in the individual papers ranges from three to ten. On the basis of a more complete analysis, it seems likely that an optimum division into activities might be between fifteen and twenty. When a class contains securities with a wide spread of maturities, it should be further subdivided by this factor. Since risk depends on the proportion of each activity in the total, the first step in measuring risk for a specific bank is to aggregate assets and liabilities into these desired classes.

3.2.2   Capital or Net Worth

The model of risk and capital adequacy starts with a measurement of net worth at the beginning of a period. This is one of the most difficult tasks in the entire process. In a way this seems surprising, since ascertaining the value of capital is a primary aim of accounting systems. In fact, however, as chapter 5 shows, finding the economic, as compared to the book, value of a bank is an extremely complex task. For a limited number of banks, valuations of capital are constantly performed by the stock and bond markets. However, this is not true for the vast majority of institutions, which are either privately held or have stocks that trade in narrow markets. For these banks, alternative methods are called for to find actual current capital.

Moreover, even for those banks for which market estimates of net worth are available, questions arise as to the accuracy of such valuations, particularly for the purposes of measuring the risks of insolvency. The degree to which stock market values reflect the facts of regulation compared with the values that would be set in free markets is unclear. Bankers claim that their net worth is reduced by restrictive regulations and capital requirements. Bank critics hold that net worth is inflated by the oligopolistic position of banks, by regulated interest rates, and by deposit insurance whose fees in specific cases may not cover the risks assumed by a bank.

Capital is required in relation to total or risk assets. Banks are among the most highly leveraged of all firms. Many of the arguments over bank capital arise from the banker's assumption that he will be better off if he can increase this leverage even more. The theory of capital structure and financial leverage indicates that this will be true only in special circumstances (Modigliani and Miller 1958; Stiglitz 1974). It will occur primarily when debt issues bring major tax advantages or when high information or transaction costs, including those of bankruptcy, make issuing stock or selling other assets expensive. To date, studies fail to show whether increased leverage is more efficient either for banks or for the economy. This is especially so because of the situation analyzed by Sharpe (chap. 8), where the existence of insurance makes it possible for the firm to increase its value to its owners at the expense of the insurer.

The idea that investors will choose portfolios composed of optimum risk return relationships to their own utilities leads to concepts of markets in which individuals shift their investments and use arbitrage and hedging to obtain optimum portfolios. Because of their ability to hedge and arbitrage, investors value the debt and equity of each institution in accordance with the amount of systematic risks they include. Except for possible tax savings and information difficulties, a firm cannot change its value by leverage. It can, however, change the risk of a particular class of assets. It can therefore alter the price these assets will sell for to people looking for and willing to pay for particular risks. Thus leverage can alter the risk and the price of common stock.

While most banks have sought to increase their leverage to the maximum, it is not clear whether this results from the current regulatory system or from forces that would exist even in a free competitive market. Taxes, bankruptcy costs, and information deficiencies can influence optimum capital/asset ratios. On the other hand, because financial markets are fluid, to the degree they are not fettered by government action they tend toward efficiency and toward equalizing costs of capital.

3.2.3   Expected Values

A third task is to project the expected level of operations and capital to the time of next evaluation. The expected value of a bank depends both on its own operations and on future movements in cash flows and expected values. The studies by Jacobson (chap. 11) and by Craine and Pierce (chap. 12) attempted to model changes in the net worth of individual banks by use of econometric models whose inputs came from movements of variables forecast by large-scale models.

The forecasting ability of such econometric models was poor. The papers show that Box-Jenkins types of techniques using recent trends in a bank's activities plus projected changes in major macroeconomic forces do a better job of estimating end-of-period values. They assume that the information contained in market forecasts will be correct. The combination of time-series models with forecasts of interest rates, GNP, and dividend policy can produce acceptable expected values for a bank.

3.2.4   Risks in Particular Activities

The fourth task is to estimate the distribution function surrounding the expected value of the bank. The spread of the distribution function depends on the weights and the volatilities of the activities in the bank's portfolio. In theory, a complete risk estimate requires finding the covariance matrix of returns for each of the bank's numerous activities. When it is recognized that what is desired are the risks arising from unanticipated events, their measurement becomes more tractable. In practice, useful estimates of risk can be made by applying a limited number of risk functions to a small group of activities.

The papers that follow estimate probability distributions of future returns for three main causes of variations. The first is interest rate risk or changes in the value of a portfolio arising from movements in the rate at which expected cash flows are discounted. Discount rates alter as spot interest rates move, as the time structure of interest rates shifts, and as the margin between rates on risk-free and risky assets alters. The second risk is that of default or losses on loans. The third is operating losses. These can occur when there are changes in interest margins, operating expenses, the sources of funds, and from income and losses in miscellaneous or non-balance-sheet operations.

Time-series and cross-sectional data of unanticipated shifts in each of these factors are used to estimate probability distributions and forecasting equations of potential losses in specific activities. With additional estimates or allowances for nondiversification and fraud or insider abuse, the knowledge of these probability distributions can be used to set outer bounds on risks in any particular bank. With more detailed data from individual banks, the reliability of these estimates could be rapidly improved.

The application of these techniques to prototype banks is illustrated in chapter 5. These examples show the degree to which risks may vary among banks. Dissimilarities are found to be economically significant. Variations appear more dependent on interest rate and maldiversification risks than on loan or operating losses.

3.2.5   Relating Capital and Risks

A final task is to combine the estimates of capital with the probability distribution of future values to obtain a measure of true portfolio risk. McCulloch shows (chap. 10) that the risk of insolvency is a nonlinear function of the amount of potential variance in a bank's portfolio and of level of capital. It decreases rapidly as the ratio of expected capital to assets increases. It also alters with the length of time between portfolio evaluations. Thus McCulloch shows that raising the capital/asset ratio from 1 percent to 10 percent decreases the risk of insolvency more than thirty-three times.

The methods of calculating probability distributions differ depending upon the techniques used to model risks. Some of the projections in the papers assume that future events follow a random process. Others predict risks conditional upon forecast changes in the macroeconomy. While use of past random movements may suffice for regulatory or insurance purposes, within a bank, analysis and projections based upon risks conditional upon forecasts of the economy may be preferable. It may be particularly useful to estimate the risks of insolvency under a graduated list of possible events. Banks may desire to cut off their risks when the probabilities of failure are at low levels (say .001) for events thought to be extremely unlikely (a major war and freezing of all assets by foreign nations).

The following discussion first considers some of the factors involved in estimating expected values, as well as the factors that can alter the expected returns. It then discusses problems in determining net worth and methods of relating capital and risks.

3.3   Activities, Expected Values, and Risks

When a bank selects its portfolio and activities, it simultaneously determines its expected future net worth and its risks of insolvency. Both of these factors must be estimated.

1. The expected future net worth can be projected from the type of activities the bank chooses, its earning record, how it handles dividends and capital investment, and its current balance sheet.

2. The distribution function around such expected values, which determines its possible losses of net worth, is also a function of the particular activities selected. In addition, however, distribution functions depend on the way such activities are likely to react to unanticipated events. Each activity will respond differently to the events that occur, according to how its values are affected by economic change.

3.3.1   Expected Values

The expected change in net worth of an individual institution can best be projected from what has been happening within the bank. Its expected level of losses and operating income depends on the loans it has made and its operating procedures. Recent data can be used to estimate expected earnings, losses, and growth. If they indicate a low expected net worth, risks can be reduced by increasing capital.

Risk analysis for the individual bank, whether for the manager, creditor, investor, or regulator, begins with the proper calculation of expected income by applying valuations based on current market data to operations. In addition to assets with market prices, such values must be applied to assets and liabilities not quoted in the market and to intangibles. In this sphere, arguments over the validity of market, as compared to nonmarket, valuations are hottest. The paper by Maisel and Jacobson (chap. 9) shows that, on the whole, banks appear to adjust their operations to the competitive market. Banking markets are not so overwhelmed by institutional and monopolistic practices that applications of equilibrium theory fail. A general financial model can be usefully employed. Book rates of return and costs for classes of assets and liabilities adjust toward each other. Marginal rates received or paid for different activities tend to equalize. The correlation among returns is high, though rates of adjustment may be slow.

While our studies show that the best estimate of a bank's expected income comes from its own balance sheet and past history, two banks with the same expected future net worth may not end up in the same position. One may prosper even as the other fails. Actual incomes will differ depending on how each one's activities react to events. The degree of risk in each bank depends on both the outcome that is expected and the relationship of probable outcomes to possible events.

3.3.2   The Distribution of Possible Losses

It is because portfolios differ in these ways that an estimate of risk and capital adequacy also requires an estimate of the specific distribution function around a bank's anticipated net worth. This requires finding the possible risks in each activity it is engaged in and then combining them to form an estimate of total risk.

As noted, the general evaluations of risks can be divided into four types:

1. Unanticipated movements in the discount rates applicable to an activity's future earnings or costs are a big factor in risks. Discounts change with movements in the default-free spot interest rate; the term structure of interest rates; and the risk premiums for individual activities.

2. The risk that loans will perform poorly is a second type. Variations in the default rates of banks around their expected values have not been large, but the departure of individual banks from this average has been considerable. Thus in 1975, the worst postwar year for unanticipated loan losses, losses as a share of net earning assets for the banking system increased by 15 basis points, or from 0.27 percent to 0.42 percent. On the other hand, about 6 percent of the banks increased their loan losses by more than 50 basis points (0.5 percent) in that year.

3. In addition, a risk exists that a bank will incur large changes in its current earnings because of a shift in liabilities, unexpected operating expenses, losses from off-balance-sheet operations, or alterations in its portfolio. Such changes are measured roughly by the variations in current operating earnings before loan losses and taxes. In the 1970s the net income of banks before loan losses and income taxes averaged about 1.55 percent of net earning assets ($1.55 per $100). The range around this average was from 1.38 percent to 1.70 percent. In each year, fewer than 3 percent of banks had negative returns before loan losses. In 1975 an examination of individual banks shows that, at the 1st percentile of all banks, the decrease in net worth from this cause was about 1.5 percent of

all earning assets. At the 99th percentile, net worth increased by an amount equal to 3.7 percent of net earning assets as a result of such earnings.

More important than the level of earnings are unexpected negative shifts that cause unexpected losses in net worth. The largest drop in operating earnings for the average of all banks was 0.23 percent of net earning assets in 1971. In other years the maximum fall in this ratio was less than 10 percent (0.02) of this amount. In 1975 slightly more than 5 percent of all banks had net operating losses, including losses from loans but excluding credits. In that year, 10 percent of all banks experienced a decline in this earning ratio of 0.4 percent or more.

For some of these banks such losses would not have been unexpected but could have been predicted from their prior record. In such cases, risks could have been reduced by requiring poorly operating banks to put up more capital and to alter their operations. Dangers arise primarily from unanticipated changes in operating losses.

4. Finally, there are risks that do not seem quantifiable in the same way. Such risks include major losses due to insider abuse, fraud, or lack of diversification. These have been among the main causes of bank failures. One would normally assume that the risk of such losses would fall rapidly with size, but this has not been the case. The number of large bank failures in this category seems to be an indictment of existing methods of examination. In most cases examinations did not eliminate the risks from lack of diversification, whether of type of loan, duration, or customers. In some cases the examiners were aware of the risks but did not have the tools to deal with them.

While some degree of success has been achieved in estimating the first three types of risk, greater progress is needed. More detailed analysis and simulation of the risks of maldiversification are also vital. Furthermore, knowledge of the covariances among risks is inadequate. From individual bank data, however, it does appear, as one would expect, that the four risks are not perfectly correlated. Therefore total risk is less than would be estimated by merely totaling their separate values.

This discussion brings out rather clearly a contrast between this volume's view of how to estimate the soundness of a bank and the methods frequently used by examiners and similar evaluators. Their estimates are usually based on examinations of individual loans and measures of trends or untoward movements in book values. They fail to estimate the risks of unanticipated events. If they estimate the gap between market and book values (and they often do not), such evaluations may properly reflect future expected values. They may show problems in a bank owing to past events. Spot checks may be useful in determining that an institution has not properly reported its poor prior performance; but the need for such evaluations is a measure of poor auditing standards. Examinations may also be useful to catch fraud or a lack of adequate diversification.

Such evaluations, however, fail to measure the actual portfolio risks. These depend upon how unexpected events may change the value of specific activities and on the weight of these activities in the bank's portfolio. To measure such risks requires modeling the way events are likely to cause unanticipated changes in values and the distribution of such movements.

3.4   The Expected Level of Earnings or Losses

Since a bank's current net worth is the present value of its expected net cash flows, projecting the expected net worth of a bank at the end of any operating period cannot be separated, in theory, from estimating the value of its capital. The same kinds of forces must be considered in each evaluation. At this point, however, we first examine the problem of estimating expected total returns or losses, then go on to the estimate of the distribution function around this projection before returning to questions concerning current capital values, which logically should come first.

As one aspect of the research for this volume, a great deal of effort was spent in attempting to examine relationships between economic events and revenues and losses in specific bank activities. We obtained individual income statements and balance sheets covering fifteen years or more for a large sample of banks. We attempted to fit both simple and complex econometric models to their earning movements. The results were inconclusive.

We found that the best explanations of movements in the net worth of individual banks could be derived most accurately by use of time series of their past actions, along with movements in a limited number of macroeconomic variables. The papers by Jacobson (chap. 11) and by Craine and Pierce (chap. 12) describe some of the positive results of these studies. The negative results of additional approaches, not reported on in detail, covered a wide variety of other sources of data, longer time periods, and more exogenous variables.

Both the theoretical and the empirical analysis indicate a strong correlation between recent net earnings and their levels in future periods. Revenues differ among banks, depending on each one's portfolio and operations. As shown by the Maisel and Jacobson paper (chap. 9), gross revenues among banks differ by more than their net revenues. Banks select a variety of techniques by which they generate interest income and their operating income and losses. Such differences and their results are mirrored in their past earning histories.

Gross revenues should, and do, include a margin to pay for expected losses. The levels of anticipated interest earnings and losses are a function of prior earnings and loan losses. Banks with higher loss ratios need not be riskier if they charge enough to cover their higher expected losses.

The estimates of anticipated levels of net worth and the distribution function of probable fluctuations around such expected levels can be analyzed in two separate categories. First come the gains and losses from the interest rates of the assets and liabilities in the portfolio. Second come the results arising from operations, which include losses from loan underwriting.

3.4.1   Anticipated Interest Earnings

At any time, interest earnings reflect the categories of assets and liabilities and the interest rate maturities in each category selected by a bank. As the papers in part 2 show, interest rates paid and received by a bank reflect the best knowledge in financial markets with respect to movements of general (risk-free) interest rates. However, earnings from loans as well as the costs of borrowing do vary somewhat from purely market-determined interest rates. But, even so, a bank's actual returns can be expected to change roughly in conformance with whatever movements occur in market rates.

Both the theory and the results of these and other studies show that in general the market's estimate of future interest rate earnings is likely to be the best available. Furthermore, the recent earning record of the bank will reflect the relationship between its selected balance sheet and overall interest returns for both market instruments and banks as a whole. The studies show, moreover, that, for a bank away from the average in any period, a slight tendency exists for its interest earnings to regress toward the median of its size group.

3.4.2   Expected Operating Earnings

Expected net income also depends on operating expenses and loan losses in addition to net interest income. Movements in earnings, therefore, may diverge from expectations if a bank's performance in its operations or its loan underwriting does not meet anticipations. An examination of past loan and operating incomes shows that, as with interest rates, it is useful in forecasting the next period's losses to start with the assumption that they will equal those of the prior period. Estimates based on the previous year mean that a bank that is experiencing losses or low operating income will need greater capital to offset its expected poor results. Losses also rise in recessions and in the aftermath of a period of high interest rates (Hoenig and Spong 1977; Spong and Hoenig 1978).

Loan Losses

No bank knowingly takes a loan that it expects will default. Some banks may select portfolios that have higher average losses, but, unless they change their selection process suddenly, their choice of portfolios will have been reflected in prior years' net revenues. A correlation exists between higher gross revenues and loan losses, but, since these offset each other, net revenues are not affected. Losses that are anticipated are charged for in the interest rate or fees quoted prospective borrowers. Expected losses merely increase the gap between gross and net revenues.

The ratio of losses to net earning assets also depends on the share of loans in the portfolio. Banks investing primarily in securities rather than loans have a lower percentage of loan losses compared with assets than banks with a high ratio of loans. The type of loans also influences the level of losses. They rise with the percentage of commercial and industrial and consumer loans and fall with the amount of mortgage loans. Large banks average more losses than small ones, but small banks are more likely to be at either extreme. A tendency exists for banks with larger than average losses to regress toward the median in the following year.

Changes in Operating Income before Loan Losses

Just as with loan losses, the best prediction for next year's income for individual banks is simply last year's income. It is difficult to improve upon such a prediction by adding other variables. The R^2s for regressions of the current year's income for individual banks, using last year's income as the only independent variable, are about 0.5. The only other obvious significant variables are those based on differences in liabilities held by a bank. If a bank has a higher share of demand deposits, its earnings are slightly higher; and, if its percentage of purchased liabilities is larger, its earnings are slightly lower than the average. The relationships are weak, however, with R^2 of under 0.1. More significantly, virtually no relationship exists between gross revenues before interest and expenses and net earnings. All of the increased revenues go to pay for larger interest payments, larger losses, or higher operating expenses. Net revenues are independent of the difference in gross revenues.

Differences in balance sheets also do not offer significant explanations for year-to-year movements in incomes of individual banks. As with loan losses, an assumption that year-to-year movements in income are unanticipated and follow a stochastic process among banks of the same size seems a good initial assumption in estimating risks.

The primary exception to a purely random relationship is again a slight tendency for individual banks' revenues to regress back toward the median of all banks in the next year. Furthermore, in years when revenues drop sharply, banks with higher revenues seem to be in greater danger of an above-average fall, but the R^2s are under 0.05.

The sections that follow examine why the expected earnings are likely to be more or less than anticipated. As in this section, the causes are divided into those movements dominated by market interest rates and those due to failure of a bank to perform its operating and lending functions adequately.

3.5   Interest Rate Risk

The most important risk of insolvency or of a fall in the net worth of a bank arises from a mismatch of the term to maturity of assets and liabilities with fixed interest rates. Samuelson (1945) and later authors have used the concept of duration to study the effects of interest rate changes on financial institutions. *Duration* is a measure of the weighted average time before payments are received from interest and principal on a security or loan. The weights used in the calculation are the relative present values of the future payments.

3.5.1   The Interest Elasticity of Net Worth

Morrison and Pyle discuss in their paper (chap. 13) both the theory of interest elasticity and some models that can be used to apply the concept to specific bank assets and liabilities. They show that under the simplifying assumption that all spot and forward rates change by the same amount and that assets and liabilities remain constant, the percentage change in a bank's net worth will be proportional to the percentage change in interest rates. The proportion or actual value of such movements in capital will depend on the duration of the bank as a whole. The bank's duration is a weighted average of the duration of its individual activities. The weights are each activity's share of the present value of the portfolio.

Morrison and Pyle also show, however, that for two reasons these simplifying assumptions are unlikely to be met:

1. The discount rates for all future payments are not likely to move together. They will diverge depending upon the time until a payment is to be received or made and also because of variations in the inherent risk in each asset or liability.

When interest rates rise or fall, the term structure (the rate paid on assets of different maturities) does not move proportionately throughout. Short-term rates usually move by more than long-term rates. Both may react differently to shifts in real interest rates and to expected inflation. The lack of correlation across the structure of rates may, according to Morrison and Pyle, reduce the simpler calculation of interest rate risks by up to 25 percent or, in some cases, even more.

In addition to shifts in the term structure, discounts for risks of different classes of loans, borrowings, and securities may widen as interest rates rise. Most calculations of term structure interest movements are based on risk-free or government securities. (The Lane and Golen paper, chap. 15, introduces the broader concept in contrast to the simpler calculations in McCulloch and in Morrison and Pyle.) Such widening of risk premiums will raise the total effect of interest movements, particularly since larger movements in risk premiums are likely to occur for loans and other nonliquid assets, which make up a large share of bank portfolios. This tendency will be heightened because added risk premiums are also likely to raise the total amount that must be paid for liabilities.

While the theory indicates that completely accurate results require that risk estimates be built up taking into account the many diverse movements arising in the term and risk structure, the empirical data seem to show that in practice modeling risks at each duration may be adequate without the need for information about the exact time path of flows. The risks caused by uneven annual returns from assets appear minor compared with those that arise from differences in the average duration of banks' assets and liabilities.

2. The second reason the simplifying assumptions fail is that not all of a bank's assets and liabilities have fixed payment streams and a well-defined maturity. Cash flows alter as the rates at which commitments are taken down change, assets are paid off more or less rapidly, and deposit liabilities shift. At the same time, interest rates paid and received on assets tied to market rates move.

The papers by both Morrison and Pyle and Nadauld (chap. 14) consider procedures by which adjustments for uneven flows may be made in the risk estimates for specific types of assets and liabilities. The empirical work makes it appear that adjustments for such movements are of a second order and not necessary for adequate risk estimates.

3.5.2 The Interest Risk Estimates

The studies do show the necessity of calculating the duration of individual activities in a bank's portfolio. The risk of an activity can then be calculated by applying to it estimates of the risk at that particular duration. The risk of the portfolio is found by combining the activities into a total using proportionate weights. Such risk estimates do not include adjustments for shifts in cash flows, for widening risk premiums, or for possible covariance among interest movements. In the studies, this latter factor more than offsets the other two. If this is generally true, the abbreviated estimates may well form an outside bound.

McCulloch in his paper (chap. 10) estimates the probability that, as a result of unanticipated interest rate movements, an asset with a specific duration will lose more than x percent of its value at some point during the year. He calculates such probable movements in the risk-free rates for assets and liabilities with maturities from three months to thirty years. He bases these estimates on the history of actual movements in the prices of government securities between 1951 and 1977. The tables and figures in the McCulloch chapter can be used to calculate the probable interest rate risk of any portfolio, under the assumption that the probabilities evidenced by these distributions will continue.

If the dynamics of changes in the values of assets and liabilities are such that they can be modeled by diffusion processes, a variance rate for such changes will serve to measure risks. The assumption is frequently made, as in the Black-Scholes option pricing model, that changes in value owing to interest rate movements follow a log-normal distribution. McCulloch and others have argued that the distribution of the prices of interest-bearing securities is far more fat-tailed, or leptokurtic. To reflect this, McCulloch has developed an option pricing formula based on a log-symmetric stable distribution (McCulloch 1978a). The distribution assumes a greater probability of extreme events. The application of the more fat-tailed distribution greatly increases the estimated risk from interest rate changes. Thus, McCulloch shows that for a twenty-year par bond the risk that the price will change by 10 percent or more during a year is estimated to be covered by a fair insurance premium of 0.06 percent if a log-normal distribution is used, compared with a premium of 1.17 percent under the log-symmetric stable distribution that he has fitted to past interest rate changes.

The papers by Morrison and Pyle, Nadauld, and Lane and Golen (chaps. 13, 14, and 15) attempt to calculate the interest rate elasticity of net worth for specific model institutions. Each selects a limited number of activities and simulates their movements based on econometric models of past lending and borrowing. Possible movements in interest rates are estimated from maximum past shifts in the spot rate and the term structure.

Many bank assets are not market instruments, and as a result they lack observable market values. Market values must be imputed adjusting expected cash flows to a certainty equivalence. These adjusted flows can then be discounted at the projected default-free rate. Morrison and Pyle describe the theory behind one form of estimation of a certainty equivalence as well as a technique for performing this task. Nadauld expands upon this concept and explains the content of a computer program that can perform this task.

All these chapters present examples of actual simulations for periods in the mid-1970s. Morrison and Pyle estimate the interest elasticity for a wholesale bank that contains business loans, demand deposits, certificates of deposits, and equity capital. They utilize a range of term structures to obtain estimated interest rate elasticities and find that they are low for a bank whose portfolio consists only of commercial loans with primarily floating rates.

These papers show vast differences in interest rate risks depending upon the activities contained in the model bank. The estimates of potential interest rate risks vary considerably among the studies in this volume. The large changes in value found as probable by Nadauld in his work with savings and loan data are similar to the earlier studies. Morrison and Pyle and Lane and Golen show both low interest rate elasticities and insurance costs. These results follow directly from the specific assumptions used in their particular applications and not from the techniques. If more general assumptions were used, the results of the different techniques would come closer together.

As noted, Morrison and Pyle measure the interest rate risk of a limited part of a bank—one in which most rates move with the market. Capital losses are minor. They also find that changes in value as a result of interest induced flows in a wholesale bank are small. This latter result may well be typical of more broadly based portfolios.

Several critical factors account for the lower costs of insurance estimated by Lane and Golen, which range from 10 to 40 percent of those found by McCulloch for similar maturities and capital ratios. In practice, each would have to be adjusted to more realistic assumptions for the particular bank being evaluated. Lane and Golen assume that all funds received during the period are invested at the rate that applies at the next examination period. The effect of this assumption is to reduce the duration by a full year. In contrast, if the rollover of investments took place evenly, the diminution of duration would be only half a year. They also assume no dividends, while McCulloch assumes that all earnings are paid out. The Lane-Golen technique increases the estimated end-of-period capital.

More significantly, the period Lane and Golen picked to develop their probability distributions was one in which capital values rose as a result of declining interest rates. Thus they measure variances around an expected capital gain. Insolvency occurs only if the initial net worth plus this expected gain is exceeded by a loss. The negative parts of their estimated distributions are considerably smaller than they would be if the variances were measured around a neutral expectation of changes in value. The Lane-Golen tables make clear, as do the prior studies, how rapidly additional capital can reduce the risk of insolvency. An examination of any of the tables shows that the cost of insurance drops rapidly as the amount of capital is increased.

3.6   Risks of Poor Performance

The risks of insolvency may rise and the future net worth of a bank may fall because of poor performance of its normal functions. A variety of causes can decrease revenues or raise expenses. Loan losses or delayed payments may expand. The bank may have to increase the share of high-priced purchased money. Operating costs may jump. Decreases or losses may occur in miscellaneous sources of income, such as from the trust department, foreign exchange or security trading, or real estate.

3.6.1 Distribution Functions Derived from Estimates of Nonperformance

The measurements of the distribution functions around expected changes in net worth arising from unanticipated movements in loan losses and operating earnings are derived from a variety of time series and cross-sectional data. The time-series data include year-to-year movements in average changes for banks as a whole, for classes of banks, and for individual large banks and bank holding companies. The cross-sectional data include movements in the levels and year-to-year changes for each bank since 1970. The data on individual banks were analyzed extensively. They are the source of knowledge concerning the relationships from one period to the next.

One form of the distribution functions used is developed from the variances of the year-to-year changes in individual bank net worths arising from loan losses and operating charges. The years used are those in which the variances were largest. The distribution functions derived from these records are based on the movements in all banks, in all large banks, and in the banks with the largest and smallest variances. The period covered is from 1965 to 1979.

As the next chapter shows, the distribution functions derived from the records of nonperformance do not indicate that these are important sources of insolvency. In a competitive economy, the average earnings for a continuing, vital industry must be high enough to maintain its ongoing performance. While variations in earnings occur with macro-events, such fluctuations are not likely to lead to insolvency in an industry with adequate capital aided by a good insurance system.

Operating revenues and loans usually do not deteriorate suddenly. It takes poor management or fraud and insider abuse to thwart normal diversification. While errors may accumulate in a bank over time, a proper analysis of the existing trends usually shows when changes in operations and capital additions are required. A failure to require that existing conditions be corrected is more likely to cause problems than is the impact of unanticipated events.

3.6.2 Are These Risk Estimates Adequate?

Because the distribution functions measuring the probabilities of poor performance do not indicate much risk in banking operations from this source, the question must be raised whether they are biased downward. For two technical reasons they may be low, but these do not appear significant. More important is the absence from the general distributions of measures of maldiversification and of the probability of fraud.

The distributions used in this study are based on years of maximum past movements and on the assumption that changes for individual banks follow a normal distribution. Both assumptions may reduce estimates of true risks. Distribution functions should be based on a complete estimate of potential events. An estimate of risks based on the maximum changes in losses or income over a fifteen-year period may not be as high as an estimate measuring risks over a longer period.

Furthermore, as with interest rates, losses and unanticipated movements do not appear to follow a completely normal pattern. The distributions, particularly among either very large or very small banks, seem skewed toward more extreme losses. They appear leptokurtic. Risk measures based on an assumption of normality may, as is shown in McCulloch's paper, understate the true values.

Nondiversification

One of the more critical questions in estimating risks is to find a logical measure of nondiversification. Theoretical concepts are quite clear. Nondiversification is measured by the correlation among individual assets and activities of possible losses in total returns from interest and capital. A portfolio in which activities are not correlated is diversified. Problems arise because, by definition, losses are unanticipated. Still, certain correlations with a resulting lack of diversification appear probable. Clearly, interest rate risks are correlated. Other classifications with high correlations also appear, such as geographic—local versus national versus international; by industry; by size of firm; by ownership.

We have examined differences among loan losses in some detail. Contrary to our initial expectations, we could not develop any general rules, perhaps because historically the rate of loss in most cases has been low. As a result, it may be possible to build a better measure of nondiversification by use of simulations rather than past data. One could assign possible distributions of loan losses and correlations to specific activities. By drawing from these distributions, one could estimate the potential costs of nondiversification in a manner similar to that used in the Lane and Golen paper (chap. 15).

Insider Abuse

Better definitions of insider abuse are also necessary. Two of the largest bank failures were related to misuse of insider positions. Congress has been legislating in this sphere. If the laws are clear enough, then protection against abuse should be a matter of proper audit. For this purpose there is little obvious reason to expect that government audits or examinations would be better than private ones. Since most of our economy and regulations are based on private auditing and accounting, it appears that those who feel it cannot work for banks ought to show what basic differences exist and why these cause a need to treat banks differently from other corporations. While special regulations may be necessary for some purposes, it is not obvious that a need exists for a government audit.

In analyzing these other risk factors, one must not overestimate their total effect. While insider abuse or fraud has caused the failure of most banks, they tend to be the small ones. Their losses, compared with either the insurance fund or payments from it, are not large. From 1 January 1934 to 31 December 1978, the FDIC total losses, including anticipated losses on assets still held, were $345 million. This does not include forgone interest, which would increase the total losses by 50 percent or so. Of the total, by far the largest share has gone to cover the losses of banks with over $100,000,000 in deposits. Later discussions show that these various factors may make it advisable to use somewhat different techniques for measuring risks in large and small banks. However, the general approach appears suitable for both.

3.7   Measuring Net Worth

In the measurement of risk and capital adequacy, most attention has been paid to measuring possible losses in income. Yet the measurement of current and projected net worth should play a role as significant as, or even more significant than, that of possible losses. Furthermore, the difficulties of measuring net worth are as great or even greater.

A key factor in total risk is the real or economic value of a bank's capital and those forces that will cause it to differ at the next evaluation. Because many gains or losses in the value of assets and liabilities are taken into the books only over time rather than when they occur, and because many intangibles are never recorded, the economic value of capital often varies greatly from that shown on a bank's books.

We can see how great the difference is between book and economic value if we are willing to assume that the value of a bank's stock in the market reflects its true economic value. In the years 1950 through 1975, the market value of the net worth of the approximately twenty-five banks and bank holding companies carried in Standard and Poor's Bank Stock Index averaged about 135 percent of their book value. In individual years, the ratio of net worth in the market to book for all of these banks ranged from 1.87 in the highest year to 0.94. Year-to-year changes in this ratio exceeded 40 percent at times. When market-to-book ratios for individual banks are examined by years, an even wider range is found. The years 1971–73 appear not untypical. We have examined the market-to-book ratios for these years for each of 135 banks; they ranged from 3.5 for the bank with the highest ratio to 0.6 for that with the lowest, around a median of 1.25.

Capital accounts in banks consist of equity capital, surplus, undivided profits, reserves for contingencies, and other capital reserves. True economic capital may differ from this total because: (*a*) gains or losses on assets from interest rate movements are not recorded; (*b*) liabilities may be overstated when regulation Q forbids payment of market interest rates; (*c*) the value of information, customer relations, and goodwill may be considerable; (*d*) reserves for loan losses may not be accurate; (*e*) the value in use or in liquidation of fixed assets varies; (*f*) commitments for future loans or foreign exchange purchases and sales may have a positive or a negative value; (*g*) other reserves, such as those for contingencies and deferred taxes, may increase real net worth.

The paper by Sharpe (chap. 8) presents the formal analysis and precise definitions that are at the heart of our discussions of capital adequacy. Sharpe uses a state preference model to make clear the theoretical underpinning of some of the more common ideas.

The first section outlines the concept of capital adequacy for an institution whose deposits are insured by a third party. An economic balance sheet that includes the FDIC's liability to the depositors is introduced and explained. It is demonstrated that, given relevant risks, an increase in capital will reduce the per unit value of the FDIC's liability. However, the relationship is nonlinear. Each additional increment of capital will cause a small drop in the FDIC's liability. Given a specific amount of risk, some level of capital exists that will make the per unit liability equal to any preselected premium.

The second part develops the idea that with fixed insurance premiums a bank can increase its value by gaming against the FDIC; in other words, it can raise its net worth by increasing the risks in its portfolio. Furthermore, the more inadequate is the initial capital (the larger the FDIC's liability), the more will a given increase in risk raise the value of net worth. The model also shows that the total increase in the stockholder's net worth or in the FDIC's liability depends upon how changes influence liabilities as well as assets. As is stressed throughout our discussion, results depend upon the covariances among the balance sheet items as well as upon their individual relationships to events.

In the course of the analysis, another example is presented of why, in complete financial markets with an assumption of no bankruptcy and no gain from the FDIC, the mix of deposits and capital should be irrelevant. No matter what mix of deposits and stock it elected to employ, an uninsured bank could raise just enough capital to pay the market value for its assets.

3.7.1 Use of Common Stock Prices

One method of measuring the value of a bank's capital is to look at the stock market's estimate of its net worth. To believers in the efficiency of financial markets, this is the only sensible way. In an efficient market, prices reflect the usable relevant information on the present value of future dividends and net worth. They summarize all the pertinent facts of the balance sheet and intangible assets.

However, serious problems arise in estimating capital from stock market data. In the first place, well-operating markets exist for stocks of only 1 to 2 percent of all banks. While these are the largest, containing the majority of all assets, a substitute technique must be found for the others. Furthermore, though the market may be efficient in projecting its own future estimate of net worth, this may differ from actual values. The market swings widely in estimates. It must consider earnings far into the future, not the resources available for payments on a given day.

While efficient in the narrow sense, the market's record of projections, both on an individual and an aggregate basis, is not good. If the market's estimates were accepted, the amount of capital would fluctuate widely. This could affect lending decisions and output. Even if public policy increased to some degree the risks assumed by the FDIC, it might be good policy if it smoothed the swings and discouraged procyclical lending. Finally, because the market is so heavily influenced by government regulations and actions, there is no reason to expect it to be estimating the true market values desirable for public policy as against the value of regulations to the individual owners.

Poor Information

Financial theory tells us that it is difficult to improve upon the market's judgment as to the value of a bank's capital—because anyone who could consistently improve upon the market would make large profits and drive the price toward equilibrium. Still, in the case of many banks, the information available to the market has been inadequate for making the best judgments. Some data have not been gathered, and some have been suppressed. Because they fear that disclosure could lead to runs from ill-informed depositors, regulators have opposed disclosure of a broad range of information, such as on poor loans and investments, misconduct, source of deposits, and similar data.

Perhaps as a result, in critical cases the market's judgment has been demonstrably poor. The stock of several of the large banks that failed in recent years sold at high levels until well after insolvency was already a highly probable outcome. Few large depositors or lenders spent time or money in attempting to judge their banks' risk, because the depositors made the correct assumption that, even though most of their loans to the banks were not covered by FDIC insurance, there was a de facto guarantee.

Based on poor experience both for stockholders and for the insuring agency, however, and as a result of pressure from the Securities and

Exchange Commission, regulators are increasing the flow of information. The justifications for withholding information have decreased. Small depositors did not withdraw their funds on receiving adverse news. They trusted the FDIC. On the other hand, stockholders and lenders on debentures suffered large losses because of a conflict of interest between the regulators' desire to keep the banks open and their duties as security regulators.

Even with added requirements, however, managements may still hide critical information. Creative accounting is not uncommon. Furthermore, even with adequate information the market fails to anticipate many events. Its forecasting record is not good.

Private versus Social Values

We also do not know how much of estimated net worth at any time reflects divergence between private and social valuations of risks and future earnings. By taking excess risks or reducing their capital below the level that would be set in a competitive informed market for an uninsured, nonregulated firm, bankers may raise the market's valuation of their net worth. The expectations of earnings might disappear if current insurance operations were altered to charge fair premiums. Similarly, some of the bank's returns and its estimated economic capital may reflect noncompetitive features in the system that should be removed.

The Market Price of Risk

Rather than requiring added capital or insurance each time the market reduces its estimate of the net worth of banks as a whole, it may be worthwhile for a public insurer to share certain risks. To avoid large variances in estimated capital, for example, the FDIC or other regulators using capital estimates on market valuations might prefer to use a moving average of some sort to iron out the effect of the largest fluctuations in overall stock prices.

Decisions on how often and how much to counter market estimates are difficult. Some movements reflect real drops in economic value. Thus banks as a whole lose net worth when interest rates rise or major industries face potential defaults. Furthermore, each bank reacts uniquely to such macro events, depending on how it has constructed its own portfolio. Changes in net worth owing to such events are a necessary part of risk calculations and should not be neglected.

On the other hand, some movements in capital values, as evidenced in tables 5.2 and 5.3, reflect the market's shifting evaluation of risk as a whole. Fluctuations occur because of rapid shifts from optimistic to pessimistic expectations of future earnings. For administrative and other reasons, it may be advantageous to smooth out some of these overall movements even if it increases the insurer's risk. Even though future movements in the market may be random and not predictable, the FDIC can assume different risks than can individuals or firms. It can afford to average out over cycles, even though this might be unprofitable for individuals.

A willingness to average market estimates of value may make additional sense because, if regulators or insurers bring added pressure on banks to increase their capital based on cyclical fluctuations, they may create difficulties both for the bank and for the economy. In recessions, equity capital is expensive and difficult to raise. Furthermore, in recessions macro conditions will improve faster if businesses can borrow money to invest. If banks are restricted in their lending because the market value of their capital has fallen, recovery will be delayed. Market values reflect a general pessimism and poor expectations. Attempts to force banks to increase capital in order to offset the market's reactions will increase the overall pressure on the economy (Orgler and Wolkowitz 1976).

3.7.2   Use of Market Related Data

Since the actual use of specific stock market data for calculating net worth is possible for only about 100 or 200 of the 14,400 banks, other techniques are necessary for the rest. One procedure is to estimate separately the present value of the individual activities in the banks from related information taken from financial markets. The individual parts can then be summed. Thus the present value of securities held, of the loan function, of the deposit function, and of miscellaneous operations can be valued separately and the bank's total net worth calculated.

The direct valuation of a bank's assets and liabilities can start with estimates taken from financial markets. For actively traded securities, marking to market is no problem. Since market quotations for equivalent assets exist, a direct estimate of any discrepancies between book and market is possible. In fact, bank annual reports currently carry such calculations. However, they appear as footnotes or appendixes to the report, not as corrections to the book capital. The market can also be used to value other liabilities and related assets such as federal funds, repurchase agreements, owned acceptances, and certificates of deposits.

The Maisel and Jacobson paper (chap. 9) shows that valuation is possible but more difficult for demand and savings deposits where neither on an explicit nor an implicit basis are market returns paid, for loan accounts where accrued information among lending officers can increase returns, and for miscellaneous income such as from trust departments.

The value of deposits, other information, and miscellaneous income can be estimated from the market for premiums paid for such assets, including goodwill. Unfortunately, the market for selling banks or their deposits is not an active one. Premiums paid vary greatly depending on how badly a firm or individual wants to enter a specific market. For these reasons, other techniques must be employed that use information from a variety of sources.

A large difference between market and book values is likely to arise from the effect of interest rate changes on the loan account. These can be corrected for by using recent lending rates—say over the past month or quarter. These rates can be used to discount the portfolio of previously existing loans after their maturity has been estimated.

Estimates are available for expected average net returns from deposits and from other activities for all banks. Such expected rates of return can be applied to specific banks, with necessary adjustments if they seem out of line. These expected returns for the individual bank can be capitalized. A faster, less rigorous procedure may be used by capitalizing overall returns through market price/earnings ratios of similar banks. While these are not rigorous methods, the degree of effort worth using in this valuation depends upon the significance of these other sources of income.

Such estimates of capital owing to a more realistic estimate of the firm as an operating entity must be added to those changes arising from the differences in the market value of assets. In most cases, returns from intangibles will be in the range of 10 to 30 percent of the total. Therefore, an error of even 20 percent in estimating them will change the total estimated capital by only 5 or 6 percent.

Would such ad hoc procedures improve on the use of either stock prices or book? The answer seems to be yes. Since capital enters into the risk calculations in a nonlinear form, even minor improvements in estimates may be important in certain critical ranges. In the same way, some adjustment for expected growth in a portfolio relative to net worth may also be worthwhile. Although the record of sophisticated attempts to project individual balance sheets is not good, in a dynamic situation rough approximations of the future are likely to be better than an assumption of no change.

3.8   Models of Risk and Capital Adequacy

The final step in the procedure for measuring capital adequacy is to derive from the separate measures of a portfolio's current and expected net worth and its distribution function a measure of its total risk or capital adequacy. Such measures either can show the fair insurance premium that would have to be paid to offset the portfolio's risk or can estimate the probability that a negative net worth will occur in a designated period.

The papers in this volume use three separate approaches to the measurement problem. In some cases the approaches are applied to actual or prototype banks. In other cases, only certain functions or certain kinds of risks are modeled. These studies develop theories while illustrating their application by specific examples. The results of such examples show how banks can avoid major risks. However, to measure complete risks and capital adequacy, more detailed information concerning the individual bank must be inserted into the models.

The first approach estimates risks through the theory of contingent claims, using variances derived from past movements of returns in the interest rate market, in loan losses, and in operating earnings. The second constructs simulation models of future net worth and failure probabilities. The distributions of risks are based on past experience or on assumptions as to extreme possibilities of movements in a period. The final approach predicts risks from regressions of measures of bank asset and liability characteristics, other annual report data, and past behavior of total stock market returns of banks.

3.8.1   Conditional Claims

Merton (1974, 1977a) has shown that many types of conditional financial claims can be analyzed in terms of option pricing theory (Black and Scholes 1973; Cox, Ross, and Rubenstein 1979). McCulloch in his paper (chap. 10) and in related work measures the variance of past interest rate movements. Both he and Merton (1977a) show that the value of deposit insurance (the risk of loss from insolvency) is equivalent to a promise by a third party guarantor to take over the assets and pay deposits in full if the value of a bank's assets falls below the amount it has promised to pay on deposits.

At a given date, a firm has a particular sum of assets and has promised to pay a given amount to liability holders. The difference is its net worth. Its liabilities at the time of the next examination are already a fixed sum based on promised interest rates, but the future value of its assets and its net worth will depend on what events occur in the interim. An insurer guarantees that, if the assets are worth less than the liabilities, it will pay them off at their face value and accept the assets as its recompense.

The insurer is offering a guarantee that is equivalent to a "put option." In an option market, the seller of the option agrees to accept shares of stock at a fixed (exercise) price set at the time of the sale. His risk depends on the probability distribution over which stock prices may range at the expiration date. His potential losses depend on the probabilities that the stock will be selling below the exercise price and how far below in each such case. If we chart his risk, the curve will be similar to that of figure 2.1.

Option pricing theory shows that the value of the put option or its equivalent, the fair insurance premium, depends only on the risk-free interest rate, the amount of liabilities at the date of next examination, the time until the examination, the current value of the firm's assets (the difference between the current values of its assets and its liabilities being its net worth), and the variance rate per unit time for the logarithmic change in the value of assets.

3.8.2   Simulations

A second approach to measuring risk is through simulations. The papers by Morrison and Pyle, Nadauld, and Lane and Golen (chaps. 13, 14, and 15) contain approaches of this type. They also discuss the underlying theories behind these and related techniques. Simulations enable one to relate the risk in particular portfolios either to a forecast of exogenous variables available from other sources or to a distribution of probable events based upon past relationships.

Morrison and Pyle, for example, model a few particular activities of a bank. They show how to measure the magnitude of interest rate risks in a particular combination of activities. In a bank that can move its lending rates promptly after the risk-free rate changes, the remaining risks—primarily those of movements in risk premiums and disintermediation—are not large.

Nadauld develops a computer model to make measurements of the Morrison and Pyle type in a more general form. His model is developed to measure probable changes in net worth that may arise from movements in interest rates. He accounts for resulting movements in both discount rates and induced changes in loan payments. Although Nadauld uses mortgages for his particular examples, the program can be applied to all types of loans and investments.

The paper by Lane and Golen develops this approach further. It shows how simulations can be used to estimate risks in more complex situations. The authors simulate the probability distributions needed for the estimation of risks, drawing from distributions based either on time-series forecasts or on past movements. The simulations use knowledge of recent events as well as history. The probability distributions that result are related to a variety of capital/asset ratios in order to measure the interaction between risks, capital, and fair insurance premiums. Specific results depend upon the initial conditions for the simulations.

As in the Morrison and Pyle paper, the activities of the bank are limited, and only interest rate risks are measured. Liabilities, on average, are assumed to cost the bank sums equivalent to the six-month Treasury bill rate. The particular period used for these simulations shows rather low risks for these activities in comparison with those estimated from the option pricing model.

3.8.3   Fundamental Risk Determinants

The third approach, in the paper by Rosenberg and Perry (chap. 16), models risk by using regression techniques. It determines prediction rules for the systematic and residual risk experienced in the market for the bank's common stock. It aims at measuring the predictive significance of a large number of variables as an indicator of risk, and hence as a target for regulation.

Using the COMPUSTAT data base, prediction rules have been developed for two aspects of risk: systematic risk (risk that is related to covariance with the market portfolio) and residual risk (the aggregate of specific risk and extramarket covariance). For each type of risk, several models have been estimated: one model employs only measures of the bank's asset and liability characteristics; a second employs these characteristics and other data taken from annual reports; a third model adds the history of the behavior of the price of the bank's common stock. The central conclusion of the study is that systematic and residual risk in banks can be predicted from predetermined data. Prediction rules estimated in this way can serve a useful function in monitoring bank risk.

3.9   Can General Financial Theory Really Be Applied?

The measures of risk and capital are based upon models derived from modern financial theory. Numerous arguments arise about whether the concepts that have been developed and tested largely in more perfect markets, such as that for bonds and common stocks, can be applied to a specialized industry and individual institutions. Banking markets do vary from those of the theory, but how significant is this in overall results?

One of the strengths of the theories arises from the fact that only a few assumptions are necessary to obtain robust empirical results even when deviations from the assumptions occur. However, since the markets for financial intermediaries deviate from the assumptions of a perfect, efficient market in many ways, as a minimum, qualitative differences will exist between actuality and the predictions of the theoretical analysis.

The following important simplifying assumptions of models have been worked out in theories:

1. Perfect capital markets exist. This means that securities are infinitely divisible; information is available to all at no cost; there are no costs for transactions, and pure competition exists among borrowers and lenders.

2. There are no legal or institutional restrictions on borrowers or lenders.

3. Taxation costs are zero.

4. Bankruptcy costs are zero.

5. Those engaged in the market attempt rationally to maximize.

6. Homogeneous expectations exist, and future earnings can be represented by a subjective random variable.

7. Lending and borrowing can be accomplished by individuals and corporations at the risk-free rate.

8. Hedging and arbitrage, including short sales, are possible in any security.

Critical for the models is the idea that financial markets are efficient and utilize available information effectively to project and value future cash flows. Based on these projections, accurate and rational prices are established for securities. These can be traded costlessly, allowing arbitrage to work. Perfect substitutes will not sell at different prices in the same market.

Arbitrage will be at work in three ways. It will tend to ensure that loans and investments with similar characteristics will have roughly equal returns. It should cause managers and bank executives to be paid what they are worth, since otherwise they can move elsewhere. It will cause substitutions of holdings among bank stocks so that a bank's value will depend upon its choice of activities.

3.9.1 Significant Differences

There are a number of ways the banking market fails to meet the assumptions. Regulations restrict competition and the free choice of portfolios. Taxes and bankruptcy costs are not zero. Information and transaction costs are important.

Regulation and Competition

Most significant variations exist with respect to competition and legal or institutional restrictions. Financial institutions do not operate in purely competitive markets. Administered prices apply to both their borrowing and their lending. Nonprice competition is not sufficient to remove distortions.

If their markets were to be classified, as are those of manufacturing or commercial firms, some banks would appear to operate in fairly competitive oligopolistic markets. Others, especially those in small, one-bank towns, have much tighter monopolies for many services. Competition is restricted by the need for a charter and permission from the regulatory authorities to open new branches. Neither type of permission is easily obtained.

There are numerous regulations over interest rates, with respect to both the amount that can be paid on different classes of deposits and the amount that can be charged on loans.

The composition of portfolios is regulated, and the assets an institution can hold are limited. These restrictions exist partly as an attempt to control risks (though it might be noted that their effect, by decreasing diversification and limiting better choices, is probably to increase risks) and partly to allocate credit that may be available to the institutions in accordance with certain priorities set by the government.

Taxes and Bankruptcy Costs

Basic differences arise in the theories of leverage and corporation finance when taxes are taken into account. Effects become less certain because of the complexities of our tax system. Some taxes push in one direction, some in the opposite.

Bankruptcy costs can also be significant. Legal and court costs rapidly diminish the value of a firm in bankruptcy. Economically illogical decisions may be made because of the need to protect the conflicting rights of numerous claimants to the estate. However, in many cases of banking insolvency, costs can be considerably reduced because of the ability of the regulators and the FDIC to move rapidly and logically. Mergers can be aided and expedited.

Information and Borrowing Costs

Other significant factors are costs of information and of issuing securities and trading assets. They influence the efficiency of the market for raising capital and for lending. They are also among the critical factors in bankruptcies. Rapid progress is being made in developing an economic theory of information. However, its numerous potential effects and the need to alter concepts when lack of information is taken into account are still only unfolding. When insiders in a firm have greater information than does the public, a moral hazard arises. It is hard for the market to devise procedures to protect lenders and investors from insiders (Ross, 1977).

There are many other informational deficiencies in the lending sphere. Many loans are small. It is not profitable to spend large sums on gathering information. As one might expect, the amount of information available rises with the size of loans. A good deal of information is specific to each existing borrowing-lending relationship. For example, on consumer loans most profits arise only from second or later loans to a customer. The need to gather information and the risk of error greatly reduce the value of an initial loan. Success increases with time and with knowledge.

Because information about the customer's past payments and ability to pay are so important, loans in many cases can be sold only at large discounts. When part of a portfolio of loans is offered in the market, the threat of adverse selection is always present. Many of the significant costs of transactions in bankruptcies seem to be related to the cost of gathering information. Factors such as the loss of existing relationships, cost in establishing new relationships, and adverse selection raise the cost of marketing loans. In turn, transaction and bankruptcy costs increase risks. They also may make some added leverage profitable.

Individuals and firms frequently lack the assumed ability to arbitrage, to create hedges, to lay off risks, or to sell short. As a result, the rates at which they borrow and lend may vary by a great deal.

There also may be considerable irrationality, or, as important, the cost of attempting to operate rationally in the market may be great. When costs of shopping the markets and of making decisions are high, actual market rates will diverge. There can be tied relationships, with a resulting sluggish response to outside action or shocks.

Even if the market is efficient, its knowledge of the future may be slight. Much of our later analysis is based on the fact that returns are stochastic. Forecasts of the future in the financial markets are usually, or at least frequently, wrong. The data in the Maisel and Jacobson paper illustrate the fact that ex post results can differ for long periods from those that probably were thought to exist at the time of lending and investment.

Transaction Costs

Another sphere in which important divergences from the theoretical assumptions appear is transaction costs. Much of the analysis assumes that necessary assets and liabilities of the type held by the bank can be sold for value in a well-operating market. While this is true for many assets, sales of commercial, farm, and foreign loans may entail sizable losses. High transaction costs may occur because of loss of information or liquidity squeezes. In the foreign sphere liquidation costs may be extreme because political forces may make it impossible to shift loans and raise funds.

As a result, loans with high potential transaction costs require maintaining liquidity through other assets. They may also require an additional risk premium that takes into account that their rates of return are not symmetrical. Because of forces external to the particular bank, their rate of loss may rise sharply at times when sales of such loans become necessary.

It is possible to estimate how expensive it would be to liquidate a portfolio. Transaction costs will vary. Government securities will have a broad market. Most municipals will be salable also, although some may be local names that can be liquidated only with extra time and effort. Confusions have arisen because at times securities can be sold only with large losses. Losses based on the difference between book and market values must be differentiated from transaction costs. While a firm may obtain far less than book value in a weak market, these losses do not reflect additional liquidation costs. The market will pay only current values, not book values; but such losses follow from prior interest rate movements.

National business loans will normally have a fairly active market, particularly if the bank has only a share of a loan, as is true for most national companies. Real estate loans of a permanent type on single-family homes also are readily salable. Permanent loans on other real properties will be slightly less liquid, but in these cases an estimate of the cost of brokerage or obtaining information sufficient to sell the loans is easily obtained from charges for this type of service by mortgage brokers. Loans to financial institutions and for carrying securities are also readily sold. In all these cases, liquidity problems or selling in a period of tight credit must be separated from the transaction-information cost of a loan sale.

Consumer loans have somewhat higher transaction costs because information is more vital. With-recourse sales of such loans create only slight problems. Without recourse, buyers will have more trouble evaluating risks.

Three spheres with high transaction costs are construction loans, commercial and farm loans to local borrowers, and foreign loans. In the first two cases, information is the key. A new lender will have to redevelop information and charge for it, as well as charging a premium for probable adverse selection. Foreign loans either to a single country or in toto are likely to go bad because of balance-of-payment difficulties, for political reasons, war, or international economic upheaval. If they do, their market will disappear. No real diversification among foreign loans is possible for losses brought on by major international stress.

In most of these cases, even if a contract calls for variable rates and short maturities, firms usually cannot pay off loans and probably cannot increase interest rates at times of economic stress. Risks on such loans are greater because, in a liquidity squeeze, chances rise rapidly that the loans will default and that costs of sales to others will become much higher.

3.9.2   Excess Profitability

One obvious question that immediately occurs to most observers is, Why, if the market works and is fairly effective, do some banks seem so much more profitable than others? Aren't the divergence in profitability and the large differences in market valuations of capital indications that the theories are wrong? When we examine average rates of return on banks' earning assets, we find numerous reasons why these should differ.

Some higher returns reflect earnings on the bank's own capital. The amount employed in earning assets depends not only on capital as reported on the bank's books, but also on a complicated relationship among nonearning assets, reserves, and intangible capital. The earnings on intangible capital will include earnings from such items as information and customer relationships developed in the past.

Other important returns may arise from oligopolistic powers. Banks have obtained such power because of limited entry into the banking business and because of the prohibition of payments of market interest rates on deposits.

Some managements may be more efficient, more innovative, or better forecasters. In a competitive market, however, greater efficiency and innovations of managers should be competed away. In addition, a better forecaster or a more efficient individual ought to be paid nearly what he is worth. It is not too difficult for one bank to hire away good managers from others, and such changes occur fairly often.

If a set of assets seems to be returning above-normal amounts, this may simply reflect luck or the fact that possible but not highly probable unfortunate events have not yet occurred. Values are based on expected returns. For periods such as this past decade, these can be badly off in either a favorable or an unfavorable direction. But over time in an efficient market, no class of assets should have returns that diverge significantly from returns for similar assets.

The most important way for a firm to alter its returns is by increasing the risks it assumes. By selecting assets, firms can determine both the return they will earn and their basic level of systematic risks. Firms can err in their operations if they improperly measure the risk of a loan and accept too low a rate of return, or if they fail to properly diversify their risks.

The amount a firm receives from any asset or class of asset depends upon the systematic or nondiversifiable risks in the asset. On the other hand, the risk in the firm's portfolio depends upon its ability to diversify and therefore upon the nondiversified risk it retains. Thus the danger of insolvency will rise to the extent that a firm increases the risks in its portfolio in a nonsystematic manner.

It is possible that a firm with proper skills can pick nondiversifiable assets so well that it can increase its expected returns corrected for risks. However, historical and anecdotal evidence from bank failures and problem banks indicate that firms attempting to specialize and not diversify are likely to underestimate the actual risks they take and to overestimate their risk-corrected returns.

Banks that are earning a good deal less than the average tend to do so either because they have not properly controlled their expenses, or because they have failed to properly underwrite their loans and are in danger of taking large loan losses, or because their forecasts have been poor and their portfolio choices react poorly to unexpected events. Those who earn less than the market because their expense controls or underwriting are bad tend to stand out. On the whole, such trends can be observed, risks can be reduced, and insolvency can be prevented by taking the necessary action to increase their capital and shake up the management.

3.10   Concordance with Concepts: Large and Small Banks

Our empirical work and theoretical developments seem to show that, while qualitative and individual differences between theories and institutional facts must be considered, analysis built upon the theories can be extremely useful. In this as in other spheres, the theories appear to give robust empirical results even when deviations from the assumptions occur.

Returns—particularly on a book basis—for categories of loans among banks do tend to equalize. Even though their task is complicated by problems of information and transaction costs, bankers do make logical choices.

While excess returns may be earned in some categories such as demand and saving deposits because of ceilings and a lack of competition, returns to these activities are far less than they appear to those, for example, who believe that the prohibition against paying interest on demand deposits makes them a free good to banks. Competition does not reduce excess returns to zero, but costs of deposits do move with market interest rates.

However, the degree to which the theories fit the facts and their usefulness for policy may differ between large and small banks. As in many parts of our economy, banking is divided into a small number of large firms, which control the bulk of the assets, and a large number of relatively small firms.

In 1980 there were approximately 175 banks with assets of over one billion dollars. These accounted for more than 60 percent of all assets. One might define small in various ways. Of the 14,400 banks in the United States, slightly more than 3,000 had assets below $10,000,000 and accounted for about 2 percent of all assets. About 8,000 banks with assets of between $10 and $50 million accounted for about 11 percent of all assets. The 1,800 between $50 million and $100 million held about 7 percent of the assets. The 1,400 banks between $100,000,000 and $1 billion held 20 percent. All together, the 1,600 largest banks held well over 80 percent of all bank assets, or over $1.5 trillion.

The problems of operation, of regulation, and of examination differ a great deal depending on size. The skills of the managers, the degree of diversification, the degree of market pressure and segmentation vary greatly.

All banks have a number of widely traded investments, returns on which are completely competitive. At the other extreme, there are neighborhood depositors and borrowers who do not shop for better prices because the importance of convenience and goodwill is so great. Returns from these customers can have a noncompetitive factor. A higher proportion of the portfolios of the larger banks will be market dominated; they will have a much smaller percentage of depositors or borrowers tied primarily because of convenience. Small banks are more likely to fail because of fraud, insider abuse, and lack of diversification, but when they fail, the average loss is not large.

Because the size of banks makes such a difference in their conformance to the basic concepts of theory, in the effect that existing forms of regulation will have on their efficiency, and in the impact of a failure on the economy and on the insurance fund, it may be sensible to separate out small banks in determining the most effective forms of regulation.

The next two chapters show the results of applying the measurement procedures to specific uses and types of risks. They describe in greater detail some of the difficulties found in actual applications. They are based on the theories and some of the specific results contained in the more detailed papers of part 2.

4   Estimates of Typical Risks

4.1   Introduction

In this chapter we examine a variety of estimates of risks in banks. We discuss three major types of risk: interest rates, shifts in operating earnings, and loan losses. The next chapter takes up problems in valuing net worth and shows how the figures of this chapter can be combined with net worth calculations to measure capital adequacy. As noted previously, our studies did not include estimates for risks of maldiversification or fraud. Therefore, the prototype risk computations exclude these risks. While the history of bank bankruptcies over the past thirty-five years reveals these factors to be a main cause of failures in small banks, the losses to liability holders of these institutions from such forces have been extremely small.

The studies show the degree to which risks vary among banks even under our existing system of regulation. Dissimilarities in risks assumed by institutions are found to be economically significant: the risks from possible interest rate movements and maldiversification appear far more likely to lead to bankruptcy than do those from loan or operating losses.

These prototype models are only illustrative. The estimates of the probability distributions are preliminary; they require more detailed information. However, the case example of the First Pennsylvania Corporation, which contains more specific data, appears to confirm the analysis. Individual banks may vary more in their choice of activities than the examples selected. The past relationships reflect a particular set of conditions that have been changing. They may change even more, particularly if the regulations and anticompetitive policies that shaped the past are removed. Just as relaxation of regulations will shift past relationships, so will differing inflation rates and changed techniques of monetary policy. Estimates must take into account any such expected shifts in the environment.

At this time, a complete estimate of the covariance matrix is far too complex for existing knowledge, and it probably is not necessary. The analytical model allows one to pick out a limited number of significant risk relationships. The empirical data, moreover, seem to indicate that an adequate system of probability functions can be built with far less than complete information. With good theory and models, it is possible that less information would be required to insure or regulate banks than is now developed in the examination process.

For example, examiners now spend a good deal of time evaluating individual loans. In small banks with inadequate managers, directors, and records, such examinations may be helpful, but they are not obviously necessary. Risk may be controlled instead through simpler and more general classifications, taken together with measures of adequate diversification and with data on nonperforming loans. Probability distributions can be applied to broad groups and to the total bank. Only if diversification is inadequate because too many loans are being made to similar industries, localities, countries, or regions may more complete data on individual loans be necessary.

Similarly, the model and the analysis of chapters 8 and 14 show that in theory a simple concept of duration may not be adequate for measuring interest rate risk because the changes in discount factors from year to year, while fairly high, are not completely correlated. In contrast, the empirical data seem to show that, in practice, duration without information for individual flows may be an adequate measure. The risks caused by uneven annual returns from assets with similar durations may be minor compared with differences in the average duration of banks' assets and liabilities.

4.2   Interest Rate Risks

The general discussion of the previous chapter showed that interest rate risks depend on a mismatch of the maturity structure of an institution's assets and liabilities. When interest rates move, banks are affected in at least four ways:

1. Their cash flows alter as the rate at which commitments are taken down changes, assets are paid off more or less rapidly, and deposit liabilities are transferred.

2. The interest rates paid and received on liabilities and assets tied to market rates move with those rates.

3. The term structure of interest rates shifts. If the term structure moves up, the value of future promises to pay becomes less.

4. The discounts for risk may widen. These changes will have the same effect as movements in the risk-free rate.

4.2.1   Approach to the Estimates

Most of the papers in part 2 are concerned with the theory and estimates of such interest rate risks. The papers by Morrison and Pyle, Nadauld, and Lane and Golen (chaps. 13, 14, and 15) consider both the theory of how movements in spot interest rates affect the term structure and how such changes influence capital values of specific activities. Nadauld also discusses the effect of interest rate movements on cash flows. However, his analysis is restricted to the mortgage market.

The paper by Maisel and Jacobson estimates the year-by-year effect of interest rate movements on the total returns to a bank that distributes its assets and liabilities in accordance with the average balance sheet for banks as a whole.

In this paper, as in much of the other analysis in this volume, lack of data leads to the assumption that rates on different classes of assets and liabilities move together with changes in the risk-free rate. Table 9.2 shows this to be a fairly good assumption. However, costs of borrowed money have a somewhat greater amplitude of rise and fall than does the risk-free rate. Offsetting such added dangers from rate changes, certificates of deposit have a fixed maturity and fixed rates. A lag occurs in their adjustment.

There is debate about whether implicit (actual) rates on demand and time deposits adjust to the market. If their rates remained constant as market rates rose, such an obvious case of noncorrelation would reduce interest rate risk. The study in chapter 9 indicates that implicit rates do move with the market. Intangible capital is created by banks, which can attract consumer and demand deposits, through the capitalization of excess earnings on deposits with regulated rates. However, the amount of such returns varies with the total amount of deposits rather than with shifting interest rates. The probability of losses from disintermediation or gains from added demand and savings deposits must be considered, but it can be part of capital analysis.

The paper by McCulloch calculates the probable variance in the risk-free interest rate applicable to assets and liabilities at maturities from three months to thirty years. He compares returns at each maturity for discount instruments, par bonds, and amortized loans. These estimates are based on the listing of actual month-to-month movements in the return on government securities between 1951 and 1977. He shows how these risk calculations apply to individual activities with different durations and how, depending on the particular portfolio of an institution, they can be combined to find the weighted total variance from interest rates.

4.2.2   Variations among Banks

Wide divergences are found in the distribution of assets and liabilities among banks and, therefore, in the interest rate risks they assume. Institutions alter their interest risk along either of two dimensions.

1. They may vary the proportion of each asset and liability in their portfolios. For example, they may choose to increase their ratio of purchased money or instead they might emphasize dependence on demand or saving deposits. Again, they may put more money into loans instead of into securities. The percentages of each category of asset and liability held by banks are widely dispersed.

2. They have a choice within each category of maturity structures. They can hold all short-term Treasury bills, or concentrate instead on twenty-year bonds. While in some cases maturities are closely related to a class of asset or liability, in many cases choices are wide. Banks appear to vary their risks either as a matter of preference—they are more or less willing to gamble—or because of ignorance—they fail to recognize that they are risking insolvency by assuming too much interest rate risk.

Table 4.1 measures some differences among liabilities and assets in banks. This table, as well as table 4.3, compares information for the top 250 banks whose average net earning assets exceeded $500 million in 1979 with the 8,400 banks with assets under $25 million and with data for all of the more than 14,000 insured commercial banks. The largest banks constituted less than 0.2 percent in number but accounted for over 60 percent of the assets of all banks. Banks with under $25 million in net earning assets made up nearly 60 percent of all banks but accounted for less than 8 percent of bank assets. The tables are weighted averages of the December 1978, June 1979, and December 1979 condition reports (with weights of ¼, ½, and ¼ respectively) and 1979 income statements for all banks.

Liabilities and Interest Expense

The first four items in table 4.1 show differences among liabilities held by banks. They also serve as rough measures of risk from the danger that interest expenses may change as a result of movements in market interest rates. When interest rates on liabilities rise, two types of danger emerge. Most types of liabilities, and therefore their average, will cost more. Equally significant, it becomes likely that one class will be substituted for another. Disintermediation may occur. More expensive liabilities may have to be substituted for cheaper ones.

Table 4.1 shows that banks vary considerably in the types of deposits they hold and in their use of borrowed money. Many small banks have large amounts of demand and savings deposits. They are net sellers of federal funds. On the other hand, some large banks have only limited net demand and savings deposits. They purchase large sums of money at

Table 4.1   **Measures of Interest Rate Risk in 1979 by Bank Size (as a Percentage of Net Earning Assets)**

Bank Size by Net Earning Assets	Banks at Specific Percentiles for Individual Item						
	1	5	25	50	75	95	99
Net Demand Deposits							
Over $500 million	0%	5.3%	14.8%	19.6%	24.2%	31.5%	39.6%
Under $25 million	8.6	12.4	18.2	23.2	29.5	42.5	64.1
All banks	8.3	12.2	17.8	22.6	28.6	39.9	57.3
Foreign Deposits							
Over $500 million	0	0	0	1.3	10.5	46.9	64.6
Under $25 million	0	0	0	0	0	0	0
All banks	0	0	0	0	0	0	1.6
Purchased Money							
Over $500 million	7.3	13.2	26.1	40.6	56.8	81.7	91.7
Under $25 million	0	0	2.7	6.4	12.4	25.3	38.0
All banks	0	0.2	4.0	8.8	16.4	33.1	51.5
Interest Expense							
Over $500 million	3.8	4.4	5.7	6.4	7.3	8.9	10.9
Under $25 million	1.0	2.8	4.0	4.5	5.1	5.9	6.5
All banks	1.6	3.1	4.2	4.8	5.3	6.1	7.1
Mortgages							
Over $500 million	0	1.9	8.3	14.6	21.8	33.9	46.9
Under $25 million	0.1	2.5	9.7	17.7	27.8	42.1	50.8
All banks	0.4	3.3	11.6	19.9	29.3	42.1	50.5
Gross Interest Income							
Over $500 million	8.4	8.9	9.9	10.4	11.1	12.2	14.8
Under $25 million	3.2	4.5	6.4	7.6	8.9	10.8	12.3
All banks	3.5	4.9	6.8	8.0	9.3	11.0	12.3
Net Interest Income							
Over $500 million	1.0	2.0	3.3	4.0	4.7	6.0	6.9
Under $25 million	0	0.4	2.0	3.0	4.4	6.4	8.2
All banks	0	0.5	2.1	3.2	4.4	6.2	7.8

Source: 1978 and 1979 call reports for all insured commercial banks in the United States.

current market rates. They raise by borrowing nearly 100 percent of the amounts needed to cover their loans and investments.

The share of liabilities that respond rapidly to market interest rates has been growing steadily for all banks. Traditionally, banks raised funds through demand deposits and through household deposits of under $100,000. These were considered stable sources, since the rates paid on them were regulated by interest rate ceilings. Banks were able to continue to carry low-yielding assets because their interest expenses did not rise rapidly when market rates changed. Even though the alteration in market rates caused real capital losses and lowered future net income, banks were able to avoid showing the losses on their books because of their stable interest expenses.

Three major changes have increased the risks that liability costs will rise. In the first place, the share of demand and consumer savings and time deposits among all liabilities has fallen rapidly, particularly among large banks. The table shows that many banks have virtually no net demand deposits. What demand deposits they do have are offset by cash, required reserves, and checks in the process of collection. The median bank funds less than one-quarter of its net earning assets by demand deposits. The larger the bank, the less likely are demand deposits to be a significant source of funds.

Instead, banks depend more and more on purchased money—deposits from abroad, large certificates of deposit, federal funds, repurchase agreements, and similar liabilities bought at competitive rates in the money markets. Item 2 shows the amounts borrowed abroad. Only the largest banks use Euro-dollars and other foreign deposits, but, as the table shows, some of these banks raise a high proportion of their funds in these markets. There is wide dispersion among banks in their dependence on purchased money, the third item in the table (which includes the previous foreign deposits). The majority of small banks use only small percentages of purchased funds; they raise their money in the traditional way, through demand and savings deposits. In contrast, large banks purchase most of their liabilities in the money markets. The larger the bank, the more likely it is to depend on purchased funds. However, the table does reveal a few exceptions; some large banks make only minor purchases, while some small banks are active borrowers through the money markets.

Second, among all banks, the costs of small deposits are rising. The 1980 Bank Deregulation Act requires that ceilings on time and savings deposits be phased out as soon as feasible. In the interim, rates are rising toward the market. At the same time, the share of accounts paying interest rates tied to the market increases. At the end of 1979, money market certificates, paying rates roughly equivalent to those on six-month Treasury bills, already made up more than 10 percent of total deposits at commercial banks.

Finally, as the Maisel and Jacobson paper shows, even before these regulatory changes, the actual marginal cost for deposits under interest rate ceilings appeared to move with market interest rates. Nonprice services expanded in order to hold funds that would otherwise disintermediate as market rates rose.

Since the new types of liabilities tend to have longer maturities, they increase the average duration of the liabilities and slightly decrease a portfolio's overall duration. Since the rates are fixed for six months or more when issued, the maturity factor furnishes a slight offset to their heightened interest volatility. However, such improvements may well be more than offset by an increased need to spend money on nonprice incentives as all depositors become more aware of the availability of nonregulated rates. Such expenses are reflected in other operating costs, not in the interest expense shown in the table.

All of these factors taken together have speeded up the rate at which liability costs react to the market. The average interest expense for all banks rose by over one hundred basis points, or more than 17 percent, in both 1978 and 1979. Beyond the change in the average are dangers that arise in individual banks because of the wide dispersion of interest costs about the average. The table shows both this wide dispersion of interest expenses and the high amounts some banks paid in 1979. While the median bank paid 4.8 percent interest to obtain the money needed to fund its net earning assets, some large banks were paying over 10.9 percent. Average interest expenses are lower the larger the amount of funds raised through capital, demand deposits, and small savings deposits. Interest expenses were nearly twice as much for banks at the 95th percentile as for those at the 5th percentile. The higher the amount borrowed through purchased money, the greater the risk. As an example of how dependence on the market can cause interest expense to vary, the costs of funds for First Pennsylvania Bank averaged about 8.9 percent per dollar of earning assets in 1979. For the first quarter of 1980, they rose to a rate of over 11.5 percent per annum.

Returns from Assets

When interest rates rise, the total returns from a bank's assets are likely to fall. What happens depends on the interest rate risk it has assumed—that is, the actual duration of its assets. The capital value of all assets with fixed maturities will fall. Although new loans will be made and new securities will be bought at higher rates, disintermediation may force a contraction of assets or limit the ability to obtain the new rates. Interest rates on some existing loans—those written with variable rates—will also rise. How a particular bank is affected depends on the percentage of its assets with variable rates and on the duration, and therefore the capital losses, of the assets with fixed rates.

The fifth item in table 4.1 carries a measure of such interest rate risk. It shows differences in the share of mortgages in bank portfolios. Since mortgages almost always carry fixed interest rates and long maturities, the higher their ratio, the greater is interest rate risk. Although not shown in the table, when the security investments of banks are compared, some portfolios are found to have maturities averaging less than two years, while others have average maturities exceeding ten years. A more complete analysis of how the average duration of the assets of banks is dispersed shows variations of well over 100 percent. Some banks as a matter of choice take far greater interest rate risks than the average.

The final two items show the distributions of gross and net interest income as a percentage of net earning assets for each bank. Again, a bank's choice of assets determines its gross rate of earnings. The net interest earned, or the bank's margin between its interest revenues and costs, varies with its choices of both assets and liabilities. Neither the gross nor the net data in the table take into account differences in loan losses or expenses, even though our studies show that both are related to the level of gross interest rates. Nevertheless, the table illustrates the wide dispersion of risks reflected by the range of interest rates among banks.

Missing from the table is any indication of changes in the market values of a bank's securities and of its loans that resulted from movements in market interest rates. Net interest incomes reported in call reports, from which the table is constructed, are based on book, not economic calculations. The following discussion shows that many of the banks that reported a positive net interest income actually had negative net interest margins even before operating expenses were taken into account. To obtain total economic returns, net interest income as reported must be corrected to account for interest that is charged to cover larger expected loan losses, for movements in capital values, and for expenses.

4.2.3   Movements of Market Interest Rates

Interest rate risks within an institution depend not only upon its portfolio choices, but also upon whatever random movements occur in market rates. The studies for this volume use two measures of probable fluctuations around expected rates. One is the simple variance of year-to-year movements in interest rates for United States government securities at particular maturities. The second is more detailed. McCulloch (chap. 10) fits symmetric Paretian stable distributions to adjusted monthly interest movements at each maturity point.

It is worth emphasizing again that the studies assume that the market at all times represents the economy's best judgment as to future interest rates. The expected value of rates in the future can be calculated from the spot rate and the forward rates contained in the term structure. The random distributions about expected rates are assumed to be symmetrical.

At times, the regulatory authorities and some decision-makers appear to accept the view that better estimates of future value can be found than those furnished by the market. When rates have been rising or seem high in comparison with past levels, many assume that rates are bound to fall back toward previous readings. Actions based on assumptions of this sort can be costly. As table 4.2 shows, in the post–World War II period it has

Table 4.2   **Interest Rate Movements as a Measure of Risk, 1965–80 (in Percent)**

Year	Interest Rate on 3–5 Year U.S. Government Securities[a]	Change in Capital Value for a U.S. Bond with 3-Year Duration[b]	Rate of Total Portfolio Return[c]
1965	4.82%	—	—
1966	4.84	−0.1%	−0.34%
1967	5.75	−2.55	1.04
1968	6.17	−1.19	2.17
1969	8.10	−5.45	−2.97
1970	5.96	5.66	6.30
1971	5.43	1.50	2.44
1972	6.12	−1.96	0.49
1973	6.83	−2.01	−0.12
1974	7.17	−0.95	−0.31
1975	7.37	−0.56	1.13
1976	5.98	3.88	4.76
1977	7.51	−4.33	−2.92
1978	9.48	−5.50	n.a.[e]
1979	10.55	−2.93	n.a.
1980[d]	13.68	−8.49	n.a.

Source: Federal Reserve Bulletin and chap. 9.
[a]Market average of prices in last week of year.
[b]The data in first column were used to measure change in value.
[c]From table 9.5.
[d]First quarter only
[e]n.a. = not available.

not been unusual for interest rates to continue to rise for four years or more. Between 1976 and 1980, the price of twenty-five-year government bonds fell by over 50 percent. People who assumed that prices were bound to rise soon because they were down 20 to 25 percent might have lost a fortune had they taken positions based on such views.

Financial theory teaches that if the average investor believed such corrections would take place, future rates would move to reflect such views. Anyone who takes a position contrary to the market is backing his own forecast against the majority. The Craine and Pierce paper (chap. 12) and related discussions of previous work on this problem demonstrate that markets appear to be efficient. The assumption appears to be logical that, at any time, future movements around expected rates are random.

Interest Rate Time Series

As is well known, the term structure of rates does not shift by equivalent percentages at all points. Yields on securities at separate maturities tend to shift in the same direction, but movements of short-term rates are usually more volatile. The Morrison and Pyle paper (chap. 13) discusses such differences and some of the implications for the usefulness of duration in estimating interest rate risks. They show that the values of activities react uniquely depending upon the duration of each.

Table 4.2 contains a series of interest rate movements with their related effects on values for the period 1965 to the end of the first quarter of 1980, when rates reached a cyclical peak. The first column shows end-of-year (last week's average) rates on United States Treasury notes and bonds with maturities of three to five years. This series is selected because its duration is roughly equivalent to that of the net portfolio of an average bank's assets.

In this period, these interest rates fluctuated between 4.82 percent and 13.68 percent. Since, within some years, rates dropped lower or went above the year-end figures, the total amount of fluctuation and the spread of rates were greater than shown in the table.

The second column reports the year-to-year changes in capital values experienced by a portfolio with a duration of three years, under the assumption that the interest rate on the portfolio shifted in accordance with column 1. As the studies of part 2 show, the averaging of durations for a portfolio with assets and liabilities of different maturities for the purpose of finding the interest rate risk is more complex than this simple assumption. In addition, rates applicable at each maturity vary. However, column 2 does give a rough indication of the changes that took place in the capital values of the net asset portfolio of a typical bank.

The most critical period was from 1977 to 1980. In this three and one-quarter years, capital values of a portfolio that averaged three years in duration would have fallen more than 20 percent. The significance of such movements becomes evident when it is recognized that the book value of the average bank's capital at the start of the period was only 6 percent of its portfolio.

The final column in table 4.2 extends beyond the movements in capital values. It takes into account that economic returns depend upon current returns and costs as well as upon changes in capital values. This column, taken from the Maisel and Jacobson study (chap. 9), measures the total returns to an average bank. These calculations are derived from movements in total returns of the activities engaged in by a typical bank. It takes into account changes both from market values and from the bank's net operating earnings. It is therefore an approximation of the total returns in each year for the average bank.

When interest rates rise, so do current earnings from assets; but capital values fall, and payments for most liabilities go up. The random changes in value from these pressures are a measure of interest rate risk. In 1969 and 1977, net losses for a typical bank were close to 3 percent. While exact calculations are not available, at the interest rate peak in 1980, many banks probably had a negative economic net worth. If a bank had earlier assumed that interest rates were bound to fall after a year or two of steady rises and therefore took greater than the average risk by increasing the duration of its portfolio, it would have suffered much larger losses than the average. Interest rate risks in the typical financial institution are high. They rise rapidly if a bank picks a portfolio with a duration that extends well beyond the average.

Probability Distributions

In chapter 10, McCulloch estimates interest rate risks in a more complex manner. He calculates probability distributions for unanticipated interest rate movements. He also calculates three related measures. He assumes that future interest rate movements will be similar to those of the past and that all income is paid out as it accrues. He then asks:

1. Given a specific portfolio consisting of an initial amount of capital, assets of a particular maturity, and the form of payment (amortization) for the assets, how often would random interest rate movements cause an institution's net worth to fall below zero?

2. Given assets of a particular maturity and payment form, how much capital would it take to reduce the probability of insolvency to specific levels?

3. Given specific types of portfolios, what insurance premium would be fair to cover the probability of losses to an insurer?

Table 10.3 provides answers to the first of these questions. It shows how the percentage of time that a bank would have a negative net worth varies depending upon its capital and the weighted average maturity of its portfolio. Assume that a bank has a portfolio equivalent to a bond; interest is received and paid out annually, and the principal is received at a fixed maturity. Assume also that the bank initially has 4 percent net worth and funds 96 percent of its assets by borrowing. If its portfolio was all invested so as to give on average a net three-month maturity, unanticipated fluctuations in interest rates would be expected to cause it to have a negative net worth once in 350 years. If under similar conditions the average maturity of its portfolios was 10 years, on average, it would have a negative net worth every 3.7 years.

Assume that the bank wanted to maintain a portfolio with bonds having an average maturity of 10 years, but wanted to reduce its chances of finding itself with such a negative net worth to once in 100 years. How much capital would it require? Figure 10.6 shows that it would need capital equal to 30 percent of its total assets. To reduce the probability of insolvency to once in 100 years, it must not borrow over 70 percent of the value of the portfolio. Figure 10.6 also shows the annual probability of failure that results from each capital/asset ratio and possible average portfolio maturities.

Finally, table 10.4 shows fair insurance premiums. If a bank with 4 percent capital maintained a portfolio equivalent to a ten-year bond, and it wanted to carry insurance that would pay off its creditors at 100 percent in case of insolvency, a fair premium charge would be 1.55 percent of its assets per year.

McCulloch explains how he derives these figures and describes the type of factors in his study that influence the probabilities. Included are such factors as the estimates of past and future fluctuations, the rate at which earnings are paid out, and the composition of assets and liabilities. He considers only the pure interest rate risks of unanticipated movements in risk-free rates. The probabilities of insolvency are actually larger because other interest factors are correlated with risk-free rates. On the other hand, most banks retain some of their current earnings. Retained earnings are equivalent to added capital and reduce risks.

4.3   Risks of Poor Performance

In addition to risks arising from interest rates, our studies furnish some estimates of the risks of insolvency owing to failures of banks to maintain their operating margins or to properly control their underwriting of loans. Table 4.3 brings out the wide contrasts in the record of banks in these other spheres. The risks from unanticipated movements in earnings and loan losses are estimated by constructing probability distributions of these factors.

In this chapter we examine past movements in loan losses and revenues to see what has affected them, their magnitudes, and their variances. We examine both cross-sectional and time-series data. For loan losses, the cross-sectional data come from the FDIC sample of all banks described in chapter 9. Estimates are based on the portfolios and losses of individual banks in 1975 and the changes between 1974 and 1975, which were the highs for the postwar period. For changes in revenue, the cross-sectional analysis is based on the FDIC sample for 1970, 1971, 1974, and 1975. These years include the largest year-to-year declines in the postwar period. Table 4.8 also reports loan losses and revenues for all 14,400 banks. Unfortunately, we do not have the changes for this broader universe.

The time-series data are derived from all banks and from a limited group of large banks. There are 98 banks in the large-bank sample, with individual time-series for each bank for thirteen years. Both the cross-sectional and time-series data are used in estimating probability distributions for unanticipated losses.

4.3.1   The Dispersion of Earnings

In 1979, the average insured commercial bank in the United States had net book income before taxes and security losses equal to 1.1 percent of its assets. This income gave a pretax book return of 20.0 percent on book (not economic) net worth. The danger of insolvency depends on variations in earnings and losses resulting from fluctuations in net interest income, in operating expenses (less miscellaneous income), in loan losses, and in changes in net worth from capital gains and losses, as well as upon payment policies which add to or subtract from net worth. Table 4.3 gives an indication of the wide dispersion among banks in 1979 of the first two of these factors.

The first item repeats the data on net interest income from table 4.1. The second item shows the large variations in expenses among banks. Given the wide dispersion of incomes and expenses, one is not surprised to see how greatly net operating income (before loan losses and taxes) varies among banks. Items 3 and 4 show the dispersion of such income as

Table 4.3   **Types of Income and Expenses in 1979 by Bank Size (as a Percentage of Net Earning Assets)**

Bank Size by Net Earning Assets	Banks at Specific Percentiles for Individual Items						
	1	5	25	50	75	95	99
Net Interest Income							
Over $500 million	1.0%	2.0%	3.3%	4.0%	4.7%	6.0%	6.9%
Under $25 million	0	0.4	2.0	3.0	4.4	6.4	8.2
All banks	0	0.5	2.1	3.2	4.4	6.2	7.8
Operating Expenses (Other Than Interest and Loan Losses)							
Over $500 million	0.7	1.7	2.8	3.6	4.2	5.4	6.9
Under $25 million	1.6	2.0	2.6	3.3	4.4	6.6	9.2
All banks	1.6	2.0	2.6	3.3	4.2	6.1	8.4
Net Operating Income before Loan Losses and Taxes							
Over $500 million	0.3	0.7	1.2	1.6	1.9	2.7	3.6
Under $25 million	−0.6	0.8	1.6	2.0	2.6	3.6	4.5
All banks	−0.1	0.9	1.5	2.0	2.5	3.4	4.3
Net Operating Income (before Loan Losses and Taxes) as Percentage of Equity							
Over $500 million	6.1	11.2	17.7	22.2	26.8	35.7	48.2
Under $25 million	−3.5	7.3	16.4	21.1	26.2	34.9	44.3
All banks	−1.0	9.1	16.8	21.3	26.2	35.4	46.2
Loan Losses as Percentage of Net Earning Assets							
Over $500 million	0	0.01	0.11	0.18	0.30	0.58	1.40
Under $25 million	0	0	0.01	0.09	0.26	0.89	2.04
All banks	0	0	0.02	0.11	0.26	0.78	1.83
Loan Losses as Percentage of Equity							
Over $500 million	0	0.2	1.5	2.7	4.3	8.9	18.7
Under $25 million	0	0	0.1	0.9	2.7	9.2	22.2
All banks	0	0	0.2	1.2	2.9	8.5	19.8

Source: 1978 and 1979 call reports for all insured commercial banks in the United States.

a percentage of net earning assets and of equity. The median bank netted 2.0 percent of its earning assets before providing for loan losses. Slightly more than 1 percent had negative returns. At the other extreme, 1 percent earned over 4.3 percent. The spread among large banks was considerably smaller. Only one large bank reported negative operating earnings before providing for loan losses. Out of the more than 14,000 banks, only 59 reported that operating losses ran as high as 1 percent of earning assets. Of these, 27 banks had losses exceeding 2 percent.

The risk from such losses depends on their size in relation to equity. The table shows that only 1 percent of banks lost as much as 1 percent of their equity as a result of operating losses. The total number who lost 10 percent of their equity or more was 53, of which one was a large bank.

The year 1979 was fairly typical in terms of bank operating earnings. In 1975, at the first percentile of all banks, the loss from operations was 1.5 percent, compared with 0.9 percent in 1979. Table 4.8 shows more detailed information about those with large losses in 1975. In that year, the number of banks with operating losses above 1 percent of earning assets or 10 percent of equity was more than twice as large as in 1979; but still, only 1.2 percent of all banks lost as much as 1 percent of their earning assets.

Loan Losses

In addition to high interest and other expenses causing poor operating results, banks can lose money because of poor underwriting leading to bad loans, failure to receive repayments, and a need to charge off the bad loans against capital. The final two items in table 4.3 show the ratio of net loan losses to all earning assets (not loans alone) and to equity. Again, the dispersion is wide. The median bank in 1979 lost only 0.11 percent of its earning assets from loan write-offs. The mean was somewhat higher at 0.21 percent. Since, typically, loans made up 65 percent of net earning assets, losses against loans alone averaged 0.33 percent. About 10 percent of operating earnings was required by an average bank to cover loan losses; 90 percent was available for profits and taxes.

The dispersion was great in this category also. Nearly one-quarter of the banks sustained no net loan losses. On the other hand, 1 percent of all banks had to charge off amounts equivalent to 1.83 percent or more of assets and over 20 percent of their equity.

The table does not show those banks—probably 20 or fewer—that were not operating at the end of the year because they had closed or merged as a result of poor operations. Of those banks with records available for the entire year, 5 had loan losses equal to 100 percent of their equity. They were able to cover such losses from other operating income, loan loss reserves, or tax credits.

The table also shows that, on average, large banks have somewhat riskier loans. Their average loan losses as a percentage of both assets and equity are greater. On the other hand, the law of large numbers works in their favor. Because they tend to have more diversified loan portfolios, they are less likely to have an extremely high loss ratio. Their losses become serious primarily when they concentrate too many of their loans in a specific activity.

In the following discussion, changes in operating income before loan losses and net loan charge-offs are analyzed separately, because valuable information may be gained from considering the two individually. On the other hand, because some correlation exists between them, for some purposes the net income after loan losses is a more suitable figure.

4.4 Estimates of Operating Risks

While only a small number of banks show operating losses before loan charge-offs, the risk that operating earnings will change significantly exceeds the risk from poor loan underwriting. Tables 4.4 and 4.5 contain estimates of operating risks.

Risk is a function of unanticipated decreases in expected earnings. The discussion of risk theory pointed out that problems arise primarily if a loss is unexpected. Expected losses can be offset by capital contributions, or the bank can be closed. In some cases, however, banks will be allowed to operate even though they are expected to have a negative net worth at the end of a period. Agreements on whether to force increases of capital, mergers, or bankruptcy are regulatory decisions.

As chapter 3 noted, the best estimate of a bank's expected operating earnings or losses is simply their level in the previous period. Table 4.4 shows the levels of operating earnings in each year for all banks, for the weighted average of the 98 large bank holding companies whose annual operating results have been reported in a consistent manner on the COMPUSTAT tape, and for the company whose reported variance of earnings before loan losses was the largest during this period.[1]

The table shows that, with the major exception of the sharp drop in earnings between 1970 and 1971, shifts in income before loan losses have been relatively minor. (The differences in percentages reported for 1976 and later are due to a change in the form of reporting. Prior years were based only on domestic activities and income. In 1976 the call reports were shifted to consolidate foreign and domestic operations. Because earnings on foreign assets are lower than on domestic ones, average consolidated earnings as a percentage of net earning assets are reduced.) Except that they are slightly smaller, on the whole, the levels and movements for the large banks do not differ much from those for all banks.

---

1. The programming and calculations from the COMPUSTAT tapes were ably performed by Etian Gurel.

Table 4.4   **Income before Loan Losses and Income Taxes as a Percentage of Net Earning Assets at Year End**

Year	All Banks		98 Large Banks		Bank with Large Variance	
	Actual %	Change	Actual %	Change	Actual %	Change
1967	1.433	−0.079	1.512	—	1.53	—
1968	1.507	0.074	1.573	0.051	1.60	.07
1969	1.719	0.212	1.634	0.061	1.80	.20
1970	1.697	−0.022	1.713	0.079	1.91	.11
1971	1.466	−0.231	1.575	−0.138	1.75	−.16
1972	1.375	−0.091	1.444	−0.131	1.47	−.28
1973	1.461	0.086	1.412	−0.032	1.23	−.24
1974	1.561	0.100	1.464	0.052	1.16	−.07
1975	1.640	0.079	1.704	0.240	0.00	−1.16
1976[a]	1.378	n.a.	1.563	−0.141	1.36	1.36
1977[a]	1.352	−0.026	1.461	−0.102	1.09	−0.27
1978[a]	1.528	0.176	1.623	0.162	1.22	0.13
1979[a]	1.586e[b]	0.058	1.633	0.010	1.17	−0.05

Source: Cols. 1 and 2 from FDIC annual reports; cols. 3–6 COMPUSTAT tapes.
[a]Fully consolidated.
[b]e = estimated.

Their reports are on a holding company consolidated basis for the entire sixteen years.

While the data for all banks are an indication of what shifts are likely to occur in the income of an average bank as a result of economic events, they do not take into account added risks assumed by individual banks as a result of nontypical portfolio choices, management, or location. To better estimate individual bank risks, we use two other sources that do contain data on individual banks.

We have examined the record for each of 98 banks from the COMPUSTAT tape. The bank with the largest variance in these earnings is shown in table 4.4. It should be noted, however, that the tape no longer includes some large banks that disappeared because of merger or insolvency. In the cases of insolvency, failure probably resulted more from fraud or maldiversification than from accepting unusual operating risks.

The Cross-sectional Data

Table 4.5 shows the distribution of banks by changes in income before loan losses that occurred between 1970 and 1971, the year of maximum fall for this item. It shows only those whose income fell, although the distribution statistics in the table are based on all banks. On average, large banks show larger movements than small ones. Over 5 percent of large banks saw their earnings drop by 1 percent or more of their earning assets. On the other hand, the dispersion of loss increases among small banks is far larger; more of them tend to be at the extremes.

The estimated risks from operating changes are somewhat higher than are those from loan losses found in table 4.7. There are two basic reasons for this greater apparent risk. One arises from the fact that a large number of factors influence earnings. If all of these turn negative, the unanticipated fall in income is likely to be greater than for loan losses. The drop in average income from 1970 to 1971 was 23 basis points per dollar of earning assets, compared with an average increase in loan losses of 15.7 basis points between 1974 and 1975, its maximum.

The second reason appears to be the much greater difficulty small banks have in controlling their expense/revenue ratios. While all sizes of banks except for the $50 to $500 million class show higher variances of income than of loan losses, the increase in the variance for the smallest bank is over 300 percent.

Time-Series Data

The risks of changes in income, as measured by the time-series data of the 98 large banks, agree with the concept that operating risks exceed those from loan losses by a great deal. The average variance in values from operating changes from 1965 to 1979 was 0.0000064 (table 5.4). At the median, the time-series data show operating risks about 100 percent higher than risks of movements in loan losses. The largest banks with lowest operating risks show a variance of about 0.000001. On the other hand, the bank with the largest variation of this income shows a risk more than thirty times higher, at 0.000031. Because we lack time-series data for individual small banks, the time-series estimates of operating risk are somewhat below those from cross-sectional data. If we had time-series data for small banks, those at the higher end would probably show a much higher probability of loss from this factor than is brought out in the table.

| Table 4.5 | Change in Operating Income before Loan Losses and Taxes, 1970–71 | | | | | | | |

Size of Bank in Millions of $	Mean	σ	Percentile				Median	Var. $\log(1+\Delta)$
			1	5	10	25		
>500	−0.35	0.44	−2.01	−1.04	−0.73	−0.53	−0.31	.000019
50–500	−0.26	0.37	−1.51	−0.87	−0.71	−0.46	−0.23	.000014
10–49	−0.06	0.53	−1.58	−0.90	−0.57	−0.35	−0.06	.000028
<10	−0.04	0.83	−3.31	−1.33	−1.06	−0.49	−0.05	.000069

Source: FDIC tape.

Other Risk Factors

The lack of time-series data for small banks is only one factor tending to underestimate loss probabilities for this group. Another is the good chance that, as a result of fraud, insider abuse, or nondiversification, a few banks each year will have a greater probability of losses than is shown in these estimates. In each year of the 1970s a few banks experienced losses greater than 5 percent, and in some cases over 10 percent of their earning assets.

If these banks are small the losses to the economy from such failures will be minor. It may well be inefficient and costly to the economy's productivity to fight to keep such losses as low as they now are (Mayer 1975). On the other hand, it may well be that improved techniques of estimating nondiversification and insider abuse through simulations could increase our knowledge of what types of portfolios contain appreciable risks from these sources. A new system might hold down such losses at a lower cost to the economy.

4.4.1   Estimate of Risks from Loan Losses

Most discussion of banks has concentrated on default risk—the inability of borrowers to pay off their loans. In fact, in a diversified portfolio this risk may be far lower than that from interest rate changes.

Loan losses are dangerous primarily if the bank concentrates too many of its loans in a particular sphere, such as construction and development loans, real estate investment trusts, loans to individual investors, or foreign loans. Table 4.3 showed loan loss ratios for 1979. We also examined in detail similar information for 1975, the year losses rose most sharply. Net charge-offs (losses less recoveries) were actually slightly less than in 1979 for the median bank. However, the mean of loan losses in 1975 was twice as high as in 1979. More banks—and especially more large banks (whose weight is much greater in calculating the mean)—suffered a sharp increase in loan losses as a result of the recession. Their loan experience was likely to be particularly adverse if they had made large loans to real estate investment trusts and on construction projects.

In 1975 loan losses exceeded 1 percent of net earning assets for 572 banks, and in over 5 percent of the cases losses exceeded currently available revenue, thus requiring that capital be drawn down. In the period 1970–75, however, only a handful of banks had losses exceeding 5 percent of assets for either a one- or a two-year period. Under existing conditions, a bank must have an undue concentration of loans or be extremely inept to fail because of loan losses alone.

It must be remembered that these favorable results have occurred under a regime when banks are examined at regular intervals. They are not as reliable a predictor of potential losses without regulations. Theory, however, does indicate that roughly similar results should be expected if other properly devised measures of risk and risk-taking are substituted for examinations and evaluation of individual loans.

4.4.2   Levels of Losses

Table 4.6 contains time-series data for loan losses derived in the same manner as those for operating losses in table 4.4. This table also makes clear why, on the whole, loan losses have not been a critical risk factor under our existing banking system. On average, loan losses were low in the 1960s. They took a series of jumps in the 1970s. Still they reached only slightly over 0.4 percent for all banks in 1976 and slightly over 0.5 percent for the largest banks. From 1976 to 1979, the net loss ratio was cut by over one-half.

Moreover, it is not the level of loan losses that is most critical. Losses that are anticipated will be charged for in the interest rate or in fees quoted prospective borrowers. Expected losses will merely increase the gap between gross and net revenue. Risks arise not from the total, but from unanticipated increases in losses and from the distribution of individual banks around the average change.

In any year, the level of loan losses will depend upon the type of portfolio and the operating skills and style of individual banks. Levels of losses from one year to the next, and therefore expected income, depend upon such individual bank factors. However, most changes in the level of

Table 4.6   Net Loan Losses as a Percentage of Net Earning Assets at Year End

Year	All Banks		96 Large Banks		Bank with Large Variance	
	Actual %	Change	Actual %	Change	Actual %	Change
1967	0.119	−0.004	0.101	—	0.058	—
1968	0.101	−0.018	0.078	−0.023	−0.063	−0.121
1969	0.116	0.015	0.087	0.009	0.285	0.348
1970	0.213	0.097	0.238	0.151	0.251	−0.034
1971	0.210	−0.003	0.266	0.028	0.293	0.042
1972	0.148	−0.062	0.162	−0.104	0.458	0.165
1973	0.170	0.022	0.191	0.029	0.615	0.157
1974	0.265	0.095	0.285	0.094	1.990	1.375
1975	0.422	0.157	0.532	0.247	2.266	0.276
1976[a]	0.355	—	0.508	−0.024	1.278	−0.988
1977[a]	0.254	−0.101	0.358	−0.150	0.288	−0.990
1978[a]	0.205	−0.049	0.264	−0.092	0.224	−0.064
1979[a]	0.179e[b]	−0.026	0.223	−0.041	0.128	−0.096

Source: Cols. 1 and 2 from FDIC annual reports; cols. 3–6 from COMPUSTAT tapes.
[a]Fully consolidated.
[b]e = estimated.

losses do not depend upon prior levels of risks or income. There is only a slight correlation between broad classifications of portfolios and movements in losses from year to year.

The ratio of losses to net earning assets obviously depends on the share of loans in the portfolio. Banks investing primarily in securities rather than loans have a lower percentage of loan losses to assets than banks with a high ratio of loans. A correlation also exists between losses and gross earnings on assets in one year and the following year's level of losses. Firms that take greater risks to earn larger sums experience more losses and are more apt to see their losses increase. But the correlation is not high. Past losses and gross earnings together predicted less than 10 percent of losses in 1974 and about one-quarter in 1975.

The type of loans in the portfolio also influences the level of losses. Using a four-way classification, we find that, as the percentage of commercial and industrial and consumer loans in a portfolio rises, so do losses. On the other hand, home mortgage loans lower the loss ratio. However, the R^2s for the level of loan losses compared with their composition was under 0.05 in 1974 and was 0.12 in 1975. From other data, we know that if loans are further subdivided into more classes, some, such as land development and construction, will show still higher rates of losses.

When a sharp jump in losses occurs, the relationship between past behavior and the level of losses becomes still more attenuated. Thus in 1974 and 1975, when losses jumped sharply, correlations of the amount of losses with beginning of the year portfolios were reduced compared with prior years when losses stayed steady. Unanticipated losses were a much higher percentage of the total.

Skewness

The distribution of loan losses in any year is not normal. It is skewed to the right. As pointed out, the median loan losses in 1979 for all banks was 0.11 percent, but the mean was at 0.21 percent. Nearly one-quarter of all banks had no loan losses. Among banks under $10 million in size, nearly half fell into this category of no loan losses. On the other hand, small banks sustained a considerably higher percentage of large loan losses.

In 1979 the percentage of small banks either with no loan losses or with losses exceeding 2.0 percent of net earning assets was 2.5 times as high as for banks in the largest size category. In 1975, when unexpected losses increased sharply, skewness was even greater. No large banks had loan losses above 2.55 percent of net earning assets, while there were 66 banks in the under-$500 million category whose losses exceeded 3 percent of earning assets, and 5 banks actually had loan losses that exceeded 10 percent of their total assets. This seems to reflect the lesser chance for smaller banks to adequately diversify their portfolios and profit from the law of large numbers. Again, these large losses skew the distribution of losses to the right. If the distribution were normal, we would expect about 7 banks in the smallest category to have loan losses higher than 1.27 percent (three standard deviations from the mean). Instead, the number of banks with losses exceeding this level was over 100. Among all banks we would expect about 18 to have loan losses exceeding 2 percent of their net earning assets, but 158 banks had losses above that point.

4.4.3   Cross-Sectional Data

We should expect that changes in loan losses from one year to the next will be largely unanticipated or random. No bank will knowingly take a loan it has reason to expect will default. Some banks will select portfolios that have higher average losses, but unless they change their selection process suddenly, their choice of a higher risk portfolio will have been reflected in higher loss rates in prior years also. There is also a correlation between higher gross revenues and loan losses in each year.

On the other hand, a tendency does exist, as one would expect, for banks having above-normal losses in one year to move back toward the mean in the next. Both managerial and regulatory pressures are exerted on banks to bring their losses into line. In 1974 the regression of change in loan losses on the previous year's level of losses was negative, with an R^2 of 0.3, while it was negative with an R^2 under 0.1 for 1975. In that year the previous level of gross revenues also had a small impact. Otherwise, changes in losses in both years seemed unrelated to previous experience. To the degree that this is true, we can estimate risks under the assumption that they are stochastic. We can measure them by fitting distributions to past unanticipated changes. Such distributions by size of bank are shown in table 4.7.

Probabilities of Unanticipated Losses

The table shows a distribution of changes in loan losses between 1974 and 1975 by size of bank. This was the year of the largest increase in losses in postwar history. The weighted average of loan losses as a percentage of

Table 4.7   Change in Loan Losses as a Percentage of Net Earning Assets 1974–75 by Size of Bank

Size in Millions	Mean	σ	Median	Percentile 75	90	95	99	Var. $\log(1+\Delta)$
>500	0.19%	0.298%	0.12	0.24	0.54	0.82	1.16	.000009
50–500	0.10	0.431	0.06	0.16	0.39	0.64	1.85	.000018
10–49	0.01	0.419	0.02	0.12	0.27	0.42	1.09	.000017
<10	−0.04	0.403	0	0.04	0.17	0.53	1.05	.000016

Source: FDIC sample tape.

net earning assets for all banks rose from 0.265 percent to 0.422 percent. When we examine the table, however, we note that the increase in losses occurred almost entirely among the relatively small number of larger banks. The unweighted mean and median of banks with less than $50 million in earning assets show that virtually no change occurred.

Even though the largest banks had on average the sharpest jump in losses, their actual risk or danger of insolvency is offset somewhat by their smaller variance around the mean. As a result, when one reaches the right-hand side of the distribution for those with the largest losses, no great difference appears in the amount of change experienced among classes of banks. The major exception is for the unusual 99th percentile figure for the banks in the $50 to $500 million class.

The standard deviation of the entire distribution is 0.413 percent. When we compare the numbers of banks whose losses exceed two or three standard deviations with the number expected in a normal distribution, we find that the fit is good for the two classes containing the bulk of banks (banks with less than $50 million), but the number with higher than expected changes in the two larger bank classes is considerable. For these classes, it might be sensible to fit a symmetric Paretian rather than a normal distribution.

A major point of the table, however, is that even in a year with maximum unanticipated changes, the total impact of loan losses on risks is not large. Risks are measured by the probability that losses will increase sufficiently to wipe out all capital. The measure of this risk is the variance of the log of the change in asset values as a result of unanticipated losses. This variance is found in the last column of table 4.7. The risks from loan losses as measured in this way not only are small, but are relatively small compared with interest rate risks.

4.4.4   Time-Series Estimates of Loss Probabilities

In addition to estimating probable loan losses by size from cross-sectional data as in table 4.7, we can also estimate these probabilities from the time-series data on individual banks shown in table 4.6.

The variance of the logs of the change in asset values as a result of the year-to-year movements in loan losses for 96 large banks from 1967 to 1979 was 0.0000031. This is only about one-quarter of the cross-sectional estimate of this same probability, which equaled 0.0000165, based on the changes in loan losses between 1974 and 1975.

When we examine the extremes among these large banks, we find a large range; but, still, even that bank with the largest variance does not reflect a high risk. Several large banks experienced virtually no net loan losses over this period. Each of them had variances of the logs of about 0.0000003. In contrast, a few had considerably larger losses than average, but the worst had a variance of 0.0000375. This amount is somewhat larger than the estimate of high risks from the cross-sectional data.

The time-series data seem to confirm the cross-sectional data. The use of a distribution based upon the worst year of unanticipated changes that occurred in the postwar period is probably a fairly good indicator of loan loss risk. One problem with both types of information of course, is that they exclude the banks that actually became insolvent in these years. These totaled four banks in 1974 and thirteen in 1975. In addition, the regulatory agencies issued a slightly larger number of cease and desist orders or actions to terminate insurance, primarily because of threatened loan losses. These stopped banks from assuming as much risk as they desired.

Similarly for the large bank sample, data are not included for United States National Bank and Franklin National Bank because they failed during this period. These banks clearly had much larger variances than the highest continuing bank, given their large losses in their final year.

4.4.5   Total Losses from Poor Performance

The next chapter contains estimates of the total risk in banks calculated to match the interest rate, operating, and loan loss risks that prototype banks have assumed by their past portfolio and operating choices.

Tables 4.8 and 4.9 give another picture of operating and loan losses. They contain information for all banks that in 1975 reported book losses of 1 percent of net earning assets, either from operations before loan losses, or 1 percent from loan losses, or 1 percent from a combination of the two. The tables were prepared from data reported for each individual bank in the United States.

About 3 percent of all banks had operating losses before loan losses in 1975. Of these, 169, or 1.2 percent, lost more than 1 percent of their net earning assets. These were heavily concentrated in the smallest banks, of which 2.5 percent lost more than this amount. The table shows a smaller and smaller number of banks as the size of operating loss increases. Before loan losses, none lost over 6 percent of assets.

The number of banks where loan losses exceeded 1 percent of earning assets was far larger, with 572, or 4 percent of the total. In this category the distribution by size of bank is considerably different. The largest banks had a higher percentage with sizable loan losses, though none had losses above 3 percent. Among smaller banks, a few had large loan losses, rising to over 10 percent of assets for three small banks.

The final sector shows losses including both those from operations and those from loans. The number is smaller than those with loan losses above 1 percent because many banks had positive operating earnings against which to offset loan losses. Eight banks out of 14,400 lost over 6.0 percent of earning assets, and each of these lost more than 10 percent.

Perhaps more important than the losses compared with assets are losses compared with book capital. In 1975, the worst year for banks, 1.9 percent lost more than 10 percent of their capital. Of these, 36 banks lost

Table 4.8   Number of Banks That Lost over 0.99% of NEA in 1975, Classified by Size and Amount of Loss

Class of Banks by Net Earnings Assets ($ Millions)	Number of Banks in Size Group	Operating Loss before Loan Losses of Net Earning Assets (%)				Loan Losses of Net Earning Assets (%)				Operating Losses, Including Loan Losses of Net Earning Assets (%)			
		1.0 to 1.99	2.0 to 2.99	3.0 to 3.99	4.0+	1.0 to 1.99	2.0 to 3.99	4.0 to 5.99	6.0+	1.0 to 1.99	2.0 to 3.99	4.0 to 5.99	6.0+
>500	203	0	0	0	0	14	3	0	0	1	1	0	0
50–500	1,778	2	0	0	0	75	13	3	1	13	5	2	1
10–49	6,853	20	7	5	4	215	67	12	2	65	31	16	3
<10	5,205	56	35	22	18	110	42	12	3	88	72	32	4
All banks	14,039	78	42	27	22	414	125	27	6	167	109	50	8
Percentage of All Banks in Class													
>500		0	0	0	0	6.9%	1.5%	0	0	0.5%	0.5%	0	0
50–500		0.1%	0	0	0	4.2%	0.7%	0.2%	0.1%	0.7%	0.3%	0.1%	0.1%
10–49		0.3%	0.1%	0.1%	0.1%	3.1%	1.0%	0.2%	*	0.9%	0.5%	0.2%	*
<10		1.1%	0.7%	0.4%	0.3%	2.1%	0.8%	0.2%	0.1%	1.7%	1.4%	0.6%	0.1%
All banks		0.6%	0.3%	0.2%	0.2%	2.9%	0.9%	0.2%	*	1.2%	0.8%	0.4%	0.1%

Note: Excludes banks not reporting assets or income for full year.
*Less than 0.05%.

Table 4.9   Number of Banks That Lost over 0.99% of NEA in 1975, Classified by Size and Amount of Loss

Class of Banks by Net Earnings Assets ($ Millions)	Operating Loss before Loan Loss, % of Book Equity				Loan Loss, % of Book Equity				Operating Loss Plus Loan Loss, % of Book Equity			
	10–19%	20–49%	50–74%	75+	10–19%	20–49%	50–74%	75+	10–19%	20–49%	50–74%	75+
>500	0	0	0	0	12	4	0	0	1	1	0	0
50–500	3	0	0	0	79	11	3	1	11	8	1	1
10–49	23	11	2	1	216	84	9	6	49	45	17	6
<10	41	14	0	0	111	39	6	3	62	42	5	6
All banks	67	25	2	1	418	138	18	10	123	96	23	13
					Percentage of All Banks in Class							
>500	0	0	0	0	5.9%	1.9%	0	0	0.5%	0.5%	0	0
50–500	0.2%	0	0	0	4.4%	0.6%	0.2%	0.1%	0.6%	0.4%	0.1%	0.1%
10–49	0.3%	0.2%	*	*	3.2%	1.2%	0.1%	0.1%	0.7%	0.7%	0.2%	0.1%
<10	0.8%	0.3%	0	0	2.1%	0.7%	0.1%	0.1%	1.2%	0.8%	0.1%	0.1%
All banks	0.5%	0.2%	*	*	3.0%	1.0%	0.1%	0.1%	0.9%	0.7%	0.2%	0.1%

Note: Excludes banks not reporting assets or income for full year.
*Less than 0.05%

50 percent or more, with one bank reporting losses of over 100 percent of capital. In addition, of course, the FDIC paid off the depositors of 3 banks and assisted 10 others by advancing funds for mergers. Some other banks merged or sold out voluntarily during the year because of losses. In many ways, table 4.8 is important for analyzing risks from defaults and operations. It shows the total distribution of banks that did badly in the banks' worst year.

4.4.6   Bank Size

The difference in losses experienced by banks of various sizes, illustrated in tables 4.8 and 4.9 and earlier tables in this chapter, is interesting but not critical. Larger banks borrow more money and purchase a higher percentage of liabilities. They take somewhat riskier loans and average somewhat higher income from loans and investments. They also engage in more miscellaneous activities. However, because they have higher operating expenses, pay more for their liabilities, and have larger loan losses, on average their income as a share of earning assets is lower. They also have a smaller amount of equity behind each dollar of assets; their income as a percentage of equity has also been lower; but in 1979 there was virtually no difference in earnings on equity by size. The lower earnings on assets were offset by less capital behind each dollar of assets.

On the surface, the large banks appear to be more likely to fail, since they have riskier assets and less capital. This factor is offset to the degree that they have more diversified assets. Diversification lowers the chances of their sustaining extremely large losses. On the other hand, when they fail to diversify, their greater inherent risk/capital ratio means that other risks dominate, and the probability of their failure rises above that of smaller banks. Such increase in risks and failures has been the experience in the 1970s. In 1975 their loan losses were a higher share of available income at all points except at the extreme 99th percentile. In 1979 this crossover point occurred at the 95th percentile.

Several factors distinguish the smallest banks. They borrow less money and have more demand deposits. As a result, they earn slightly more than average from net interest. They also have somewhat higher operating expenses and considerably lower loan losses. When these various factors are put together, the smallest banks may earn above-average amounts as a percentage of both earning assets and equity. This was true in most years, but in 1979 there were only slight differences in average earnings on equity by bank size. However, the smallest banks still had a greater chance of unfortunate outcomes. Their variances of losses and changes in operating incomes are greater.

The risk that operating earnings will deteriorate seriously is more than twice as great for a bank with assets under $10 million as it is for a larger bank. Clearly, because they lack the self-insurance arising from the law of large numbers, smaller banks are much more likely to experience either changes in liabilities and total assets, without the ability to lower expenses, or relatively larger shifts in losses. This is one of the critical reasons why a different system of regulation and insurance may make sense for small banks.

4.4.7   Are the Estimates Adequate?

The use of distributions of past movements to estimate future unanticipated changes may either understate or overstate actual probabilities. The estimates take no account of the probabilities of fraud or maldiversification. Furthermore, though we would like to estimate what risks would prevail in a free market, this is difficult to do. Bank examiners have probably reduced risk-taking below the level that would prevail if they were absent.

On the other hand, the flat charges of the FDIC, which does not penalize added risk, probably increases the amount of risk many banks can and do take. Furthermore, the estimates of this chapter are based on cross-sectional data in years of maximum change or on time series from the riskiest of large banks. To some this might appear to overstate normal risks, on the assumption that one ought to use average rather than extremes for measurements. But, as was pointed out in the previous chapter, risk calculations should be based on a complete estimate of potential events covering a long period. Insurance reserves should be built up in periods of low losses to offset more extreme shifts. The use of an estimate of risk based on the maximum change in losses or income in fourteen years may not be high enough to offset the actual maximum that might be experienced in a period two or three times as long. On the other hand, this estimate would have overstated average risks during the fourteen-year period. We do not know whether there would be a shortfall or overage over a similar future period, but it is clear that, by the use of maximum variances, some provision is being made for the probability of larger unanticipated movements in the future than occurred on average in the past.

Another problem is that, except for McCulloch's interest rate risk estimates, all the others assume a log-normal distribution. The actual distributions appear to be somewhat skewed. The next chapter gives an indication of the types of errors this can lead to. However, past movements of operating and loan losses are small enough so that even another form of distribution would not make much difference in the magnitude of the estimates.

It should also be recognized, moreover, that the assumption of a normal distribution of expected changes depends upon the bank's having a properly diversified portfolio. Any significant concentration of loans means that the future can be heavily influenced by one or a few exogenous changes. It will be unlikely to follow the same type of random process that results from a wide variety of assets. A typical portfolio is likely to follow a random process because, while the level of reaction will depend on major macro movements of the economy, the degree of reaction will be limited by the need of the government and the Federal Reserve to maintain a generally viable financial system.

Banks as a whole are profitable. Bank profits have been increased by aid from the government through interest rate ceilings and limitation on competition. When these aids are removed, we would still expect the banking system as a whole to earn average profits equal to the risks it assumes. While variations in earnings occur with macroevents, such fluctuations are not likely to lead to insolvency in an industry with adequate capital bolstered by a good insurance system.

This relatively favorable view that normal risks are not unduly high is enhanced by the fact that operating revenues, even for individual banks, usually do not deteriorate suddenly. It takes poor management or fraud and insider abuse to thwart normal diversification. While errors may accumulate over time, advance warnings signal that changes in operations and capital additions usually are required.

Among small banks, most failures have resulted from fraud, insider abuse, or an accumulation of poor operations. When larger banks have failed, unanticipated interest rate changes accompanied by a concentration of loans have been more significant. The analysis in this volume shows that this is what should be expected. Risks arise primarily from a lower than normal level of capital, from a lack of proper diversification, or from continuing subnormal operations.

5 Estimates of Capital and Its Adequacy

5.1 Introduction

Measures of capital adequacy require estimates of the level of expected net worth. To accomplish this task, one must first make an estimate of the level of economic capital, then add or subtract the expected amount of net earnings and of capital contributions less dividend payments.

In simplified financial theory, one should be able to obtain a useful estimate of a unit's net worth from its market value. This would then be available as a starting point, to which estimates of expected changes could be added. However, as already noted, the direct estimate of values from market observations may not be possible. Only a limited number of banks have active markets for shares of their common stock or other liabilities. Furthermore, the prices paid for bank stock may depend upon government regulations or insurance procedures, or other artificial forces. The cost and availability of information may lead to inaccurate valuations. The prices quoted may be inordinately influenced by cyclical or other expectational forces that do not affect the risks of insolvency but rather result from expectations that future returns will be lower or have an increased volatility.

This chapter adds information on the problem of determining net worth and on how this influences risks. It considers some of the factors that enter into a proper capital definition and the procedures used to measure and project banks' net worth. It discusses some of the tensions that exist between banks and their regulators over a proper level of capital.

The previous analysis showed that estimates of capital could be improved by using market information to estimate the value of individual activities, which could then be summed to obtain the value of the portfolio, of liabilities, and of net worth, which is the residual between assets and liabilities.

This chapter considers in greater depth:

1. Proper definitions of capital.
2. The economic costs of capital to a bank and the economy.
3. Some market estimates of net worth compared with those based on book figures.
4. Measures of capital adequacy and fair insurance premiums.

The concluding discussion in this chapter uses past experience and the resulting probability estimates of changes in net worth to show how they affect specific prototype banks. Such banks include those at the average and at the extremes of risk-taking. In place of an attempt to measure the net worth of specific banks, the estimates of fair insurance premiums for the prototype banks are calculated for a range of possible net worths. The information for the prototype banks is supplemented by a specific case example, that of the First Pennsylvania Bank.

Capital is risk-offsetting because it can cover losses. It can bridge negative cash flows and pay off creditors. It also earns returns but does not require cash payments or engender interest rate risk. Yet banking history reflects a steady decline in the ratio of capital to assets. Why has this occurred? Why has leverage—the ratio of borrowed money to capital—steadily increased?

Financial theory offers two conflicting answers. One emphasizes the advantages to stockholders of increasing leverage—advantages arising out of the tax and regulatory system. While, in theory, arbitrage among investors and lenders should wipe out any profits from leverage, this probably does not happen under existing conditions.

In contrast, traditional theory posits a falling cost curve until leverage reaches some optimum point. It pays to reduce the capital ratio until that point is reached. If leverage continues to expand among banks, it is an indication that the market judgment is that leverage has not reached the optimum.

In this latter view, failure to pick the optimum point of capital reduces welfare by wasting scarce resources. On the other hand, if leverage has expanded primarily because it is subsidized by the government, regulations that prevent it from expanding as far as the market wants do not create a social loss. While neither view can be proved, many believe that bank capital may be far lower now than it would be in a completely free, competitive market. In banking, unlike other industries where excess capital and fixed assets are wasted, most capital is lent out. There are no obvious advantages to substituting one form of liquid capital for another, in contrast to whatever ratio a free market would select.

5.2   Capital and Capital/Asset Ratios

Capital is desired as an offset to risks of fluctuations in the value of assets and liabilities. Capital must earn an adequate return if it is to be invested. For analysis of the risks of individual banks, the amount of capital per se is not significant; the important thing is its relationship either to the bank's total assets or liabilities or to a subcategory such as assets at risk or earning assets.

In our studies, we primarily compare capital with net earning assets. When we seek a measure of capital adequacy, we consider the ratio of these two items. Both these totals must be defined if we are to understand what they include and exclude. It is recognized, however, that what constitutes an adequate ratio may differ considerably from bank to bank based on their individual risks.

5.2.1   Defining Capital

Capital accounts in banks consist of equity capital, surplus, undivided profits, reserves for contingencies and other capital reserves, and perhaps capital notes and debentures. Of these, all but the last clearly fit a proper criterion for capital. In addition, reserves for bad debt losses and other reserves on loans and securities are available to offset losses. Deferred taxes also can reduce risks. At a minimum, these offset assets and require no cash outflow. If the firm is in an unprofitable situation, they usually work their way into other accounts.

Over the years, a major debate has developed about whether capital notes and debentures should be counted as part of capital. The answer depends on the purpose for which capital is being defined. If capital is to protect the FDIC and uninsured depositors when a bank becomes insolvent, then subordinated notes and debentures serve as capital. But if capital is to protect against the occurrence of a negative net worth this need not be true.

The prime advantage of debentures in reducing the risk of insolvency is that they usually have fixed interest rates and payment dates and a longer duration than other liabilities. Their interest rate risk tends to be negatively correlated with that of assets. If interest rates rise, the economic liability of debentures to the bank will fall. Since their usefulness follows from their duration, a debenture coming due shortly or with variable rates is equivalent to any other liability and should not be counted as capital.

For most analyses, notes and debentures are not a significant factor in banks. If included as part of bank capital, they make up less than 6 percent of the total. They have been issued by an even smaller percentage of banks than this. On the other hand, most large banks have raised between 25 and 35 percent of total equity plus bond capital through debentures, and in some the ratio is as high as 50 percent. In most of this volume, we have included debentures as capital in much of our analysis, even though we recognize their inability to substitute for equity capital in particular cases. In most of the statistical analysis, because so few banks have issued capital notes, results depend primarily upon banks without existing debentures.

5.2.2   Net Earning Assets

We are rarely concerned with the amount of capital per se. Bank A could have one hundred times the capital of bank B, but if its deposits were two hundred times as large, it would not be in as strong a position. Capital must be related to the risks it is expected to absorb. Assets are also a useful base in analyzing earnings. While recognizing the arbitrariness of a particular definition, in our studies we primarily work with the ratio of capital to net earning assets (NEA), the primary assets at risk. The regulatory agencies frequently use total assets or total deposits. They also use the concept of risk assets, which excludes government securities from NEA. To measure net earning assets, we exclude from total assets cash and due from banks (except interest-earning deposits), fixed assets, other assets, and acceptances. On the liability side, to offset these subtractions, we have also excluded acceptances and have subtracted cash and due from banks from demand deposits to arrive at net demand deposits.

The exclusion of acceptances from both sides is straightforward. The pertinent balance-sheet item should be the value of the put option that the bank writes when it accepts a bill. It also seems clear that cash items in process of collection (float) should be subtracted from both sides.

However, more questions can be raised about the other adjustments. Banks receive some services from their reserves and the balances they hold with other banks. Fixed and other assets also furnish services and incidental income. In contrast, currency and coin are an expense. The particular definition we use may bias income and expense statements slightly, but in most cases we have compared analysis based on the use of total assets in place of NEA and have found no significant differences. Risks of loss from the items excluded are slight. Using net earning assets gives a better measure of risk as well as a more accurate base for analyzing earnings and losses.

A more difficult problem arises from the fact that some of the condition reports used for much of our analysis and for that in many banking studies contain information only for the bank and its domestic subsidiaries. Until 1976, most series excluded data for branches and subsidiaries abroad. For many large banks, foreign assets and liabilities are critical. More than 17 percent of the total earning assets of the American banking system are now held abroad. Many published statements of the ratio of equity to net earning assets for the banking system are biased upward by a failure to include foreign assets. As an example, the ratio of capital to domestic net earning assets for our five largest bank holding companies in 1979 was about 8 percent. When their foreign earning assets are added, the ratio of capital to net earning assets falls to about 4 percent. Yet figures based only on the banking system's domestic assets are frequently cited in capital ratios.

In our study we have used domestic balance sheet and earnings data for analysis when we felt this would not bias the results. For the larger banks and the past four years (when more foreign data are available), we have used data that include foreign operations whenever available.

To give some indication of differences, when domestic net earning assets are used as a base compared with total earning assets, the reported capital ratios increase by about 20 percent. The ratio is about 40 percent greater than if worldwide total assets are the base. The use of domestic NEA gives a ratio about 18 percent higher than if worldwide net earning assets are used, with of course much larger differences for the biggest banks.

5.3   End-of-Year Capital/Asset Ratios

The risk of inadequate capital, as we saw in figure 2.1, is that negative variances will affect the expected net worth; that is, the value of liabilities will exceed the value of assets. In addition to the initial net worth, the expected change in net worth between examinations must be analyzed. Changes in net worth depend on net earnings and on a bank's dividend and capital policies. Since risk depends on the ratio of capital to liabilities, the growth in liabilities must also be estimated.

In the 1970s, for banks as a whole, net earnings on equity have been in the neighborhood of 12 percent. Dividends have averaged about 40 percent of earnings, so that undistributed profits have been over 7 percent of net earning assets. In addition, however, banks raised capital and added to their reserves. As a result, in an average year, total capital and reserves available to absorb losses have grown at a rate of 10 to 12 percent a year. Since earning assets grew at a somewhat faster pace, the ratio of capital to total assets fell.

Chapter 11 discusses procedures by which the expected capital/asset ratio for a bank can be calculated. The technique explained there is the use of time-series transfer function analysis. This allows one to extract the maximum information from the recent history of the bank, but it also enables one to use projected or ranges for significant exogenous variables, such as the occurrence of a recession or sharp movements in interest or inflation rates. In any case, the most critical factor is to find the actual value of the bank's net worth and assets. When these have been determined, the projection to the end of the year is likely to be a second-order problem.

The procedures outlined may illumine some of the uses for and problems with existing bank examinations. Much of the examination process can be thought of as an attempt to project a capital/asset ratio. In effect, examiners project losses in capital by their loan classifications. If well done, this is a useful function, particularly when accompanied by suggestions for improving operations and increasing capital.

The process, however, remains too subjective. Measurements of capital and of liquidity are not modeled carefully or correctly. Knowledge of potential losses needs to be embedded in a more complete model if it is to be of maximum benefit.

5.3.1 Costs of Capital and Leverage

The higher the percentage of capital compared with assets or liabilities, the lower the risk of insolvency. The steady downward trend in this capital ratio is demonstrated in table 5.1. In 1939, the banks that survived the depression were extremely cautious. Their equity capital was 10.33 percent of their total assets. During World War II banks expanded their assets rapidly, but most of the expansion was in government securities. Their capital ratio fell to 6.86 percent, but they were deemed not to have increased their risk excessively because their ratio of capital to loans was still over 25 percent.

During the 1960s and 1970s, the ratio of capital to assets kept declining, and the ratio of capital to loans fell even more rapidly as the share of loans in portfolios rose. Of course the increased loan percentage may not have added to risk as much as conventional wisdom believed if it simultaneously lowered the duration, and therefore the interest rate risk, in portfolios.

When we examine banks by size, as in the second half of table 5.1, we note that the distribution of capital is very uneven. The ten largest banks

Table 5.1   **Bank Equity Capital as a Percentage of Total Book Assets for All Banks in the United States**

By Year		By Bank Size in 1979	
Year	Percent	Bank Size	Percent
1939	10.33	<$100 million	8.07
1949	6.86	$100 million to $1 billion	6.89
1959	7.90	Over $1 billion	4.63
1969	7.45	Ten largest banks	4.02
1979	5.75		

Source: Federal Reserve and Comptroller of the Currency.

had 4.02 percent of capital to total assets. In contrast, banks with under $100 million in assets averaged over 8 percent in capital. National banks have tended to hold less capital than other banks. The percentage of capital to assets for the five largest national banks in 1979 was 3.80 percent. Capital adequacy has become a question of prime concern because some observers, including bankers, fear that the level of capital may have fallen too far. A constant battle is waged as regulators try to encourage or to force banks to increase their capital ratios.

Obviously, forces are at work tending to drive capital ratios down below prior levels and under those that regulators believe are adequate. What are these forces? Do such pressures arise from the normal operation of a free market, or are they the result of the special regulatory environment of banks? If the pressure to reduce capital is based on market forces, will the market, left to itself, bring about an optimum capital ratio? Or are there problems such as those of information and transaction costs that can either lead to a market failure or mean that a regulated market will perform better than one left to itself?

Answers are not simple. Financial theory offers two conflicting views on the forces that determine the optimum capital/asset or capital/liability ratio (leverage). However, both views agree that our existing regulatory and tax system may make it profitable for banks to reduce their capital below the level that would be set in an unconstrained market. Thus the pressure from regulators to increase capital may reflect their view of what a free market would demand. However, it may also reflect lack of knowledge. There have been no objective standards in establishing sound capital ratios. As a result, critics of the existing system believe that significant costs arise both for a bank and for the economy when regulators insist on more capital than is optimum.

5.3.2 The Optimum Level of Leverage

Van Horne (1977) gives an excellent exposition of two main views in the theory of finance as to leverage and the cost of capital. He discusses them as the traditional and the Modigliani-Miller (MM) theories. Under the traditional theory, up to a point, the marginal and average costs of capital fall as the ratio of debt to equity increases. After that point they rise. This U-shaped cost curve results from two separate pressures. Initially the rates paid for liabilities such as deposits, federal funds, or debentures are less than the cost of equity. As a bank raises money from such liabilities, its average cost of capital, which depends on the ratio between the more expensive equity and the lower-cost borrowings, falls.

This decrease in average borrowing costs cannot go on forever. As the bank increases its leverage, risk—and therefore the rate it must pay on its equity—rises. After a point, the cost of borrowing rises also. Lenders demand higher rates as their risk increases with higher leverage. The average cost of financing the bank starts to rise when the effect of the increasing costs from added risks exceeds the falling costs that result from mixing cheaper debt with more expensive equity. Under the traditional concept, a competitive market will force the firm to operate at an optimum point where its average costs of funds are at a minimum.

In contrast to this view, Modigliani and Miller (1958) show that, under the particular assumptions they posit and ones commonly adopted in financial theory, the value of the firm and its cost of capital are independent of its financing decisions. The leverage decisions or financial structure of the bank are irrelevant to its value or to the cost of its capital. In perfect competitive financial markets, individuals, providing they have equal access to the market, can undo any leverage decision of the firm.

One explanation of the irrelevance of corporate financial structure draws upon the concept of arbitrage. If there were an optimum level of debt equity and the firm failed to choose it, individuals could make a profit by buying the optimum ratios of the firm's debt and equity in the market and issuing new securities against them. Based on issuing at this optimum ratio, they would receive more than they had paid. Since such arbitrage profits are inconsistent with equilibrium, opportunities for them should not exist in a well-operating market. The value of a bank should be constant across all leverage ratios. Stiglitz (1974) has shown that corporate financial policy is irrelevant under still broader conditions. His proof is based on the fact that, under rather general conditions, individuals' decisions are independent of the debt equity ratio of firms, and they can undo any firm decisions by shifting their relative debt equity ratios.

5.3.3   Leverage in the Banking System

Since banks seem under constant pressure to increase their leverage, something must happen when the theories are applied to the facts. Why do bankers believe they can improve profits by increasing their leverage? Why do they believe their minimum cost of capital or the maximum value for their stock to be at a point with greater leverage than in the past?

Modifications of the Theories

For a number of reasons, the theories must be modified in application. The literature is full of such debates. Some major qualifications generally agreed to as potentially important are listed in Van Horne as the following:

1. Bankruptcy costs may be significant. If they are, as they seem to be for banks, then, as leverage increases, the new, more highly leveraged financial packages threaten losses that make them less attractive. As the possible cost of bankruptcy grows with leverage, so does the bank's borrowing cost. The risk to managers may rise even faster. To the degree

that this is so, strong internal pressures should develop against borrowing even the amount optimum from the shareholder's point of view. Many observers believe that this accounts for the relatively low leverage of nonfinancial firms.

2. The capital markets may not work as well as assumed. There may be high transaction costs when banks, especially small ones, try to issue stock or bonds. This raises their cost of capital compared with deposits and leads to pressure for increased leverage.

3. Institutional factors and market imperfections similarly may raise individuals' borrowing costs even more than those of banks. The arbitrage process may be much more difficult than theory assumes. If the perceived risks of personal leverage exceed those of corporations, optimum arbitrage would be still further reduced.

Also significant are (4) taxes, (5) information deficiencies, and (6) deposit insurance. More detailed discussions of these last three items follow.

The Corporate Income Tax

The MM theory applies in a world without corporate income taxes, or at least in a world where taxes are neutral with respect to payments for raising funds through debt or equity. This is not true of the United States. Under our system, since interest payments are tax deductible, greater leverage lowers the after-tax cost of capital. In fact, many observers believe that, given the high rate of corporate taxation, the minimal cost of capital would be achieved when all or nearly all funds were borrowed.

This is somewhat less true for banks. In comparison with other corporations, banks have extremely high leverage. Also, banks on average have lower corporate taxes. These can frequently be reduced to zero because of special provisions for items such as state and local bonds, leasing income, and taxes paid abroad. Thus banks may not achieve as large tax advantages for their stockholders compared with other corporations by increasing their leverage. When all things are considered, however, the form of the corporate income tax probably does serve to increase the optimum level of leverage even for banks.

Information Deficiencies

Another factor not considered in the simplified theories is the cost and amount of information available to depositors and lenders in comparison with that possessed by managers or owners. Ross (1977) and others have shown that when there are problems of disparate information, and particularly when moral hazards can exist, the amount of leverage may be a significant factor in determining the cost of capital.

Information has been a particularly troublesome question for banks. On the one hand, regulators seemed to feel, until recently, that the public ought to depend on regulations rather than try to obtain information on the soundness of banks. The less the public knew, the better. On the whole, depositors and lenders went along with this thesis. They depended on the regulators either to establish capital levels adequate to ensure solvency or to bail out even the uninsured depositors if something went wrong.

Risk and Insurance

In chapter 8, Sharpe demonstrates what happens as the FDIC offers insurance to all banks at the same rate irrespective of their risk level. It is profitable for banks to increase both the riskiness of their assets and their leverage. As a result, under existing procedures the regulators must impose limits on the banks. Bank profits increase to the extent that they are able to exceed the regulator's limits.

An assumption that the regulators are guaranteeing the safety of a bank's debt lowers its cost even at extreme levels of leverage. The increase in the cost of debt with rising risk, which is assumed to limit leverage in corporations, would not be effective for banks if their deposits are insured or their safety guaranteed.

5.3.4   The Costs of Increased Capital

We have pointed out important advantages gained by banks that expand through borrowing. As long as depositors are insured or believe they are insured, stockholders can profit by increasing leverage. Under the present insurance system, normal market operations do not work to hold down leverage. There are, however, at least two major unresolved issues in this generalization.

Managers may believe that they will not be fully compensated for increasing risks in their banks. Even though profits rise with risk and leverage, managers' inability to spread risks because so large a part of their wealth may be tied to a single bank should make them more cautious. Heavy losses, a requirement for a large capital infusion, a forced merger, or bankruptcy will be far more traumatic the larger is the share of the bank in an individual's wealth or income.

Lenders on capital notes or subordinated debentures are also not protected by insurance. Yet in recent years many large banks have been able to increase their stock leverage by issuing debentures. Such issues took place even though it was often recognized that the issues were requested by regulators who felt that the bank's ratio of capital to deposits or risk assets was falling too low. Either (1) the purchasers were poorly informed and the market was not performing well, or (2) the level of leverage deemed inadequate by the regulators was not worrisome to the bond market or at least was adequately covered by a higher promised return, or (3) bondholders placed a low probability on regulators' allowing a large bank to fail. (While interest rates paid were higher than those paid by other corporate borrowers, they were not much higher. In 1980, yields on bonds of banks were 40 to 70 basis points, or 4 to 6 percent, higher.)

It is not clear which explanation is correct. Evidence exists that those who bought bonds of the banks that failed in 1973–75 had not given sufficient attention to the risks involved. The purchasers of debentures, who included among their number some large and theoretically sophisticated lenders, were unaware of the degree of risk they were assuming. On the other hand, even after it became clear that bank debentures were far more risky than deposits, the rates for most banks did not move out of line with those of other securities. The market apparently is willing to accept very high leverage ratios.

A number of empirical studies have been conducted on the effect of leverage on the cost of bank capital. The results have been mixed. In most cases, added leverage did not seem to increase the cost of debt capital—nor, however, did it significantly reduce the average cost of funds. But, as in so many empirical tests, specific results depend greatly upon the specification of the model and the choice of variables (Orgler and Wolkowitz 1976; Weaver and Herzig-Marx 1978).

Overcapitalization

A critical question in the debate over leverage is who gains or loses if regulators demand and succeed in enforcing either too high a level of capital or, conversely, too low a level of leverage. The models of risk show that the dangers of insolvency and costs to the insurer and society fall rather rapidly as capital ratios are increased. The functions are nonlinear, so at critical points risk is reduced greatly by small additions to capital, whereas, at levels not too much higher, additional capital has very little effect.

Bankers clearly believe they lose if they are forced to increase their capital needlessly. They lose tax advantages. They lose whatever gains they are now making at the expense of the FDIC. Raising additional capital is costly. There are marketing costs for new issues. In addition, prices must be sufficiently below the market so that the issue will sell. For most banks, markets are extremely limited. Selling new stock may mean diluting control. Selling bonds, except to correspondent banks, may be almost impossible.

It is not as clear that the costs to the public or society of overcapitalization of banks are serious or even positive. Part of the argument depends upon how closely the theory of MM fits the facts in this case.

There is a basic difference between the investment of capital in a financial institution and investment in fixed assets. Excess investment in fixed assets means that resources are standing idle. Added capital to a financial institution does not reduce the amount of real resources. It simply means that intermediation takes place in a different form than it otherwise would. The analysis in this case requires dealing primarily with the theory of capital structure and the theory of intermediation.

The gains to banks from monopoly positions and from gaming against the FDIC are costs to the public that we would be better off without. The tax breaks also probably cost the public. By law we have created tax expenditures (some prefer the term subsidies) to increase the use of debt over equity. If regulators require excess capital, they force banks to give up this tax break. The Treasury would gain. Tracing whether a cost to the public arises from such an action depends upon a complex analysis of the reason this particular tax expenditure was established, and of what gains and losses were expected.

Santomero and Watson (1977) believe they have shown that there may be serious costs for both under- and overcapitalization. Undercapitalization increases the risks of insolvency and therefore imposes whatever social or public, as opposed to private, costs appear when a bank fails.

Their argument for costs of overcapitalization seems weaker. They argue that, if banks are required to lower their leverage, individuals must hold more bank capital and fewer deposits. If individuals substitute bank capital for loans in their portfolios rather than deposits, interest rates will rise and investment and capital accumulation will fall.

A similar but somewhat less complete argument is made by Scott and Mayer (1971). They say, in effect, that forcing investment in a low-risk or risk-free asset causes a deadweight loss of the difference between the rate a firm can earn on its capital and the risk-free rate.

These arguments, however, seem in conflict with the MM thesis. The irrelevancy argument will apply. As is demonstrated in chapter 8, in a complete financial market there is no "optimal" financing mix. In more general terms it is not clear why there should be a social loss if banks are required to issue somewhat less risky capital than they would otherwise prefer. Depending on their attitude toward risk, investors will shift their portfolios so that some will hold more and some fewer bank stocks. Investors can also adjust their other holdings. There would not seem to be a loss to the economy if a high percentage of bank stocks are held by widows and orphans or risk averters, as opposed to risk-seeking institutions.

The strongest argument for a social cost, but one financial economists tend to disbelieve and downplay, stems from the possible existence of highly segmented and noncompetitive markets. Banks and savings and loans cannot buy common stocks or, frequently, corporate bonds. If markets are not efficient, excluding potential sources of funds could make a difference in availability and in what borrowers in these sectors must pay. Conversely, restricting savings and loans primarily to the mortgage market by tax inducements or regulation is assumed to lower interest rates on mortgages.

If segmentation occurs, it is most likely to affect small, high-risk borrowers in local markets. In these markets, competition and efficiency are constrained by a limited number of lenders, together with poor information for those at a distance who might be willing to enter.

Specific information on segmentation is scarce enough so that regulators frequently make (but usually not simultaneously) two common but opposing arguments. One states that requiring excess capital is dangerous for banks because it will increase their capital costs and thereby affect their ability to compete with other types of financial institutions. The second argument is that requiring excess capital with its higher costs is dangerous because banks, as a noncompetitive group, will raise their charges or make more risky loans to cover these costs. If markets are not highly segmented, neither of these situations should occur. Depositors and investors can alter their choice of assets and liabilities in such a manner as to equalize financial investing and lending rates among markets. There should not be any basic alteration in real capital or the physical investments of the economy.

Arguments against change that depend for their validity on the existence of segmentation are frequently, in fact, disguised arguments in favor of more change and more competition.

5.3.5   Measuring Capital

While most discussions of capital ratios are based on calculations like those in table 5.1, which show the relationships between book capital and a bank's assets also valued at book, the figures actually needed to measure risks may be quite different. It is the true, or economic, net worth that protects a bank's liability holders or the FDIC, not the values shown on a bank's books. To measure risks, the economic net worth must be estimated. Valuable intangible assets may not be entered on the books, while the recorded value of assets may differ considerably from their actual or market value. As a partial list of differences between book and economic capital, there may be:

1. Unrecorded gains or losses in the portfolio, depending upon past interest rate movements.

2. Because of interest rate ceilings (regulation Q), liabilities for deposits as shown are higher than their true liability to the bank. Payments against them will not rise as fast as market interest rates because crediting interest on demand deposits is prohibited, and interest rate ceilings on savings and consumer time deposits have been below the market in most years. The capitalized difference between their cost and market rate adds net worth to the bank.

3. The value of customer relationships, goodwill, knowledge of individual loans, and similar information, which has been paid for in the past and serves to reduce future costs, is usually not shown on the bank's books.

4. The reserves against loan losses may be over- or underestimated. In their examinations, regulators decrease estimates of available capital by, requiring additions to reserves in accordance with the amount of loans classified by the examiners.

5. The balance sheet also contains furniture, fixtures, computers, and fixed assets. Regulators in the past have assumed that investments in such forms are not available to serve capital needs. While these items may have only slight liquidity, their actual earnings value and ultimate worth may be as large as or larger than that of other assets.

6. Many balance sheets also contain other reserves, such as for deferred taxes or contingencies. These also serve to decrease the probability of insolvency.

7. In contrast, certain types of commitments, such as for future loans or for foreign exchange, are likely to be drawn upon when they will be costly to the bank. They serve to lower net worth.

Chapter 3 pointed out some of the advantages and disadvantages of attempting to measure capital values by use of market quotations of both common stocks and bonds. Many experts believe that the market is the best and truest measure of net worth. However, because of the lack of data for most institutions and because of questions on how to relate the risks reflected in changes in stock values to the risks of insolvency, other techniques have been suggested to measure net worth.

Market quotations of rates of return on bank securities can be used as guides to value the assets and liabilities of banks whose securities lack a market. At the coarsest level, the average price/earnings ratio for bank stocks obtained from the market can be used as a multiplier applied to the reported book earnings of an individual bank in order to secure an estimate of its net worth. Since the reported earnings are on a book basis in both cases, the multiplier provides a rough equivalent of economic value. However, the dispersion of price/earnings ratios of individual banks is very wide. Consequently, this procedure results in estimates over a similar broad band. It is difficult to judge where in this range the individual bank under consideration would fall. In addition, this method suffers from whatever general disabilities apply to market quotations for individual institutions.

Somewhat more accurate would be the use of rates of return in the market applied to individual similar activities within a bank. Applied to an institution's own activities, these can be used to adjust the values of classes of assets and liabilities from a book to a market basis. A big problem is the difficulty of finding the values of intangibles and determining how much difference they make for individual banks. Still, this procedure can be used as an alternative to the grosser technique.

A third method is described in the papers by Morrison and Pyle and Nadauld (chaps. 13 and 14). It utilizes the concept that the generalized price of risk can be estimated from market quotations. The values of future cash flows depend on their certainty equivalencies and on the discount rate currently being applied to funds that will be received in the future. This discount rate is measured by the term structure of risk-free interest rates. If the comparative risk can be calculated for each activity by adding to the risk-free rate a factor for its added risk, then its expected cash flows can be capitalized by using the market rates of return for activities with equivalent risks.

5.3.6   Market-to-Book Value Ratios

The past movements of common stock prices compared with book values yield a general picture of how market and book values have been related and how the relationships have varied. Such data are shown in table 5.2.

Table 5.2   **Relationship of Market Value of Bank to Book Value**

Part 1: Banks Included in Standard and Poor's Bank Stocks Index

Year	Ratio	Year	Ratio	Year	Ratio	Year	Ratio
1950	0.986	1957	1.074	1964	1.652	1971	1.444
1951	1.056	1958	1.372	1965	1.436	1972	1.584
1952	1.367	1959	1.556	1966	1.345	1973	1.615
1953	1.107	1960	1.403	1967	1.270	1974	0.943
1954	1.291	1961	1.874	1968	1.743	1975	0.967
1955	1.493	1962	1.529	1969	1.439		
1956	1.220	1963	1.641	1970	1.345		

Part 2: Percentile Distribution of Banks with Data Available
on COMPUSTAT Tape

Years	Percentile						
	1	5	10	50	90	95	99
1968–70	0.93	1.01	1.09	1.43	2.07	2.36	2.66
1971–73	0.64	0.82	0.84	1.25	2.05	2.40	3.51
1974–76	0.33	0.40	0.47	0.65	1.03	1.53	1.66
1977–79	0.30	0.42	0.49	0.66	1.00	1.10	1.36

Source for Part 1: L. Goodman and W. Sharpe, "Perspective on Bank Capital Adequacy: A Time Series Analysis," NBER Working Paper, tables A–3–1 and A–3–2. Includes nine New York banks (bank holding companies) and sixteen outside New York banks (bank holding companies) in 1976.
Note: Part 2 is based on COMPUSTAT tape data for 1968–79. By 1977, most observations were for bank holding companies.

The first part of the table shows the year-to-year movement in the ratio of market value to book value of the banks in Standard and Poor's Stock Indexes of New York City and Outside New York City Bank Stocks (Goodman and Sharpe 1978). The combined weights are based on 1976 book values. During most of the past thirty years, the market valued banks at about 135 percent of their book value. Sharp fluctuations occurred around this average, such as the nearly 46 percent jump from 1967 to 1968 and the more than 40 percent fall from 1973 to 1974.

Such differences are even clearer when we examine the second part of the table. It shows the distribution of market-to-book ratios of individual banks at selected percentiles. It contains average market-to-book ratios for the three-year periods 1968–70, 1971–73, 1974–76, and 1977–79.

The table reflects a major shift during this period of the market's valuation of individual banks, of banks as a group, and of common stocks as a group. In the period 1968–70, the average or median bank had a market-to-book ratio of 1.43 (the mean was 1.49), and fewer than 5 percent of banks showed ratios under 1.0. For the next three-year period, a minor drop of 13 percent, to 1.25, occurred in the median (the mean fell less, to 1.40). The spread of the distribution increased considerably. The top 10 percent of banks had higher ratios than the top 10 percent in the previous period, while the bottom 10 percent fell by more than the average.

The year of the big drop was 1974. In comparison with 1971–73, the market's valuation of book assets fell nearly half. Furthermore, the amount of decline was approximately the same all across the distribution. It was not a case of riskier banks being assigned a higher cost of risk after the insolvency of several large banks in 1973 and 1974. Rather, all banks were judged to be far riskier. While data for individual banks show some movement in the following five years, through 1979 the average bank continued to be valued in the market at about two-thirds of its book value. Either intangibles were considered to be negative, or they were heavily outweighed by losses of capital values not taken into the books.

5.3.7   Price/Earnings Ratios

A major factor explaining the large drop in the valuation of banks can be found in table 5.3. It contains data that show the weighted average market price/earnings (P/E) ratio for 81 large banks from 1967 through 1979. It also presents information on the average return these banks earned on their book assets, as well as the price/earnings ratios of stocks in the Standard and Poor's Stock Index.

The market's valuation of intangible capital can alter either because banks are earning less on their tangible and intangible assets or because the market capitalization of such earnings falls. In turn, an increase in discount rates can reflect a general marketwide increase or one applicable to a particular industry.

Table 5.3   **Stock Market Valuation of Income (Price/Earnings Ratios)**

Year	Banks[a]	Standard and Poor's 500 Stocks[b]	Price/Earnings Ratios of Banks to Standard and Poor's 500	Bank's Percentage Earned on Book Value[c]
1967	11.7	17.7	.66	11.2
1968	15.8	18.1	.87	11.0
1969	14.7	15.1	.97	11.5
1970	11.9	16.7	.71	12.0
1971	11.7	18.3	.64	12.2
1972	13.8	19.1	.72	12.0
1973	11.6	12.3	.94	12.4
1974	6.6	7.3	.90	12.5
1975	7.3	11.7	.62	11.7
1976	9.3	11.0	.85	11.3
1977	7.3	8.8	.83	11.6
1978	6.1	8.3	.73	13.0
1979	5.5	7.4	.74	13.9

Source: Cols. 1 and 4, COMPUSTAT tape; col. 2, Standard and Poor's.
[a]End-of-year stock prices
[b]December average stock prices.
[c]After taxes.

The decline in the stock market's valuation of bank assets was not caused by any decrease in the yield that banks reported earning on their assets. Column 4 of table 5.3 shows the reported book net income after taxes as a percentage of banks' earning assets. In 1974, market values took their sharpest drop even though the return on assets remained stable. By 1979 the rate of reported book earnings was at a high for the period and 13 percent above the rate of earnings reported for 1973, but the market valuation of bank assets was less than half that of the former period.

Most of the large decrease in the valuation of earnings appears to have been a general market phenomenon. The price/earnings ratio on the Standard and Poor's 500 stock average dropped more than 55 percent between 1971–73 and 1979. In this period, bank reported earnings became somewhat suspect because they failed to include losses in capital values from higher interest rates. Still, the drop in the P/E ratios for banks was almost identical to that for the overall market. This drop in the valuation of book earnings more than accounts for the entire fall in estimated net worth shown in table 5.2. The market capitalization rate for earnings was far lower than the reported percentage return on book values.

Because the difference between book earnings and real earnings probably fluctuates more for banks than for other industries, or at least has a different timing, one would expect to see banks' P/E ratios move independently of stocks as a whole. The table shows that this is the case, but differences appear to average out.

5.3.8   Estimating Risks in Prototype Banks

When they select their portfolios, banks alter the degree to which they risk insolvency. Their choices of assets and liabilities, their operating procedure and expense, their off-balance-sheet commitments, and their capital policy, determine their expected end-of-period ratio of net worth to assets as well as the possible variance in this proportion. If their assets end up less than their liabilities, they will be insolvent. Their risk of failure depends on their expected capital/asset ratio, on the potential variance in their portfolios, and on the time period under consideration.

Table 5.4 shows how banks might vary the volatility of their assets and how such choices influence their risks and fair insurance premiums. The table is only illustrative. It brings out differences that can arise when banks select activities with interest, credit, and operating risks that diverge from the average. The table employs somewhat arbitrary

Table 5.4   **Example of Risks and Fair Insurance Premiums**

	Bank A	Bank B	Bank C
Section 1			
Interest rate risk	.0006539	.0008627	.0021111
Credit risk	.0000002	.0000031	.0000375
Operating risk	.0000010	.0000064	.0000309
Sum of variances	.0006551	.0008722	.0021795
Fair Insurance Premiums per $ of Liabilities			
5% capital/NEA	.0002210	.0005206	.0033026
10% capital/NEA	.0000001	.0000010	.0002308
Section 2			
Interest rate risk	.0006539	.0008627	.0021111
Credit risk	.0000090	.0000165	.0000185
Operating risk	.0000298	.0000320	.0000683
Sum of variances	.0006927	.0009112	.0021979
Fair Insurance Premiums per $ of Liabilities			
5% capital/NEA	.0002630	.0005670	.0033390
10% capital/NEA	.0000002	.0000020	.0002110
Section 3			
Fair Insurance Premiums with Interest Risk Based on Chapter 10			
5% capital/NEA	.0047[a]	.0065[a]	.0090[a]
10% capital/NEA	.0028	.0039[a]	.0054

Source: See text. Fair insurance premiums for sections 1 and 2 are based on table 1, Merton, *Journal of Banking and Finance*, 1 (1977): 3–11.
[a]Interpolated.

assumptions with respect to variations among risks and in net worth. The chapters in part 2, which contain other assumptions, illustrate how vital are measurements of maturities and duration in obtaining specific risk estimates.

Table 5.4 measures degrees of risk, first by summing the variances of the three types of risk contained in the portfolios assigned to the prototype banks. It then uses these variances to calculate the fair insurance premium that would be needed to guarantee full payment to liability holders despite any shortfall in assets at the end of a year (Merton 1977 a).

5.3.9   Time-Series Estimates of Variances

Section 1 of the table shows estimates constructed from the variances of movements in time series of total returns in a bank's activities. In the table, the portfolio of bank A includes activities with minimum risks. Bank B represents an institution that conducts its operation in a manner closer to the averages for the banking system. Bank C is assumed to take risks at the high levels of the risk spectrum.

Examine the components of possible future changes for bank A. It takes an interest rate risk equivalent to that existing in an average net portfolio with a duration of not quite two years. Its probable fluctuations are assumed to equal the variance recorded between 1965 and 1976 in the log of the end-of-the-year prices of a two-year government note. The estimate of operating and credit risks for bank A is based on the year-to-year movements in operating earnings and loan losses experienced from 1967 to 1979 by the bank at the low end of the banks contained on the COMPUSTAT data.

Bank B's activities are more typical of an average bank. Its interest rate risk is assumed equal to that experienced by the holder of a three-year government note. Its estimated variances for operating and credit risks are derived from the weighted average of the banks shown in tables 4.4 and 4.6.

Finally, bank C—the riskiest—is assumed to accept an interest rate risk equal to that on a five-year government note. Its operating and credit risks are those experienced by the bank with the largest variances contained in the final columns of tables 4.4 and 4.6.

Although total returns on government securities at different maturities are used to measure interest rate risk, we do not know exactly what movements in net worth typically result from interest changes. Chapter 10 illustrates that the interest elasticity of bank net worth depends on a complex averaging of the duration effects of both assets and liabilities. The next example—that of the First Pennsylvania Corporation—demonstrates that a specific estimate of duration requires an examination of each of the major components of the bank's balance sheet. It also depends, as later chapters show, on what assumptions are made about whether the cash inflows received during a period are paid out or, if they are not, at what rates new assets are bought.

In addition to differences among prototype banks shown by the sum of their variances, the bottom data in each section estimate fair insurance premiums per dollar of liabilities based on their variances and capital/asset percentages of 5 and 10 percent. These premiums are taken from tables prepared by Merton under the assumption that the Black-Scholes option pricing model applies (Merton 1977a).

Examining section 1 of table 5.4 lays out at least three important factors. In the first place, the danger of adverse interest rate movements engenders by far the largest share of the risks. The past variances of interest rates account for 95 percent or more of the total.

Second, wide differences exist in the risks accepted by different types of banks and therefore in the costs to the economy or an insurer for protecting each against defaults. If the expected ratio of capital to net earning assets is 5 percent, the premium for insuring bank C with its risky portfolio choices is more than six times as large as for bank B—the average bank. Moreover, these differences are sufficiently large so that banks may appreciably increase their profitability by taking excess risks.

Finally, we note that the amount of capital compared with assets or liabilities is extremely important in determining total risk. Given the type of variances shown for the prototype banks, the risks of insolvency fall rapidly as the expected net worth rises. At a 10 percent capital-asset ratio, the estimated risks for banks A and B become almost negligible. Even bank C, which chooses a portfolio with much greater variances, can offset most of the added changes by increasing its expected capital/asset ratio to 10 percent.

5.3.10   Other Estimates of Risks

Sections 2 and 3 of table 5.4 are based on alternative methods of calculating the variance in the prototype banks. In section 2 the prototype banks use the same estimate of interest rate risk as in section 1. However, the estimates for credit and operating risks are based on cross-sectional data. The variances are based on the logs of changes in asset values arising from loan losses of individual banks between 1974 and 1975, and changes in operating income before loan losses and taxes between 1970 and 1971. These are the years of maximum changes in the postwar period. Bank A uses banks with over $500 million in assets; bank B uses the data for all banks; and bank C uses data for banks under $10 million in assets, which have the greatest variance. This method of calculating the variances raises the estimates for these risks considerably, but they remain minor compared with the risks from interest movements.

In the techniques used here, how the credit and operating risks are calculated makes little difference. However, an examination of the underlying data indicates that, as with interest rate movements, the actual changes may not follow a normal distribution. Especially among smaller banks, outliers in the negative direction exceed normal expectations. If possibilities of fraud and insider abuse were added, the risks from these and other factors would also be somewhat greater than shown in the table.

Some idea of the rapidity with which risks can rise if one takes account of these other factors is shown in section 3. It presents an estimate of the fair insurance premiums required if one believes that a log-symmetric stable distribution rather than a log-normal distribution ought to be fitted to project possible future movements in yields. According to McCulloch's tables (chap.10), with a capital-to-net earning asset ratio of 5 percent the symmetric distributions show an estimated risk of failure ten to thirty times as great as under an assumption of a normal distribution.

The amount of risk will also exceed that shown for the banks in sections 1 and 2 if other distributions are used for credit and operating risks, and if adjustments are made for maldiversification and for moral hazard. Unfortunately we do not have estimates of how much these will raise the possible variances. It does not seem likely, however, that they will increase so much as to make these other hazards equal to interest rate risk.

While we cannot check the accuracy of the data from information about past insolvencies, they appear to be consistent with past events. Actual failures occur primarily among small banks and among banks with high moral hazards not caught by auditors or the examination system. The critical question is whether the present complex system of regulation is necessary to perform this task or whether alternative systems of measuring the risks and of insuring properly could arrive at a more efficient technique for guarding against large numbers of insolvencies and a threatened breakdown in the banking system.

In our examination of the measures needed to improve the system, the biggest gap appears to be in the estimates of future net worth. Except among small banks, the risk estimates seem to be reasonable, as do the techniques for relating variances to expected capital/asset ratios.

5.4   The First Pennsylvania Bank

This case of the First Pennsylvania Bank could be substituted almost without alteration for prototype bank C—the high risk-taker. It also demonstrates some of the difficulties in measuring net worth for a bank. The case is a particularly appropriate example of capital inadequate to meet risks. It illustrates why better analysis of capital adequacy is needed. It took place in the manner predicted by our studies well after they had been submitted to the regulatory authorities and had appeared in journals.

From the published record, the bank appears to have decided that risk-taking was profitable. For a time, its shareholders and management profited from this policy decision. Their gaming—whether deliberately or not—against the FDIC by increasing the risks of the portfolio well beyond those of the average bank appeared to pay off. But when a run of adverse economic events occurred, the risk positions the bank had assumed worked against it. Its operating earnings fell and loan losses increased. In what appeared, at least to outsiders, as an attempt to recoup, the bank continued to increase its risks, particularly those of interest rate changes. The result was a disaster. This was by far the largest bank to require the assistance of the FDIC.

The $325,000,000 below-market loan made by the FDIC to the First Pennsylvania Bank was made in accordance with section 13(c) of the Federal Deposit Insurance Act. This act authorizes the FDIC to lend money only when it has determined that action is necessary to prevent the bank from closing and "when . . . the continued operation of such bank is essential to provide adequate banking service in the community." In this case, the FDIC recognized that it was assuming the risks that more money would be lost, and therefore it acted to recover part of its costs by requiring stock warrants that would gain value if its rescue operation was successful (see the next chapter).

5.4.1 The Record in Brief

During the 1970s, First Pennsylvania Corporation (the bank made up 85 to 95 percent of its consolidated corporation) prided itself on breaking new ground as an innovator. It steadily increased the risks in its portfolio. It raised its dependence on purchased money with a high degree of interest sensitivity. It increased its leverage by reducing the ratio of capital to assets. It raised the share of riskier loans in its portfolio. It purchased securities with longer maturities, thereby widening its exposure to interest increases.

This strategy appeared to be successful until 1973–74 brought both high interest rates and a recession. At the end of 1972, the common stock of First Pennsylvania traded at 2.7 times its reported book value and 16.6 times its reported after-tax earnings. Both of the multiples were among the highest for any bank with an actively traded stock.

In 1972, as shown in table 5.5, the bank reported earnings before loan losses and taxes equal to 1.77 percent of its earning assets. Its net charge-offs for loan losses were 0.28 percent of these assets. Its net earnings on assets were above average. Because of heavy leverage, its

Table 5.5   First Pennsylvania Corporation Operating Earnings and Loan Losses (in Millions of Dollars)

Year	Equity as Percentage of NEA[a]	Net Interest Income	Ex-penses[b]	Provi-sion for Loan Losses	Net Loan Losses Charged	Net Earn-ings[c]	Net Earn-ings as Percentage of NEA	Net Loan Losses as Percentage of NEA
1967	8.7	72	37	3.8	1.9	35.1	2.21	0.12
1968	7.9	78	43	4.1	2.1	35.3	1.94	0.12
1969	7.4	95	50	4.8	2.5	44.7	2.20	0.12
1970	7.0	106	55	6.2	4.0	50.8	2.21	0.17
1971	6.2	113	59	7.0	8.6	54.4	1.91	0.30
1972	5.3	131	68	8.9	10.0	62.5	1.77	0.28
1973	5.1	147	79	11.1	11.5	68.2	1.55	0.26
1974	4.7	156	85	32.0	24.4	71.4	1.29	0.44
1975	5.0	168	106	61.5	30.0	62.1	1.06	0.51
1976	5.0	168	105	52.8	66.0	63.4	1.08	1.12
1977	4.5	177	102	51.1	54.4	75.3	1.12	0.81
1978	4.6	193	112	42.8	40.5	81.0	1.11	0.56
1979	4.2	179	128	46.8	42.5	50.8	0.61	0.51
1980[d]	4.5	122	119	63.7	92.2	3.4	0.00	1.56

Source: Annual reports.
[a]Net earning assets and book capital.
[b]Less other income and excluding loan losses.
[c]Before loan losses and taxes.
[d]Estimated annual rates based on preliminary six-month data.

reported earnings on equity were high. It earned 16.8 percent on its equity. Between 1967 and 1972, the price of its stock rose about four times as fast as did the average for other banks. (It rose by 200 percent, compared with an average of 50 percent.)

Those who follow such a strategy apparently fail to realize the ever-present possibility that a string of adverse events can occur. In fact, interest rates rose in seven of the eight years from 1972 through 1979, culminating in extremely large increases in the first quarter of 1980. Table 5.5 shows that changes in the economy caused sharp declines in operating earnings and an increase in loan losses from 1972 to 1976, when net loan charge-offs exceeded earnings. However, because of tax credits and differences in when losses were taken into the operating statement, the corporation was able to report after-tax earnings of $18 million and a return on equity of 6.4 percent for 1976.

Reported earnings continued to be weak. In 1979, net earnings before tax credits dropped to 0.10 percent of earning assets. Again, however, with tax credits, earnings after taxes were reported as $16.5 million, or 4.7 percent of book equity. The price of a share of common stock at the end of 1979 was only 0.4 times its book value and 8.2 times reported earnings. The market/book ratio was among the lowest for all banks, while the price/earnings ratio was near the highest.

This was the record at the start of 1980. In the first three months of that year, short-term interest rates rose 32 percent, while the interest rate for a ten-year maturity government bond rose 24.5 percent. Given the interest rate risk the bank had assumed, these interest movements were sufficient to cause a negative real net worth, the start of a run by uninsured depositors on the bank, and the need for an FDIC rescue. How this situation developed can be seen in the following tables and the related discussion.

5.4.2   Interest Rate Risks

Interest rate risks result from a mismatch of maturities in a bank's assets and liabilities. The longer the maturity of its assets compared with that of its liabilities, the greater the danger. When a bank buys a fixed-rate security or makes a fixed-rate loan, its interest revenues are frozen until the investment matures. Furthermore, because no asset will sell for more than its present value, if interest rates rise the value of its portfolio falls. When the discount rates for future receipts go up as a result of increased current and projected higher future interest rates, the economic values of all future returns decline. The amount of loss grows the further into the future is the expected payment.

Current Interest Returns

A rise in interest rates in a bank with a mismatched portfolio shows up initially in higher payments for liabilities, accompanied by only a small growth in receipts. The spread narrows between what is earned on assets and what is paid on liabilities. Net interest income falls. If the spread decreases sufficiently, interest earnings will not cover operating expenses. The bank will suffer losses.

Tables 5.5 and 5.6 illustrate one aspect of First Pennsylvania's increasing interest risk. Note in table 5.6 the steady growth in the amount and percentage of interest-sensitive borrowings. After 1967 the bank expanded rapidly, but it based its growth almost entirely on borrowing in the money market. Less than 10 percent of the bank's 400 percent growth in earning assets was funded by demand and saving deposits. Such deposits have been considered safer because their rates were held down by regulations.

What happens to banks that fund their assets through borrowing is demonstrated in the last column of table 5.6. The ratio of net interest return to assets fell steadily, from 4.7 percent in 1969 to 2.1 percent in 1979. Note especially 1974 and 1979 and the spring of 1980, when interest rates jumped. The rates paid on liabilities rose much faster than those received on assets, many of which have fixed yields. These movements

Table 5.6   **First Pennsylvania Corporation Borrowing, Interest Rates, and Net Yields 1967–79**

Year	NEA[a] (in Billions of Dollars)	Interest-Sensitive Borrowings		Average Interest Rates (in Percent)			Net Interest Revenue	
		Amount (in Billions of Dollars)	Percentage of NEA	On Earning Assets	Interest-Bearing Liabilities	Spread	(in Millions of Dollars)	Percentage of NEA
1967	1.59	0.42	26.4	7.3	4.7	2.6	72	4.5
1968	1.82	0.49	26.8	7.7	5.0	2.7	78	4.5
1969	2.03	0.59	29.1	8.9	5.8	3.1	95	4.7
1970	2.30	0.86	37.6	9.2	6.3	2.9	106	4.6
1971	2.85	1.39	48.6	8.4	5.6	2.8	113	4.0
1972	3.54	1.97	55.5	8.3	5.3	3.0	131	3.7
1973	4.40	2.71	61.7	9.6	7.2	2.4	147	3.3
1974	5.53	3.62	68.7	11.0	9.4	1.6	156	2.8
1975	5.88	4.07	69.3	9.2	6.8	2.4	168	2.9
1976	5.87	3.95	67.3	8.4	5.9	2.5	168	2.9
1977	6.71	4.21	70.2	8.1	5.8	2.3	177	2.6
1978	7.28	5.30	72.8	9.5	7.4	2.1	193	2.7
1979	8.34	6.24	74.9	11.3	10.0	1.3	179	2.1
1980[b]							122	1.7

Source: Annual reports, 1979 and 1975. Data before 1975 are not exactly comparable owing to minor adjustments from mergers, etc.
[a]Net earning assets.
[b]Estimated annual rate based on preliminary six-month data.

narrowed the spread and caused a sharp drop in net interest earnings. In the first six months of 1980, net interest income dropped to a rate of about 1.7 percent of net earning assets. Net earnings before loan losses and taxes were close to zero. The squeeze on interest rates meant that, even with only normal loan losses, the bank would lose money.

5.4.3   Estimating Declines in Capital Values

A second effect from interest rate moves is felt through shifts in the bank's wealth or net worth. The degree of impact depends on the degree of mismatch or, more correctly, as shown in chapter 10, on the weighted anticipated variances of a banks' assets and liabilities.

The Portfolio's Maturity Structure

It is somewhat easier to estimate the maturity of liabilities than of assets. An examination of the balance sheet of First Pennsylvania at the end of 1979 shows that earning assets were funded by four principal components. About 6 percent of earning assets were financed by the difference between non-interest-bearing liabilities (demand deposits) and non-interest-bearing assets (cash, etc.). A second component, equity plus long-term borrowings, equaled 8 percent of earning assets. Savings accounts and certificates made up about 10 percent. Finally, the great bulk, 76 percent, come from purchased money. Most, but not all, the rates paid for the 76 percent of borrowed money change daily with the market. The study in chapter 9 shows that even though some borrowings have slightly longer maturities of one week to six months, the marginal costs of all but the equity and long-term borrowings are likely to move with market rates. If one estimated roughly that the payments on 85 to 90 percent of liabilities had a one-day maturity and moved with the market, while the remainder had fixed payments with long maturities, he would probably not be far off base.

Again, there are four principal components on the asset side. Footnotes to balance sheets report the average maturity and amount of the investment portfolio. Table 5.7 shows that, at the end of 1979, the average maturity for this component was 123 months. On average, about 20 percent of earning assets were in this category. (The table presents data for total assets.) At the opposite extreme, about one-quarter of the portfolio consisted of time balances with banks, trading account securities, federal funds sold, and resale purchases. These all have rates that move generally with the market.

The average maturity of the loan portfolio is far more difficult to measure. It is divided into two components—those with fixed rates and those with variable rates. The bank reports that approximately one-third of earning assets are loans written with rates that adjust with the prime. On the other hand, experience shows that where rates rise rapidly, as in 1974 or 1979, many customers cannot pay added amounts. Either they default, or the loans are renegotiated, allowing them to pay at lower rates and decreasing the percentage with floating rates.

Approximately one-quarter of assets are loans carrying fixed rates. Banks do not estimate specific maturities for this category, which consists of some commercial loans, consumer loans, and mortgages. Based on prior studies of portfolios of these types, one may guess that the average maturity—considering amortization—for these loans lies between two and three years. Using this estimate for the fixed rate component, the average maturity for the three components outside the investment portfolio could be between six months and one year.

Putting the Components Together

To find the interest rate risk of portfolios, one must be able to calculate the average weighted duration of both the assets and the liabilities. Most bank balance sheets do not carry enough information to determine the interest elasticity of the bank's portfolio. First Pennsylvania's is no excep-

Table 5.7   **First Pennsylvania Corporation Investment Security Portfolio (in Millions of Dollars)**

| | Years to Maturity | | | | | | Average Maturity (in Months) | Percentage of Assets |
	Within 1 year	1 year– 5 years	5 years– 10 years	Over 10 years	Total Book	Total Market		
1979								
U.S. governments and agencies	109	325	245	498	1,177	1,015	118	13.1
States, municipals, other	34	135	64	179	412	383	138	4.6
Total book	143	460	309	677	1,589	1,398	123	17.7
1975								
U.S. governments and agencies	121	170	—	—	291	292	21	4.1
States, municipals, other	28	91	121	145	385	386	108	5.5
Total book	149	261	121	145	676	678	71	9.6
1970		Combined						
U.S. governments and agencies	15	124	—		139	n.a.	33	4.2
States, municipals, other	41	96	177		314	n.a.	82	9.6
Total book	56	220	177		453	445	67	13.8
1965								
U.S. governments and agencies	48	93	20	—	161	156	28	10.3
States, municipals, other	—	35	2	20	57	n.a.	76	3.7
Total book	48	128	22	20	218	n.a.	40	14.0

Source: Annual reports.

tion. However, even without complete data, one can make gross estimates of how net worth is affected by interest movements.

In the last section we reduced the number of components with diverse interest effects from eight to four. Rates on all of the liabilities except equity and long-term debt can be assumed to move with market rates. The average maturity (and approximate duration) of the investment portfolio can easily be calculated, and it is given in footnotes to balance sheets. The remaining assets are estimated to have an average duration of six months to a year; how long depends on the share of assets at market rate, on what percentage of loans move with the market, and on delays occurring before rates move.

Using a variety of weighting systems for the unknowns and accepting the duration of the investment portfolio as seven years, we estimated durations for the total portfolio at the end of 1979 to be from 1.3 to 2.5 years. Between the last week of December 1979 and March 1980, a bond with a constant one-year duration lost about 3.2 percent of its capital value. The loss for securities with a seven-year duration was about 16 percent. An estimated loss in the value of First Pennsylvania's investment portfolio for this quarter was somewhat over $125 million. (In 1979, when interest rates rose 45 percent as much, the unrecorded loss in the value of the investment portfolio was $89 billion.)

To avoid an appearance of unjustified exactitude, we use only two estimates of how far the bank's net worth may have fallen as a result of interest rate movements. Column 2 of table 5.8 subtracts from the company's book net worth the difference between the market and book values of the security portfolio as shown in the footnotes to the balance sheet. This would be the total decline in value if all other interest rate effects in the balance sheet just canceled each other out.

However, it is unlikely that interest rate risk will be limited to that in the investment portfolio. Mortgages and other loans also fall in value. To take these into account, assume that one-quarter of the portfolio carried no risk because it was funded by equity, long-term debt, and other liabilities whose values rise as interest rates rise. Also assume that the duration of the remaining portfolio was 2.5 years. If these conditions prevailed, the loss in value of the portfolio from an increase in interest rates would be somewhat more than twice as large as the decline in value of the security portfolio alone.

The first column of table 5.8 shows the value of First Pennsylvania's net worth as reported in its balance sheet with all assets carried at book. The second column subtracts from the reported net worth the difference

Table 5.8   **Estimates of the Economic Net Worth of the First Pennsylvania Corporation (in Millions of Dollars)**

Year	Book Value	Corrected for Market Value of Securities	Corrected for Possible Losses on Other Assets	Market Price of Equity
1977	304	279	254	220
1978	348	246	144	204
1979	350	159	−32	136
1980 (31 March)	343	28	−287	109

Source: See text.

between market and book security values. The third column doubles this reported decline to give a weight to other probable losses in the portfolio. The fourth column shows the value of net worth as estimated from the price of the common stock.

Three key points stand out:

1. The stock market's valuation in 1977, 1978, and 1979 fell between columns 2 and 3.

2. According to any of the three last columns, the bank had only a small ratio of net worth to assets at the end of 1979. Column 2 shows a net worth of $159 million, which was 1.75 percent of total assets, while column 3, of course, showed a negative net worth.

3. Even though the official balance sheet showed a minimal change in net worth and an actual increase in the ratio of capital to total assets, columns 2 and 3 show sharp drops in value by March 1980, and an almost certain negative equity.

5.4.4   Operating and Loan Loss Risks

Tables 5.5 and 5.6 contain data reflecting the bank's operating and loan loss risks in addition to those from interest rates. Even as the share of purchased money increased, the bank raised the proportion of loans in its portfolio, particularly those in which high gross rates were paid to compensate for high risks. The gross rate of revenue from the bank's portfolio was among the highest for all banks. While loan losses went up, reflecting greater risk, net earnings on the bank's assets both before and after loan losses stayed high.

In addition to accepting riskier loans, the bank compounded its risks by increasing its leverage. As table 5.5 shows, stockholders' book equity as a percentage of net earning assets measured 8.7 percent in 1967, 5.3 percent in 1972, and 5.1 percent in 1973. Stock market valuations for the equity were higher, resulting in ratios of market-estimated net worth to earning assets of 16.6 percent in 1967, 14.3 percent in 1972, and 8.2 percent in 1973.

The high interest rates and recession of 1974 dealt a body blow to this high-risk strategy. Table 5.6 illustrates the sharp decline in the margin between earnings on assets and payments on liabilities. The bank attempted to avoid the squeeze by increasing volume even more sharply, with only slight additions to capital. Interest revenues were maintained, but with smaller margins and much greater risks.

The recession also caused nonperforming loans to balloon upward. They reached $400 million in 1975, lowering margins still further. Net revenues were reduced more than $30 million a year by this factor. The same forces led to much higher loan losses. Note in table 5.5 that the provision to cover loan losses shot up sharply in 1975. The big increase in actual charge-offs occurred in 1976. Although revenues fell and losses rose, because of tax credits in 1975, 1976, and 1979 net income after taxes showed less variation than appears in this table. Reported net income after taxes was $18.3 million in 1975, rose to $29.0 in 1978, and fell back to $16.5 million in 1979.

From knowledge of how operating earnings and loan losses vary, as shown in this and the previous chapter, we can see that the type of fluctuations shown by the bank should have been anticipated. The year-to-year variances were below those shown for type C banks in table 5.4. The sharpest dip in operating earnings was the 0.5 percent experienced in 1979. The largest loan loss increase was 0.61 percent in 1976. Only in that year did the combined earnings and losses become negative before the debacle.

In the first quarter of 1980, interest rates rose sharply from the previous high levels. Net interest income of the bank dropped by 40 percent compared with the same quarter of 1979. This brought about a sharp decline in earnings. The bank reported a net loss of $7 million in the first quarter and $30 million for the first six months. These figures were before security losses and taxes, but the six-months figure almost certainly included some excessive provision for loan losses.

In summary, the operations of the bank were obviously risky. Purchased money, risky loans, and leverage were all high. Even so, with potential tax credits and adequate loan loss reserves, the bank would not have become insolvent as a result of operations alone. As is indicated by table 5.4 and the discussion of the prototypes, for a large bank to fail a good deal of maldiversification must exist. In the case of First Pennsylvania, the critical factor was the undue interest rate risk arising from an excess concentration in long-maturity securities.

5.4.5   Market Valuation of Earnings

As First Pennsylvania increased its operating risks from 1967 to 1973, the stock market welcomed the changes. The market for a firm's stock provides independent valuations of both its earnings and capital. Although related, the prices fluctuate independently. Dividing the closing market price of a share of stock by after-tax net earnings per share yields the price/earnings ratio. Dividing the price per share by its book value gives a market estimate of the value of equity. Tables 5.2 and 5.3 show average data for these measures for the major banks with easily available information. The information they provide can be compared with that for First Pennsylvania.

For the six years, 1967–72, as growth and risks accumulated, the price/earnings ratio for the First Pennsylvania Corporation averaged 14. Although about ten percent above the bank average, this ratio was well below that of common stocks in general. In 1972, its P/E ratio was 20 percent above the bank average and close to that for all stocks.

In 1973 and 1974, rising market interest rates and a recession caused a sharp fall in the market's valuation of earnings. The average bank P/E ratio dropped from 13.8 in 1972 to 11.6, and then more drastically to 6.6 in 1974. First Pennsylvania's record was similar. It dropped from 16.6 in 1972 to 12.1, and then more sharply to 5.0. From well above the bank average, it fell below.

After 1974, First Pennsylvania's P/E ratio moved up and down along with the overall market. On the whole, it exceeded the bank average. At the end of 1979 it was 8.3, compared with the average bank's 5.5.

5.4.6   Estimating the Bank's Net Worth

The market estimates the economic value of the bank's equity. As chapters 2 and 3 explain, the bank's net worth can also be measured indirectly by using related market information. How did the market price of equity adjust to the movements in risk? From 1969 through 1973, the market valuation of net worth was high. Apparently the bank's common stock reflected a market view that important intangible sources of future earnings not carried on its books existed within the bank. A high degree of leverage and high after-tax yields on equity fostered such views. Return on equity ranged between 16 and 17 percent. For the six years 1967–72, the market value of the firm was more than twice its book value. Its market/book ratio ranked it in the top 10 percent of major banks.

However, as earnings turned downward, the market revised its estimates of capital values. The market-to-book ratio of First Pennsylvania dropped from 2.7 in 1972 to 2.0 in 1973, and then to 0.6 in 1974. Instead of selling at a premium in 1975–77, the market price averaged about 70 percent of book value. This decline was not an obvious reflection of any capital losses the bank had neglected to take. In this period, any differences between the book and market values of individual accounts were slight. Although the bank had a large volume of nonperforming loans, they improved steadily, and potential losses were covered by reserves. The market's reevaluation of the bank's equity seemed more closely related to a general disenchantment with common stocks. The discount from book for First Pennsylvania averaged about the same as for all major banks.

This situation changed drastically in 1978 and 1979. Because of the large interest risks it had assumed, rising rates hit this bank especially hard. At the end of 1979, the ratio of market to book value was only 0.39—among the lowest for any major bank.

Table 5.8 shows how the market's valuations of equity compared with those reported in the bank's balance sheet. It also shows valuations based on the indirect use of market information. The middle columns estimate values from the known interest effects on a bank's assets. They indicate much sharper declines in net worth. Although the indirect estimates show a probable negative net worth in 1980, the stock market still assigned a positive value. This is not surprising—even in bankruptcy, the stock of corporations sells at a positive price. Stockholders' liability is limited, whereas they retain claims that may gain value during the process of reorganization in bankruptcy.

5.4.7 The Need for Rescue

The drop in economic capital led to a dangerous situation for the bank. Because it was in amounts that exceeded the insurance limits, much of the purchased money was not insured by the FDIC. Lenders recognized increased danger. If the bank were closed, long delays would occur in repayment, and losses would probably ensue. As the increased risks became more apparent, uninsured depositors began to withdraw their funds. Between 1 July 1979 and 23 April 1980, the bank lost approximately half the funds it had obtained through large certificates of deposit. Its foreign deposits also began to decline sharply.

Insured depositors did not run. They trusted the FDIC insurance and left their funds in the bank. Borrowing was also possible through sale and repurchase agreements and from companies sufficiently in debt to the bank to be able to offset any deposit losses.

Still, the bank needed to borrow heavily from the Federal Reserve to pay off fleeing lenders. When it became obvious that the probabilities were low that it would be able to repay the Federal Reserve from normal operations, the FDIC was called in. Under Pennsylvania law, a satisfactory merger or purchase was almost impossible. Faced with the prospect of a far greater liquidation task than it had ever attempted before, and recognizing the danger that a failure to bail out one of the oldest and largest banks could lead to runs on other banks, the FDIC put together its largest rescue program.

5.5   Conclusion

This chapter pinpoints some of the difficulties of measuring economic net worth. The First Pennsylvania case highlights the necessity of estimating net worth. It also indicates that, with additional effort, procedures to use market data indirectly can be developed for this purpose. The examples of the prototype banks demonstrate how existing knowledge of probable distributions of declines in value owing to interest rate movements, loan losses, and operations can be brought together to estimate the total danger in a portfolio. The variances of different portfolios can then be related to the level of economic capital in order to measure adequacy and the remaining risk.

The First Pennsylvania rescue operation worries many observers. As is noted in chapter 8, it is not illogical for managers to take excessive risks because they can profit from the FDIC guarantee. Such prospects became even more likely if the losses that normally would accompany a poor policy are limited. Critics fear that this rescue marks another instance of unwillingness to see a large corporation pay fully for the losses engendered by its policies. They question the ultimate results of removing the threat of losses from the profit system. The next chapter discusses several related issues of this type.

6　Some Issues in Bank Regulation

6.1　Introduction

In addition to our wish to improve bank management of risks, one of the driving forces behind the studies for this volume was a desire to reexamine some features of the system of bank regulation and point up areas in which procedures could be improved.

Complaints are widespread that government regulation of banks reduces productivity and raises the costs of borrowing and lending. Bank regulations are accused of weakening competition while giving rise to a plethora of wasteful non-price-competitive practices. As bankers shape their operations and lending, their decisions are said to be warped to circumvent regulatory constraints. Risk-taking is artificially reduced even as capital is wasted (Scott and Mayer 1971; Edwards and Scott 1979; Black, Miller, and Posner 1978).

But regulations, particularly in banking, did not arise capriciously or primarily as the result of bureaucratic pressure. They developed because of major crises in the economy and in financial markets. Regulations were imposed to avoid bankruptcies caused by failures of financial markets to regain stability. These market failures appeared to result from natural and inevitable features of our competitive system. Regulations have been continued because they have created a number of public benefits.

Existing regulations and the bank examination system attempt to control capital, liquidity, diversification, and risks while promoting sound management. However, controls are based on tradition, industry norms, and subjective evaluations. How to measure risks and what constitutes adequate capital have not been formulated in objective terms. The ratio of capital to assets has declined steadily. It is unclear whether this is due to market forces or to weaknesses in the regulatory system. In critical cases, problem banks have ignored regulatory constraints because suggestions for change could not be formulated in an enforceable manner.

Yet the need for some regulation is widely recognized. Without regulations, an undue percentage of financial institutions are likely to take excessive risks. Because of the large amount of leverage, the difficulty of depositors' policing risk levels, the high cost of information, and the number of small, uninformed depositors, an institution can profit by raising its risk ratio. Moral hazards are also high; it is hard to protect against conflicts of interest and self-dealing.

The introduction of federal deposit insurance was a major reform. It reduced fear among depositors, ended bank runs, and helped stabilize the economy. It also potentially increased competition and choice among borrowers and lenders by making entry easier. Depositors do not have to seek size to ensure the safety of their claims.

However, the existing system has several actual and potential flaws. Because insurance premiums are fixed and flat at all levels of risk or capital adequacy, bank managers and stockholders can profit by increasing their risks at the expense of the FDIC. As a result, to curtail excessive risks, detailed regulations and examinations are necessary. It would be more efficient to protect the public by greater use of the market and through insurance properly priced to reflect risks rather than through regulations (Scott and Mayer 1971; Barnett 1976). Insurance should be expanded to cover unsecured depositors.

6.1.1 Special-Purpose Regulations

The criticisms of banking regulations are part of the general attack on government interference, but they are also specific with respect to the procedures that have evolved in banking.

The banking regulatory system is recognized as one of the most complex. With three federal and fifty state agencies, there is a large amount of overlap. The lack of centralization and absence of clear authority have been retained, primarily as a result of industry pressure. Bankers believe that competition among regulators ensures them more freedom and thus enhances the public welfare. In contrast, on the whole, bankers have opposed competition in interest rates and in location.

The regulatory system is expensive. Furthermore, it seems to have some built-in conflicts. The FDIC, Federal Reserve, and Comptroller of the Currency found themselves with considerably different interests and statutory requirements in the cases of the United States National Bank and Franklin National Bank. Each has been concerned over attempts of the Securities and Exchange Commission to protect investors furnishing nondeposit liabilities to banks. Inadequate understanding of the risks in banks and poor information systems lead to unnecessary regulations.

Problems and costs may be reduced if the market is allowed to handle what it can do efficiently. At the same time, productivity may be increased by determining what regulatory information is necessary and useful and what is not. With a more complete understanding, management of banks and their functioning in the economy can be improved.

It is claimed that regulatory regimes not carefully controlled become costly and inefficient. Regulations will tend to aid the existing firms in an industry at the expense of the public. Limits on chartering, branching, and many activities are maintained primarily as methods of reducing competition and creating monopolistic profits for banks. Our studies examined this issue only peripherally. We assumed that a better understanding of the underlying problems or risks might lead to a diminished fear of competition. This in turn might remove from the anticompetitive ranks those who support controls and regulations because they fear that competition unduly increases bank risks.

Many economists have concluded that interest rate ceilings increase instability and cause a redistribution of income, probably from lower- to higher-income groups. This is not a desirable or necessary result of regulation. These ceilings are now in the process of being phased out.

This volume has not attempted to evaluate another use of the regulatory system, that of allocating credit by controls over portfolios. In theory, programs that allocate portfolios to particular purposes can be paid for by charging the program whatever cost of insurance is adequate to handle the less-than-satisfactory portfolio diversifications that such programs create. If, for example, it turns out that portfolio regulations for savings and loans or credit unions lead to an unduly high need for insurance, such costs might be subsidized.

We are also not concerned with those regulations whose primary purpose is control over financial institutions on the assumption that they are powerful and are prone to misuse their power. Such excess power is more likely to arise from a lack of competition rather than from increased competition. If there are enough lenders, the excess power of any one is likely to be small.

Finally, while regulations also attempt to prevent fraud and insider misconduct, we do not deal with this problem either. Halting this type of action requires auditing and the enforcement of legal regulations. In other spheres, more use is made of the courts. Under existing procedures, competition is limited in its ability to prevent conflicts of interest and other malpractice. If there were no danger of monopoly profits, the need for regulations designed to control them would be eliminated.

Our emphasis has primarily been on the analysis of potential improvements in the regulatory process that could result from a more thorough application of the ideas developed in portfolio theory. We have searched for concepts that could improve the analysis of risks, on the assumption that the regulatory process could be made more efficient if they were properly applied.

The next section takes up some of the reasons for the existence of banking regulations. Key questions concern whether the form of regulations is optimum and particularly the logic of the existing methods of examination, which is the fulcrum of the regulatory system. We scrutinize in more detail the examination system. We also analyze some of the issues related to when a bank should be declared insolvent and how much aid it should be given by the government either to remain open or to merge with another institution.

The concluding chapter in part 1 considers the possibilities of substituting a more general form of risk rating for that now used. It also cites specific examples where the model of capital adequacy and portfolio risk can improve existing regulatory procedures.

6.2 Reasons for Regulation

There are many reasons why our regulatory system arose and is maintained. Regulations can create significant public and private benefits. Much of the argument over the form of regulation starts from the basic fact that the banking system has been unstable. Our history is full of bank crises and financial panics. However, during the 1960s, the belief (common in earlier periods also) grew that the problem of instability had been solved. From 1946 through 1970, bank failures averaged slightly over five a year. Banks that failed were primarily small ones. The largest bank that closed had $40 million in deposits, while the average one had about $14 million. Many felt that regulators had been overcautious, that the economy would be aided if risk-taking by banks was less vigorously controlled.

The situation changed rather sharply in the 1970s. The percentage of banks failing did not rise appreciably, but their average size did. Under the pressure of inflation, sharply fluctuating interest rates, and recession, fourteen banks failed in 1975 and sixteen in 1976. For the other years in this decade, the average number of failures remained at five. Between 1971 and 1980, including the emergency merger of Security National Bank and the aid to First Pennsylvania Bank, twenty large banks with assets totaling over $20 billion required regulative assistance. The FDIC, according to Chairman Wille, was forced to make major decisions based on the possibility that its insurance fund was in danger of depletion.

6.2.1 Risk Levels

Past experience is only one of the reasons why regulation and deposit insurance of financial institutions appear to be justified. Equally important is the basic fact that an undue percentage of unregulated financial institutions are likely to take on excessive risks. Moral hazards exist. Given the large amount of leverage and the fact that much of the money comes from relatively small, uninformed lenders, it may be worthwhile for an institution to increase its risk ratio above that which would be determined by an efficient market with perfect information. Given a lack of information, owners or managers of institutions can reap large potential gains with limited losses. As a result, even though they are basically risk-averters, they may push risk beyond the level optimum for society as a whole.

Such tendencies are fostered by the difficulty of policing the level of risks. Financial institutions can change their risk levels rapidly between reporting or auditing periods. In contrast to other types of corporations, it is difficult to protect the lenders to a financial institution by covenants, secured loans, and similar agreements, such as those found in the manufacturing or commercial sector. It is also far harder to protect against conflicts of interest and self-dealing. Regulation or insurance becomes a worthwhile policy because it substitutes a strong third party for weak depositors.

6.2.2   Information

Another basic reason for regulation is the high cost of information. While private suppliers of such information could arise, experience has shown that, to many small depositors or other small creditors, the cost of information may appear high compared with its value. Even for large lenders, problems of evaluating risk and the probabilities of fraud and mismanagement are such that it may be more efficient to have a monopoly source of information. This is particularly so if the monopoly can enforce rules and regulations against fraud and against the issuing of misleading information more simply than a variety of private information sources. In addition, analysis shows that, at times when a bank is in trouble, a single regulator may be able to find an efficient solution not possible to competing lenders (Shoven and Bulow 1978).

6.2.3   Instability

Regulation potentially can halt cumulative movements in credit and the money supply. Costs of instability have been high. General agreement exists that it is worthwhile to maintain the stability of the money supply by avoiding the cumulative bank failures that have occurred in the past. Even if one were not afraid of cumulative movements, large public benefits are realized when an average person is given the opportunity to purchase a simple risk-free asset, particularly if this asset is the medium of exchange. Financial intermediaries create benefits to the economy by simplifying borrowing and lending and increasing the level of risk-taking at lower costs. They can gather information more cheaply because of economies of scale. They allow divisibility of assets to an almost unlimited degree. They lower transaction costs. They make it simpler for small savers to obtain adequate diversification (Kaufman 1975; Mayer 1975).

While arguments have been made that concern with individual institutions could be obviated if the central bank properly maintained the level of the money supply and acted as a lender of last resort, these are based upon an unwarranted assumption of stability. Many would argue, in contrast, that the problems of inflation and of exogenous shocks are so large that it is preferable for the central bank to concentrate its attention on problems of inflation and similar matters rather than on the safety of individual banks. One wants a system where the ability of the central bank to deal with macroeconomic problems is not constrained by its need to act as a lender of last resort at an early stage in the policy cycle.

The existence of deposit insurance is also an aid to competition and to potential entry into the banking system, while it ensures the continuance of significant information and banking relationships.

6.2.4   Public Benefits

There are major advantages to competition in lending. The fear of concentration of power is not unfounded. Economic and political democracy is enhanced when potential borrowers are able to present their cases to as many potential lenders as possible. A system of insurance makes it possible to increase competition by sharing risks. More significantly, lenders and borrowers can deal with small banks because they need not spend large sums in checking them out.

While regulations and insurance may be necessary and worthwhile, there is no necessary reason why the risks of deposit insurance could not be assumed by private firms. However, their record has been dismal. Furthermore, they lack the certainty of payoff granted to a government insurer. Without such a guarantee, search and information costs to find the best insurer would rise. There might well be a tendency to choose on the basis of size. When offered a choice, knowledgeable consumers have picked government-insured over private-insured or uninsured institutions. They have voted with their dollars (Scott and Mayer 1971; Merton 1979).

Other social costs might also increase if the government left the deposit insurance field. Private insurers would exclude from their decision-making the social and public benefits that are part of the existing system. Questions of power in private hands would arise. It would be disadvantageous to substitute a limited number of private insurance decision-makers for the present mixed system with over 14,000 potential bank lenders. Finally, private insurers might find it more expensive to control fraud, since they would find it more difficult and expensive to invoke the final sanction of the legal system (Scott and Mayer 1971).

6.3 Conflicts in Goals and Procedures

Perhaps more significant than the debate over the need for regulation is controversy over its form. Even supporters of a need for regulation and its division among several agencies question the methods used. Regulations deal primarily with the type of activities banks can undertake, their portfolios, and their capital; with controls over chartering and branching; with price-fixing of their charges and interest rates they can pay (regulation Q); and with insurance of their deposit liabilities. The regulations are enforced by bank examinations, by the requirement of charters, permits, or approval, and by private lawsuits.

6.3.1   Protection of the Deposit Insurance Fund

A critical issue, and one raised constantly by the studies, is the degree to which current regulations are required because of the form deposit insurance has followed. Many types of insurance adjust the premium to the risk assumed by the insurer. This is not true of the FDIC. Insurance premiums are based on the volume of insured deposits and not on potential losses. As a result, unregulated banks could increase their profits at the expense of the FDIC (cf. chap. 8).

Since deposit insurance is deemed worthwhile by most observers, the ability of banks to gain at the expense of the fund implies some need to control risks or capital. It clearly does not, however, imply a need for the existing forms of control. This is a major reason for a careful reexamination of the existing system. Are there simpler and more efficient procedures that can protect the insurer, depositors, borrowers, investors, and the public from the dangers of instability and bankruptcy as effectively as—or better than—the existing methods?

6.3.2   Regulation of Risk and Capital

In this volume we have primarily examined knowledge and existing or potential regulations relating to the measurement of risk and capital adequacy and insurance premiums. These are among the regulations many have claimed are both arbitrary and restrictive. In attempting to control unsatisfactory practices, regulators may penalize progressive managements. In attempting to establish minimum levels of competence, regulations may reward primarily those firms that are mediocre and remain faithful to older traditions. Many critics have argued that the FDIC and the other regulators have maintained too many inefficient banks while also lowering national productivity by restricting the investment decisions allowed to financial institutions (Meltzer 1967; Gibson 1971; Mayer 1965). Abolition or complete reform of the insurance system has been urged.

What we have tried to find is the logic of existing rules and the degree to which they are necessary to restrain those who would profit by taking excess risks at the expense of the public. Concern over risks of insolvency has led to regulations with respect to:

1. The types of activities banks can undertake.
2. Requirements over liquidity and diversification in the bank's portfolio of assets and liabilities.
3. Insider misconduct through loans.
4. Capital requirements.
5. Classification of loans by examination.
6. Information to stockholders.

The most important of these regulations deal with limitations on types of activities, requirements of liquidity, diversification, and capital (Edwards and Scott 1979). Proposals for reform require a great deal more knowledge of what risks exist in a particular portfolio policy, and of how these relate to the amount of capital. This is the key matter we analyze in the remainder of this volume.

Although the concepts are closely related, we tend to analyze the problem from the point of view of the depositor or insurer, not the stockholder. The protection of stockholders by regulation is a special problem. In the past they have been given inadequate information because of the fear that, if adequate information were made available to them, it would cause a flight of depositors or other lenders and thus might lead to the failure of the institution.

This type of argument has been carried over from the preinsurance era. It makes sense in the current context primarily because of the failure to clarify who is really insured. If institutions are required to maintain a proper level of information on their capital and risks, the facts should be available to both the uninsured depositors and the stockholders. Failure to make such information available can only lead to unnecessary risks of panic withdrawals, higher costs, and inefficiency. It is likely to increase, not diminish, the remaining residual risks of runs on a bank.

6.3.3 Regulation of Risks

The principal regulatory control over risks in banks has been through the process of bank examination. The examination aims at judging the bank's compliance with existing rules and regulations. Equally, or more important, the examiners attempt to judge the soundness of the bank, its prospects of avoiding insolvency, and its ability to meet current and future needs of its community. The soundness of the bank is a function of its management, ownership, and operating procedures; its liquidity or ability to meet future demands for cash; and, above all, its capital adequacy. The examination report is the basis for numerous approvals banks may need from their regulators (Sherman 1977).

However, important questions have been raised with respect to the efficacy of the examination process and methods of improving it. The system has been criticized as too backward-looking, too concerned with detail, ineffective, and lacking in objective standards.

The examination system has been characterized as aimed primarily at measuring trends on the basis of past actions. The current situation of the bank is analyzed, and suggestions are made for improvements. Examiners have not attempted to measure portfolio risks that arise from exposure to possible future events (Flannery and Guttentag 1979). Too little attention has been paid to possible movements in interest rates.

Many believe that the system places too much emphasis on detailed analysis of individual loans. The stress is on record-keeping and on delays in loan payments. The amount of specific detail employed may make sense with respect to small banks, but even here it is not clear why private auditors and enforcement by courts of legal restrictions cannot do as good a job or better. Other related industries do not depend on similar detailed regulatory examinations.

The Comptroller of the Currency, recognizing that the traditional examination process may not suffice for large banks, has established a National Bank Surveillance System and Divisions of Special Projects and Multinational Banking to analyze operations of all banks with over $2 billion in deposits or of those having special problems.

What are required are techniques for measuring the actual changes in banks, as well as measures of capital adequacy that can be applied objectively. Current procedures have placed too much emphasis on finding the status of a bank, while giving some weight to trends in loan losses and earnings. If a bank has inadequate capital at the time of examination, the regulatory solution has been to urge its managers to increase its capital or decrease its risk.

For many years, regulators had great difficulty enforcing such requests for added capital or other actions. However, under the Financial Institutions Supervisory Act of 1966, strengthened by the Financial Institutions Regulatory and Interest Rate Control Act of 1978, regulators were given cease and desist powers that greatly enhance their enforcement ability. These powers do not, however, reduce the need for standards to be applied. The examination process continues to pay too little attention to the overall portfolio risk.

6.3.4 The Regulatory Background

All insured commercial banks are under the authority of more than one regulatory agency.[1] National banks are under the authority of the Federal Reserve, the Comptroller of the Currency, and the Federal Deposit Insurance Corporation (FDIC). State member banks are under the authority of the Federal Reserve, the FDIC, and the state banking commis-

---

1. Most of the rest of this chapter was prepared by Dr. Laurie Goodman.

sioner. State nonmember banks are under the authority of both the FDIC and the state banking commissioner. However, the examining agency has the primary responsibility for regulating the banks it examines.

Commercial banks are examined at least once a year, more often if they are believed to represent special risks (Benston 1973). National banks are examined three times in two years by the Office of the Comptroller of the Currency. State member banks are examined once a year by the Federal Reserve. The FDIC examines state nonmember banks every eighteen months. The banking commissioner's office in each state examines all state banks, generally about once a year. In about half of the states, no attempt is made for the FDIC and the state banking commissioners to conduct their examinations jointly or concurrently. To avoid duplication of effort, the FDIC has begun a pilot program in some states in which it would rely upon the state banking commissioner's examination reports. The FDIC would check only on bank compliance with pertinent federal statutes (White 1976a).

The bank examiners will make sure that the assets and liabilities actually held by the bank correspond to the detailed statement of assets and liabilities that the bank is required to submit four times a year. Most of the examination time is spent studying the bank's loan portfolio and determining its credit quality. The examination also evaluates the quality of the bank's management and its system of internal controls. The reports of the bank examiners are discussed with the bank's top management. Frequently the managers are told to raise more capital or to stop various unwise business practices. These requests are often ignored, as Lucille Mayne points out. In 1972 she sampled 364 banks in the Fourth Federal Reserve District to determine if they had been requested by regulating agencies to provide additional capital between 1961 and 1968. Of those who replied, 30.3 percent indicated they had; of these, only 43.2 percent fully complied; 27.2 percent partially complied, and 29.6 percent did not comply at all.

The three federal bank regulatory agencies have adopted a uniform interagency system for rating the condition of commercial banks.[2] Previously, the three agencies used different systems for bank evaluation, which made interagency comparisons difficult. The new system involves an assessment by bank examiners of five critical aspects of the bank's operations. These critical factors are then aggregated in an overall rating of the bank condition. The five dimensions that are examined include "the adequacy of the bank's capital; the quality of the bank's assets (its loans and investments); the ability of the bank's management and administration; the quantity and quality of the bank's earnings, and the level of

2. Board of Governors of the Federal Reserve System. Press Release, 11 May 1978, and Federal Financial Institutions Examination Council, *Annual Report 1979* (Washington, D.C.).

its liquidity." Each of these performance dimensions is rated on a scale of 1 to 5, with 1 representing the highest level of operating performance and 5 the lowest. A rating of 1 indicates strong performance; a rating of 2 means satisfactory performance, reflecting the sound operation of the bank; a rating of 3 represents fair performance, flawed to some degree; a rating of 4 reflects marginal performance that, if left unchecked, could threaten the viability of the institution. A rating of 5 reflects unsatisfactory performance in need of immediate attention. The composite rating is also on a scale from 1 to 5. The composite rating is not a mere average of the ratings on the five dimensions; the interrelationships among the aspects of the bank's operations are considered. Banks rated 4 or 5 are deemed to have "financial, operational or managerial weaknesses so severe as to pose a serious threat to continued financial viability."

6.3.5   The Troubled Bank

If the condition of the bank deteriorates to the point where it needs to be monitored more closely, the FDIC will put the bank on its problem bank list.[3] The FDIC has three classes of problem banks: (1) "other problem," (2) "serious problem," and (3) "serious problem—PPO."[4] The "other problem" banks are those that have significant weaknesses and require more than ordinary concern. "Serious problem banks" reveal weaknesses that urgently need correction. PPO—potential payoff situation—is the most serious problem state. Banks in this condition are judged by the FDIC to have at least a 50 percent chance of requiring financial assistance from the corporation in the near future. At year end in 1978, there were 342 banks on the problem list, or about 2.5 percent of all insured banks. Of these, 249 were "other problem" banks, 82 were "serious problem," and 11 were "serious problem—PPO."

If the bank ignores repeated informal correction procedures, cease and desist proceedings may be used by the examining agency. The trend is toward more frequent use of formal actions. The first cease and desist order was issued in 1971; there were seven that year, eight in 1975, forty-one in 1976, forty-five in 1977, and more than one hundred in 1978. The examining agency may issue a cease and desist order when the bank "is engaged . . . or the agency has reasonable cause to believe that the bank is about to engage in an unsafe or unsound practice in conducting . . . business, or is violating or has violated or the agency has reasonable cause to believe that the bank is about to violate, a law, a rule or regulation . . .

3. The Comptroller of the Currency and the Federal Reserve Board also have problem bank lists. The FDIC's list overlaps but does not duplicate these lists. The FDIC is not concerned with supervisory problems that pose little risk to the fund.

4. The composite ratings of 3, 4, and 5 do not, as of now, directly correspond to the three classes of problem banks. It is not clear what the correspondence will be when the uniform system goes into complete effect. The FDIC has indicated that it will maintain its problem bank list for purposes of insurance exposure.

or any written agreement entered into with the agency" (12 U.S.C.A §
1818b). When a bank is served with a cease and desist order, a hearing is
held from thirty to sixty days later. If the bank defaults or consents to the
order, it will become effective immediately. If the bank does neither and
the hearing rules in favor of the agency, the order will become effective
after a thirty-day lag. The main regulatory agency may also issue a
temporary cease and desist order. This is effective upon serving, and,
unless a federal court orders otherwise, it is enforceable until the underlying cease and desist proceedings are resolved. A temporary cease and
desist order should be issued only when the sixty- to ninety-day delay
might seriously harm the interests of depositors.

The FDIC wields the power to terminate a bank's insurance. This
power is rarely used. The FDIC may issue notice of an "unsafe and
unsound practices situation" when it finds the bank is not in sound
condition to continue operations as an insured bank (12 U.S.C.A. §
1818a). From 1934 to 1978, this action was taken against 243 banks. If the
necessary corrections are not made within 120 days, the FDIC may give
the bank thirty days notice of an intent to terminate its insured status. If
the FDIC finds in a hearing that the practices are indeed unsatisfactory,
and corrections have not been made, it may terminate the bank's insurance. According to the FDIC Annual Report of Operations, 1978, of the
243 cases from 1934 to 1978, 240 had been closed by year end 1978. In
slightly less than half the closed cases, corrections were made, and in
most of the other cases the banks were absorbed by another insured bank
or ceased operations before a date was established for insurance termination. In only thirteen cases was a date for insurance termination set. The
termination order is subject to judicial review, but the broad wording of
12 U.S.C.A. § 1818a makes this merely a formality. It provides that the
FDIC may issue such an order when it finds that the bank is engaged in
unsafe or unsound practices, is not in safe or sound condition to continue
operating as an insured bank, or has violated a law, regulation, or any
condition imposed in writing by the FDIC.

For national banks, termination of insurance means that the Comptroller of the Currency must declare the bank insolvent and appoint a
receiver. For state member banks, termination means loss of Federal
Reserve membership. This power theoretically allows the FDIC rather
than the Comptroller of the Currency to pull the plug on national banks.
In practice, this has yet to happen. The Comptroller is a member of the
FDIC Board of Directors, and national banks are placed in receivership
long before termination of insured status.

6.3.6 Lack of Effectiveness

Several studies question the effectiveness of the bank examination
process (Mayne 1972; Benston 1973; Graham and Humphrey 1976).

These studies do not question the ability of examiners to find weak loans on a bank's books. Wu (1977) found that examiners had criticized about two-thirds of the loans charged off in a period in a sample of banks. Almost 10 percent of loans rated substandard and doubtful were fully charged off, while additional criticized loans led to partial losses.

Critics question whether examinations improve or hinder an efficient lending process. Many if not most of criticized loans are known to the banks. There is no indication that knowledge of the examiner's results improves the ability to predict future loan losses beyond mere knowledge of the bank's previous loss experience.

On the other hand, the process is expensive and time-consuming. It is believed to inhibit bankers in the lending process. As in football, Monday morning quarterbacking is not thought to be helpful, and it may make performance more timid. Bank examinations preceded the use of outside auditors. It is possible that any advantages of an outside review of problem loans could be obtained in a more efficient manner. In this as in other parts of the regulation process, more differentiation between large and small banks may be sensible.

6.3.7   Subjective Standards

Regulators' decisions on capital adequacy are primarily subjective. No clear standards have been developed. In fact, over the past decade the Comptroller of the Currency has frequently stressed the necessarily subjective nature of the decision. The FDIC and Federal Reserve banks used somewhat more objective standards, but in the final analysis their decisions, too, appear to be subjective, even though they have paid somewhat more attention to balance sheets and accounting ratios.

Recently all three regulators have placed greater emphasis on industry norms or standards. The ability of computers to maintain and analyze a tremendous amount of data has enabled the regulators to set up "surveillance systems" that can rapidly spotlight outliers on any of a large number of accounting ratios or examiners' evaluations. Unfortunately, however, for optimum usefulness in applications, the systems require, but do not contain, standards for what constitutes adequacy (Martin 1977).

Sherman (1977) and Orgler and Wolkowitz (1976) contain descriptions of the primary factors considered by each of the regulators. The Office of the Comptroller, for example, has emphasized a subjective evaluation relating capital adequacy to the risks assumed by a particular bank. This requires evaluating management, ownership, and operating procedures; liquidity related to the deposit structure and ability to borrow; the earnings history in comparison with dividends, fixed expense, and amounts due on capital notes or debentures; loans classified by examination into substandard, doubtful, loss, or reported as nonperforming.

The FDIC has placed more emphasis on capital/asset ratios. They adjust both capital and assets for classified loans. They also consider management, earnings, and past loan losses in determining a bank's rating.

The Federal Reserve System has had a far more complex "Form for Analyzing Bank Capital" (ABC) form. This form attempts to make a judgment concerning capital related to liquidity and to asset risks. Both credit and market (interest rate) risks are included, but the determination of what risks are involved remains arbitrary. Improvements have been made in measuring risks for investment securities; but, on the other hand, all loans are grouped together and are assigned a high capital requirement.

The Federal Reserve has additional standards for the capital requirements of bank holding companies. A number of proposed acquisitions or new holding company formations have been turned down on the grounds that capital was inadequate. The board examines the needs of the components of a banking organization as well as the overall leverage. In typical cases, proposals have been rejected because capital in a bank or banks has been considered inadequate, or because the structure of the proposal threatened the availability of capital to a bank.

In these, as in most, decisions the lack of objective standards creates difficulties. Except when a bank is asking for a privilege, regulators can only urge or attempt to convince a bank that more capital is required. Arguments about what is or is not adequate are difficult if not impossible to resolve. With the exception of bank holding companies where regulation is unified, banks have felt free to disregard requests for additional capital. They have recognized that competition among regulators reduces the risks of firm action. The lack of any objective capital standards has meant that the agencies have problems in enforcing requests for added capital. The list of enforcement proceedings shows long delays when a bank decides not to cooperate. Examiners do find illegal and illogical actions, but they also miss many. In large banks, they can be overwhelmed by details. Attempts are being made to centralize judgments on large credits and foreign exposures, but, again, these attempts cannot work without better standards and measurements of the risks involved.

Regulators strongly believe that examinations are useful and necessary. They point out that examiners do find bad loans, poorly operating banks, and banks that take excessive risks. We do not question these results. The critical issues are whether a better model and theory of risks and capital adequacy could make the examinations less onerous, improve their results, or substitute more efficient forms of regulation.

6.3.8   Early Warning Systems

Attempts are in progress to mechanize some of the examination process by using computers to pinpoint banks whose assets, liabilities, or capital ratios deviate from those of the bulk of similar institutions. Thus far the attempts have not been very successful. Inequalities may indicate a risk of insolvency, but do not necessarily do so. Theories are needed to explain what is wrong with the banks the computer unearths.

That probabilities of insolvency can be measured through a limited number of factors on a firm's balance sheet and operating statement has been recognized. Beaver (1966, 1968) and Altman (1968, 1977) have examined the use of financial ratios in predicting bankruptcy among various types of corporations. The application of these techniques to banks has been studied at the FDIC and the Federal Reserve Bank of New York, among others.

Martin (1977) has summarized much of this information. Like the other firms, banks can be classified on the basis of a limited number of financial ratios into those likely to fail and those not as likely to fail. As they obviously should be, these factors are closely related to those that theory says induce insolvency.

Altman (1977) show that, for firms in general, risks depend upon levels and variance of earnings, upon leverage, liquidity, and size. For banks, Martin finds that the significant ratios are earnings as a percentage of assets, loan losses as a percentage of earnings, some measure of asset risk, such as either the percentage of commercial loans or liquid assets in total assets, and the ratio of capital to risk assets.

The problem with these techniques is that they classify very broadly and cannot discriminate accurately enough. Thus Martin shows that, applying the early warning system that he and others at the Federal Reserve have developed to the 5,500 or so Federal Reserve member banks in any year, predictions are obtained that about 650 specific banks are likely to fail. In actuality, of these banks for which failure is predicted as likely, only 10 to 15, or about 2 percent of the total predicted, will fail (counting forced sales or mergers of banks in trouble as failures in addition to those requiring aid or payment by the FDIC). Furthermore, the selected group will not include 10 to 20 percent of the banks that actually do fail.

Although these predictions can be useful, the error rates are so high that they cannot be used either to replace current examinations or as a basis for insurance. While they make more specific the spheres of recognized risk, they also indicate that a great deal more information about individual banks is necessary if an accurate system of risk measurement is to be developed.

6.3.9   Behavior toward Insolvent Banks

When a bank is believed to be insolvent, four courses of action are available to the primary regulator and the FDIC:

1. Close the bank and pay off deposits.

2. Cause a merger or consolidation with another bank.
3. Delay a declaration of bankruptcy in the hope that conditions will improve.
4. Not only delay bankruptcy, but make sufficient funds available to ensure the bank's viability.

Selecting any one of these actions is difficult for the regulator and the FDIC. Regulators do not like to close banks. There are potential social losses to the community from unnecessary bankruptcy charges and other disruptions in established borrowing and lending patterns. Frequently a political outcry arises purporting to show that the failure was due to poor regulatory actions. Stockholders, bondholders, and uninsured depositors all lose money and are unhappy. As a result, regulators will often risk future losses to avoid closing or merging a bank. Since the costs to the insurance fund will not be borne by the regulator with the responsibility of declaring the firm insolvent, such delays are even more likely to occur.

In cases where the fact of insolvency is not clear but rather requires a decision based on judgment, difficult choices face the regulators, particularly the FDIC. What is the optimum time to declare a bank bankrupt? If a bank cannot stay open under existing conditions, should the FDIC lend it money to stay open, or should it pay another bank to assume its deposits or merge with it?

These decisions require not only an analysis of the law but, even more, a basic theory that can enable the decision-makers to take full account of economic reality and the public welfare. The FDIC can act to support a bank or pay out funds to aid in a merger if it believes the bank is essential to the community or, according to 12 U.S.C.A. § 1823e, if "in the judgment of the Board of Directors [of the FDIC] such action will reduce the risk or avert a threatened loss to the corporation and will facilitate a merger, consolidation." This was interpreted over the years by the FDIC to mean "only if it's cheaper." The FDIC always has the option of simply paying off the depositors. If it does this and a merger (purchase and assumption) would have left more for the stockholders and/or general creditors, neither group has legal recourse. If a purchase and assumption was done and deposit payoff would have left more for the equity holders or other subordinated debt holders, they may seek legal recourse. For example, in one case the FDIC excluded some contingent and suspect claims to determine that purchase and assumption was cheaper. The stockholders are challenging this.

It should be noted that the decision between deposit payoff and merger is not always very simple. "Only if it's cheaper" does not have a ready interpretation when the value of the assets and liabilities is uncertain. If purchase and assumption has a slightly lower expected loss to the FDIC but a considerably higher variance, should it automatically be picked?

Often in the case of fraud, where contingent claims are extensive, the FDIC prefers a deposit payoff, since it places a limit on their liability.

In recent years the law has been interpreted more flexibly. The number of mergers or support to remain open has grown rapidly as deposit payoffs have diminished. In determining the public benefit in such cases, the concepts of portfolio risks, of the economic as opposed to the book value of the loans, and of the probability of future variances around expected values are particularly important. In deciding whether to give aid and, if so, how much, there should be a careful analysis of the actual economic costs involved. Failure to take into account the difference between book and economic values and what the market is forecasting about the future makes it probable that decisions will not be optimum from the point of view of either the regulators, stockholders, uninsured lenders, or the public.

6.3.10   Deposit Payoff

Title 12 U.S.C. § 1821c provides that whenever the Comptroller of the Currency appoints a receiver "other than a conservator" of a national bank, the FDIC is to be the appointee.[5] The Comptroller will appoint a conservator only if there are strong reasons not to appoint the FDIC (in practice this happens rarely, if at all). A conservator has essentially the same duties as the receiver, except that, subject to the Comptroller of the Currency's approval, a conservator may allow the bank to continue in limited operation. The FDIC is required to accept the job of receiver if it is offered. With state chartered banks, the position falls either to the FDIC or to the state superintendent, as determined by state law. (In New York and California, it falls to the state superintendent.)

To maintain public confidence, the FDIC must pay off insured depositors as soon as possible after the bank fails (12 U.S.C. § 1821f). The FDIC regulations state that one or more "claims agents" are to maintain a temporary office at the site of the closed bank in order to receive claims for insured deposits. The FDIC may choose either to pay in cash, to make a deposit in another bank, or to make a deposit in an FDIC-operated new bank.[6]

The FDIC, as receiver, will now begin to liquidate the assets of the bank. At various stages of liquidation, creditor dividends will be paid;

---

5. This presentation relies very heavily upon the presentation in White (1976a).

6. White (1976a) states "Under 12 U.S.C. 1821h, the FDIC may own and operate a bank whenever "it is advisable and in the interest of the depositors of the closed bank and the public." The new bank must be in the same community as the old bank. This bank is operated as a nonstock corporation and is managed by an executive officer appointed by the FDIC. The bank must be sold or terminated within two years, and during that time the FDIC will cover any losses. This power is rarely relied upon; the FDIC will operate a bank only if the community the failed bank served would be deprived of any banking services."

these are prorated by the creditor's forced loan to the bank. The FDIC, in the case of a national or district bank, will count as a creditor to the extent of the insured deposits it has paid off, and as such it will be eligible for the creditor dividends. Before it makes a payment to insured depositors of state banks, it must be assured of its right to subrogate; that is, it must be assured that it will be considered the equal of other creditors.

If there is any money left over after all creditors are paid with interest, it will go to the stockholders. 12 U.S.C. § 197 provides that, after all creditors have been paid off, the FDIC will call a stockholders' meeting to determine whether the FDIC will continue as receiver and wind up the affairs of the bank, or whether an agent will be elected for that purpose. If they decide to elect an agent, an election will take place. "Wind up the affairs of the association," as the phrase is used in 12 U.S.C. § 197, means to sell all remaining assets. When state banks assets are being liquidated, state law governs the proceeding.

Even during liquidation, there are several thorny issues: What exactly are insured deposits? and Which creditors, if any, have priority? According to 12 U.S.C. § 1813m, an insured deposit is "the net amount due to any depositor for deposits in an insured bank (after deducting offsets) less any part thereof which is in excess of $100,000 . . . and, in determining the amount due to any depositor, there shall be added together all deposits in the bank maintained in the same capacity and the same right for his benefit either in his own name or in the names of others except trust funds." Needless to say, "in the same capacity and the same right" has led the FDIC into the courts many times.

Offsets can be very important. If an uninsured depositor has a loan with the bank, the deposit will be offset by the amount of the loan. This is especially significant in the case of large banks. Barnett (1976a) points out that "examination of the Franklin failure shows how significant a factor loan offsets could be, particularly in a large bank failure. We estimate that about three-fourths of the uninsured demand deposits and one-third of all uninsured domestic deposits remaining at Franklin at the time it closed were protected by loss offsets" (p. 161).

Title 12 of the United States Code does not attempt to answer the question whether secured creditors are to be treated differently. The courts have generally held that secured creditors may share in the total distribution of assets pro rata, according to the total value of their debts and despite the fact some portion of the debt may be satisfied by the collateral held. Say that a secured creditor has made a forced loan of $200. Also assume that his or her security is worth $150, and the creditor dividend is 20 percent. The secured creditor will get $150 + (.20 × $200) = $190. It appears that a secured creditor can never get more than the credit and interest.

6.3.11   Merger or Consolidation (Purchase and Assumption)

In a merger of purchase and assumption, another insured commercial bank will take over the liabilities and often the assets of the failed bank.

The FDIC Annual Report of Operations, 1978, notes that since 1934 a total of 548 insured banks have failed. In 304 of these, depositors were directly paid off, and in 244 the FDIC arranged a merger. However, 90 percent of the deposit dollars were in bank failures handled by purchase and assumption. From January 1976 through December 1978, only 4 out of 29 failed banks were handled by deposit payoff.

Purchase and assumption cases are not handled nearly as mechanically as deposit payoff cases. In bank failures such as those of Franklin National and United States National Bank of San Diego, the packages put together to make the failed banks look palatable to other banks are truly a tribute to the creativity of the FDIC and the Comptroller of the Currency.

The Comptroller of the Currency (in the case of national banks) and the FDIC will approach banks they think may be interested in taking over the failing bank. There are three basic methods by which the FDIC can sweeten the deal, according to 12 U.S.C. § 1823e. First, they can lend money secured at least in part by the assets of the failing bank. While the wording of this statute does not prevent making the loan to the failing bank or its receiver, it is clear in context that the failed bank cannot receive the loan. This loan may be subordinated to the claims of deposits and other general creditors. This is equivalent to adding capital to the assuming bank. Second, the FDIC can purchase all or part of the assets of the failing bank, and the cash paid by the FDIC would go the purchasing bank. A third type of assistance takes the form of guarantees against loss extended to the purchasing bank (if you, the purchasing bank, lose more than $100 million on liquidation of assets, the FDIC will cover any additional losses). This guarantee is a guarantee of the FDIC as insurer, not as receiver. Usually, a combination of the approaches is used.

The merger or consolidation usually occurs after a receiver is appointed. The Comptroller of the Currency or state banking commissioner will not officially declare the bank insolvent until the arrangements for the purchase and assumption are final. Hence the bank will be in the hands of the receiver for several hours, or perhaps overnight. The next morning, when the bank reopens, it will look to the public as if the bank has merely changed names.

6.3.12   How Much Is a Merger Worth to the FDIC?

In theory, the FDIC's decision to use its own funds to sweeten the terms of a merger should depend on a potential saving for the insurance fund. In fact, the FDIC has paid increasing attention in recent years to political realities as well as to a broader view of costs to the public beyond those to the fund. In either case, the FDIC should be aware of the costs both to the fund and to the public under either alternative. One problem, however, arises from the difficulty of determining the long-run effects of increased government aid to an industry.

What causes costs to differ between a deposit payoff and a merger? A bank is insolvent when it cannot meet demands for cash or when the economic value of its liabilities exceeds that of its assets. If the FDIC pays out funds to insured depositors, it has a claim against a share of the assets. The remaining share belongs to the uninsured depositors, depending on their proportion of the total deposits when bankruptcy occurs. If the value of the assets finally exceeded deposit liabilities, excess funds would go to bond- and stockholders. If the FDIC pays for an assumption or merger, the uninsured depositors suffer no losses. Any bank assuming the deposit liabilities will insist that it be made whole for all deposits. The uninsured depositors in effect are paid off in full. The FDIC must cover their potential losses as well as those of the insured. This factor becomes important only if the uninsured deposits are a sizable share of the total. If they are, and a deposit payoff occurs, the FDIC's losses will be reduced by those of the uninsured depositors in comparison with what happens if a merger occurs.

Opposing pressures unfavorable to a payoff arise because assets in a merged bank are usually worth more than those same assets are worth to a receiver in liquidation. At least three reasons are found for such differences in value. The FDIC accrues administrative costs both to pay off the depositors and to liquidate assets. More important in most cases are losses in intangible values in a case of a payoff. A successor bank in a merger takes over the deposits as well as customers for loans and other services. Because relationships of these types are costly to develop de novo, such intangibles sell well in the market. On bids, the FDIC usually receives offers of sizable amounts above the book value of deposits. Finally, asset values drop when they are placed in the hands of a liquidator in comparison to their value to a going firm. Loans are harder to collect when they are not held by someone with a continuing business relationship. In some cases, borrowers require future infusions of funds to maintain their viability and their ability to continue payouts. Since the FDIC is not an ongoing lender, it has difficulty in meeting these needs. This further reduces asset values.

Since the gains to the FDIC at the expense of the uninsured depositors are usually relatively small, the existing system of having some insured and some uninsured depositors is awkward and perhaps really dangerous. It has value primarily because it adds a group of nonregulators to those examining and evaluating banks' risks and capital. Its value is diminished because most uninsured lenders recognize that they have a form of de facto insurance. In all large bank failures, the FDIC has arranged a merger and assumption covering all deposits. There is only slight evidence that the existence of uninsured deposits performs the function intended and leads to additional evaluations and greater caution.

The present system may be dangerous if it forces the regulators to declare a bank insolvent at an awkward time. If an institution whose solvency is suspect faces a large cash outflow, regulators may be forced to act when they otherwise would not. Under our current system, the uninsured group includes large depositors, those holding deposits in foreign branches, and uninsured creditors such as those who make federal funds available. Any or all of these groups may withdraw funds because of fear. If these withdrawals are large enough, insolvency can follow unless the Federal Reserve or the FDIC steps in as lender of last resort.

Allowing these uninsured creditors to force the foreclosure of insolvent banks may or may not be useful. That they have funds at stake should mean that they are more careful, and therefore their surveillance should work to improve that of the regulators. On the other hand, when they become frightened, these funds can flow out rapidly and thus bring about the danger that insurance was formed to avoid. One can easily imagine a situation in which uninsured funds flow rapidly from all institutions that are even slightly suspect. We might be back at the preinsurance situation. Maintaining uninsured depositors and lenders retains the possibility of runs. If this fringe is maintained, they need a better information system so that they can properly evaluate the risks they take.

However, these depositors do serve a purpose. If their demands lead to a lack of liquidity, it is easier for the regulators to close the institution if they so desire. When closed, most institutions show positive book balance sheets. If there is a run, the lenders need not examine as carefully the question whether the economic balance sheet of the firm is actually negative. They can use the lack of liquidity and the fact that the firm cannot meet its cash demands without loans as a reason for closing it.

It is the presence of these depositors and the possibility of runs that give the Federal Reserve increased importance in determining when a bank should be declared insolvent. Paul Horvitz (1975) has argued that, in the case of large member banks, the Federal Reserve and not the Comptroller makes the insolvency decision. The Federal Reserve is legally allowed to make loans to any bank facing a temporary liquidity crisis, whether or not it is a member bank. It does not, however, have the power to make long-term loans to sustain a failing bank. The failing bank is unable to borrow federal funds, so its only source of borrowed money is the Federal Reserve's discount window, which lends on a day-to-day basis. The Federal Reserve can simply refuse to renew the loans. The Federal

Reserve as the central bank has a responsibility to provide ultimate liquidity to the *system*, but not to a given bank. The Federal Reserve can, if it chooses, totally ignore the Comptroller's wishes to keep the bank open a bit longer and the FDIC's wishes for more time to work out a merger. Horvitz believes, as many others do, that having three agencies with different objectives involved in large bank cases makes it impossible to attain optimal solutions in short periods of time. The need for regulatory reform in this area is crucial.

6.3.13   Delaying Bankruptcy

Even more difficult than the FDIC's decision on how much to pay to have a viable bank assume the liabilities of an insolvent one is the decision on how long to delay the actual declaration of bankruptcy. The potential social loss to the community from unnecessary bankruptcy charges and other disruptions argues for delays. So do the pressures from stock- and bondholders who will lose their funds. Opposition to delays arise because, after the point of economic insolvency, the public, through the FDIC insurance fund, bears all future losses, while any gains will go to the stockholders. Furthermore, agreement is quite general that a system that fails to penalize bad management will become far less efficient over time.

In cases of undeclared insolvency, insurance premiums are being used to underwrite insolvent firms. The FDIC is accepting additional risks without additional opportunities to recoup. If the market value of the firm's assets improves, stockholders will profit. If the market value falls, the insurer will lose. If the firm is not really insolvent, either stockholders should be willing to put up more capital, or the firm should be able to sell assets or borrow on them. In most cases, of course, if a positive net worth still exists, this is what does happen when capital falls to low levels.

Difficulties arise because some assets lack market value. A lack of liquidity can force the firm to sell off assets at below actual values. Valuation problems are compounded because the existence of low capital implies past losses and is an indication of poor management. Risks of hidden losses are greater for a firm that has shown itself less able than other banks in recent operations. Still, it may be worthwhile for all to keep insolvent firms alive. A private creditor might do so, but it would demand compensation for its extra risks by sharing in future profits if bankruptcy were successfully avoided (Shoven and Bulow 1978).

Just as the FDIC assumes undue risks and may create future problems each time an insolvent bank is allowed to stay open, in the hope that it may recover, so a bank allowed to decrease its liquidity unduly may create problems for the Federal Reserve. Since nonliquid loans and investments pay premium rates, banks that choose them can gain at the expense of the government.

The Federal Reserve and the FDIC should not be willing to furnish liquidity freely because, if they do, institutions can gain at their expense by increasing the maturity and the average duration of their assets. An institution assured that the regulators will not force it to value depressed securities at their true market values can assume large interest rate risks. Losses from a lack of liquidity are among the risks that arise from mismatched maturities of assets and liabilities. A bank making such a decision should have to pay for its improper balancing.

6.3.14   Monetary Assistance to Existing Banks

Still more difficult decisions, with respect to both economic analysis and potential adverse precedents, arise when the FDIC faces the question whether to lend or give money to an existing bank to help it avoid bankruptcy. If the FDIC agrees to furnish funds, what claims should it make against the future profits? In the First Pennsylvania case, for example, the FDIC lent $325 million on a five-year subordinated debenture. The loan was interest-free for the first year and at below market rates for the remaining term. For this loan, the FDIC received warrants to purchase 13 million shares of common stock at $3 a share. This was well below the market price that prevailed up to the agreement, since the market had underestimated the bank's severe difficulties.

While the Federal Reserve does not have the authority to make long-term loans to sustain a failing bank, the FDIC, under the powers granted to it by 12 U.S.C. § 1823c, can "make loans to, or purchase the assets of, or make deposits in [the] insured bank, upon such terms and conditions as the Board of Directors may prescribe, when, in the opinion of the board of directors, the continued operation of such bank is essential to provide adequate banking service in the community." This has happened only five times since 1950, when the FDIC was granted this power. In the case of Bank of the Commonwealth of Detroit, monetary assistance was provided because, owing to the oligopolistic nature of Detroit banking, there were only three other major banks, and Commonwealth made a significant contribution to bank competition and provided essential services to the Detroit community. In the case of Unity Bank and Trust of Boston, the FDIC felt the black-owned bank was essential to provide banking services to the black community of Boston. In the case of American Bank and Trust of Orangeburg, South Carolina, there were several branches that were the only banking establishments in their communities. The Farmers Bank in Delaware was the second largest commercial bank in Delaware and the sole legal depository for state funds. Under Pennsylvania law, there were no available merger partners for First Pennsylvania Bank.

The FDIC reads § 1823c to ban direct loans unless the bank's services are absolutely essential to the community. Failing banks frequently request monetary assistance from the FDIC. It is in the interest of their shareholders to do so. If the insolvent bank is merged or a deposit payoff occurs, the shareholders rarely get anything. If the FDIC can be pressured into making a loan, and the bank winds up as a solvent entity, the gains go to the stockholders. If the bank fails after the loan is made, the stockholders are no worse off than if the loan had not been made.

6.3.15   Monetary Assistance versus Deposit Payoff and Merger

If there are real bankruptcy costs, situations may arise in which monetary assistance is, in the short run, the cheapest course of action open to the FDIC.[7] The rationale for this anti-intuitive result is that, if the bank recovers, the FDIC will get its loan back with no other monetary outlay. In a merger or deposit payoff case, the FDIC will never get back the money it puts in. If the probability of recovery is sufficiently high and there are real bankruptcy costs, monetary assistance may prove to be cheaper than a merger or deposit payoff. But, even though monetary assistance may be cheaper for a particular case, the FDIC may be setting a dangerous precedent that could be expensive. Other banks may fail to put up more capital on the assumption that the FDIC will lend them money when things get bad.

In reality, there should be few cases in which monetary assistance is actually more profitable. A failing bank usually has serious problems in managing assets and liabilities. Furthermore, if the FDIC were allowed to make loans whenever it was the cheapest action available, the problems of estimating the probability of loan recovery would be enormous. Banks would be appealing this decision if they were allowed, fighting the FDIC forecasts with their own. Furthermore, shareholders have had plenty of opportunities to put up capital before the bank reaches the point of insolvency. They chose not to, even though they must give up any right to intangible assets when the bank is declared insolvent.

Given that there are real bankruptcy costs, there is room for negotiation between the FDIC and the shareholders. The FDIC could offer to make a loan if the shareholders put up more capital. This is exactly what happened in the case of Bank of the Commonwealth. If, however, the FDIC did this consistently, banks would not get capital earlier, but would wait for the FDIC to bail them out. In the long run this could be far more expensive for the FDIC than occasionally incurring bankruptcy costs.

Another situation in which monetary assistance makes sense from a social viewpoint occurs when there is a unique social cost if the bank fails. This will happen if the bank is the only bank in the community, or if its loss will have a severe impact on the competitive banking structure in the community. Most of the FDIC's support decisions have been based on such reasoning.

---

7. A similar point is made by Shoven and Bulow (1977), who note that it may be in the interests of the creditors that a firm stays in business despite negative net worth.

6.3.16 Summary

The likelihood that our system of banking regulations can be entirely abolished is slight. A completely free banking system, such as that attempted in the nineteenth century, is unlikely to be sound. The costs of obtaining information with respect to bank risks and their control in a fully competitive banking system are probably unduly large compared with those of our existing system. The reduction that regulations have brought about in the risks of runs, of sharp shifts in credit and of money are of great value to the public. Deposit insurance is a sound and efficient concept.

However, the regulatory system has failed to integrate traditional techniques with all the potential values of the insurance system. Regulations, the examination process, and decisions on how to handle banks at or approaching insolvency can be improved if more attention is paid to possible future dangers. The risks to a bank are as likely to arise from its overall portfolio and operating structure as from individual loans. Yet regulations and examinations have been aimed primarily at control of individual activities rather than at portfolio risk.

Decisions on whether a bank is insolvent and the degree to which it should be helped to continue can be improved by a more realistic appraisal of economic balance sheets. While in some cases the existence of insolvency is obvious, in most an examination of a bank's current status as reflected in its books may be ambiguous. Insolvency depends on the values of the intangibles not shown on the books and on correctly calculating the over- or undervaluation of assets, as reflected in a comparison of book values with values determined by the marketplace.

7   Conclusions:
       Risk-Related Insurance

In this final chapter of part 1, we summarize some prior results and conclusions, while at the same time examining a few additional issues in more depth. We pay special attention to what knowledge would be essential if a system of risk-related insurance premiums were to be substituted for the current flat FDIC rates that depend on regulations and examinations to hold down risks.

Portfolio theory offers general techniques that can improve analysis of bank risks and capital adequacy. It enables managers and regulators to be more objective in their evaluations. As more information becomes available and techniques improve, decision-makers should be able to increase their use of the price-market system. Such methods can be substituted for the regulatory tradition that forms the basis of the existing procedures.

7.1   Risk and Capital Adequacy

We have analyzed dangers of insolvency to find methods of measuring such risks. A system based on reliable estimates would make risk-free deposits possible (through a fair insurance) while allowing managers and owners of banks to select those risks they feel are appropriate to the circumstances. For every level of potential portfolio volatility there is a related sum of capital sufficient to reduce its risk to a predetermined level.

To determine whether capital is adequate, we must be able to define and measure it. The basic protection capital offers against the risk of insolvency depends not on a firm's book net worth, but on the true economic value of its capital. A difficult but necessary first step in measuring capital adequacy is estimating a bank's true expected net worth. Capital is adequate when it reduces risk of future insolvency to an acceptable level or, alternatively, when the premium the firm pays to an insurer is fair.

To determine capital adequacy, this volume models the risk of insolvency. Portfolio theory furnishes us the necessary tools. A bank selects a particular portfolio consisting of a variety of activities. These activities include assets, liabilities, non-balance-sheet operations, including foreign exchange and loan commitments, and capital and reserves (net worth). The expected rate of return on these activities together with the bank's capital policy give an anticipated end-of-period economic net worth. However, this expected net worth is unlikely to eventuate. Economic events will cause returns to fall short or to exceed their expected levels. Risk depends on the probable variance of the returns in the particular portfolio selected by the bank. More specifically, risk depends on the likelihood that returns will be so negative as to cause the firm to be insolvent, and on the expected losses in case of such failure.

7.1.1 Variances in Returns

The volatility of each portfolio depends upon the weight of the activities within it, the underlying variance of each activity, and the correlation among them. Fluctuations become most dangerous when a bank concentrates its assets or liabilities into relatively few activities, each of which experiences wide swings as the economy shifts.

In most bank portfolios, the number of securities and individual loans is large enough so that activities can be combined into broad classes for analysis. Activities are sufficiently comprehensive so that within them the diversifiable risks of the individual components offset each other. Such groupings become the basis for estimating nondiversifiable risk of the portfolio. These are the losses likely to occur as a result of the market, shifts in the GNP, price changes, and variations in interest rates.

The most probable causes of shortfalls in income are found to be changes in interest rates and risk premiums, unexpected loan losses, and variations in operating income and expenses. Interest rate risks are by far the largest.

Obvious and seemingly evident dangers are not among the major risk factors. Activities with high systematic or market risks also carry high gross margins that tend to lower their danger. Insolvency occurs when a bank selects too high a level of nonmarket risks or fails to diversify. A concentration of loans in an industry, region, or foreign sphere or to insiders can be expensive. Such portfolios carry a higher probability of large variances.

Financial theory emphasizes the differences between shortfalls of revenues on individual assets, which are expected to occur and are paid for through larger gross charges, and portfolio risks, which carry a higher return because they cannot be diversified away. Since the risks of individual assets can be diversified away by proper choices, they carry no incremental return. In banks, returns on activities that require higher gross rates to yield a net return equal to the market are part of the level of current earnings. Examinations of past experience can be used to measure expected future trends. The current level and trends in earnings are the basis upon which net worth is analyzed. If capital is expected to be negative under current conditions, it must be supplemented. To fund portfolio risks, however, one must do more than make certain that a bank does not have negative expected capital. One must calculate the probabilities of shortfalls in returns and of insolvency by applying to the entire portfolio estimates of interest, operating, and credit risks determined by the bank's specific activities.

In determining portfolio policies and adequate capital, it is not necessary to reduce volatility per se. Risk-takers should be welcome as long as they assume the full costs of their activities. Our financial system will work best when financial intermediaries are allowed a wide choice in determining their own most effective risk level. They should be able to judge—backing their judgment with their own funds—whether the gross return on any asset is sufficient to cover its specific risk. Regulatory concerns should be limited to the risk of insolvency. What is necessary is that a bank's nondiversifiable risks be reduced to where its capital adequately supports its choices. If its capital is inadequate, a bank should be required either to reduce its risks or to increase its capital to a level that just makes fair the insurance premium it pays.

7.1.2   Actual Measurements

Critical measures include both the expected level of net worth and probable fluctuations around it. Although our studies expended a great deal of effort trying to utilize the market to estimate expected net worth, our results were somewhat disappointing. The Rosenberg and Perry, Morrison and Pyle, and Jacobson papers (chaps. 16, 13, and 11) report some progress, but other results were negative.

Chapter 5 notes that difficulties arise because of possible conflicts among the risks being evaluated by the market. Some changes in stock or bond prices reflect risks of insolvency. In contrast, other movements are based on variations in the degree of uncertainty of other returns. However, these may not be so large as to alter significantly the probability of failure. Bankruptcy sets one limit to the fluctuations in net worth and influences market prices. In addition, however, investors may adjust their willingness to purchase securities on the basis of risks arising from uncertainties over future rates of return other than those affected by insolvency.

The analysis clarifies the unsatisfactory nature of book net worth as a measure of capital. Book values fail to reflect many events that have already occurred. This is obvious in the First Pennsylvania case, as in many others. The differential movements of market to book stock values have ranged over a wide area and furnished a good deal of useful information. The changes in stock market values reflect at least partially the result of movements in the expected income from intangibles, securities, and loans.

A better estimate of net worth than that contained on the books can be derived by applying movements in market prices to the separate activities of a bank. Current practice is for footnotes to financial statements to show the relationship between market and book values for the bank's investment portfolio. They also include a statement about the interest rate sensitivity of parts of the loan portfolio and of some liabilities. However, these sensitivity footnotes are rarely in a form useful for estimating either current or net worth or the net duration of the bank's assets and liabilities.

Net worth calculations require more complete descriptions of loan portfolios, as well as a more detailed analysis of commitments and intangibles. However, even when this desired data is lacking, the application of market prices to individual activities can improve upon net worth estimates that use book values alone. Market-based projections employ the information contained in the markets' own estimates of future values in place of the arbitrary assumptions about what will happen contained in unadjusted book values. While estimates using techniques based on the market will not be exact, experience should show the extent of probable errors and enable them to be improved.

Our ability to estimate potential fluctuations in returns seems somewhat better. The studies for this volume make major contributions to the theory of such risks and methods of calculating them as well as to estimating orders of magnitude. Movements in interest rates cause capital values and cash flows to change. Movements in current cash flows affect reported earnings from operations. Changes in expected flows alter current values. Shifts both in levels of interest rates and in the term structure cause values to move. McCulloch's calculations contain estimates of the effect of both types of movements on the distribution functions.

The analysis of loan losses and operating earnings highlights the important differences between predictable and unpredictable movements in returns. A good deal of effort was expended in attempting to devise models and more complete classification systems for loans in order to improve the predictability of losses. The market, however, appears to be highly efficient in its pricing of returns that can be predicted. The more complete models made only marginal improvements in estimates of expected returns. Differences do exist in the likelihood that, on average, some classes will experience greater losses than other types—for example, average losses on consumer loans run more than ten times as high as those on residential mortgage loans. However, the Maisel and Jacobson paper (chap. 9) shows that, though results will diverge for one or several years, on the whole differences in predictable outcome are already reflected in gross interest rates and current earning experiences. Classifications of loans yield minimal information about the likelihood of unexpected movements.

The estimates of the probable distribution of changes in loan losses and operating earnings contained in chapters 4 and 5 are based on time series of past changes and on cross-sectional data in the years of maximum upheaval. Both approaches indicate that well-diversified portfolios and operations do not contain large risks from these factors. The type of reserves already found in most banks are sufficient protection against them.

These risk estimates do not, however, take into account poor diversification or fraud. Both theory and history show that such risks are found primarily among small firms. They are among the reasons that large and small banks should be differentiated in examinations and regulations. However, maldiversification can also cause large banks to fail. They can speculate in futures, take undue country risks, or concentrate too many loans to a few related firms. Such possibilities seem to call for better accounting and auditing principles or a change in examination practices to put more emphasis on diversification and the possible correlations among loan and security losses resulting from interest rate movements or other economic events.

7.1.3 Some Inferences with Respect to the Regulatory Process

The final section discusses in greater detail procedures that might make it possible to substitute fair payments for risks in place of the restrictions over activities and decision-making now contained in the regulatory process. Such a change would aim at removing the dangerous flaw that makes it profitable for banks to increase their risks because their costs of insurance are not based on their capital adequacy.

Before proceeding, we again observe some possible improvements in the regulatory and examination process brought out in previous discussions. Probably most important are changes in how the regulatory system evaluates bank operations and risks. Both the theoretical work and the empirical work emphasize a need to differentiate between predictable and nonpredictable future movements and between economic and book values in calculating effective capital. In these areas, the present regulatory system appears weakest. The examination process often succeeds in requiring that banks charge off actual losses that have occurred or that have a high probability of occurring. The examinations also form a base for estimating whether the earnings trend of a bank is up or down. Such analysis can find weak performances, and it can become the base upon which demands for additional capital or improved procedures can be made.

However, it appears that the current procedures miss dangers that are equally serious. They fail to estimate the probabilities that portfolio choices may lead to large-scale future losses. Such losses become probable when portfolios are too sensitive to unpredictable events. These changes are distinct from past losses or trends in earnings. Needed reforms would place greater emphasis on the possible distribution of returns around expectations and on evaluating those changes that have already reduced the level of capital. Such movements are reflected in market prices and can be used to calculate a bank's economic net worth.

7.1.4   Size of Bank

Another possibility arises from the potential regulatory advantage to be gained from recognizing the differences between the risks faced by large and small banks and treating them separately. Fewer than 100 banks hold more than half the assets of the banking system. The 1,600 banks with over $100 million in assets (as of the start of 1980) held 80 percent of total assets. Because their portfolios are larger, the normal degree of diversification for these banks is greater. Their record-keeping is more likely to be handled in a satisfactory manner. They can afford good internal and external auditing.

If large banks assume too much risk in relation to their capital, it is probably because they follow faulty theories and have an inadequate understanding of how insolvency is likely to occur, or because they desire to increase their profits by assuming a position of maximum leverage with a high-risk portfolio. The form of examination needed to monitor their performance should be quite different from that applied to smaller banks.

The Comptroller of the Currency has established special units to work on issues of direct concern to larger and multinational banks. It is not clear how successful these units have been in interfacing with the traditional examination process, or what theories they have developed to help carry out their tasks.

The problems facing the nearly 13,000 remaining banks with 20 percent of the assets may be quite different. Because they are small, a successful diversification program may require constant effort. Their policies are far more likely to be dominated by a single individual, a fact that greatly increases their risk of maldiversification. An executive who merely expresses strong opinions on what constitutes sound investments and loans is likely to reduce diversification. If the views are wrong, undue concentration, whether in a type of loan, in an industry, or in maturity structure, can lead to dangerous risks. In addition, of course, record-keeping among smaller institutions is more likely to fall short of adequate standards. Furthermore, if either external or internal fraud occurs—and it probably will, even if only through random chance—a loss of any given size will be harder to absorb without insolvency the smaller the bank and the less the capital available to offset the loss.

7.1.5   Uninsured Depositors

Another potential danger also pointed out previously is the ambiguous position of uninsured depositors. Those in large banks have been insured de facto, while those in small banks have suffered losses. However, since protection is not a matter of law, unless changes are made the future may witness major runs together with all the difficulties the deposit insurance system is supposed to avoid.

One of the reasons advanced for maintaining uninsured depositors is that procedures for determining insolvency are less than satisfactory. When a regulator fails to close an insolvent bank, both stockholders and the public may gain. If it is closed too soon, all may lose. But it is also possible that delay will be at the expense of the public, both now and in the future. With a more careful analysis of the dangers of improper timing, a better decision process should be possible.

7.1.6   Liquidity

When our analysis of risks is compared with the traditional literature and examination process, there seems to be a huge gap. We appear to have neglected an analysis of liquidity. This topic plays a critical role in existing practice. Since banks can be, and in the past frequently were, closed when they could not meet current demands for payment, an examination of potential liquidity has been an extremely important part of examinations. What is behind our seeming omission of this crucial topic? The apparent neglect is, in fact, primarily a difference in nomenclature. Liquidity remains a vital part of our analysis, but we believe that a study of the concepts that underlie the problems lumped together under the term liquidity provides a more useful approach to this issue.

Liquidity can be divided into two factors, either of which can present a threat to a bank's solvency. Such a division makes it easier to avoid its dangers. When divided, liquidity appears either as a problem of interest rate risk or as one of potential transaction costs. The term liquidity is used in two related but entirely different senses: (a) The first considers the balance or lack of balance of interest rate risks that arise from holding assets with a duration closely related to or far different from one's liabilities. Under this concept, a bank can improve its liquidity either by shortening the average maturity of its assets or by lengthening the average maturity of its liabilities. (b) The second is the ability to obtain cash when necessary from an asset or a liability, while experiencing only minor transaction costs or low interest penalties.

Liquidity as an Interest Rate Risk

The first concept—that it is necessary to protect against interest rate risk by matching the maturities of a bank's assets and liabilities—is an integral part of our analysis. In fact, the ability to measure such risk specifically rather than covering it under the general rubric of liquidity can, we feel, lead to a major improvement in bank planning and regulation.

The relationships between interest rate risks and transaction costs are frequently confused because of conventional accounting and examination procedures. In these, the actual loss to the bank as a result of an interest rate shift is not taken into account (except in a footnote to the balance sheet for marketable securities) at the time it occurs. Instead, depreciated assets are carried on the balance sheet at original cost. If such an asset has to be sold, both the loss that occurred earlier from interest rate movements and the loss from the transaction cost of the final liquidation are added together. They are thought of as a liquidation cost.

Cootner (1969) analyzed the difference between these two factors. His presentation makes the concepts clear. The loss from an interest movement occurs at the time the market shifts, not at the time of liquidation, when it is entered on the books. He also showed how confusion over a real or economic loss and what was shown on the books could lead to uneconomic decisions.

The whole discussion in the 1940s of the "locked-in effect" assumed that banks did not react to economic values. Changes in tax laws, accounting regulations, and pressure for better information have all improved current practice, but errors are still common. Increased emphasis on the economic balance sheet and interest rate risk can, we hope, improve analysis and practice in protecting against this form of liquidity risk. It is necessary to reemphasize that this interest rate risk applies to loans as well as securities. The duration of a loan depends on when and if its interest rate can be shifted as the market moves.

Liquidity and Transaction Costs

If cash is required to meet adverse deposit flows or takedowns against loan commitments, or to allow a bank to avail itself of a profitable investment opportunity, it would like to obtain the funds without undue costs. This need to manage liquidity, or the ability to obtain funds without high transaction costs, is an important function. The better it is performed, the higher the bank's profits.

There many ways to obtain funds. A well-operating bank models and plans liquidity carefully. It may sell some assets or, more commonly, it may borrow. In fact, large money market banks in recent years have carried more liquid liabilities than liquid assets.

Many observers of the growing use by banks of liability management and the increased ratio of borrowed money among bank liabilities consider liquidity a constant and heightened danger. As an example, Kane (1978) draws a gloomy picture of an increasing threat of financial panic as liability management expands. He differentiates between the day-to-day adjustment of liquidity, which he agrees is a necessary and useful function for a financial intermediary, and the growth of higher ratios of nontraditional borrowing.

Implicit in such views is the fear that, because of ineptness or in a desire to contract the economy to fight inflation, the Federal Reserve and the FDIC will cause or allow financial markets in general to collapse. If markets do not fail, banks can obtain funds by shifting assets to others. They may be penalized by transaction costs, but not to an undue extent.

A government-induced market collapse is neither useful, necessary, nor (we hope) likely. The Penn Central bankruptcy and its threat to the commercial paper market and bank lending demonstrated that the Federal Reserve can furnish the economy with required liquidity (Maisel 1973). The threats to individual banks in 1974 that were aborted is another example.

In fact, increased liability management can potentially increase the effectiveness of monetary policy. Without large fixed-rate liabilities, banks find it necessary to adjust the price of their loans to market rates more rapidly. They are less likely to expand credit by offering their customers below-market rates.

7.1.7   The Ability to Shift Funds

In general, liquidation costs should not be large. Dangers exist only to the extent that cash flows are so great that a bank has to start liquidating assets with high transaction costs. (Recall that capital losses from interest or default risks of borrowers need not be considered; they have already led to an economic loss.)

General financial theory points out that in a well-operating market, it should be possible to raise funds without major transaction costs (Stiglitz 1974). Problems arise when lack of information creates moral hazards, or when there is no lender of last resort for the system. The lender of last resort need not lend directly to the needy borrower. The Federal Reserve has for many years had contingency plans calling for the use of pass-through lending.

Two primary dangers exist: (*a*) Customers with existing loans may not be able to afford market rates. (*b*) Because of the lack of 100 percent deposit insurance, large lenders to banks may be unwilling to ascertain the institutions' safety. They will either flee to a few large banks on the assumption that the Federal Reserve and the FDIC will allow middle-sized, but not larger, banks to fail; or they will concentrate their funds in the government securities market. Both dangers depend upon a failure of the government to furnish adequate liquidity to allow shifts among banks of assets and liabilities. As corporations transfer funds from a bank or banks to governments or large banks, the Federal Reserve, by substituting loans to the banks needing liquidity for securities in its own portfolio, can furnish unlimited liquidity.

Even in tight circumstances, extremely large amounts can be raised rapidly by banks. In the Franklin Bank case, several billion dollars were obtained. Insolvency arose not from transaction costs, but because prior losses in assets were still carried at inflated book values. The bank was also faced with much higher market rates on its liabilities. Its current earnings were low or negative because it had to pay market rates to others but appeared to be earning below-market rates on its assets. This illusion occurred because it was carrying its assets at book values that far exceeded their true economic values. Failing to recognize losses in market values did not affect the bank's economic earnings, and it fooled few. The market, including the Federal Reserve, recognized that its capital was low or negative, even though the losses were not shown on the books. The bank could borrow only on secure collateral, which was valued currently on an economic basis far below its face or book value.

Difficulties of smooth transitions will be worsened if potential lenders, whether other banks, the Federal Reserve or the FDIC, feel constrained not to lend because they fear they will be subsidizing the borrower as a result of quoting below-market rates. If banks believe that subsidies from below-market rates will be granted, they need not calculate the true cost of liquidity. They can gain at the expense of the lender. If the Federal Reserve or FDIC, as a result of improper pricing, refuses to lend, troubles could follow. A small penalty rate on emergency borrowing should exist (as is now possible at the Federal Reserve), with its amount known in advance so banks can estimate what it will cost them to obtain the necessary funds. In such circumstances, an apparent lack of liquidity resulting from an inability to earn market rates would primarily reflect a failure to diversify properly. A bank holding a typical portfolio should find its costs and revenues moving with the market. It should not face undue problems from transaction costs.

The possible costs of having to borrow or sell assets when interest rates have moved are true risks. They are part of the general risks of operations. Lack of liquidity can mean interest rate penalties and potential losses from operations. Such risks must be and are measured in the models developed in this volume. However, there is no need for or advantage from double counting by showing liquidity as a separate factor over and above interest rate risks and potential costs of liability management.

7.2   The Insurance System

One of the principal suggestions on how to improve our existing regulatory system is to increase its flexibility. A possible procedure is to reshape deposit insurance so that it depends more on prices and less on detailed regulations. An analysis of some of the changes necessary if insurance rates were to vary with risk will enable us to bring together again some of the main points made in the analysis of the previous chapters.

Before any major shift is possible, it may be necessary to have interested policy-makers rethink the purposes of the existing regulatory system. One of the great advantages of being able to measure risk more accurately is the potential ability to separate policies needed to maintain a safe banking system from those regulations that maintain monopolistic power or unequal income distributions. Since the latter are undemocratic and counter to our usual political thrust, it is likely that the political influence of those supporting the regulatory system for their own ends would decrease if it were recognized that we could have a safe financial system without the existing form of regulations.

Another problem would be to convince policy-makers to think of the FDIC as a true insurer, charging rates and building reserves related to real risks. If the FDIC were recognized as primarily an insurer covering its own costs and perhaps earning a profit, no one would be shocked when it experienced an occasional loss as a result of a bank closing. There is no need for people to worry each time a bank fails. The government pays out on crop, housing, flood and many other types of insurance without its being considered unseemly. Such acceptance of bank failures, however, would also require movement to 100 percent deposit insurance.

Perhaps one reason for the current view that a bank failure reflects a critical error in regulatory judgment is that too much emphasis is put on the examination process. The regulators take too much responsibility, which they can fulfill only at decided costs to the system. It is also recognized that, under the existing system, many failures reflect an attempt by banks to profit at the expense of the FDIC and others. If banks fail, a suspicion arises that they went too far in expanding risks in an attempt to profit at others' expense. If they were forced to pay for their true costs when they took excess risks, failures might be recognized as already paid for and either part of normal business or an act of nature.

7.2.1   Potential Changes

Suggestions on changes in the FDIC primarily discuss either the advantages of relating rates for individual banks to the real value they and their depositors receive from the insurance or the advantages of creating private competitive firms, as has been accomplished in the mortgage insurance business, which, not too long ago, was also a government monopoly (Scott and Mayer 1971).

Four basic topics dominate discussions of the need for change: (*a*) The belief that regulators require arbitrary amounts of capital. With a changed system, banks and the market could be given more freedom of choice. (*b*) The idea that the present examination system and portfolio regulations dissuade banks from making venture or risk loans that they should make. Too few or improper risks are taken. (*c*) The fear that a failure to charge properly for differences in risks penalizes the well-managed bank in favor of the poor ones. (*d*) The assumption that any lasting government agencies become overly bureaucratic and that their functions could be performed more efficiently by private profit-making firms.

There is general agreement that the existing system has numerous built-in conflicts between market efficiency and regulatory needs or desires. Because the regulators have only a subjective measurement of the proper relationship between risk and capital adequacy, their ability to enforce their standards is limited, even though it entails a vast panoply of exams and analysis. Banks are under constant pressure to invent schemes and procedures that will enable them to live and profit under the existing network of regulatory constraints. Much of this effort is costly and lowers the economy's productivity and welfare (Kane 1978).

Insurance against What?

It is not clear whether banks ought to be charged only for normal year-to-year risks, with the government making funds available through other sources in major financial crises, or whether the insurance fund should be able to withstand all losses. Currently, the FDIC returns to banks two-thirds of the amount by which annual assessments exceed FDIC expenses. Such a policy, in effect, accepts recent developments as typical of what should be insured against. Yet, as many of our studies make clear, in pursuing such a policy the FDIC fails to charge for major risks. Crises arise because rare events do occur. The reckless firms are those that fail to plan for unusual economic events. Insurance funds and rates should be set so that they cover the rare event, not merely the normal. Both, in fact, are probable and expected. We build our sewers for rains expected to occur only every one hundred years, not for the yearly average.

The Fund

When one examines past FDIC expenses and losses, the existing insurance fund seems ample, even though it is small compared with the funds insured. Total FDIC losses, including interest not earned, were about $460 million from 1934 through 1978.

In terms of needs and expenses, we can think of 1978 as a typical year. Total domestic deposits of insured banks were over $1,000 billion. The deposit insurance fund was $8.8 billion, or less than 1 percent of deposits. The gross revenues of the fund in 1978 were $1.39 billion, including $0.81 billion from assessments and $0.58 billion from interest earnings on the fund's assets. However, $0.44 billion was returned to banks so that net revenues were $0.95 billion consisting of $0.37 billion (0.81 − 0.44) in net assessments and $0.58 billion in interest.

Against these revenues, the FDIC paid out $42 million for insurance losses plus expenses of $103 million, primarily for bank examinations and supervision. The deposit insurance fund was increased by $803 million. Actual losses in 1977 were under 4/10,000 of 1 percent of total deposits and about 5/1,000 of 1 percent of net revenues after expenses. These ratios are low compared with past years, but not extremely low. From 1941 through 1977, only in four years did losses exceed 0.01 of 1 percent of deposits. The largest single year's loss was $100 million in 1974. This was 0.012 of 1 percent of total deposits in that year and was about 15 percent of the FDIC's income in that year. For the five years of heaviest losses, 1973–77, the total cost to the FDIC averaged about $48 million a year. This was about 0.005 of 1 percent of average deposits in this period and about 7 percent of the FDIC's average income in these years. These were, of course, additional bank supervision expenses for the Comptroller of the Currency, the Federal Reserve, and state bank commissioners.

Thus, if experience were to be the major guide to needs, insurance premiums would appear adequate and even high. But this reasoning neglects the infrequent event. In 1974 the total fund appeared low compared with possible near-term requirements. In 1980 there were about twenty banks that each had liabilities larger than the insurance fund. Had any of these collapsed, the FDIC of necessity would have had to arrange a merger into another very large bank.

Furthermore, in chapter 5, we saw that, while most banks are paying higher insurance rates than they would have to if premiums were based on their true risk, this is not the case for banks that have picked riskier portfolios. In many cases banks may be paying half or less of their fair charges. If regulations were removed without any techniques to ensure fair charges, the number of high-risk banks might well increase rapidly.

7.2.2 Public Functions of Insurance

There are numerous possible debates over the public functions of the insurance system, but we have not analyzed them. Questions have been raised whether the regulators are too close to those being regulated, and therefore whether the public or the industry is being benefited. Observers seem to see fluctuations in agencies' attitudes, depending partly on the administration in power and partly on the individuals in charge of the agencies.

In other related areas of government, agencies similar to the FDIC have been used to promote rather than hinder competition, to increase entry, to aid small businesses. These types of factors lead to support of public insurance. Their importance, weighed against the value of profit-making incentives, must be evaluated.

Experience seems to say that if the purpose of the government regulations is clarified and if the existing agency makes more use of market mechanisms, then it may seem possible to consider splitting off specific functions and operations. Competition from the private sector would become more feasible.

7.2.3   Insurance Terms

In addition to risks of insolvency, another variable in the value or cost of insurance is the terms under which it is written or operated. Terms include such factors as the frequency of examination, the rapidity with which capital and risk are required to come into line with the standards of the insurer, and the point at which an institution is found to be insolvent and is shut down.

The amount of losses an insurer will have to pay will depend upon how much the bank's liabilities exceed its assets and upon transaction, liquidation, and bankruptcy costs. In theory, if exams were frequent enough and were sufficiently accurate, and if macrovariable changes were smooth, institutions could be closed at the moment they reach insolvency. In that case the liquidation would cover all costs. Creditors and insurers would not lose, even if stockholders would.

In fact, however, examinations are not that frequent. The estimation of the value of the balance sheet is not that accurate, and there may be negotiations over required changes in capital and risk. This means that the regulator allows potentially insolvent firms to continue to operate. In such circumstances, the stockholders have a great deal to gain by continuing operations without adding capital. If events improve, the value of their stock will increase. On the other hand, if events deteriorate they have no more to lose. Only the losses to the insurer will increase. Thus, the terms of the insurance are a significant variable similar to the premiums, the amount of capital, and the amount of risk.

7.3   Variable Rates

Many observers have argued that charging deposit insurance premiums that vary with actual risk to the insurer is a necessary step in solving many regulatory problems (Barnett 1976*b*; Scott and Mayer 1971). If charges were related to the risks they assumed, individual banks could have far greater freedom in deciding what were and were not logical loans. Our system of intermediation would improve. The amount of required regulation would fall. The straitjacket within which the system operates could be removed.

Some believe that a goal of variable premiums is impossible to achieve, even if desirable. They feel we do not know enough to accurately classify banks into risk classes. As a result, they fear that too much authority would be given to those establishing the classification system. Decisions would be arbitrary and even less acceptable to banks than the existing ones. An added disadvantage would arise from political pressures to change the classification system. Although the present system is arbitrary and creates subsidies and maldistributions of income, as a flat rate it is simple to explain. It is set by Congress, thought to be insensitive to problems of fairness or efficiency. Critics fear that a variable rate system would be subject to constant political interference (Scott and Mayer 1971).

The discussions in the previous chapters indicate that we may be close to understanding how a more logical system of deposit insurance could be established. They also show the type of knowledge that would still need to be developed if a variable system were to be introduced.

7.3.1 Risk Rating

In theory, if it were decided to use variable rates, the premium could be set so it would return a sum just sufficient to pay for any combination of capital and risk a bank desired. While not foolish as an ultimate goal, so complex a system would make little sense at first. It would be sufficient if variable rates could be set initially for a limited number (five to ten) of risk classes. Each class would consist of a range of equivalent risk/capital trade-offs. Banks could choose a specific risk class by picking any of the combination risk/capital trade-offs within the class.

As an example of how a variable scheme might work, think of a form somewhat similar to the Federal Reserve's ABC form. It could be filled out by the bank, certified by the bank's auditors, and spot-checked by the regulators. Initially, bank supervisors could furnish the necessary instructions and offer help in filling out the form similar to that granted when reserve requirement forms have changed.

As a starter, the form might break risks down into four separate classes that would then be added together. Another section would estimate the level of economic capital relative to either liabilities or earning assets, also in several steps as discussed in chapter 5. The level of risk would then be measured against the capital ratio. The resulting index number would place the bank in a specific class with a specified premium.

7.3.2   Risk Classes

While more complex schemes are possible, the prior studies indicated that it may be satisfactory initially to use only a limited number of risk categories. They show that because market rates and competition already are forcing banks to charge for the necessary trade-offs between expected losses and expected returns, the critical problem is to evaluate the risk of unanticipated changes or higher variances and, therefore, possible insolvency. Less concern is needed over existing high or low losses. These and their projected earnings show up as part of economic capital and the expected end-of-period capital/asset ratio. What must be insured against is those portfolios of loans and investments that have a greater probability of a concentration of unanticipated negative returns. It is this variance, not the higher or lower expected rates of loss, that requires insurance.

Interest Rate Risk

The first and most important division of the portfolio for insurance underwriting is into groups based on interest rate risk. Chapters 10 and 13 discuss in detail and illustrate the type of analysis required to measure interest rate risk. Both assets and liabilities must be divided into a limited number of maturity or duration groups. Loans as well as securities must be included. Potential changes in risk premiums, as discussed in chapters 14 and 15, must also be added to simple interest rate risk. Each group has a risk factor. These can be aggregated to obtain the total interest rate risk for the bank.

Loan Loss or Credit Risk

Although information is skimpy, the studies indicate that the measurement of credit risk can start with three basic concepts: (a) The amount of unanticipated losses can be estimated from existing distributions of past changes in loan losses, based on either cross-sectional or time-series data. Again, a major point is that this distribution appears to be independent of expected losses. In fact, banks with high expected losses are likely to have a somewhat reduced probability of large unanticipated losses, since they are likely to regress back toward the overall mean. (b) A system of penalties for nondiversification is another critical component. Risks arise from an undue concentration of any type, whether by industry, locality, domestic-foreign, related companies or individuals, and so forth. (c) It is likely that some penalty should be assessed or credit granted for an unusual distribution of loans by major classes. The rate of return for a whole class of assets may be far lower than anticipated as a result of related but unexpected losses. Such surprises were apparently true of nonhome real estate loans for the past decade. They were also obvious in loans to real estate investment trusts. The three factors influencing credit risk can be summed to obtain the total expected variance of the portfolio and a single value for the bank's risk of unanticipated loan losses.

Changes in Operating Earnings or Margins

Again, as for credit risks, operating risks can be considered under several headings. (a) In chapter 4 we saw measures of income before net charge-offs for loan losses. High gross earnings may be reduced by collection and loss expenses. We also noted the possibility of using a general probability distribution for unanticipated changes in earnings. As with loan losses, high or low past earnings enter directly into expected values but have little obvious influence on unanticipated changes. Again, however, a slight tendency exists for earnings to regress toward the mean. Whether this is important enough to use in projections is not clear. Perhaps banks in the upper range of high earnings should be penalized on the assumption that they contain a slight additional risk, even if no credit is given those with low expected earnings. (b) However, those with anticipated low earnings should also pay a premium. The early warning systems indicate that continuous low earnings are a critical factor in predicting certain types of bankruptcy. Such firms have less room for error, since unanticipated decreases will take the firm into the loss sphere more rapidly. At this point, penalties should be assessed for firms that show up in the danger category from past failures to earn normal sums. These firms should be required to make improvements in their operations and capital and should also pay higher insurance premiums. (c) We assumed initially, as does much of the literature, that there were major risks in borrowed liabilities—the traditional fear of illiquidity. As discussed previously, however, such risks may arise only at the extremes of imbalance or of market collapses. Whether borrowed liabilities are safer than demand or savings deposits depends on the likelihood that the market will stop lending compared with possible outflows from disintermediation. It also depends on a possible large increase in margins on market funds compared with the cost of replacing lost demand and savings deposits at market rates. (d) We also saw that size influences variances in earnings; small firms experience more unanticipated decreases. Whether they should be charged for their lack of size is a policy decision. Their value to the economy may make a small subsidy worthwhile.

Fraud or Defalcations

A final category of risk is from insider abuse, or from fraud and major losses in single "stings." These losses definitely are a function of size, with risk from this factor falling steadily and then disappearing as banks grow large enough and sufficiently bureaucratic. The risk penalty for fraud can also be made a function of the degree to which these risks are underwritten by private insurance. For example, the level of bonding and the form of audit could be used to differentiate various degrees of risk. In fact, new forms of private audits might be devised to replace most examinations. Many types of risk and liability that are not now covered in a traditional audit could be shifted to auditors for a fee.

7.3.3   Estimate of Capital or Net Worth

As significant as measurement of risk for setting fair insurance premiums is the estimate of what capital is expected between examinations. The risk of insolvency depends on the capital/asset ratio and how it is expected to change between examinations. This means that both the present net worth and expected movements in it as well as in earning assets must be estimated.

Net Worth is the present value of expected earnings. The greater the share of the capital estimate that can be made from market data, the more accurate the results are likely to be. Most securities and loans, as well as several types of liabilities, can be valued at the market. Part 2 also discusses methods of making such estimates by discounting the expected returns from individual assets or classes of assets.

Intangibles are harder to value. For most banks, the most important intangibles are the bank's holdings of demand and saving deposits. The expected earnings from these must be capitalized. Chapter 9 indicates the possibility of arriving at general values for such factors. Further analysis of individual situations is necessary to find the degree to which it would be proper to apply average values for such deposits to individual banks. It may be that estimates of both expected deposits and their correct capitalization rates require a more complete breakdown by size, type, and region than we used in our analysis.

Finally, some banks achieve large additional earnings from other intangibles. These revenues must also be capitalized. Again, the discount rate selected can be developed either from the variance of such earnings based on the bank's own experience, or from that of a class of similar banks.

Changes in the Ratio of Capital

Net worth may increase or decrease compared with assets for several reasons. A bank has an expected rate of return on its assets. This may be estimated from prior periods' earnings adjusted for any major shifts in portfolio. Some of these earnings will be paid out in dividends. Additional capital may be raised in the market.

As noted, risk depends not on the amount of capital, but on its ratio to net earning assets. Therefore, along with expected changes in capital, the volume of net earning assets must be projected. It is the expected capital/

asset ratio that is pertinent in determining a fair insurance premium. While a good deal more study is required, either simple techniques of projections from past trends or more complex forecasts of the type detailed in chapter 11 can be used for this purpose.

7.3.4   Calculating Insurance Premiums

Fair insurance premiums depend upon balancing capital/asset ratios and the risk of insolvency. A bank's estimated risk and expected capital must be merged to get a fair premium. Examples of such calculations and tables of trade-offs are found in chapters 5, 10, and 15. Although any number of specific premiums could be charged, initially only a limited number of different premium classes, perhaps five to ten, might be optimum. The object should be to give a wide enough range of classes so that rates vary significantly from the high to the low. On the other hand, there should be a wide enough spread of risk within each class so that no undue impression of exactness is implied.

Initially, ratings and premium charges would have to be somewhat arbitrary. For this reason, it might be well if each bank were allowed to choose its own risk class, based on a form and calculations of the type just detailed. However, each bank should be experience-rated retrospectively. Penalties that increase rapidly with the extent of underestimates should be charged if, upon the date of the next examination, the bank falls into a higher risk class than the one it paid for at the start of the period.

7.3.5   Retrospective Experience Rating

In retrospective rating, it would be important to differentiate between those changes in net worth that were included in the original insurance calculation and have already been paid for and those the bank created as a result of shifting its risks and becoming riskier between examinations, or from wrongly estimating the growth in its capital or earning assets.

It is because risks are not linear that the penalties for shifting risk classes should rise more rapidly the larger the underestimate. For purposes of evaluation, it might be sufficient to compare the estimated interest rate risk of the beginning and ending portfolio and the change in the capital/asset ratio resulting from the movements in net earning assets and retained earnings or added capital. While the amount of variation to allow without penalty requires detailed analysis, as an example, no penalty might apply if the ending portfolio's risks were no more than 10 percent larger than those on which premiums were paid. Similarly, a capital/asset ratio 10 percent less (i.e., no penalty if the initial agreed-on ratio was 5 percent and the final was 4.5 percent) might not be subject to penalty. If risk was added or capital/asset ratios declined, each 5 percent greater error would be paid for at increasing rates.

There should be no penalty for changes in net worth from unanticipated interest rate movements because these would already be paid for in the insurance premium. It is added average risk duration of the portfolio that creates added risk. Given the 10 percent leeway, if the risk duration average rose from 3.0 to 3.3, there would be no penalty. However, if the risk duration rose from 3.0 to 3.4 there would be an extra fee, since the bank would have increased its interest rate risk by extending the average maturity of its portfolio.

In experience rating, it would not be necessary to consider separately loan losses above those anticipated, a drop in other revenues, or an increase in costs. These are already paid for in the initial risk estimates. However, unexpected changes in dividends or excess growth would lower the anticipated capital/asset ratio and therefore could increase the actual risk. Some leeway, such as a 10 percent variation above estimated risk, is logical because the insurance premium already anticipates that some variance will occur as a result of unexpected events. The fee should be increased only if the bank assumes added risk not included in the projection for which it paid. Such added risk could reflect faster than projected growth, riskier types of loans, longer maturities, or a failure to retain earnings.

7.4   Other Knowledge

The suggestion of a variable insurance premium is only one form of increasing the objectivity of regulatory standards. Other techniques can be used by both bankers and regulators to measure risk and to make certain that risks are not accepted unknowingly and without adequate capital to offset them.

Some observers believe that, given the rapid decrease of the risk of insolvency as the ratio of capital rises, rather than changing the insurance system, it may be more efficient to enforce minimum capital asset ratios strictly. What is an adequate minimum level of capital clearly depends upon what is a maximum level of risk that an individual bank assumes in any period. This means that a risk/capital measurement form of the type just described is necessary for this type of change also.

It may be argued that the regulatory system in effect at present attempts to set a minimum of capital adequacy. It does this, however, in an extremely awkward, arbitrary, and subjective manner. A key point of this volume is that the existing examination and regulatory system is not estimating the level of capital adequacy very efficiently. It retains inadequate concepts of illiquidity, diversification, and capital. It fails to make optimum use of knowledge gained through examinations.

We recognize that this volume is only an introduction to ways of improving our thinking about and measuring each of the relevant concepts. More work is needed both to clarify the analysis and to measure the pertinent risk distributions. The techniques that have been outlined do, however, seem capable of solving many of the problems. The methods of measuring risk and capital can be improved. Through the models introduced, the relationship between risk and capital adequacy can be far more explicit and easier to understand than it has been under current practice.

II   Research Studies

8 Bank Capital Adequacy, Deposit Insurance, and Security Values

W. F. Sharpe

8.1 Introduction

Since the first owner of a gold depository discovered that profits could be made by lending some of the gold deposited for safekeeping, there has been concern for the "capital adequacy" of depository institutions. The idea is simple enough. If the value of an institution's assets may decline in the future, its deposits will generally be safer, the larger the current value of assets in relation to the value of deposits. Defining capital as the difference between assets and deposits, the larger the ratio of capital to assets (or the ratio of capital to deposits) the safer the deposits. At some level capital will be "adequate"—that is, the deposits will be "safe enough."

In most countries depository institutions are regulated and examined periodically by regulatory authorities, and much of this effort is directed toward ensuring capital adequacy, broadly construed. However, the concept of capital adequacy is generally left undefined, making it impossible to specify an explicit criterion by which one can judge whether capital is adequate.

This chapter provides a formal setting for the analysis of the capital adequacy of an institution with deposits insured by a third party. We emphasize the case in which the insurer charges a fixed premium per dollar of deposits, since this is the policy of federal insurance agencies in the United States. However, most of the analysis is applicable to cases in

Reprinted from *Journal of Financial and Quantitative Analysis*, November 1978.

W. F. Sharpe is Timken Professor of Finance, Stanford University Graduate School of Business. Comments and suggestions from Paul Cootner, Laurie Goodman, Robert Litzenberger, Sherman Maisel, Huston McCulloch, James Pierce, David Pyle, Krishna Ramaswamy, Barr Rosenberg, Kenneth Scott and Robert Willis are gratefully acknowledged.

which insurance premiums vary with deposit risk, and much of it is also relevant for cases in which deposits are uninsured.

To avoid circumlocution, we will refer to the depository institution as a *bank*, but most of the analysis also applies to savings and loan companies and other depository institutions. Similarly, we will refer to the insurer as the *FDIC* (Federal Deposit Insurance Corporation), although the analysis applies as well to the Federal Savings and Loan Insurance Corporations and similar agencies.

8.2   The Value of the Insurer's Liability

A highly simplified view of the balance sheet at time t is the following:

bank

| Assets $= A_t$ | Deposits $= D_t$ |
| | Capital $= C_t$ |

All amounts are *economic values*—the prices for which the assets (A_t) or claims on assets (D_t, C_t) would sell in a free market. Throughout, we assume that values are calculated in this manner and that we are dealing with *economic balance sheets*, not traditional (accounting) balance sheets.

If there is any risk that the bank might not pay its depositors' claims in full and on time, the economic value of such claims will be less than it would be if there were no such risk. Define DF_t as the amount the deposit claims would be worth at time t if they were *default-free*. An insured depositor has, in effect, two claims: one on the bank and another on the FDIC. One way to portray the situation is shown in figure 8.1.

The depositors consider their claims default-free, with a corresponding value of DF_t. Since the bank may in fact default, its liability to the depositors is only worth D_t. The difference, $L_t(= DF_t - D_t)$, is the *present value of the FDIC's liability*.

Another way to portray the situation is the following:

bank		FDIC		depositors
A_t	D_t ←- - - - D_t	DF_t ←- - - -DF_t	net worth $= DF_t$
	C_t reserves	net worth	

To avoid a negative net worth, ex ante, the FDIC should charge a premium that will bring in reserves equal to the present value of its liability. Conversely, if the premium is predetermined, the FDIC should require that the value of the deposit claims (D_t) differ from the default-free value (DF_t) by no more than the premium.

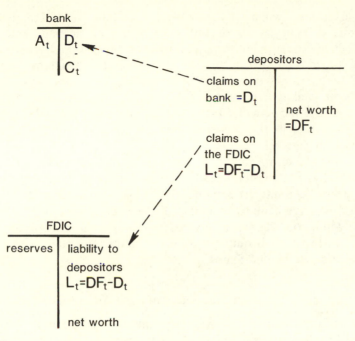

Fig. 8.1

Assume that for the relevant period the insurance premium is ρDF_t. Then the required condition is

$$\rho DF_t + D_t \geq DF_t$$

or

$$\frac{DF_t - D_t}{DF_t} \geq \rho.$$

If this condition is met, capital is adequate; if not, capital is inadequate. As we will see, the ratio on the left is a function of capital coverage and risk. The determination of a bank's capital adequacy thus requires both an assessment of the economic values of all assets and liabilities (including intangible assets such as the value of a charter, monopoly power or superior management, and options such as acceptances and lines of credit) and the estimation of all relevant risks.

The second depiction of the relationships among the three parties is particularly useful in one respect: it highlights the fact that the FDIC has the major interest in monitoring and policing the behavior of the bank, since it must bear the consequences of any default.

In the United States there is both explicit and implicit deposit insurance. The FDIC insures only some deposit claims; excluded are foreign deposits, claims owned by other banks (most of the "federal funds"), and portions of deposits above \$40,000 per private account and above \$100,000 per government account. However, the Federal Reserve system often provides de facto insurance for its member banks by furnishing liquidity to a troubled bank so that uninsured depositors can be paid off before the bank is actually closed. Moreover, the FDIC tries, whenever possible, to avoid actually closing a bank; arranging instead for another bank to assume all the deposit claims. One way or another, almost all deposits are insured.

The cost of such insurance is the explicit FDIC premium—a percentage of (virtually) all deposits, including those nominally uninsured—plus at least part of the interest forgone on reserves required to be held at a Federal Reserve bank by members of the Federal Reserve system.

We will ignore these complexities, assuming that all deposits are insured. In fact, this is quite an accurate characterization of the actual situation in the United States.

8.3   Capital Coverage and the Value of the FDIC's Liability

We assume that the FDIC insures a bank for one period. At the end of the period the bank is *reviewed*. At that time, if the economic value of assets is less than the default-free value of deposits, the FDIC must cover the shortfall in some manner; otherwise it bears no cost. The FDIC's problem is to ensure that ex ante, the economic value of its liability is no larger than the premium charged to insure the bank during the period.

Assume that the bank issues certificates of deposit (CDs) that promise total payments of $[P_1, P_2, \ldots, P_N]$ at times $1, 2, \ldots, N$ (the current time is denoted 0 and the bank is reviewed at time 1).[1]

At the beginning of the period depositors pay DF_0, the current value of default-free CDs paying $[P_1, P_2, \ldots, P_N]$, to the bank, since the CDs are insured. However, the bank receives a smaller amount, since it must pay ρDF_0 to the FDIC for insuring the deposits. In addition, the bank issues common stock for which it receives C_0' dollars. The net amount received is invested in an asset mix with a current value of $A_0 = (1 - \rho)DF_0 + C_0'$. If the insurance premium is set correctly, the economic value of the deposits (D_0) is equal to $(1 - \rho)DF_0$ and C_0, the economic value of the capital, is equal to C_0'. In any event, at time zero the economic balance sheet is:

assets $= A_0$	deposits $= D_0$
	capital $= C_0$

1. Demand deposits can be considered one-period deposits, since services are provided during the period and the existence of insurance gives depositors little incentive to withdraw funds before the FDIC review. Under this interpretation the value of services provided during the period could be assumed to be included in P_1 or to be placed in escrow at the beginning of the period.

At the end of one year, the assets will have a value of $\tilde{A}_1 = (1 + \tilde{r}^a)A_0$, where $\tilde{r}^a$ is the rate of return on the asset mix between time zero and time 1 and tildes indicate variables whose actual values are uncertain ex ante.

At time 1, the value of a set of default-free CDs promising payments $[P_1, P_2, \ldots, P_N]$ will be $D\tilde{F}_1$, a value that is uncertain ex ante, since the term structure of default-free interest rates that will prevail at time 1 is not known with certainty at time zero.

At time 1 the bank is reviewed. In effect the FDIC guarantees that the CDs will be paid as promised. To simplify the analysis, we assume that if A_1 exceeds DF_1 the depositors are paid in full and the stockholders retain the difference $(A_1 - DF_1)$. Otherwise the depositors receive all that is available (A_1), the FDIC makes up the difference $(DF_1 - A_1)$, and the stockholders receive nothing.

Our interest is in D_0, the economic value of the CDs at time zero, and its relationship to DF_0, the value of an otherwise similar set of default-free CDs. As we will see, the ratio $(DF_0 - D_0)/DF_0$ is a function of both the relative amounts of deposits and capital and the riskiness of the bank.

The issues that concern us can be analyzed using alternative paradigms, with roughly similar results.[2] We choose to employ a complete market, state-preference approach because it is both simple and powerful. This may seem an unusual choice, since in such a market the existence of financial intermediaries, though possible, is not essential. Of course such institutions do exist, and few would argue that they are redundant. Transaction processing and information gathering and transmittal do cost money, and financial institutions provide locational economies and economies of scale as well. However, our goal is to describe relationships among the values of financial institutions' assets and claims on those assets, not the choice of the assets and claims or the nature of the operation of such institutions. We hope that many of the qualitative conclusions obtained by analyzing these issues in a market free of transaction costs and information costs apply as well to institutions operating in real financial markets.

Assume that there are S possible states of the world at time 1. A *state* has the following attributes:

r_s^a: the return on the bank's assets from time zero to time 1 if state s obtains (i.e., $A_{1s} = (1 + r_s^a)A_0$

$\pi_{11s}, \pi_{12s}, \ldots, \pi_{1Ns}$:   where π_{1ts} is the present value at time 1 if state s obtains of a default-free promise to pay \$1 at time t ($\pi_{11s} = 1$ for all s).

---

2. For a partial analysis using stochastic dominance, see Sharpe (1977); for analyses using option valuation theory, see Merton (1977a, b) and Ramaswamy (1978).

Given $[\pi_{11s}, \pi_{12s}, \ldots, \pi_{1Ns}]$, the default-free value of deposits at time 1 can be determined directly:

$$DF_{1s} = \sum_{t=1}^{S} \pi_{1ts} P_t.$$

Define r_s^{ℓ} as the "default-free" return on the bank's deposits in state s; that is, $(1 + r_s^{\ell}) DF_0 = DF_1$. Then the payment to depositors in state s will be

$$D_{1s} = \min [A_0 (1 + r_s^a), DF_0 (1 + r_s^{\ell})],$$

and the payment to stockholders will be

$$C_{1s} = A_0(1 + r_s^a) - \min [A_0 (1 + r_s^a), DF_0 (1 + r_s^{\ell})].$$

If, by buying and selling existing securities, an investor can obtain any desired proportions of payments in different states, the financial market is said to be *complete*. Equilibrium in such a market is characterized by a series of implicit or explicit prices for state-contingent claims—prices that are the same whether one wishes to purchase or to sell such claims (since transaction costs are assumed to be zero).

Now, let:

p_s = the price in time zero certain dollars of a default-free promise to receive \$1 if and only if state s occurs one year hence.

Then the present value of a dollar certain to be paid at time 1 is

(1) $$\pi = \sum_{s=1}^{S} p_s .$$

Note also that:

$$A_0 = \sum_{s=1}^{S} p_s (1 + r_s^a) A_0$$

and

(2) $$\sum_{s=1}^{S} p_s (1 + r_s^a) = 1 .$$

In such a market the value of the bank's CD would be

(3) $$D_0 = \sum_{s=1}^{S} p_s \{\min [A_0 (1 + r_s^a), DF_0 (1 + r_s^{\ell})]\} ,$$

and the value of its common stock would be

(4) $$C_0 = \sum_{s=1}^{S} p_s \{A_0 (1 + r_s^a)$$
$$- \min [A_0 (1 + r_s^a), DF_0 (1 + r_s^{\ell})]\} .$$

Clearly,

(5) $$C_0 + D_0 = \sum_{s=1}^{S} p_s \{A_0 (1 + r_s^a)\} = A_0 .$$

Thus an uninsured bank could raise just enough capital to pay the market value for its assets, no matter what mix of deposits and stock it elected to employ. Moreover, each source of capital would be priced appropriately. While this is almost tautological, it serves to emphasize the well-known point that in a complete financial market there is no "optimal" financing mix.[3]

Given our formulation, the relationship between relevant values and capital coverage can be derived. Note that

(6) $$DF_0 + \sum_{s=1}^{s} [p_s \, DF_0 \, (1 + r_s^\ell)]$$

and

$$\sum_{s=1}^{s} [p_s \, (1 + r_s^\ell)] = 1 \ .$$

Thus:

(7) $$D_0 = \sum_{s=1}^{s} p_s \, \{\min \, [A_0 \, (1 + r_s^a), \, DF_0 \, (1 + r_s^\ell)]\} \le DF_0 \ .$$

Now, define the net worth in state s as

$$NW_s = A_{1s} - DF_{1s} = A_0 \, (1 + r_s^a) - DF_0 \, (1 + r_s^\ell) \ .$$

Without loss of generality, we will assume that the S states are numbered in order of increasing net worth; that is:

$$[A_0 \, (1 + r_s^a) - DF_0 \, (1 + r_s^\ell)] < [A_0 \, (1 + r_{s+1}^a) - DF_0 (1 + r_{s+1}^\ell)] \ .$$

Given A_0 and DF_0, there will be a set of states $1, \ldots, K$ in which net worth will be negative and depositors will receive less than DF_1. In the remaining states, $K + 1, \ldots, S$, net worth will be positive and depositors will receive the full amount DF_1. Moreover, as A_0/DF_0 increases, K will decrease (but only at discrete points).

The definition of K ensures that

$$(1 + r_s^a)A_0 < (1 + r_s^\ell) \, DF_0 \qquad s = 1, \ldots, K$$
$$(1 + r_s^a)A_0 > (1 + r_s^\ell)DF_0. \qquad s = K + 1, \ldots, S$$

Thus:

$$D_0 = \sum_{s=1}^{K} [p_s(1 + r_s^a)A_0] + \sum_{s=K+1}^{S} [p_s \, (1 + r_s^\ell)DF_0]$$

and

(8) $$\frac{D_0}{DF_0} = \sum_{s=1}^{K} [p_s(1 + r_s^a)] \, \frac{A_0}{DF_0} + \sum_{s=K+1}^{S} [p_s(1 + r_s^\ell)]$$

3. This assumes that no resources are lost in the event of bankruptcy. If this assumption is dropped, with all others maintained, *any* situation that could lead to bankruptcy in *any* state would be suboptimal, as shown in Karaken and Wallace (1977).

Now, define

$$\frac{d(D_0/DF_0)}{d(A/DF_0)} \equiv m_k$$

as the slope of the curve relating D_0/DF_0 to A_0/DF_0 when default occurs in states $1, \ldots, K$. Then

(9) $$m_K = \sum_{s=1}^{K} [p_s(1 + r_s^a)]$$

and

(1) m_K is constant for ranges of asset values over which
      K is unchanged
(2) $m_K \leq 1$
(3) m_K is smaller, the smaller is K
(4) $m_S = 1$
(5) $m_O = 0$.

These relationships imply that the curve relating D_0/DF_0 to A_0/DF_0 is piecewise linear, concave, and bounded by both the 45° line from the origin and the horizontal line for which $D_0/DF_0 = 1$, as illustrated in figure 8.2.

The larger the number of states, the larger the number of linear segments and the closer the piecewise linear curve in figure 8.2 will approach a smooth concave curve such as that shown in figure 8.3. As in

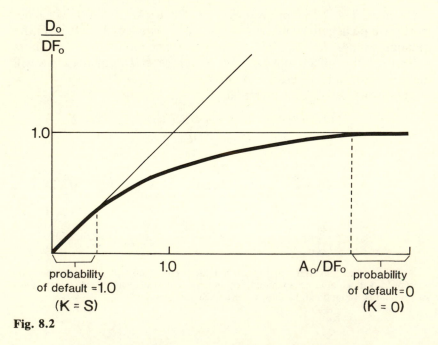

Fig. 8.2

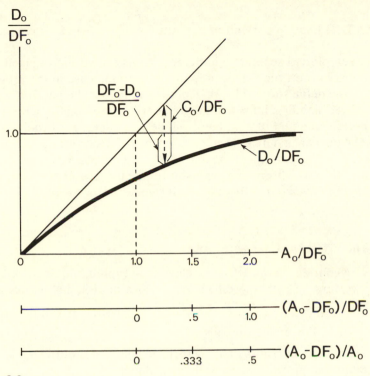

Fig. 8.3

figure 8.2, the primary scale for the horizontal axis is the ratio of assets to the default-free value of deposits, but monotonic transformations can be used to obtain scales for capital/deposit and capital/asset ratios, if the present value of net worth—the amount obtained by subtracting the *default-free* value of deposits from the economic value of assets—is utilized.

$$\frac{A_0 - DF_0}{DF_0} = \frac{A_0}{DF_0} - 1$$

$$\frac{A_0 - DF_0}{A_0} = 1 - \frac{1}{A_0/DF_0} \, .$$

As shown in figure 8.3, ceteris paribus, the greater the amount of assets covering deposits, the smaller will be the difference between the actual value of the deposits and the default-free value. Of course the balance sheet must balance, since the sum of the claims on a set of assets is worth neither more nor less than the assets. Thus C_0 must equal $A_0 - D_0$, and C_0/DF_0 must equal $(A_0 - D_0)/DF_0$, as shown. The distance between the curve and the horizontal line is of particular interest—it is the value of the FDIC liability per unit of deposits $\left(\dfrac{DF_0 - D_0}{DF_0}\right)$. For emphasis it has been plotted separately in figure 8.4. As shown there, given the relevant risks (i.e., the values of r_s^a and r_s^ℓ), an increase in the ratio of assets to the default-free value of deposits will reduce the per-unit value of the FDIC liability; however, this value will decrease at a decreasing rate. For any amount of risk, there will be some amount of capital that will make the per-unit liability equal to any preselected premium (e.g., in fig. 8.4, given a per-unit premium of ρ^*, the appropriate amount of capital is that which provides an asset-to-default free deposit ratio of $(A_0/DF_0)^*$). Given our definition, this is (precisely) an adequate amount of capital.

8.4   The Effects of Changes in Risk

Having considered the effects of changes in capital, holding risk constant, we now turn to the effects of changes in risk, holding capital constant.

8.4.1   Value-Preserving Spreads

In a complete market the risks associated with states of the world are reflected in the prices of state-contingent claims $[p_1, p_2, \ldots, p_S]$. Any economywide change in risk is likely to affect these prices. In this chapter we take a partial rather than a general equilibrium view, assuming that such prices do not change as the risks relevant for a bank change. Instead, we deal only with changes in the returns associated with various states.

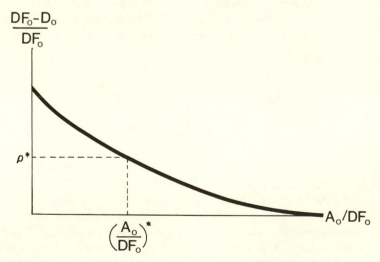

Fig. 8.4

Risk is generally considered to have increased when a set of returns becomes more "spread out." This can be given a precise meaning in the present context. Assume that states have been numbered in order of increasing magnitudes of return; that is:

$$r_s < r_{s+1}.$$

Let primes denote the set of returns after a change. Then we can say that risk has increased unambiguously if state-contingent claim prices do not change and

(10) $$r_s' = r_s + R\Delta_s,$$

where

$$\Delta_s \leq 0 \qquad s = 1, \ldots, s^*$$
$$\Delta_s \geq 0 \qquad s = s^* + 1, \ldots, S$$

and

$$R = \text{a positive constant.}$$

We wish, however, to consider only a subset of such changes in risk. Probabilistic approaches often consider *mean-preserving spreads*, in which expected return is held constant.[4] This type of increase in risk will usually lead to a change in value. In the present context this is an inappropriate ceteris paribus condition. Moreover, the concept of expected return requires the addition of some notion of (consensus) probability assessments to our set of assumptions. For both reasons we will hold *value* constant instead. Thus we require:

(11) $$\sum_{s=1}^{S} [p_s R\Delta_s] = 0.$$

Equations (10) and (11) define a concept we will term a *value-preserving spread*. Note also that they imply:

(12) $$R \sum_{s=1}^{K} [p_s\Delta_s] \leq 0 \text{ for all } K.$$

Any change conforming to (10) and (11) will be considered an increase in risk. Moreover, given a vector $[\Delta_1, \Delta_2, \ldots, \Delta_S]$ the magnitude of the change in risk will be proportional to R.

8.4.2   The Effects of a Value-Preserving Spread in Return on Net Worth

As before, assume that states have been numbered in order of increasing net worth at the end of the review period, with

$$NW_s < 0 \qquad s = 1, \ldots, K$$
$$\text{and } NW_s > 0 \qquad s = K + 1, \ldots, S.$$

---

4. See, for example, Rothschild and Stiglitz (1970).

Let L_s be the liability of the FDIC at the end of the review period if state s obtains. Then:

$$L_s = \begin{cases} - NW_s & \text{for } s = 1, \ldots, K \\ 0 & \text{for } s = K + 1, \ldots, S + 1, \ldots, S \end{cases}$$

Similarly, let C_s be the value of the claim of capital-holders at the end of the review period if state s obtains. Then:

$$C_s = \begin{cases} 0 & \text{for } s = 1, \ldots, K \\ NW_s & \text{for } s = K + 1, \ldots, S \end{cases}$$

The present values of net worth, the FDIC liability and capital are, respectively:[5]

$$NW_0 = \sum_{s=1}^{S} [p_s NW_s]$$

$$L_0 = - \sum_{s=1}^{K} [p_s NW_s]$$

$$C_0 = \sum_{s=K+1}^{S} [p_s NW_s] .$$

And

(13) $$NW_0 = C_0 - L_0.$$

Now, define r_s^n, the return on net worth in state s by

$$1 + r_s^n \equiv \frac{NW_s}{NW_0} .$$

Then the states are also ordered on the basis of r_s^n.

Assume that there is a value-preserving spread in net worth, and that the spread is small enough to leave unchanged the number of states in which default occurs. Letting primes denote values after the change:

$$L_0' = - \sum_{s=1}^{K} [p_s(1 + r_s^{n\prime})NW_0]$$

$$= - \sum_{s=1}^{K} [p_s \, s(1 + r_s^n + R\Delta_s)] \, NW_0$$

(14) $$= L_0 + \left\{ - NW_0 \left(R_s \sum_{s=1}^{K} [p_s \Delta_s] \right) \right\} .$$

Note, from (12) that the expression in braces is negative. Thus $L_0' \geq L_0$, and a value-preserving spread in net worth will either increase the value of the FDIC liability or leave it unchanged. Moreover, the magnitude of the change in L_0 will generally be greater, the greater the increase in risk (R).

5. Note also that $L_0 = DF_0 - D_0$.

Formula (14) can also be used to derive an empirically useful relationship between the effect of a shift in risk and the initial riskiness of deposits.

The change in the value of the FDIC liability is

$$\Delta L = L_0' - L_0 = - R \left[\sum_{s=1}^{K} (p_s \, \Delta_s) \right] NW_0 \; .$$

But we are considering only spreads that leave the total value of net worth unchanged. Thus, from (13):

$$\Delta C = \Delta L$$

$$\Delta C = - R \left[\sum_{s=1}^{K} (p_s \, \Delta_s) \right] NW_0$$

and

(15)
$$\frac{\Delta C}{NW_0} = - \left[\sum_{s=1}^{K} (p_s \Delta_s) \right] R \; .$$

Figure 8.5 plots the relationship between $[(\Delta C/NW_0)/R]$ and K. As implied by (10) and (12), the function is nonnegative throughout, nondecreasing over the range for which $K < s^*$, and nonincreasing over the range for which $K > s^*$.

Recall that K represents the number of states in which default occurs. As long as this is not large (i.e., $K < s^*$), the following relationship holds:

The larger the number of states in which default occurs, the greater the increase in capital value per dollar of net worth induced by a given increase in risk, ceteris paribus.

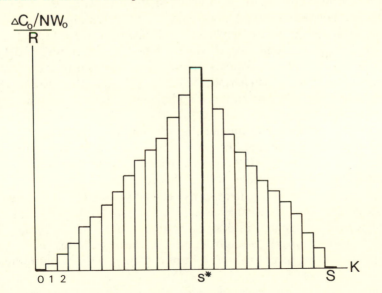

Fig. 8.5

As established earlier, $[(DF_0 - D_0)/DF_0]$ is positively related to K. We have now shown that for $K < s^*$, $[(\Delta C/NW_0)/R]$ is positively related to K. Thus, unless a bank's deposits are extremely risky:

> The larger the initial value of the FDIC liability per dollar of deposits, the greater the increase in capital value per dollar of net worth due to a *ceteris paribus* increase in risk, and vice-versa.[6]

This suggests that the response of the economic value of a bank's equity to a shift in risk may provide some information about deposit risk and hence the value of the associated FDIC liability. Ceteris paribus, the greater the effect of such a "risk shift" on capital value, the less adequate the bank's capital.

8.4.3 The Effects of a Value-Preserving Spread in Return on Assets

The uncertainty associated with a bank's net worth at the end of the review period derives from uncertainty about both the value of its assets and the default-free value of its liabilities at that time. To assess "net worth risk," one must in general consider asset risk, default-free liability risk (i.e., "interest rate risk"), and the relationship between the two.

For a financial institution with deposit liabilities extending beyond the review period, it is difficult to make general statements about the effects of changes in risk. For example, a value-preserving spread in asset returns unaccompanied by a change in default-free liability returns may not cause a value-preserving spread in return on net worth. The value of net worth will remain the same, but unless the ordering of states on the basis of NW_s conforms to the ordering on the basis of r_s^a, the changes in NW_s will not satisfy (10). Moreover, for such an institution, changes in asset returns may be accompanied by changes in default-free liability returns. In the extreme case in which a bank's assets consist of default-free bonds providing payments greater than or equal to the promised deposit payments in each period, the bank will be completely immunized, and L_0 will equal zero no matter what happens to the set of possible asset (and liability) returns.

Loosely speaking, the smaller the correlation between asset and default-free liability returns, the greater the effect of an increase in asset risk on the value of the FDIC liability. And the shorter the duration of the bank's deposits, the smaller will be this correlation.

The effects of a change in asset risk can be assessed unambiguously in one case. Assume that a bank has only deposits maturing at the end of the review period; then only asset risk is relevant. Moreover, ordering of the states in terms of NW_s is equivalent to ordering in terms of r_s^a, and a value-preserving spread in asset returns will make both r_s^n and r_s^a smaller

---

6. Except that changes in the value of the FDIC liability over a range in which K is unchanged do not affect $(\Delta C/NW_0)/R$.

or unchanged in states $1, \ldots, s^*$ and larger or unchanged in states $s^* + 1,$ $\ldots, S.$

As before, let Δ_s be the spread in state s stated in terms of return on net worth. If Δ_s^a is the spread stated in terms of return on assets, then

$$\Delta_s^a \, A_0 = \Delta_s \, NW_0 \,.$$

Substituting in (15):

$$\frac{\Delta C}{NW_0} = \left[-\sum_{s=1}^{K} \left(p_s \, \Delta_s^a \, \frac{A_0}{NW_0} \right) \right] R$$

or

(16)
$$\frac{\Delta_C}{A_0} = \left[= \sum_{s=1}^{K} \left(p_s \, \Delta_s^a \right) \right] R.$$

Given a value-preserving spread in asset returns, the expression in braces will, by (10), (11), and (12), be positive, nondecreasing for $K < s^*$ and nonincreasing for $K > s^*$. Since K is inversely related to the FDIC liability per dollar of deposits, we can conclude that unless deposits are extremely risky ($K > s^*$):

> For a bank with deposit liabilities that do not extend beyond the review period, the greater the increase in capital value per dollar of assets owing to a ceteris paribus increase in asset risk, the larger the initial value of the FDIC liability per dollar of deposits, and vice-versa.

8.5   Conclusions

Any agency insuring a bank's deposits should be concerned about the present value of the associated contingent liability. Ex ante, this value should be no larger than the premium charged for the insurance. In general, the present value of the insurer's liability depends on (*a*) the risk of the bank's assets, (*b*) the interest rate risk associated with the deposits, (*c*) the relationship between the two, and (*d*) the ratio of the economic value of the bank's assets to the default-free value of its deposits. Given the relevant risks, the present value of the insurer's liability can be reduced by increasing the value of assets by an infusion of new capital. When the value of the insurer's liability is no larger than the insurance premium, the bank can be said to have "adequate capital."

Our analysis emphasizes the importance of estimating *economic* values. It also emphasizes the importance of estimating all relevant components of risk. While these are difficult tasks, substantial progress could be made if bank regulatory authorities were to devote more effort to such goals.

Although the effects of changes in risk are complex, our discussion suggests a potentially useful new way to gain information about capital adequacy. An econometric model could be developed with the change in the market value of a bank's equity as the dependent variable (since this provides a good estimate of the change in the economic value of capital). Independent variables could include (*a*) surrogates for changes in asset values, (*b*) surrogates for changes in default-free values of liabilities, and (*c*) a surrogate for changes in asset risk multiplied by the value of assets. The coefficient associated with the latter variable would provide an estimate of the expression in braces in formula (16)—that is, the sensitivity of capital to a value-preserving spread in asset risk. It is plausible to assume that the larger the magnitude of this "risk shift sensitivity," the less adequate the bank's capital (i.e., the larger the FDIC's liability per dollar of deposits).

Unfortunately this magnitude cannot be readily translated into a numeric estimate of the FDIC's liability. However, a major increase over time in the sensitivity of a bank's equity to changes in risk might suggest a deterioration in capital adequacy. And, within a group of banks, those displaying a high sensitivity of capital to changes in risk might be considered worthy of special concern.

A procedure of this type would, at best, be simply an additional tool in the bank examiner's kit. But it might well be a desirable one.

9   Interest Rate Changes and Commercial Bank Revenues and Costs

Sherman J. Maisel and
Robert Jacobson

9.1   Introduction

In this chapter we statistically examine several issues. These are concerned with the degree to which banks react to changes in their rates of return from different activities. How closely and over what time periods do banks adjust their assets and liabilities to equalize expected risk-corrected marginal rates of return? A major related question is the degree to which interest rate ceilings influence bank returns. Given regulation Q, do banks gain or lose as interest rates shift? In seeking answers, it is useful to differentiate between wealth effects and income effects. Thus, with rising rates a bank might gain from ceilings if fixed cost deposits funded higher yielding assets (a wealth effect), but the bank might lose as much or more if the shift in rates caused most of its deposits to leave (an income effect).

The degree and rapidity with which financial institutions react to new information and shift funds among asset and liability classes so as to equalize marginal costs and returns is critical in the study of financial markets. Many analysts assume that markets are efficient, that transaction and information costs are negligible or unimportant, and that borrowing and lending, hedging and arbitrage are simple and are available at or at close to risk-free rates. As a result, they believe that they can successfully predict the results of all types of market actions and reactions without concern for institutional forces.

On the other hand, large numbers of observers believe that the markets within which financial institutions operate are so far removed from these assumptions that different theories and analyses must be applied. This is particularly true with respect to competition, legal and institutional restrictions, and information and transaction costs.

Our results fall between the extreme views. Rates of returns and costs adjust toward each other, as they should in a competitive market. On the other hand, the rates of adjustment are slow, particularly if we estimate total (in contrast to book) returns. Average book returns for classes of assets over the past sixteen years are not too far apart, but this is not true for total returns. Furthermore, no indication exists that over this period the net returns of classes of assets were related to their risk (their variance of returns).

Since the data include corrections for operating costs as well as for defaults and losses, it does appear that institutions adjust rather readily to costs they record on their books. A few major exceptions to such adjustment exist, as, for example, the low indicated return on nonhome mortgages in years such as 1973 to 1975. This seems to be an obvious result of the general euphoria and speculation that characterized this sphere in the early 1970s. The net return on consumer loans also does not respond rapidly to sharp movements in costs.

While major problems arise in measuring year-to-year fluctuations in actual returns caused by shifting interest rates, such movements have been significant. In critical years such as 1969, 1973, 1974, and 1977, for example, the rate of return on earning assets for an average bank fell 100 to 500 basis points below that reported based on book values. Since net book returns (before taxes) as a percentage of loans and investments for an average bank were about 1.20 percent of assets in this period, in these years the typical bank probably ran a true deficit that ranged up to 3.0 percent of assets. Such losses must be evaluated in light of a capital asset ratio of 9 percent, which the average bank held during this period.

Since such losses tended to decrease or even reverse in the next year for a typical bank, they were not too critical. However, the same is not true for banks that varied far from the average either in their portfolio or in capital. The variation in net returns or losses among classes of assets in a year can be large. In the past, many institutions were in jeopardy from interest rate movements. In the future, for those with unbalanced portfolios or low capital, potential dangers appear to be sizable.

9.2 The Basis of the Estimates

Our study is based upon estimated statistical cost and revenue curves for a cross section of banks in the years 1962–77 (with the exception of 1969). These estimates are of net rates of income and costs based upon book values of assets. The rates are net of servicing, processing, overhead costs, and so forth. The rates are estimated in each year from the fact that each individual bank holds a somewhat different mix of assets and liabilities. When the actual costs and revenues are regressed on the differing assets and liabilities, the regression coefficients estimate the effect on rates of return of placing a dollar in a particular class of assets or liabilities under the economic conditions of the given year. Net rates are obtained by subtracting the costs for an asset from its estimated gross revenues. The estimated cost and revenue curves are shown in table 9.1.

These statistical cost and revenue curves for a cross section of banks follow a technique used and explained in detail in studies by Hester and Zoellner (1966) and Hester and Pierce (1975). This study differs from theirs by using a national sample over a large number of years and in the methods of estimation.

The basic model used in estimation consists of two equations:

(1)
$$\frac{R_i}{A_i} = \frac{b_0}{A_i} + b_1 \frac{A_{li}}{A_1} + \ldots + b_k \frac{A_{ki}}{A_i} + \frac{e_i}{A_i}.$$

(2)
$$\frac{C_i}{A_i} = \frac{c_0}{A_i} + c_1 \frac{A_{li}}{A_i} + \ldots + c_k \frac{A_{ki}}{A_i} + c_{k+1} \frac{L_1}{A_i}$$

$$+ \ldots + c_{k+j} \frac{L_{ji}}{A_i} + \frac{u_i}{A_i}.$$

The first equation shows the gross revenues (R_i) from earning assets in a given year from a particular bank (i) related to the book value for each class (k) of assets (A_{ki}) for that bank in that year. The second equation relates the operating expenses (C_i), including actual net loan losses less income from deposit service charges, to the book value for categories of assets (A_{ki}) and liabilities (L_{ji}). The coefficients of the equations are estimates of the gross revenues and costs for each type of asset and liability. The difference between costs and revenues for an asset is its net return.

In each case the variables on both sides have been divided through by the level of assets in the year to correct for the heteroskedastic nature of banks with their widely varying sizes. This correction means that, with the exception of the first right-hand variable, which is $1/A_i$, all other variables are expressed as a percentage of total assets. A Goldfeldt-Quandt test (1965) for heteroskedasticity was employed, and the assumption of homoskedasticity could not be rejected.

While Ordinary Least Squares (OLSQ) run separately on equations (1) and (2) would give unbiased estimates of the coefficients and standard errors, they would not be efficient. It is known that the error terms across equations for corresponding observations are likely to be correlated. Variables that influence bank behavior but that are not included as independent variables and so show up in the error terms are likely to be partly the same for both equations. This knowledge can be used and efficiency increased by taking account of the correlation across equations. This has been done by using Zellner's seemingly unrelated equation

Table 9.1   Rates of Book Returns and Costs of Classes of Assets and Liabilities for a Sample of Commercial Banks (in Percent per Year)

Class of Asset or Liability	1962	1963	1964	1965	1966	1967	1968	1969	1970	1971	1972	1973	1974	1975	1976[a]	1977[a]
Securities																
U.S. Treasuries and agencies	3.43	3.50	3.77	3.86	4.30	4.54	4.57		5.62	5.60	5.43	5.42	5.91	6.00	6.31	6.23
Federal funds and other securities	2.34*	3.35*	2.17*	2.36*	3.50	4.70	3.50		5.04	4.19	4.83	7.46	9.14	6.10	5.24	4.87
State and local securities	3.38	3.13	3.29	3.36	3.27	3.69	4.16		5.02	4.55	4.74	4.79	5.35	6.13	5.72	5.71
Loans, net																
1-4 family mortgages	3.89	4.00	3.98	4.08	4.55	4.61	4.77		5.43	5.70	5.49	5.20	5.66	5.57	6.38	6.22
Other mortgages	3.79	3.43	4.01	3.72	4.15	4.34	4.56		5.03	5.61	5.26	5.54	4.45	4.19	6.13	6.57
Commercial, industrial, financial, farm, other loans	3.85	4.00	3.87	3.79	4.13	4.58	4.92		5.28	5.22	5.17	5.62	6.57	6.17	6.10	6.47
Consumer loans	3.23	3.76	4.09	4.06	4.56	4.85	5.44		4.66	5.30	5.42	5.84	6.00	5.73	4.40	4.88
Interest-bearing balances with banks															5.43	4.21
Liabilities																
Demand deposits	1.45	1.53	1.61	1.52	1.73	2.01	2.21		2.37	2.72	2.73	2.84	3.24	3.93	2.96	2.97
Time and savings deposits	3.18	3.43	3.44	3.47	3.85	4.11	4.31		4.66	4.84	4.77	4.79	5.23	5.16	5.38	5.26
Purchased money, including federal funds									4.22	3.52	3.49	6.25	8.48	4.75	7.05	7.20
Loans, gross																
1-4 family mortgages	5.03	5.12	5.28	5.43	5.61	5.41	5.53		6.03	6.21	6.64	6.82	6.86	6.89	7.87	8.14
Other mortgages	6.94	6.24	6.56	6.50	6.41	6.85	6.88		7.29	8.32	8.04	8.83	9.46	9.21	8.89	9.35
Commercial, industrial, financial, farm, other loans	5.63	5.86	6.02	6.01	6.29	6.52	6.98		8.44	7.57	7.15	8.56	10.60	8.90	8.91	8.94
Consumer loans	8.18	8.21	7.83	7.86	8.13	8.23	8.92		9.87	10.41	10.10	10.46	10.78	11.57	11.36	11.22
Interest-bearing balances with banks															9.10	6.40
Rate on three-month Treasury bills	2.77	3.16	3.54	3.95	4.86	4.29	5.34	6.68	6.39	4.33	4.07	7.03	7.84	5.80	4.98	5.27

Note: 1962–75 based on data from an FDIC 980-bank sample. Rates are the coefficients from a regression of revenues on loans and investments and costs on liabilities. All coefficients are significant at the 0.99 level, with the exception of those marked with an asterisk.
*Not significant at the 0.99 level.
[a]Data are from consolidated statements (cf. text and p. 446, *Federal Reserve Bulletin*, June 1978).

estimation (1962). The differences from OLSQ are rarely large, but they are significant.

9.3 The Data

The data used in this study for the years 1962–75 come from the Federal Deposit Insurance Corporation's stratified sample of Reports of Condition and Income. This sample covers 978 identical banks for the period 1961–68 and a somewhat different group of 980 banks for 1969–75. It includes the end-of-year and midyear call reports. There was a change in reporting between the 1968 and 1969 reports that has some influence on the choice of variables and causes the omission of much data for 1969 from the analysis. An additional change occurred for the years 1976–77. Data are from a 20 percent sample of all banks. Data are from consolidated balance sheets and income statements. Interest from balances with other banks is shown separately, and over $100,000 certificates of deposit are included in purchased money rather than in time and savings deposits. These changes for 1976 and 1977 affect the comparability of the costs for all liabilities.

In 1975 the sample contains 186 banks with over $500,000,000 in assets; 195 banks between $200,000,000 and $500,000,000; 196 between $50,-000,000 and $200,000,000; 252 between $10,000,000 and $50,000,000; and 151 banks under $10,000,000 in assets. The sample is approximating random within categories with some adjustments to ensure continuity. Such a sample, it is well known, gives unbiased estimates.

The income data cover the entire year as reported in the annual Reports of Condition (calls), the asset data are weighted averages of the final and midyear reports for the designated year and the final report for the previous year, with weights of ¼, ½, and ¼, respectively. Cash, bank balances, and items in process have been subtracted from reported demand deposits as an estimate of net demand deposits.

The data were run for the entire sample and for five subclasses by size. Chow tests indicated that one could not reject the hypothesis that there were no significant differences in net revenues and costs among the different size groups. The results for the smallest size group are more erratic than the results for the others and also on the whole show higher revenues and costs, but they still fall within the normal distribution for the entire sample.

Various problems are known to exist with the data that cause less than ideal results. Most important is the fact that the data report book income, costs, and asset values. These differ from economic variables because rates of return and the amount of assets are not corrected for changes in market values. Furthermore, economic periods of adjustment are unlikely to equal a year. Table 9.5 and the discussion of it show how rough corrections can be made to get actual economic returns and the considerable difference in analysis that result.

Because of window dressing, reported assets on call dates are known to be biased estimates of daily averages. The biases are small for most assets and liabilities, but they are significant for items such as federal funds. Miscellaneous assets or liabilities have been grouped together to decrease this problem, but biases almost certainly remain for these items. Total estimated rates of return and costs are perhaps 2 percent (about 5 to 10 basis points) less as a result of this problem.

Some sources of income and expense cannot be directly related to items on the balance sheet. This is true, for example, of income from fiduciary activities. To correct partially for such income and related costs, we have used as gross revenue the sum of all income reported for each type of earning asset. We have subtracted this amount from reported income to estimate that from other sources and have then subtracted this sum from both revenues and expenses. In effect, this assumes that banks break even on their miscellaneous activities and that costs and revenues for their loan and investment activities can be estimated with only minor biases from this correction. Since this gross correction is less than 7 percent of the total, any bias arising from a net difference between costs and revenues for these miscellaneous items is likely to be small.

A related problem arises in attempting to allocate investment expenses among classes of securities. From Federal Reserve *Functional Cost Analysis* we find that expenses for portfolio investments are less than 0.01 percent of the total. The difficulties of estimating the distribution of this small sum are great enough so that we exclude the costs of managing the securities' portfolio from our estimations, even though this means that net revenues from securities are overestimated by 3 to 10 basis points. This may approximately offset the opposite bias from use of call dates, but there will be small variations from year to year.

The most important difference between the data for 1962–68 and those for 1970–75 is in the treatment of sales and purchases of federal funds. In the earlier period, such sales are included in commercial and other loans, while in the later period they are included in federal funds and other securities owned. This is done to follow bank reporting that included sales of federal funds as part of loans to financial institutions in the earlier period but reported them separately in the later period. Purchases of federal funds in the earlier period were included in other liabilities. This causes a major difference in estimates of purchased money for the earlier period, and for this reason the results are not shown. Other minor definitional changes also occurred in 1969, but their effect is believed to be slight. The 1976 changes primarily affect the 145 large banks with foreign deposits as well as the definition of time and savings deposits and purchased money.

9.4   Results

Tables 9.1, 9.2, and 9.3 report the results of the statistical analysis of book returns. Table 9.1 shows the net and gross revenues for seven classes of assets (eight in 1976–77), three classes of liabilities, and the market rates on three-month Treasury bills, by year. Table 9.2 shows the means and standard deviations for each asset, both for the entire period and for the two subperiods. There was a major shift in the level of rates between the two periods. Thus, even though they cover a shorter period, the data for 1970–77 appear of greater interest and more relevant at present.

Table 9.3 shows the correlations between the returns on United States securities and the various other rates both for the entire period and for the two subperiods.

Table 9.2   **Average Rates of Book Returns and Costs for Classes of Assets and Liabilities**

Class of Asset or Liability	1962–68 Mean	1962–68 S.D.[a]	1970–77 Mean	1970–77 S.D.	1962–77[b] Mean	1962–77[b] S.D.
Securities						
U.S. Treasuries and agencies	4.00	.475	5.81	.348	4.97	.985
Federal funds and other securities	3.13	.906	5.85	1.659	4.59	1.861
State and local securities	3.47	.349	5.25	.565	4.42	.994
Loans, net						
1–4 family mortgages	4.28	.350	5.71	.400	5.04	.801
Other mortgages	4.00	.390	5.35	.799	4.72	.900
Commercial, industrial, financial, farm, other loans	4.16	.428	5.83	.573	5.05	.956
Consumer loans	4.29	.731	5.29	.582	4.81	.786
Liabilities						
Demand deposits	−1.72	.284	−2.97	.461	−2.39	.720
Time and savings deposits	−3.68	.414	−5.01	.275	−4.39	.736
Purchased money, including federal funds			−5.62	1.881		
Loans, gross						
1–4 family mortgages	5.34	.212	6.93	.735	6.19	.947
Other mortgages	6.62	.267	8.67	.744	7.72	1.154
Commercial, industrial, financial, farm, other loans	6.18	.452	8.63	1.034	7.49	1.439
Consumer loans	8.19	.360	10.72	.616	9.54	1.348
Rate on three-month Treasury bills	3.99	.917	5.71	1.310	4.91	1.372

[a]Standard deviation.
[b]1969 was not included in the calculations.

Table 9.3   **Correlations between Book Rates of Returns on United States Securities (Governments and Agencies) and Other Assets and Liabilities**

Class of Asset or Liability	Actual			First Differences	
	1962–68	1970–77	1962–77[a]	1963–68	1971–77
Securities					
U.S. Treasuries and agencies	1.00	1.00	1.00	1.00	1.00
Federal funds and other securities	.71	−.02	.74	.34	.08
State and local securities	.73	.85	.95	−.19	.21
Loans, net					
1–4 family mortgages	.97	.88	.98	.53	.77
Other mortgages	.90	.29	.80	.67	−.06
Commercial, industrial, financial, farm, other loans	.84	.79	.95	.18	.44
Consumer loans	.95	−.43	.70	.07	−.48
Liabilities					
Demand deposits	−.91	−.46	−.91	−.39	.14
Time and savings deposits	−.97	−.93	−.99	−.41	−.85
Purchased money, including federal funds		−.60			−.37
Loans, gross					
1–4 family mortgages	.85	.80	.91	−.03	.09
Other mortgages	.33	.60	.90	.35	−.01
Commercial, industrial, financial, farm, other loans	.93	.54	.90	−.05	.49
Consumer loans	.53	.84	.95	.27	.16
Rate on three-month Treasury bills	.92	−.02	.69	−.06	.04

[a]1969 was not included in the calculations.

Several facts stand out from the tables. (It should be recalled that all results in these tables are for book income.)

1. While net returns to a class of assets differ considerably from year to year, they are fairly close when a number of years are averaged together. In fact, one cannot reject the hypothesis that on average their rates are the same.

2. These convergences in net returns occur despite wide divergences in gross returns. The higher gross payments reflect higher costs. This is particularly true for consumer loans and nonhome mortgages.

3. Some classes of assets with high risks (for example, nonhome mortgages) have among the lowest returns. Decisions are based on expectations that can turn out to be very wrong.

4. Except for federal funds and other securities, any relationship between book rates of return and the standard deviation or variance of these returns is weak or nonexistent.

5. The correlation among the assets and liabilities and even their year-to-year changes tends to be high. There are two major exceptions. In the period 1970–77, returns on consumer loans and on federal funds had inverse correlations.

6. In the recent period also, the year-to-year movements of rates on three-month Treasury bills have been far more volatile and have not been well correlated with movements of other rates. Part of this difference occurs because the other returns are reported on a book basis rather than on a market basis. These book data tend to even out some of the year-to-year fluctuations in actual returns. This averaging process does not affect the return on the short-term Treasury bills.

7. While movements in the costs of demand and time deposits correlate well with changes in market rates, the effect of regulation Q in holding these costs down is evident. Some, but far from all, of the advantages of regulation Q to banks are given up to depositors or borrowers.

The average rate of return for the entire period for holdings of United States government securities, for most loans, and for Treasury bills are close. While significant differences occur on a year-to-year basis, they average out.

The sharpest year-to-year movements occur in the cost and revenues for federal funds and other securities and in the cost of borrowed money, which in the later period is dominated by purchases of federal funds. These returns move with changes in short-term Treasury bills. Superficially it appears that in recent years lending federal funds is the most profitable activity for a bank. This may well be true, but unfortunately these numbers have considerable bias, since the asset numbers are heavily influenced by window dressing on call dates.

Among the other assets, major divergences exist for the returns on nonresidential mortgages and consumer loans. Nonresidential mortgage loans show low returns, particularly in the years 1974–75. As noted, this reflects the fact that investment decisions are based on expectations that can be heavily influenced by market sentiments and that can turn out to be very wrong. Banks as a group were carried away by the real estate investment boom. Such errors with a lag led to the low returns of 1974–75 as losses, caused by the prior overenthusiastic lending, had to be charged off.

The lower reported return for state and local securities is expected, the only unusual feature being the high returns for the years 1975–77. Such very high returns are shown in the reports of individual banks.

Costs of money move with interest rates. This is particularly true for purchased money, but market rates also influence the costs of time and savings deposits. Regulation Q was completely removed for large certificates of deposit in 1973 and did not apply to most large certificates after mid-1970. Of course, during the earlier period, the ceilings were at times above market rates.

9.4.1   Deposit Rates

On the other hand, regulation Q apparently does hold the costs for demand deposits through services granted well below amounts paid for other funds. It is not true that costs adjust so that demand deposits have the same marginal costs as other funds. Whether because the ceiling acts as a form of price leadership or because of other oligopolistic features, banks do not completely compete away the advantages they gain from interest rate ceilings.

An examination of asset returns also makes it appear that the advantages gained through regulation Q are not given up in the form of lower returns on loans to particular classes of borrowers. There is no evident difference between the net rates earned on separate classes of loans. Net income earned from customers who would be expected to hold large balances do not differ greatly from rates charged those who walk in to borrow over the counter. Banks as a whole appear to be competitive in their loan terms even if not in payments on demand deposits.

On the other hand, a relationship may exist between the general level of rates on loans and the fact that banks need to attract deposits. Loan rates as measured in these tables do not appear to compensate fully for their additional risk of possible losses in comparison with the rate of return on Treasury securities. If they could have obtained the same amounts of funds without having to be in the loan business, banks would have earned as much money with less risk by investing primarily in government securities. As we will note shortly, however, these differences in returns may also reflect the fact that during the entire period lenders and investors were poor forecasters. The anticipated rates of return may have been in accordance with expected risks and returns. Because of large unanticipated movements, the ex post relationships probably do not reflect those lenders held when they decided to lend.

Over this period, despite the fact that loans earned the same as or less than securities, particularly in comparison with risks, banks continually increased the percentage of their loans and decreased the share of government securities in their assets. United States government and agency securities fell from over 25 percent of the total in 1961 to about 13.5 percent by 1975. Loans rose from 45 to 52.5 percent of the total. Whether this shift occurred because there is a significant interrelationship between types of assets and liabilities or simply because rates of return differed from expectations is not clear. Most bankers assume that if they made fewer loans they would attract fewer depositors.

9.5 Total Returns

The returns discussed thus far are accounting or book returns as reflected in reported balance sheets and income statements. For many purposes, however, we would like to know what happened from year to year in actual or total or market-corrected returns. The return on an asset may be positive or negative. It equals the sum of an interest component plus any change in the present value of future cash flows owing to a shift either in market interest rates or in the observed probability of default.

For an asset traded in an active market such as a listed common stock or bond, the measurement of actual return is simple. We take the dividend or coupon payments received during the year, then add or subtract changes in the market price to get the total return to the asset. If we were able to get the change in market values during the year for each of a bank's assets or classes of assets, we would be able to estimate total returns in this same manner. Unfortunately we cannot. Therefore, to obtain some idea of how risks and returns have varied, we must construct rough approximations of such numbers.

9.5.1 Duration

We have assumed that the market value of each class of assets changes in accordance with the average "duration" of the class multiplied by the change in market yields of government securities of the same approximate duration. These estimates follow from the known general relationship (cf. chap. 13) that the change in price of a bond or loan is equal to the change in expected market interest rates for similar bonds times the negative of its duration, or

$$(3) \qquad \frac{d\,\text{Price}}{\text{Price}} = \frac{d(1+r)}{(1+r)} \cdot -\text{duration},$$

where r is the rate of interest or yield to maturity (Boquist, Racette, and Schlarbaum 1975). A bond or loan's duration is simply the time until its payments will on average have been received. Thus duration is the average of the present value of each future interest or principal payment times the length of the period until it will be received.

There are well-recognized difficulties with this formulation. No allowances are made for variations in uncertainty or the risk related to the specific asset class. No adjustments are made for changes in the term structure of interest rates. We have not taken into account the fact that some changes in value may have been taken into the books during the year through the sale or purchase of assets. We have not accounted for changes other than interest rates.

While recognizing that all these factors can affect the value of an asset, we have been forced to work primarily with those changes that result from movements in the basic interest rate. However, it should be noted that changes in defaults and related costs are already reflected in the estimated book returns for that year. Moreover, a number of simulations (cf. chap. 15) of the effect of changes in market values indicates that movements in the interest rate on government securities usually account for most value changes.

As important as these other factors is the lack of exact estimates of the duration of the typical bank's assets. Duration has been estimated in a rough manner from the FDIC reports, Treasury bulletins, and the balance sheets of several large banks. The most that can be claimed is that these estimates probably are in the proper rank order and that the magnitudes are in the ball park. To avoid any sense of undue accuracy, we have rounded the estimated durations to full years. By happenstance, this results in the duration for assets of different types being roughly spaced from one to six years. The assigned duration in years are as follows: consumer loans (1 year); commercial and industrial (2); United States government and agencies (3); nonhome mortgages (4); home mortgages (5); and state and local bonds (6). It is also assumed that rates of return and costs of federal funds, other securities, and purchased money equal the market rates on federal funds and that the duration for these categories is insignificant.

9.5.2   Interest Rate Movements

Changes in interest rates are measured from the end of the year before that for which the rates of return have been estimated to the end of the year covered by the income data. In each case, the rate for the particular yield to maturity is taken from yield curves estimated for the last business day of the year by McCulloch's cubic-spline term structure curve-fitting program for United States Treasuries (McCulloch 1975a).

Table 9.4 shows the estimated changes in capital values for each class of asset. This is in accordance with equation (3). The percentage change in the yield to maturity at the assumed duration for the class of assets is multiplied by the duration of that class.

Table 9.5 is the result of combining the estimated book rates of return in Table 9.1 with the year-to-year change in capital values of table 9.4. Thus it is an estimate of the total return to a class of assets by year. As noted, these may differ from actual changes in values since the durations may not be accurate, since the specific risks of the different classes may have altered, and since changes in the assets held during the year may

Table 9.4   Changes in Capital Values by Class of Assets for Banks, by Years (in Percent per Year)

Class of Asset or Liability	1962	1963	1964	1965	1966	1967	1968	1969	1970	1971	1972	1973	1974	1975	1976	1977
Securities																
U.S. Treasuries and agencies	.75	−1.62	−.84	−1.11	−3.12	−.24	−.03	−5.76	5.19	1.02	−1.77	−2.54	−1.94	−.22	3.99	−4.80
Federal funds and other securities	0	0	0	0	0	0	0	0	0	0	0	0	0	0	0	0
State and local securities	.98	−2.27	−.69	−2.36	−4.36	−2.90	−.34	−8.45	5.42	1.62	−.68	−3.39	−5.11	−2.34	7.62	−7.74
Loans, net																
1–4 family mortgages	1.10	−1.93	−.72	−1.97	−3.78	−2.28	−.48	−7.85	5.73	1.18	−.76	−3.3	−4.08	−1.81	6.35	−6.75
Other mortgages	.92	−1.84	−.80	−1.56	−3.52	−1.16	−.32	−6.73	5.72	1.16	−1.48	−3.00	−2.96	−1.04	5.40	−6.04
Commercial, industrial, financial, farm, other loans	.35	−1.24	−.70	−.72	−2.10	−.06	−.16	−3.52	4.46	.56	−1.06	−2.12	−1.02	.37	2.64	−3.56
Consumer loans	−.02	−.69	−.40	−.31	−.97	−.27	−.05	−1.94	2.48	.41	−.65	1.96	.05	1.04	1.23	−2.04

Table 9.5   Rates of Total Returns for Classes of Assets for a Sample of Commercial Banks (in Percent per Year)

Class of Asset or Liability	1962	1963	1964	1965	1966	1967	1968	1969[a]	1970	1971	1972	1973	1974	1975	1976	1977
Securities																
U.S. Treasuries and agencies	4.18	1.88	2.93	2.75	1.18	4.30	4.54	-.66[a]	10.81	6.62	3.67	2.90	4.00	5.78	10.20	1.43
Federal funds and other securities	2.34	3.35	2.17	2.36	3.50	4.70	3.50	4.27[a]	5.04	4.19	4.83	7.46	9.14	6.10	5.24	4.87
State and local securities	4.36	.87	2.60	1.00	-1.09	.79	4.50	-3.85[a]	10.45	6.20	4.07	1.40	.25	3.79	13.34	-2.03
Loans, net																
1–4 family mortgages	4.90	2.17	3.26	2.11	.78	2.33	5.25	-2.75[a]	11.17	6.87	4.73	1.90	1.59	3.76	12.73	-0.53
Other mortgages	2.87	1.59	3.21	2.16	.63	3.18	4.89	-1.94[a]	10.76	6.78	3.77	2.54	1.48	3.14	11.53	+0.53
Commercial, industrial, financial, farm, other loans	3.51	2.76	3.17	3.07	2.03	4.52	4.79	-1.58[a]	9.68	5.77	4.10	3.51	5.85	6.53	8.95	2.91
Consumer loans	3.21	3.07	3.70	3.75	3.59	4.58	5.39	3.11[a]	7.13	5.71	4.76	3.88	5.94	6.78	5.63	2.84
Total portfolio of assets and liabilities	2.44	0.21	1.10	0.76	-0.34	1.04	2.17	-2.97[a]	6.30	2.44	0.49	-0.12	-0.31	1.13	4.76	-2.92
Rate on three-month Treasury bills	2.77	3.16	3.54	3.95	4.86	4.29	5.34	6.68	6.39	4.33	4.07	7.03	7.84	5.80	4.98	5.27

	Means		Standard Deviations
	1962–77	1970–77	1962–77
U.S. Treasuries and agencies	4.19	5.30	3.15
Federal funds and other securities	4.59	5.86	2.17
State and local securities	2.91	4.92	4.35
1–4 family mortgages	3.79	5.28	3.96
Other mortgages	3.57	5.06	3.58
Commercial, industrial, financial, farm, other loans	4.35	5.91	2.89
Consumer loans	4.56	5.33	1.73
Rate on three-month Treasury bills	5.02	5.71	1.95

[a]There are no data for book returns in 1969. The estimates are the average of 1968 and 1970 book returns plus the estimated change in capital values for 1969.

have meant that some of the reported book returns reflected changes in the assets.

The data show that over this entire period economic (as opposed to book) rates of return had a much broader dispersion. Also, using standard deviations as a measure of risk, we find not much relationship between risks and returns. Risk-corrected rates of return did not equalize.

For the period 1970–77, commercial, industrial, farm, and other loans corrected for capital changes did much better relative to other yields and to their book-value estimates. They exceeded, as theory says they should, the rate of return both on more liquid United States Treasuries and on all other activities.

This entire period was dominated by unexpected increases in both long- and short-term interest rates. With only a few exceptions, rates at every maturity rose each year from 1963 through 1969. From that year through 1975, increases were less universal and were decidedly smaller, but yields on all maturities of three years and over were higher in December 1975 than in December 1969 and nearly as high in December 1977.

9.6   Portfolio Rates of Return

A bank's earnings depend upon how each of its assets and liabilities reacts to events, but also upon how each changes as a result of these same events. Disintermediation and a shift in assets might be as significant in threatening insolvency as a loss from interest rate movements. We can consider each of these dangers separately.

We have defined the change in the value of the portfolio caused by changes in the rate of discount applied to the initial expected cash flows from both assets and liabilities as a "wealth effect." Thus, at the end of one year, the value of assets and liabilities and of the bank depends upon the projected cash flows (based upon loan agreements, expected defaults, expected processing costs, etc.) and the discount rates applicable to these future cash flows. During the course of the year, these rates of discount will change as a result of movements in spot interest rates, in forward rates, and the risk premiums for each class of assets and liabilities. Thus the wealth effect depends upon the distribution of assets in the initial portfolio and upon the way each one's rate of discount alters.

The "income effect" on the portfolio's values results from changes in the expected cash flows. These are influenced by movements in the macroeconomy. During the course of the year, cash flows will differ from those expected at the start because market interest rates will apply to new or refinanced loans or investments, because cost of operations will alter, default rates and nonaccruing loans may increase, and the amount of effort required to collect on loans may differ, and because liquidity problems may lead to transaction costs to liquidate part of the portfolio.

In addition, future cash flows will alter because the amounts of each type of asset and liability in the portfolio may differ. The rate of expansion or decline in holdings of the portfolio will react to movements in interest rates, in the money supply, and in the gross national product and to competitive pressures. How banks react to these movements will differ depending upon such factors as the bank's type of customers, its region, its past commitments, and the way different categories of assets and liabilities react to the economy.

Our study gives rough estimates of these two influences on banks with different weights of assets and liabilities. Our estimates are inexact because in table 9.4 we have not included estimates of shifts in risk premiums or shifts within the term structure, but instead have used the concept of duration and yield to maturity.

9.6.1   Wealth Effects

As examples of wealth effects for an average bank, the losses in capital values as a percentage of its total earning assets were 4.8 percent in 1969, 2.4 percent in 1973, 1.9 percent in 1974, and 4.2 percent in 1977. These are the weighted average of typical portfolios in those years times the rate of loss shown in table 9.4. These losses would have been increased to the extent that risk premiums widened and decreased to the extent that the value of existing deposits rose. However, table 9.1 shows that the cost of deposits rose at about the same rate as the value of money during this period. As a result, since deposits had only a slight influence, we can estimate that in these years the net wealth effect reduced capital values somewhat more than would be estimated from the impact of government interest rates alone.

9.6.2   Income Effects

In contrast to wealth effects, effects on the capital of the average bank from changes in income seem to be small. However, again our data are incomplete. We do not have estimates of shifts in duration from operations, and, as noted earlier, because of changes in the reporting forms we lack information on changes in book income in 1969. What we do have are estimates of changes in value arising from alterations in the mix of assets and liabilities and from movements in book earnings for the other years.

The income effects on a bank's capital value turn out to be rather minor because of offsetting pressures. Earnings on newly purchased rolled-over loans and investments rise, as do costs of liabilities. The chief danger to a bank is likely to be from a need to borrow at much higher rates while the return on assets is moving up more slowly. For the average bank, this problem was not great. Its costs for demand time and savings deposits rose at roughly the same rate as returns on assets. The costs of purchased money rose rapidly, and their share of total liabilities rose also, but an average bank does not have a large ratio of these liabilities. Table 9.4 shows that, except for a large gain in 1969 and then a sharp fall in 1971, earnings of banks on a book basis did not fluctuate much.

9.6.3   Total Portfolio Earnings

A bank's total return depends on the economic rate of return of each asset and liability and on the amount of each in its portfolio. We estimate the variation in such returns for an archetypal bank by assuming it had a portfolio equal to the mean distribution of assets and liabilities for all banks.

The line in table 9.5 labeled "total portfolio of assets and liabilities" is an estimate of how this typical bank would have fared. From table 9.1 we note rather mild fluctuations in book rates of return on assets, while payments on liabilities moved with market interest rates. When book returns are corrected for changes in capital values, as in table 9.5, except for 1969 most assets showed positive returns.

The picture is nearly, but not quite, the same when the shifting costs of liabilities are added. From the total portfolio line, we note that the typical bank probably lost money on an economic basis in 1969, 1973, 1974, and 1977. But only the first and last of these movements were sufficiently large so that losses were serious. Again, however, the difference between a typical bank and those with very different portfolios could create problem banks.

9.7   Summary

Bank returns from individual activities tend to equalize at the margins. However, equality is far from exact, nor are adjustments rapid. Banks cannot shift their portfolios too suddenly. They have existing commitments to their customers and communities. They can, however, alter their investments more rapidly while slowing down or speeding up lending. The ability of the entire financial system to shift lending plus competition among lenders leads to changes in rates and a tendency for rates among different activities to equalize.

The rate of adjustment of marginal returns is greater on a book basis than on an economic basis. It is simpler for banks to predict book returns. Still, unanticipated losses in a particular class of loan may lead to sizable year-to-year shifts even on a book basis.

The movements in total returns are much sharper. Year-to-year divergences are far greater. In this period, changes in economic returns were dominated by interest rate movements. In the years of maximum interest increases, most banks lost money. For the entire period, total returns in an activity were negatively correlated with its duration. Since the end of 1969, however, with smaller increases in market interest rates such correlations are less. Returns on commercial, industrial, and related loans have been higher than others in the 1970s.

In contrast to reported book year-to-year earning movements of about 5 basis points, the economic return on net earning assets fluctuated widely. Although exact data are not available for 1969, the shift in returns from 1969 to 1970 was probably over 9 percent. This shift reflects the fact that the three-month Treasury bill rate was 5.92 percent in December 1968, 7.72 percent in December 1969, and 4.86 percent in December 1970. Similarly, from 1976 to 1977 returns fell by nearly 7.75 percent.

While not extreme for the average bank, losses would rise rapidly if a bank maintained a portfolio with a duration far above average. Furthermore, it should be noted that for an average bank the shift in returns from interest rate risks far exceeded variations in defaults or loan losses for even those banks at the high end of the loan loss distribution.

Other significant forces appear to be at work in determining the costs of deposits (net of service chages). Banks' costs of deposits are held down by interest rate ceilings. Even though by law no interest can be paid on demand deposits, their cost is far from zero. Banks that hold deposits gain intangible capital as a result of their profitability. However, no indication exists that significant additional gains or losses arise from interest rate movements. The marginal costs of deposits seem to rise and fall in the same way as returns on assets.

Appendix

We need to differentiate among four separate approaches to estimating costs and revenues of banks.

1. As noted, this study is based upon statistical cost and revenue curves. Reported costs and revenues are regressed on differing amounts of assets and liabilities for each unit in the cross section. The regression coefficients estimate the effect on returns of placing a dollar in one class rather than in another.

Thus the estimated rates of return are closely related to marginal revenue and costs, with the estimated variations in returns depending upon differences among classes. This technique specifically accounts for the interrelationship among the banks' assets and liabilities. The influences of all assets and liabilities are considered simultaneously. One estimates the effect on revenues of placing funds in loans rather than investments in securities while simultaneously considering the effect of such differences on costs. Overhead and partially variable costs are distributed among assets and liabilities in accordance with the way they cause costs and revenues for classes of assets and liabilities to vary among banks rather than in an arbitrary manner.

2. Closely related to this study are the operating data reported by the FDIC and the Federal Reserve in their annual *Bank Operating Statistics*. Reported data in those publications are unweighted averages of individual banks. This gives a decided bias, because most banks are small while most assets are held by large banks. The sample we used is weighted more heavily to banks with more deposits, but it results in unbiased coefficients. The Federal Reserve–FDIC studies show average costs and revenues for aggregated assets, for specific types of costs, and for gross and net income before and after various types of adjustments. They do not show the interrelationship of costs and revenues. They do not show the net returns for loans or categories of loans. They do not estimate the cost of demand deposits. On the whole, estimates for the few comparable series in this study and *Bank Operating Statistics* are in general agreement. In 1975, however, this study shows a higher return on municipals and lower costs for time and savings deposits. The reason is unclear, but it may be related to the special impact of New York City bonds.

3. Types of data similar to those of the Federal Reserve–FDIC but with more complete breakdowns are found in the annual reports of larger banks. These are the kinds of data used by stock analysts and those in the market concerned with rating the safety of individual banks. Analysis of annual reports tends to emphasize net interest earned or the relationships between rates of interest earned on assets (including the effect of volume and rate changes) and the costs of money available for lending. Payments of interest are estimated for time and savings deposits and for other purchased money. Net interest earned is then compared with the noninterest costs of operating the banks.

4. An entirely different approach is followed by the studies of "functional cost analysis" (FCA) performed by and for Federal Reserve member banks. This approach uses especially prepared detailed cost accounting information. Banks in a sample period report information about personnel and other types of costs assigned to specific functions such as check clearing, account maintenance, and lending. The specific cost functions for four types of loans, for investments, and for types of deposits are estimated. Overhead costs are allocated to each. Gross yields and expenses are then estimated.

To obtain net revenues by class of assets, the FCA studies subtract the average cost of funds from the gross revenue after expenses for a specific class of assets. Similarly, gross revenues after specific expenses are calculated for the entire portfolio, and the average income is credited to each class of liability to get an estimate of net earnings by type of liability and asset.

The basic difference between the cost and revenue data in this study, in contrast to the others, is that the allocations of revenues and costs depend upon the total relationships among classes of assets and liabilities. The estimates are made statistically by regression so that a best estimate is obtained of how costs and revenues vary in accordance with the way sums earned and spent relate to differing distribution of assets and liabilities among the 980 banks in the sample. In almost all cases (the exceptions being noted by asterisks in table 9.1), the resulting estimated coefficients are highly significant (at a 99 percent level).

10 Interest Rate Risk and Capital Adequacy for Traditional Banks and Financial Intermediaries

J. Huston McCulloch

10.1 Introduction

In this study we investigate the interest rate risk confronting banks and thrift institutions. We do not deny that other types of risk are important, often more important than pure interest rate risk. However, the interest risk is particularly interesting in view of the traditional practice followed by financial intermediaries of "transforming maturities" by borrowing short and lending long. We quantify the value of insurance against this risk empirically, using a Paretian stable option pricing model.

These results can be applied in either of two ways. Currently, banks all pay a given premium to the insuring agency and are subjected to a more or less arbitrary set of regulations regarding capital structure and activities, intended to make them fairly safe from failure. Mayer (1965) has proposed a graduated deposit insurance plan, under which banks would be allowed (within reason) to take whatever capital position and risks they choose and in exchange would be required to pay a variable premium that covered the fair value of insurance for the risk category chosen. Given the riskiness of the bank's activities, the fair value of such insurance will decline as the bank's capital/asset ratio increases, because the more capital the bank has, the larger the share of any losses on the assets that will be borne by the bank's stockholders, rather than by the insuring agency. Therefore, for any given premium and riskiness of operations there will be some amount of capital that will be adequate to make the premium in question cover the fair value of insurance for the bank. Sharpe (chap. 8) has proposed that this be the criterion for deciding whether a bank's capital is "adequate," given the premium it pays and the

J. Huston McCulloch is associate professor of economics and finance at Ohio State University.

risks it takes. There is no essential difference between the two proposals, since they are just two ways of interpreting the same underlying relationship between permissible risk, adequate capital, and fair premium, which we here attempt to quantify.

10.2   Capital and the Division of Losses

To simplify the analysis, we will concentrate on a "traditional bank," which has demand or virtually demand liabilities and longer-term assets. We will assume that these assets are perfectly marketable with no transactions costs and that there is no risk of default or possibility of being called before maturity. At first we will assume that the bank's entire portfolio is invested in one type of asset and in one maturity. Later we will relax many of these assumptions.

Let A_0 be the initial value of the bank's assets and L_0 be the initial value of its liabilities, so that

(1) $C = A_0 - L_0$

is the initial economic value of its capital. Define

(2) $q = C/A_0$

as its initial capital/asset ratio, so that

(3) $L_0 = A_0(1 - q)$.

Let $\tilde{A}$ be the random value of the bank's assets when it is next examined. If $\tilde{A}$ is greater than A_0, so that the bank has excess capital, we assume the bank will be allowed to distribute this excess capital to shareholders in order to return its capital/asset ratio to q. If it is less than A_0, the examiners will require the shareholders to restore the deficient capital. If they do not, the bank will be liquidated. The shareholders could restore the capital by putting up more money of their own, by selling new stock on the open market so as to dilute their own stock, or by following a policy of retaining some of the anticipated return on the assets as a buffer against unanticipated capital losses. As long as $\tilde{A}$ is above L_0, so that their stock has positive net worth, they will choose to replenish the capital by one of these means. However, if $\tilde{A}$ is below L_0 (that is, if $\tilde{A}/A_0$ is below $1 - q$), they will (abstracting from the value of the bank's charter and customer relationships) prefer to abandon the bank and let the insuring agency pay off the depositors, taking a loss of $L_0 - \tilde{A}$. Since the shareholders reap the unanticipated capital gains if $\tilde{A}$ is unusually high but do not take all the losses if $\tilde{A}$ is unusually low, the insuring agency would have to charge some positive insurance premium I to compensate itself for the risk of having to take up part of the losses.

This premium should be retained by the party guaranteeing the deposits even in years when there are no failures, since the risk cannot be expected to average out over banks in any given year. Insurance against loan default or against embezzlement may behave to a large extent like casualty insurance, in which the premiums can be expected to pay off the losses in each year, but insurance against interest rate risk is undiversifiable. In most years, no banks will fail from this cause, but occasionally—once every ten or one hundred years, depending on the risks the banks take—all the banks will be in trouble.

10.3   The Value of Deposit Insurance

Formally, deposit insurance is equivalent to an option on the bank's assets. Deposit insurance essentially gives the banking firm (construed to include both depositors and shareholders) a "put" option, entitling it to sell the bank's assets to the insurer at a prearranged "execution price," determined by the nominal value of the bank's liabilities. The liability/asset ratio, $1 - q$, may therefore be thought of as the execution price/current price ratio in a put option contract.

Robert Merton (1977a) has thus applied the well-known Black-Scholes option pricing formula to the problem of evaluating bank deposit insurance. However, this formula relies on the strong assumption that $\tilde{A}$ is log *normal*. The distribution of most prices, including the prices of interest-bearing securities, seems to be much too fat tailed or leptokurtic to be consistent with a simple normal or log normal distribution.

We therefore assume that the logarithm of $\tilde{A}$ is instead distributed according to the symmetric Paretian stable class of distributions, whose use in financial applications has been pioneered by Mandelbrot (1963), Fama and Roll (1968, 1971), and Roll (1970). If $\tilde{A}$ itself had a symmetric stable distribution, there would be a small but positive probability that the value of the assets would actually go negative. By making its logarithm symmetric stable, we eliminate this possibility.

Symmetric stable distributions are characterized by three parameters: the *characteristic exponent* α, which governs how fast the tails taper off, the *standard scale c*, which roughly equals the semi-interquartile range, and the mean.

The characteristic exponent may range between 0 and 2, though in financial applications it is ordinarily assumed to be between 1 and 2. When it equals 1, the Cauchy distribution results, and when it equals 2, the normal (Gaussian) distribution is obtained. Except in the limiting normal case, the variance is infinite, which is why we must use the standard scale in place of the standard deviation to characterize its spread. If we were to restrict ourselves to the normal distribution, we would greatly underestimate the probability of a sudden large change in the value of the bank's assets and hence would greatly underestimate the fair value of insurance.

Figure 10.1 shows how the bell-shaped probability density function of the symmetric stable distribution changes with α. In all three cases, the standard scale is chosen to be 1.0, so that the probability is roughly 0.5 that $\tilde{X}$ will lie between $+1$ and -1 on the horizontal axis. When α is less than 2.0, the curve has a higher mode, lower shoulders, and higher tails

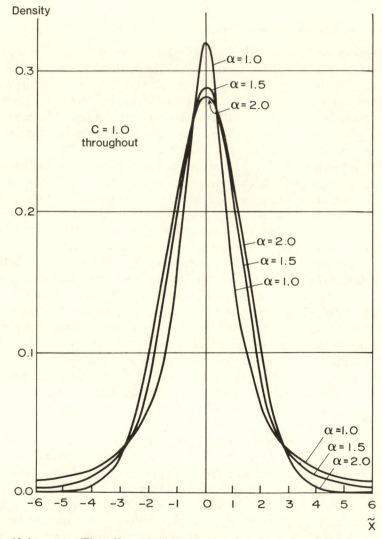

Fig. 10.1   The effect of the characteristic exponent.

than the familiar normal distribution. Note that the normal density virtually disappears by $\tilde{X} = 5.0$.

Figure 10.2 shows how the stable density function is affected by the scale parameter c. In each case, the characteristic exponent equals 1.5, the intermediate case of figure 10.1. If c is 2.0 instead of 1.0, the distribution has the same shape but is twice as spread out (and has only half as high a mode, in order to continue to integrate to unity). When c is 0.5 instead of 1.0, it is more squeezed together. The mode is now at 0.576, which is off scale in figure 10.2. Note that the tails are still perceptibly

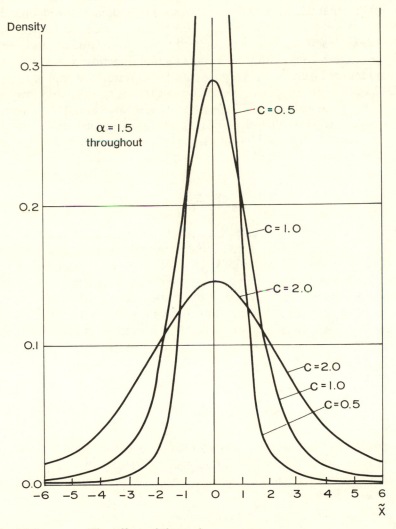

Fig. 10.2   The effect of the scale parameter.

above zero at $\tilde{X} = 6.0$, which corresponds to 12 standard scales. For the normal distribution ($\alpha = 2.0$), the standard scale exactly equals the standard deviation divided by $\sqrt{2}$, so that 54.7 percent of the probability density lies between $+c$ and $-c$.

In two papers, I have developed some of the properties of stable distributions in a continuous time context and have developed an option pricing formula based on the log symmetric stable distribution. In continuous time the sample path of a process governed by these distributions is full of discontinuities. Therefore, even if the regulators are constantly vigilant—essentially examining the bank continuously—there is some possibility that the value of the bank's assets may change so suddenly that net worth will be deeply negative before they have a chance to close it. If the bank's assets fell in value, but not by enough to wipe out its capital, the regulators could either insist on a capital injection or else raise the premium for insurance in keeping with the deteriorated capital ratio of the bank. Therefore, with continuous examination, the only way the bank could fail is through a single discontinuity large enough to wipe out the bank's capital; that is, a change in log $\tilde{A}$ greater than log $(A_0/L_0) = -\log(1-q)$. In McCulloch (1978a), it is shown that the annual rate of occurrence of such discontinuities is

$$(4) \qquad \lambda = \frac{k_\alpha}{2}\left(\frac{c_0}{-\log(1-q)}\right)^\alpha,$$

where c_0 is the standard scale of log $\tilde{A}$ that accumulates in one year, and k_α is a constant (depending on α) that is tabulated in that article. For the sake of illustration, $k_1 = .6366$, $k_{1.5} = .3989$, and $k_2 = 0$. (Since $k_2 = 0$, a normal diffusion process never, with probability 1, has discontinuities.)

When a change in the value of the bank's assets sufficiently large to close the bank suddenly occurs (or is suddenly perceived to have already occurred), the change is likely to have been more than large enough to have wiped out the bank's capital, imposing some losses on the insuring agency. McCulloch (1978b) shows that the fair value of these losses is given by

$$(5) \qquad \frac{I}{A_0} = \lambda H(1 - q, \alpha)dt,$$

where $H(\ )$ is a function that is tabulated in that article, I is insurance, and dt is the life of the "option" (or examination period), which approaches 0. Thus the value per year of insurance, computed (as is conventional) as a fraction of liabilities, is

$$(6) \qquad \pi = \frac{I}{L_0 dt} = \frac{\lambda H(1 - q, \alpha)}{1 - q}.$$

This equation, in conjunction with (4), tells us how to compute the fair value of insurance from q, α, and c_0.

10.4   The Data

To evaluate formulas (4) and (6), we need empirical values for c_0 and α for idealized default-free, perfectly marketable assets, of various maturities. United States Treasury securities are default-free, and very highly marketable, so we will use their empirical behavior as a proxy for the idealized assets we desire.

For each of several key maturities, we would like estimates of c_0 and α for three types of assets a bank or thrift institution might hold: single payment or "discount" instruments, "par bonds," by which we mean coupon bonds that happen to be selling exactly at par, and "amortized" loans that pay a constant amount each month with no balloon at final maturity. We cannot use raw Treasury securities price behavior to estimate these parameters directly, since the Treasury issues no marketable amortized securities, since its discount instruments (Treasury bills) have maturities only out to one year, and since most outstanding Treasury bonds are ordinarily selling substantially above or below par, depending on their coupon rates, and in any event do not coincide with the key maturities we would like to investigate.

However, we can bypass this problem by curve-fitting a "discount function" to empirical Treasury quotations and using this smooth function to construct a synthetic price for any type or maturity of security we care to define. For this purpose we employ my cubic-spline term structure curve-fitting program, developed while at NBER-West. This version of the progam is a modification of the tax-adjusted term structure program developed in 1973 for the United States Treasury and described in McCulloch (1975a). The new modifications account precisely for the fact that the coupons on Treasury bonds arrive semiannually. For the sake of convenience and computational speed, the version developed for the Treasury assumed a continuous stream of coupons, which slightly distorts the shape of the term structure in the maturities where bonds and bills interface.

The data base we have available consists of bid and asked quotations for United States Treasury securities for the last business day of each month, from the end of December 1946 to the end of May 1977, a total of 366 months. Since these dates represent the dividing line between two months, they could equally well be associated with either month. We will refer to them as representing the "beginning" of the subsequent month, that is, January 1947 to June 1977. In fact, the quotations are for actual delivery and payment early in these months, about two business days after the quotation date. The data for January 1947 to April 1966 were collected by Reuben A. Kessel from the quotation sheets of Salomon Brothers and were processed by Myron Scholes under the supervision of Merton H. Miller. The data for May 1966 to June 1975 were collected from Salomon Brothers quotation sheets by Joel Messina and obtained with the assistance of Jay Morrisson. The data for July 1975 to June 1977 were collected from *Wall Street Journal* composite dealer quotations by Krista Chinn under my direction.

All tax-exempt securities were rejected as being nonrepresentative of the market as a whole. (By the mid-1950s all but a handful of these had disappeared.) "Flower bonds" often sell at a price premium because they can be surrendered at par value in payment of estate taxes if they are owned by the decedent at the time of his death. It was not practical to omit all of them, because for many years they constituted most if not all of the long-term securities. The following compromise was adopted for flower bonds: Those that were selling below par; matured after 1982; and were selling within $4 per $100 of face value of the lowest-priced flower bond were excluded. Any that did not meet all three of these criteria were included.[1] No attempt was made to compensate for the price discount that existed on many bonds in the earlier part of the period because of their ineligibility for commercial bank purchase. This discount was greatly reduced after the Accord of March 1951, and most of these bonds became eligible by the mid-1950s. Except for the tax-exempt and selected flower bonds, almost all United States Treasury bills, notes, and bonds were included. It would have been desirable in principle to exclude callable bonds, but this was not practical, since they constitute almost all of the longer-term securities for many years. Therefore they were treated as maturing on the final maturity date if selling below par, and as maturing on the call date if selling above par.

For each time t, a discount function $\delta(t, m)$ was fit to the bid/asked mean prices of the securities available. This function gives the present value, as a fraction of unity, of a dollar to be repaid after maturity m, that is, at future time $t + m$. The price $a(t, m)$ of an amortized loan paying $1 per year in continuous installments for m years can be derived from the discount function as follows:

$$(7) \qquad a(t, m) = \int_0^m \delta(t, \mu) \, d\mu.[2]$$

Finally, the par bond yield $y(t, m)$ that gives the coupon rate (as a fraction of unity) that would be necessary to make a continuous-coupon bond sell just at par can be derived as follows:

$$(8) \qquad y(t, m) = \frac{1 - \delta(t, m)}{a(t, m)}.$$

1. See McCulloch (1975*a*, pp. 817–22) for further discussion of these estate tax bonds.
2. For technical reasons, $a(t,m)$ was not calculable to adequate precision for the three-month and six-month maturities. Therefore no results are reported for amortized loans of these maturities.

10.5 Parameter Estimates

At time t, a pure discount security with maturity Δt can be purchased for $\delta(t, \Delta t)$ dollars. At time $t + \Delta t$, it can be sold (i.e., cashed, since it has just matured) for \$1. The log price relative on this investment is

(9)
$$\log \frac{1}{\delta(t, \Delta t)} = -\log \delta\,(t, \Delta t).$$

The log price relative over the same holding period of duration Δt on an investment in a security with any longer maturity is random, since it depends on an unknown future price. However, its expected value will approximately equal (9), since investors have the option of investing in any maturity and will compare expected returns on all of them. In practice, the expected log price relative will be slightly higher the longer the maturity, because of a reliable, but small, liquidity premium (see McCulloch 1975*b*). Therefore the realized log price relative on a longer maturity security, minus expression (9) (i.e., plus $\log \delta(t, \Delta t)$), will equal the unanticipated return plus a small, relatively constant liquidity premium. For a pure discount security with initial maturity m, this difference is given by

(10)
$$\log \frac{\delta(t + \Delta t, m - \Delta t)}{\delta(t, m)} + \log \delta(t, \Delta t),$$

since, after Δt has elapsed, it can be sold for $\delta(t + \Delta t, m - \Delta t)$.

For coupon bonds and amortized loans, our problem is somewhat complicated by the payments that arrive during the holding period, that is, between t and $t + \Delta t$. We will therefore consider the log price relatives of modified bonds and amortized loans that have had these first few payments removed. Such a modified par bond can be purchased at time t for $1 - y(t, m)\, a(t, \Delta t)$. When it is sold at $t + \Delta t$, its principal is worth $\delta(t + \Delta t, m - \Delta t)$, and its coupons are worth $y(t, m)\, a(t + \Delta t, m - \Delta t)$, so the amount by which its log price relative exceeds that on a discount security with maturity Δt is given by

(11)
$$\log \frac{\delta(t + \Delta t, m - \Delta t) + y(t, m)\, a(t + \Delta t, m - \Delta t)}{1 - y(t, m)\, a(t, \Delta t)}$$

$$+ \log \delta(t, \Delta t).$$

Our modified amortized loan can be purchased at time t for $a(t, m) - a(t, \Delta t)$ and sold at $t + \Delta t$ for $a(t + \Delta t, m - \Delta t)$, so the relevant difference is given by

(12)
$$\log \frac{a(t + \Delta t, m - \Delta t)}{a(t, m) - a(t, \Delta t)} + \log \delta(t, \Delta t).$$

The monthly standard scale c_{1mo} and the characteristic exponent of the unanticipated returns were estimated for each of the three types of asset using the methods suggested by Fama and Roll (1971), for both the entire post-Accord period (roughly the past twenty-six years), and for the past ten years. Before the Accord of March 1951, the Federal Reserve System artificially stabilized interest rates on United States Treasury securities. Since that period is not representative of what may be expected in years to come, we did not make any use of that part of our data set. Table 10.1 shows our standard scale estimates, based on the .28 and .72 fractiles of the distributions of expressions (10)–(12). In table 10.1, these values are multiplied by 100 in order to express them as percentage unanticipated changes. These figures mean that in roughly half the months observed, the unanticipated capital gain or loss on the asset indicated was within the value indicated, as a percentage of the initial value of the asset. The standard scale for unanticipated changes accumulated over one year, c_0, can be computed from these values by equation (13), to be introduced presently.

In Figures 10.3 and 10.4 these standard scale estimates are plotted versus maturity on double logarithmic graph paper. We see that for

Table 10.1   **Standard Scale of Unanticipated Logarithmic Returns (100 c_{1mo})**

Maturity	Months	Discount Instruments	Par Bonds	Amortized Loans
		Past 26 Years (Post-Accord)		
3 mo	314	.0282	.0281	**
6 mo	314	.0698	.0695	**
1 yr	314	.141	.1378	.0686
2 yr	314	.280	.268	.1435
5 yr	314	.588	.523	.277
10 yr	314	.861	.698	.481
20 yr	274	1.29	.878	.648
30 yr	64	1.28	.849	.605
		Past 10 Years		
3 mo	120	.0462	.0459	**
6 mo	120	.1159	.1137	**
1 yr	120	.253	.247	.1241
2 yr	120	.492	.465	.264
5 yr	120	.866	.730	.492
10 yr	120	1.280	.945	.695
20 yr	85	2.91	1.437	1.132
30 yr	0	—	—	—
20 yr		1.887*	1.223*	.980*
30 yr		2.45*	1.422*	1.199*

*Extrapolated.
**See note 2.

maturities under one year, discount instruments and par bonds are virtually indistinguishable, but that the difference becomes important after five years or so. Amortized loans behave very much like par bonds with half the terminal maturity.

For the post-Accord period, we have a full 314 observations for maturities ten years or less, 274 observations for the twenty-year maturity, and only 64 observations for the thirty-year maturity. In figure 10.3, which is based on this period, we see that the twenty-year maturity standard scales lie almost on a straight line extrapolated from the five- and ten-year points, at least for discounts and par bonds. The thirty-year standard scales seem not to lie on the curve derived from the shorter maturities. I attribute this to the fact that we have only a highly curtailed sample for the thirty-year maturity, which apparently is not representative of the

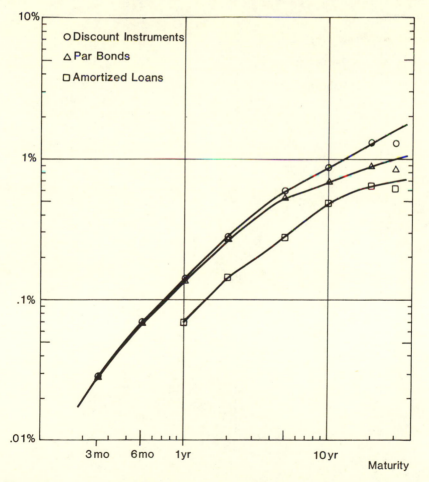

Fig. 10.3   Standard scale of unanticipated returns (post-Accord).

period as a whole. We therefore believe that if we had a full 314 observations for the thirty-year maturity, its standard scale would lie on a relatively straight line, or at least on a smooth curve, with the shorter maturities, when plotted on double logarithmic graph paper.

For the past ten years, the sample falls off even faster. We have a full 120 observations for maturities ten years or less, 85 observations (some 30 percent fewer) for the twenty-year maturity, and no observations at all for the thirty-year maturity. We see from figure 10.4 that here even the twenty-year maturity standard scales do not seem to line up with the shorter maturity standard scales. We attribute this to the fact that the twenty-year maturity sample size is more curtailed, in percentage terms, and therefore less representative, here than for the post-Accord period. If we had a full 120 observations for the twenty- and thirty-year matur-

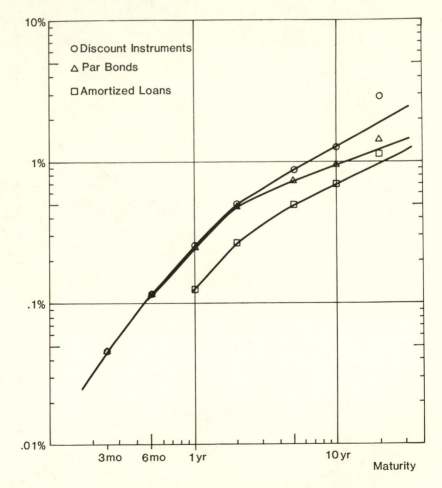

Fig. 10.4   Standard scale of unanticipated returns (past ten years).

ities, it seems reasonable to believe that they would lie on a straight line extrapolated from the five- and ten-year points. These maturities are of potential interest, especially in the case of thrift institutions, so it is important that we have reasonable estimates for these values. The straight-line double logarithmic extrapolations seems more reasonable than the curtailed-sample actual estimates, so we will use the extrapolated values to evaluate our formulas for these maturities. These extrapolated values are indicated with asterisks in table 10.1.

Table 10.2 shows estimates of the characteristic exponent, using the estimator $\hat{\alpha}_{.95}$ suggested by Fama and Roll. This estimator of α is computed from the .05 and .95 fractiles of the observed distribution. Except for the curtailed-sample thirty-year maturity, most of the estimates for the past twenty-six years lie in the range 1.24 to 1.39. The values for the past ten years are somewhat higher. Except for the curtailed-sample twenty-year maturity, most of the estimates lie in the range 1.35 to 1.52.

Examination of the raw data suggests that the volatility of interest rates has been relatively constant over the past ten years, whereas it has undergone significant changes over the past twenty-six years. The early 1950s and 1960s were periods of relatively low interest rate volatility, whereas the late 1950s and the most recent ten years were periods of relatively high interest rate volatility. When stable variables having the same characteristic exponent but different standard scales are mixed

Table 10.2   **Characteristic Exponent (α)**

Maturity	Months	Discount Instruments	Par Bonds	Amortized Bonds
		Past 26 Years (Post-Accord)		
3 mo	314	1.36	1.36	*
6 mo	314	1.43	1.44	*
1 yr	314	1.25	1.24	1.24
2 yr	314	1.27	1.29	1.31
5 yr	314	1.35	1.35	1.24
10 yr	314	1.28	1.28	1.35
20 yr	274	1.33	1.38	1.36
30 yr	64	1.49	1.62	1.59
		Past 10 Years		
3 mo	120	1.54	1.54	*
6 mo	120	1.52	1.51	*
1 yr	120	1.41	1.41	1.45
2 yr	120	1.47	1.47	1.52
5 yr	120	1.35	1.35	1.48
10 yr	120	1.39	1.32	1.36
20 yr	85	1.70	1.60	1.69
30 yr	0	—	—	—

*See note 2.

together, the resulting sample distribution tends to have fatter tails than do the distributions of the variables thus mixed. The estimator $\hat{\alpha}_{.95}$ would therefore tend to come out lower than the true characteristic exponent of the distributions generating the variables mixed. This may explain why the estimates for the past twenty-six years come out lower than for the past ten years: Unanticipated returns may have had a relatively constant characteristic exponent in the range 1.35 to 1.52, but a standard scale that has changed gradually over time, giving biased estimates of α when the whole period is pooled. It is therefore reasonable to assume that, in the immediate future, unanticipated returns will have roughly the standard scale of the past ten years, with α in the range 1.35 to 1.52. The probability of default and fair value of insurance are sharply declining functions of the characteristic exponent (except for extremely risky banks), so, in order not to overstate these values, we will use a relatively high value of α in this range, namely 1.5, in all our calculations below.

In the long-run future, we may expect the standard scale of unanticipated changes to either rise or fall from its level of the past ten years. We could probably approximate this compound distribution with a stable distribution using the standard scale and (apparently biased) characteristic exponent values estimated for the entire post-Accord period. However, this could actually give higher estimates of bank riskiness than would obtain using the past ten years' estimates, in spite of the lower standard scales, because of the powerful effect of the lower α we would be forced to use in order to capture the uncertainty in the standard scale. In the interest of keeping our estimates of the risk on the downward-biased side, we will therefore use the standard scale estimates for the past ten years (as extrapolated in the case of the twenty- and thirty-year maturities), in conjunction with an α value of 1.5 for all maturities and types of asset.[3]

10.6   Capital Adequacy: The Probability Criterion

Formula (4) above is based on the one-year standard scale c_0, while our monthly data have given us the one-month standard scale c_{1mo}. For stable distributions the standard scale accumulates according to the rule

(13) $$c_0^\alpha = 12\, c_{1mo}{}^\alpha.$$

Therefore, in place of (4) we may use

(14) $$\lambda = 6k_\alpha \left(\frac{c_{1mo}}{-\log(1-q)} \right)^\alpha$$

to evaluate the annual rate of failure. Recall that $k_{1.5} = .3989$.

Table 10.3 shows the probability per year of failure for various capital/asset ratios and eight key maturities, using formula (14). At the high

3. In footnotes 4 and 5 below, the effect of alternate values of c_0 and α will be illustrated.

Table 10.3   **Average Annual Rate of Failure as a Percentage (100λ)**

Capital/ Asset Ratio	Maturity Asset							
	3 Months	6 Months	1 Years	2 Years	5 Years	10 Years	20 Years	30 Years
Discount Instruments								
1%	2.35	9.38	30.2	82.0	191.4	344.	617.	911.
2	.827	3.29	10.60	28.7	67.1	120.7	217.	319.
4	.288	1.145	3.69	10.02	23.4	41.8	75.4	111.3
7	.1216	.483	1.558	4.23	9.87	17.73	31.8	46.7
10	.0695	.276	.890	2.42	5.64	10.14	18.14	26.9
15	.0363	.1443	.465	1.260	2.94	5.29	9.49	14.01
Par Bonds								
1%	2.34	9.10	29.3	75.3	148.3	218.	321.	403.
2	.821	3.19	10.25	26.5	52.0	76.6	112.5	141.4
4	.285	1.112	3.57	9.20	18.11	26.7	39.3	49.2
7	.1206	.469	1.503	3.89	7.64	11.25	16.56	20.8
10	.0689	.269	.860	2.22	4.37	6.44	9.47	11.87
15	.0360	.1400	.450	1.158	2.28	3.36	4.94	6.18
30	.01108	.0431	.1382	.357	.702	1.031	1.520	1.904
60	.00269	.01046	.0335	.0866	.1704	.251	.369	.463
90	.000675	.00263	.00843	.0218	.0428	.0629	.0926	.1161
Amortized Loans								
1%	*	*	10.38	32.2	82.1	137.6	231.	312.
2	*	*	3.64	11.31	28.8	48.2	80.9	109.4
4	*	*	1.268	3.94	10.03	16.80	28.2	38.1
7	*	*	.535	1.660	4.23	7.09	11.89	16.06
10	*	*	.306	.949	2.42	4.05	6.79	9.19
15	*	*	.1598	.495	1.262	2.12	3.54	4.79

*See note 2.

extreme, we see that a bank with 1 percent capital and a portfolio consisting of nothing but hypothetical thirty-year "Treasury bills" would have a failure rate of 911 percent per year. By this we mean that we would expect it to fail about 9.11 times per year, assuming it were reorganized immediately after each failure. At the low extreme, we see that a bank with 90 percent capital that rolls over from month to month in three-month par bonds has a failure rate of 0.000675 percent per year. That is, the expected time until its next failure is $1/0.00000675 = 148,000$ years, or something like twenty-five times the length of recorded history.

Between these extremes, we find more down-to-earth values. The average capital/asset ratio for the domestic operations of United States commercial banks is about 7 percent. If such a bank held a portfolio of one-year maturity par bonds (which is actually somewhat less than the present average maturity of United States commercial bank assets), its mean rate of failure would be 1.503 percent per year, and its expected life to next failure would be about 66 years, so that it would probably outlive its present management and depositors.[4] If it were to reduce the maturity of its assets to six months, its failure rate would fall to 0.469 percent per year, giving it an expected life of some 213 years.

On the other hand, a thrift institution with 7 percent capital and a portfolio of twenty-year amortized mortgages has an annual rate of occurrence of insolvency of 11.89 percent. For such an institution, a year sufficiently bad to actually make its net worth (based on market value) negative would come about once every eight years. The years 1966 and 1969 may have been recent examples of this. The authorities did not actually close the savings and loans en masse in those years, but rather imposed ceilings on the rates they were allowed to pay when competing for deposits. The monopolylike profits these ceilings gave to the thrift institutions helped to restore their battered capital positions.

Throughout table 10.3 we see that the probability of failure increases sharply with asset maturity and declines dramatically with capital/asset ratio. There is therefore a considerable trade-off between capital and this measure of risk.

The data from table 10.3 for par bonds are plotted on double logarithmic graph paper in figure 10.5. A smooth curve has been fitted to the points for each capital/asset ratio. This diagram essentially depicts a relationship between three variables: maturity, capital/asset ratio, and probability of default. We can use this diagram to derive another way of looking at this relationship, as follows: for any probability (or, equivalently, expected longevity) that we are particularly interested in, say 1 percent (one hundred years) or 4 percent (twenty-five years), we can pick off a set of maturity/capital asset ratio points that give just the probability selected. Figure 10.6 shows the results of this procedure. This diagram essentially tells us how much capital is adequate to keep the probability of default below any given level chosen, as a function of maturity. For example, 9.0 percent capital would be necessary to reduce the probability of default to 1 percent for a bank with a portfolio of one-year par bonds. A mere 2.0 percent capital would be adequate for this bank if we were content to let it fail once every ten years, but 34 percent capital would be necessary if we insisted that it fail only once in a millennium. Similar diagrams could be constructed for discount instruments or amortized loans.

10.7   Capital Adequacy: Fair Insurance Criterion

Table 10.4 shows the annual value of deposit insurance, expressed as a percentage of liabilities. At the upper extreme we see that our bank with

4. Using the same ten-year c_{1mo} of .00247 and the actual point estimate of α of 1.41, this failure rate would instead be 2.30 percent. With the twenty-six-year c_{1mo} (.001378) and α (1.25) it is 2.25 percent.

1 percent capital and thirty-year Treasury bills would have to pay the FDIC at the rate of 15.4 percent of its liabilities per year to compensate the FDIC for the risk it would run by insuring it. Again, the lower extreme is given by a bank with ninety percent capital and a portfolio of three-month par bonds. This bank would have to pay only a sum equal to 0.000444 percent of its liabilities per year (i.e., 0.0444 basis points) to fully compensate the FDIC.

Our bank with 7 percent capital and one-year par bonds should be paying a premium of 13.9 basis points.[5] The fair value of insurance

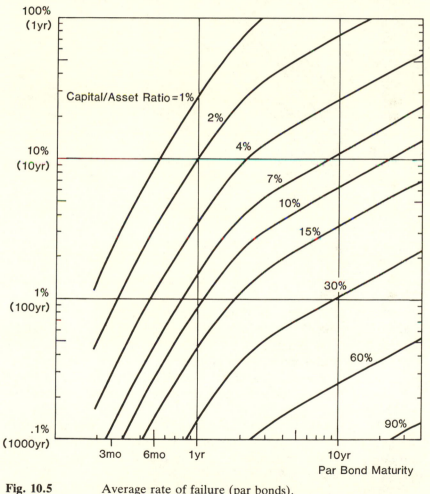

Fig. 10.5   Average rate of failure (par bonds).

5. With the same c_{1mo} but $\alpha = 1.41$, this value becomes 23.4 basis points. With $c_{1mo} = .001378$ and $\alpha = 1.25$, it becomes 27.3 basis points. Thus our estimates are, if anything, definitely on the low side. Compare footnote 4.

Capital/Asset Ratio (q)

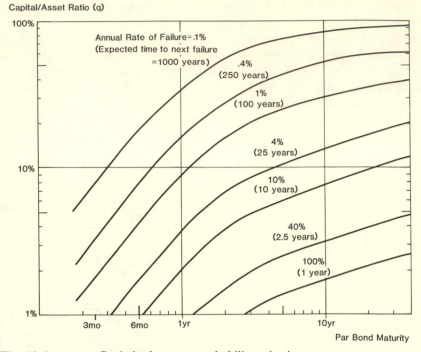

Fig. 10.6   Capital adequacy: probability criterion.

increases sharply with asset maturity in table 10.4. The hypothetical thrift institution discussed in the previous section, with 7 percent capital and a portfolio of twenty-year mortgages, imposes a liability worth 110 basis points on its insuring agency. This high a premium would make a substantial dent in the gross return it makes on its assets. If it were actually charged this premium, it would quickly try to change the structure of its balance sheet. (In practice, United States thrift institutions have an averge capital ratio more like 6 percent which would make the fair premium even higher. On the other hand, many mortgages are paid off early, making their effective maturity considerably less than their nominal maturity.)

The data for par bonds from table 10.4 have been plotted in figure 10.7. This graph can be used to find combinations of maturity and capital that generate any particular insurance value we might be interested in. This derived relationship is shown in figure 10.8.

From Figure 10.8 we see that 14 percent capital would be necessary to make the actual premium of 1/12 percent adequate for a bank whose assets consist of one-year bonds. In order for 7 percent capital to be adequate, its assets could have no more than 0.73 year (8.8 month) maturities.

Table 10.4   **Annual Value of Insurance as a Percentage of Liabilities (100 π)**

Capital Asset Ratio	Asset Maturity							
	3 Months	6 Months	1 Year	2 Years	5 Years	10 Years	20 Years	30 Years
Discount Instruments								
1%	.0397	.158	.510	1.39	3.23	5.81	10.4	15.4
2%	.0262	.104	.336	.909	2.13	3.82	6.87	10.1
4%	.0167	.0665	.214	.582	1.36	2.43	4.38	6.46
7%	.0113	.0448	.144	.392	.915	1.64	2.95	4.33
10%	.00860	.0341	.110	.299	.698	1.25	2.24	3.33
15%	.00616	.0245	.0789	.214	.499	.898	1.61	2.38
Par Bonds								
1%	.0395	.154	.495	1.27	2.51	3.68	5.42	6.81
2%	.0260	.101	.325	.839	1.65	2.43	3.56	4.48
4%	.0165	.0645	.207	.534	1.05	1.55	2.28	2.86
7%	.0112	.0435	.139	.361	.709	1.04	1.54	1.93
10%	.00852	.0333	.106	.275	.540	.796	1.17	1.47
15%	.00611	.0238	.0764	.196	.387	.570	.838	1.05
30%	.00314	.0122	.0392	.101	.199	.292	.431	.540
60%	.00125	.00487	.0156	.0403	.0794	.117	.172	.216
90%	.000444	.00173	.00554	.0143	.0281	.0413	.0608	.0763
Amortized Loans								
1%	*	*	.175	.544	1.39	2.33	3.90	5.27
2%	*	*	.115	.358	.912	1.53	2.56	3.47
4%	*	*	.0736	.229	.582	.975	1.64	2.21
7%	*	*	.0496	.154	.392	.658	1.10	1.49
10%	*	*	.0378	.117	.299	.501	.840	1.14
15%	*	*	.0271	.0840	.214	.360	.601	.813

*See note 2.

In figure 10.8 we also include a line for a premium of 1/48 percent. This value is of interest, since in recent years the FDIC has rebated approximately half of the official premium to the banks, making the total premium more nearly 1/24 percent, and this reduced premium has to cover many other types of risk beside pure interest rate risk. If these other types of risk use up half of the reduced premium, that leaves only 1/48 percent (2.08 basis points) to cover interest rate risk. We see that asset maturities would have to be reduced to about 0.34 year (4.1 months) to make 7 percent capital adequate with this low an effective premium. One-year assets would require 51 percent capital.

Using the rival normal assumption, Merton (1977a, pp. 10–11) estimates the fair value of insurance for a bank with 10 percent capital and a portfolio of long-term United States government bonds as being in the neighborhood of 6 basis points (setting Merton's τ equal to 0.003), if the bank is annually inspected. We see from table 10.4 that with 10 percent capital and twenty-year par bonds, the value of the risk is actually more like 117 basis points per year. As the bank becomes safer, so that we are concerned with events even farther out on the tail of the distribution, the difference becomes still more striking. With 15 percent capital and twenty-year par bonds, we estimate 83.8 basis points, while Merton's estimate drops below 1 basis point. Thus, the normal assumption leads to substantial underestimation of the value of bank insurance.

10.8   Mixed-Maturity Portfolios

The fair premium formula for a bank with a given capital/asset ratio is proportional to c_0^α, where c_0 is the annualized standard scale of the

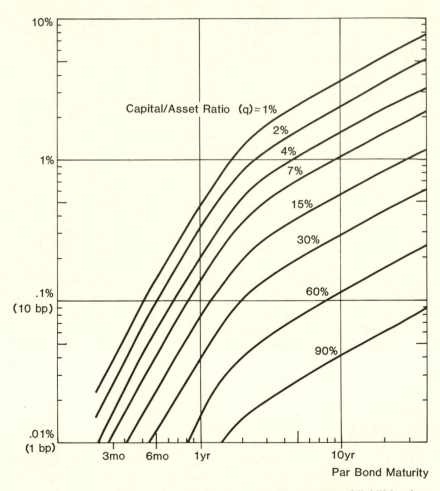

Fig. 10.7   Annual value of insurance as a percentage of liabilities (par bonds).

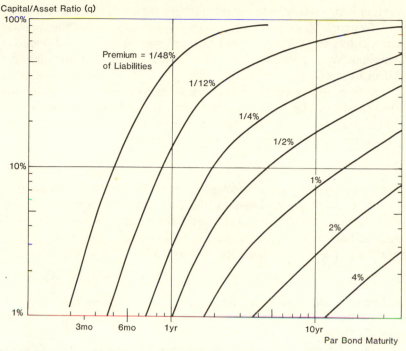

Capital/Asset Ratio (q)

Premium = 1/48% of Liabilities

1/12%

1/4%

1/2%

1%

2%

4%

100%

10%

1%

3mo   6mo   1yr   10yr

Par Bond Maturity

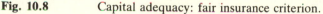

Fig. 10.8   Capital adequacy: fair insurance criterion.

unanticipated change in the logarithm of the value of the bank's assets, assumed thus far to be of one type. If the bank has a mixed portfolio of assets, we must instead base our calculation in the variability of the mixed portfolio. While the *product* of n log stable variables with the same α is log stable, their *sum* is not precisely log stable. Nevertheless, the sum is *approximately* log stable. I will therefore treat the mixed portfolio as if it really were log stable, with standard scale c_p.

Consider a bank with n types of asset, each of whose returns are log stable, and demand liabilities with fixed value. Asset i, which by itself has annualized standard scale c_i, forms fraction θ_i of the bank's assets, where

$$(15) \qquad \sum_{i=1}^{n} \theta_i = 1.$$

The effective standard scale of the approximately log stable mixed portfolio depends in a complicated way on the correlation of unanticipated returns for the different assets. Two cases are mathematically tractable: that of zero correlation, in which case we would have

$$(16) \qquad c_p^{\alpha} = \sum_{i=1}^{n} \theta_i^{\alpha} c_i^{\alpha},$$

and that of perfect positive correlation, in which case we would have

$$(17) \qquad c_p = \sum_{i=1}^{n} \theta_i c_i.$$

In actual fact, interest rate movements are highly (though by no means perfectly) correlated across maturities, which means that the unanticipated returns for different maturities will also be highly and positively correlated. We therefore regard (17) as a much better approximation to the truth than (16).

Therefore, either equation (17) can be used directly for a bank with mixed assets, or else a "pure" fair premium π_i can be found from table 10.4 or figure 10.7, and these pure premiums mixed to obtain a premium π_p for the entire portfolio, by using the formula

(18) $$\pi_p = \left(\sum_{i=1}^{n} \theta_i \, \pi_i^{1/\alpha} \right)^\alpha .$$

For example, suppose a bank with 7 percent capital held 90 percent of its assets in three-month Treasury bills (which would require a premium of 1.13 basis points by themselves) and 10 percent of its assets in ten-year bonds selling near par (requiring 104 basis points by themselves). The composite premium required for pure interest rate risk would then be

(19) $$\pi_p = (.9(1.13)^{1/1.5} + .1(104)^{1/1.5})^{1.5} = 5.69 \text{ basis points.}$$

Interestingly, this is less than 10 percent of the 104 basis point premium required for a pure ten-year bond portfolio, because of the nonlinear form of (18).

Formula (18) has an important implication for reserve policy. Consider a bank that holds fraction r of its assets in the form of cash reserves and the remainder in a portfolio that by itself would require premium π. Formula (18) then implies that its composite premium should be

(20) $$\pi_p = (r \cdot 0 + (1 - r)\pi^{1/\alpha})^\alpha$$
$$= (1 - r)^\alpha \pi.$$

Differentiating this formula with respect to r yields

(21) $$\frac{\partial \pi_p}{\partial r} = -\alpha(1 - r)^{\alpha - 1}\pi ,$$

so that cash reserves reduce the bank's fair premium, but by an amount that diminishes as r increases. The maximum reduction therefore occurs at $r = 0$:

(22) $$\left. \frac{\partial \pi_p}{\partial r} \right|_{r=0} = -\alpha\pi.$$

Let i be the expected return on the bank's risky assets. If cash reserves pay no interest, this is essentially the opportunity cost to the bank of holding reserves. As long as i is greater than $\alpha\pi$, as it almost surely would be, the bank only stands to lose by holding reserves, even the first few dollars of reserves that have the greatest impact on its fair premium. With a fair premium, the only reason the bank would voluntarily hold zero-interest cash would be to minimize transaction costs (which we have assumed away in this paper). The size of the inventory it would hold for this purpose could be modeled along the lines of the Baumol or Miller and Orr cash balance models. Zero-interest cash reserves therefore seem to be a relatively expensive way of providing bank safety. As long as banks pay a fair premium, coaxing them into short maturity assets, there seems to be no safety-related reason to require them to hold any cash reserves at all.

10.9   Liability Management

In this paper we have dealt only with a "traditional bank" that has only demand or virtually demand liabilities. In recent years, banks have relied increasingly on longer-term liabilities or certificates of deposit to partially hedge their long-term assets. This is a desirable development that would greatly reduce the riskiness of banks. If a bank perfectly matched its asset and liability maturities, it would have no interest rate risk at all. With a little capital, it would have the flexibility of not having to match perfectly and could still maintain zero interest rate risk, provided each contracted disbursement was preceded by contracted receipts. However, bank capital is limited, so the match would have to be relatively close.

If all intermediaries tried to match maturities in this manner, they would have to juggle the term structure of interest rates until savers and borrowers were coaxed into the same maturities. Elsewhere I have argued that this matching would improve the efficiency of the intertemporal economy. I argue that the traditional practice of mismatching maturities (which I call "misintermediation") actually disequilibrates macroeconomic activity.

We have made no attempt in this paper to deal with the difficult problem of how the fair premium should be calculated for a bank with mixed asset and liability maturities. Average duration is of only a little help, since the asset and liability payment profiles could have very different shapes and still represent the same average duration. If all the assets have one maturity and the liabilities have another maturity, the bank is roughly equivalent to one with demand liabilities and assets with maturity equal to the difference. Thus a thrift institution with twenty-year assets and one-year liabilities is roughly equivalent to one with nineteen-year assets and passbook liabilities.

10.10   Indexed and Variable-Rate Loans

Much of the volatility in interest rates in recent years has been due to the uncertainty of inflation. Long-term loan assets that are indexed to the cost of living would therefore probably have a substantially more certain return over a short holding period and therefore might justify lower insurance premiums, provided they were offset on the balance sheet by an equal value of indexed liabilities.

Indexed loans would have the additional advantage of reducing default risk, since a sudden unanticipated end to inflation today when nominal interest rates contain a substantial inflation premium would make it just as difficult for borrowers to repay as it was for them in 1929–33, when there was a sudden unanticipated *de*flation, while homeowners and farmers were committed to interest rates that would have been appropriate for constant prices. Defaults on such loans were a major cause of the wave of bank failures during those years. A sudden end to inflation could cause comparable problems today, unless bank balance sheets are indexed to the cost of living.

In spite of their desirable properties, indexed loans have apparently been, until very recently, illegal and unenforceable in the courts, under the second sentence of the 1933 Gold Clause Joint Resolution. It was not until October 1977 that this law was repealed.[6]

Denied indexed loans as a means of avoiding inflation uncertainty in long-term nominal interest rates, many banks have turned to "variable rate loans," whose nominal interest rates are tied to some index of short-term nominal interest rates. These loans substitute a series of relatively accurate short-run inflation forecasts for a relatively inaccurate long-run inflation forecast, so they do reduce inflation uncertainty to a degree, though not entirely. The effective maturity of these variable-rate loans is ambiguous for our purposes. If they had the same default risk as ordinary loans, they could be taken as having maturity equal to their interest computation interval, rather than the longer actual maturity of the loan. However, since they leave the real interest rate on long-term loans uncertain, the real portion of the interest rate risk is borne by the borrower rather than by the bank. On paper the bank does not face real interest rate risk from these loans, but in practice the real interest rate risk may simply be disguised as default risk. All in all, these variable-rate loans are inferior substitutes for fixed-rate indexed loans. Unless there are other hidden legal barriers to indexation, variable rate loans will probably soon disappear.

10.11   The "Going Business" Value of the Bank

For the calculations above, I have assumed that as soon as a bank has negative net worth (based on current market value of assets), the stockholders will take the option of allowing the bank to be liquidated, so that their stock becomes worthless and the insuring agency pays off the depositors in full. In practice, a bank with negative net worth may

6. See McCulloch (1980).

actually be financially viable, in the sense that eventually it may be able to pay off its liabilities with interest out of the income from its assets.

There are two reasons it may be able to do this. The first is the value of its customer relations. In fact, financial markets are not perfect, so that the bank receives a sort of rent from the fact that it has evaluated the credit worthiness of certain customers who are unknown to other banks. To the extent that this is true, the shareholders will be willing to put up additional capital or to dilute their own stock with outside capital in order to prevent the bank from being liquidated. Market imperfections are the stuff day-to-day business is made of, so it is important that a bank with negative net worth based on tangible assets be given a fair chance to raise more capital before liquidating it.

The second reason is the monopoly value of the bank's charter. Since 1935, entry into banking has been severely restricted. The value of the existing charters has been further enhanced by the 1933 ban on checking accounts interest, and the lingering interest ceilings on time and savings accounts and on the newly authorized NOW accounts.

These restrictions on competition cannot be considered in isolation from the issue of bank safety. They were originally introduced shortly after the massive bank failures of 1929–33 in hope that greater profitability would make banks safer. This hope was illusory. Pouring profits into a bank to make it safer is like trying to carry water across a room in a sieve. The profits may just flow out of the bank in the form of dividends to shareholders. The monopoly profits might instead be retained and added to economic capital, and to that extent they would indirectly make the bank safer. But the bank would be just as safe if the capital were raised by any other means.

If banks paid competitive interest on deposits but were charged a fair premium for deposit insurance, they would be forced to pass the premium on to depositors in the form of reduced interest. Therefore fair insurance would cost the demand deposit owner several basis points, depending on the maturity of the bank's assets. The above restrictions on competition, on the other hand, cost the depositor several *hundred* basis points. They are therefore an extremely costly means of providing bank safety. In a study of bank risk and capital adequacy, they cannot be taken as immutable institutional background, since they exist in the name of bank safety. If they were abolished, a large part of the "going business" value of the bank would be eliminated. The simple model we have used above would then be a more realistic one.

10.12   Conclusion

It should be remembered that the estimates in this paper are only point estimates derived from a few quartiles of the data. By using as high a value for the characteristic exponent as seemed justified by the data, we have tried to make our estimates of the fair value of insurance err, if anything, on the low side. I plan at some time in the future to improve upon these estimates by means of maximum likelihood estimates of the stable parameters. This procedure will give confidence intervals for the risk estimates in addition to improved point estimates. In the meantime the burden of proof should be on the banks to show at a high level of significance that the premium they are paying to government insuring agencies is at least sufficient to cover the fair value of insurance for the risks they are incurring.

11   Forecasting Bank Portfolios

Robert Jacobson

11.1   Introduction

The risks in a bank can be divided into wealth effects and operating or income effects. Chapters 9 and 10 analyzed possible changes in value as a result of unanticipated movements in interest rates, risk premiums, and loan losses, and from aggregate net income. These risks and probabilities depend upon the portfolio of assets and liabilities in the bank at its initial examination.

A bank, however, is a dynamic organization. Changes will occur between examinations. Both the policies of the bank and the impact of macroevents will cause shifts. The economy and individual banks wax and wane. If interest rates rise, cash flows may alter because of disintermediation or increased loan takedowns. The rates that apply to new or renewed loans or liabilities will differ from initial ones. This may lead to losses or to increased profitability. Some loans such as mortgages may be extended beyond their initial expectations, or they may be paid off more rapidly than seemed likely.

Projections of the bank's portfolio aid in risk measurement for several reasons:

1. The risk of insolvency depends directly on the expected capital/asset ratio. Therefore, estimates are needed for the expected increase or decrease in both capital and assets.

2. Risk depends upon the share of each activity in the total portfolio. We would like estimates of portfolio movements.

3. The risk of high transaction or liquidation costs depends upon the likelihood of major outflows of liabilities.

Robert Jacobson is an economist at the Federal Reserve Bank of San Francisco. Work on this chapter was done while the author was a research assistant at the National Bureau of Economic Research.

4. In obtaining present values of future flows as analyzed in chapters 3, 13, and 14, the value of an asset can shift either because discount rates move or because the time frame of expected flows after the end of the period alters. Therefore these measures should be based not only on cash flows expected initially, but also on whatever expectations alter during the period.

In this chapter time-series analysis is used to forecast various bank assets and liabilities. Although the analysis was used only for short-term forecasting of selected portfolio items, the techniques and results presented can be extended for other necessary purposes such as prediction of the capital/asset ratio. The analysis, which appears to forecast bank portfolios well, indicates that macroeconomic variables are extremely unimportant compared with the portfolio item's past values in determining the forecast.

11.2   Macromodeling

Theories of why portfolios alter are detailed in numerous economic and financial studies. Portfolios are thought to be sensitive to a variety of macro variables. Included as potential causes are such factors as the level of long- and short-interest rates; relative rates such as the difference between commercial paper and prime interest rates or between long-term and short-term rates; the amount of money or reserves; macro demand factors such as income, output, or employment; micro factors such as internal funds available to nonfinancial corporations, investment in plant and equipment, inventories, or housing. The relationship between the dependent and independent variables can be lagged and can depend on the rate of stock adjustments. A few extremely complex models have been developed for aggregate movements in bank portfolios, as for example by Hunt (1976), Bosworth and Duesenberry (1975), and Data Resources Incorporated.

11.2.1   Regression Models

With the cooperation of the Federal Reserve Board and the Federal Reserve Bank of San Francisco, we developed a data base of the series of portfolio changes for individual banks. We applied to these data standard regression models of the form:

$$(1) \qquad Y_t = B_0 + \sum_{i=1}^{k} B_i X_{it} + \varepsilon_t \, ,$$

where X_i consisted of one to ten variables in an equation and there were weekly, monthly, or quarterly observations covering more than ten years.

We tested literally hundreds of different models using the variables of the traditional theory. We concluded that at this time we could not develop an adequate econometric forecasting system for the portfolios of individual banks. One of the major problems is that there is a high probability that error terms are not independent from one period to the next. While we attempted traditional econometric corrections of first differencing and simple autoregressive error processes, they do not seem to be as effective as more complicated error processes.

Second, it seems plausible to expect past values of both the dependent and independent variables to influence current values of the dependent variable. Economic theory says very little about logical patterns of the distributed lags necessary to handle this problem. Finally, the number of specific factors influencing the movements in individual banks is large. These specific factors are likely to be much less important when their effect is averaged over a number of individual banks into large aggregates.

Some fairly adequate models have been built for more aggregated data. Thus chapters 14 and 15 contain models of demand for commercial loans and demand and time deposits. Other fairly satisfactory equations can be found for the aggregate mortgage flows and for consumer loans. However, we encountered great problems in applying these models to the more complex situation of individual institutions.

As a result, we turned to the more tractable approach of time-series analysis. It has been developed by Box and Jenkins (1976), Granger and Newbold (1977), Haugh (1972), and others, and used in bank modeling by Cramer and Miller (1976). The tools are autoregressive moving average (ARMA) and transfer function analysis. ARMA analysis allows for the modeling of a series based solely on past values of that series. By using autoregressive and moving average terms, the series can be parsimoniously modeled. Transfer function analysis uses univariate techniques but allows for the inclusion of other series. This analysis is similar to standard econometrics in that it relates one group of variables to another variable. It differs from standard econometrics in that the structure of the model is determined entirely by the data. The analysis allows for the identification, estimation, and checking of a wide variety of distributed lag and error structures. Economic theory is used to suggest possible relevant variables and "plausible" specifications.

11.3   Transfer Models

The transfer function model is

(2) $$Y_t = C + V(B)X_t + \psi(B)\eta_t ,$$

where C is   a   constant, η_t is   the   error   term, $V(B)$ $= (v_0 + v_1B + v_2B^2 + v_3B^3 \ldots)$, the transfer function (a polynomial in B, the backward shift operator such that $B^kX_t = X_{t-k}$). The transfer function is relating input (exogenous) variables to the output (endogenous) series. The v_k are called impulse response weights and indicate how the input series X_t is transferred to the output series Y_t. The obvious problem in estimating (2) is that it requires an infinite series. To overcome this problem it is necessary to approximate the transfer function by the ratio of two lower-order polynomials. The same is true for $\psi(B)$, so that (2) can be rewritten as:

$$(3) \qquad Y_t = C + \frac{\omega(B)}{\delta(B)} X_{t-L} + \frac{\theta(B)}{\phi(B)} \eta_t ,$$

where $\omega(B)$, $\delta(B)$, $\theta(B)$, ϕB are polynomials in B of degree s, r, q, and p, respectively and L is the lag time before any effects are felt.

The first step in the estimation is to make a crude guess at $V(B)$. This is done on the basis of cross-correlation analysis. The cross-correlations between two series are usually hard to interpret because of autocorrelation. However, by transforming the exogenous (input) series to white noise, the cross-correlation function becomes easier to interpret. With the input series white noise, and under the assumption that the two series are not cross-correlated, the cross-correlations will be asymptotically distributed $N(0, 1/N)$.

Starting with $Y_t = V(B)X_t + \psi(B)\eta_t$ (assume Y and X are stationary with zero mean), the exogenous series is modeled via autoregressive and moving average parameters to transform it to white noise (i.e., $\varepsilon_t = \theta(B)\phi(B)^{-1}X_t$). Multiplying through, prewhitening, by $\theta(B)\phi(B)^{-1}$ and letting $Z_t = \theta(B)\phi(B)^{-1}Y_t$ yields:

$$(4) \qquad Z_t = V(B)\varepsilon_t + \theta(B)\phi(B)^{-1}\psi(B)\eta_t.$$

Since by definition ε_t and η_t are uncorrelated, multiplying (4) by ε_{t-k} and taking expectations gives

$$E(Z_t, \varepsilon_{t-k}) = V_t \text{ var } (\varepsilon_t), \text{ or}$$

$$V_k = \text{cor } (Z_t, \varepsilon_{t-k}) \left[\frac{\text{var } (Z_t)}{\text{var } (\varepsilon_t)} \right]^{1/2} .$$

In other words, the V_ks can be tentatively identified because they are constant multiples of the cross-correlations between Z_k and ε_{t-k}.

Thus the transfer function modeling procedure is:
1. Transform the data via differencing, logs, and so forth to produce stationary time series Y and X.
2. Build a univariate model for X_t, the exogenous series, to obtain white-noise residuals (ε_t).
3. Transform the output series, the bank variables, by the same parameters used in the univariate modeling of X, the macro variable, to obtain $\hat{Z}_t$.

4. Calculate the correlation between $\hat{Z}_t$ and $\hat{\varepsilon}_{t-k}$ and obtain an estimate of the transfer function ($\hat{V}(B)$).
5. Use the estimate of $\hat{V}(B)$ to suggest the appropriate order of the polynomials $\hat{\omega}(B)$ and $\hat{\delta}(B)$. The V_k will have a certain grouping, based on the true values of (r, s, L). The size and pattern of the groupings will provide identification clues.
6. Identify the error structure polynomials $\theta(B)$, $\phi(B)$ by using the standard univariate modeling technique on the series $U_t = Y_t - \hat{\omega}(B)\hat{\delta}(B)^{-1}X_{t-L}$.

11.3.1 Diagnostic Check

Once a model is tentatively identified, numerous diagnostic checks can be employed to test for adequacy and possible changes. First, since the residuals should be white noise, autocorrelations of the residuals should be compared with $2/\sqrt{N}$, and Q (the Box-Pierce statistic) $= N \sum_{j=1}^{k} \hat{p}_j^2(\hat{\alpha})$ should be distributed $\chi^2(k-p-q)$ under the null hypothesis of no correlations between the residuals and the pre-whitened input series should be distributed $N(O, 1/N)$. Last, t-statistics can be checked and parameters can be dropped or added to see if the model can be improved. The model can then be reestimated and diagnostic checks can be employed on the new model.

11.3.2 Multiple Inputs

The transfer function model in (2) and (3) can easily be extended to include multiple inputs by putting a summation sign in front of the X_t to give:

$$(3') \qquad Y_t = C + \sum_{i=1}^{k} V_i(B)X_{it} + \psi(B)\eta_t$$

$$(4') \qquad Y_t = C + \sum_{i=1}^{k} \omega_i(B)\delta_i(B)^{-1}X_{it-L_i} + \theta(B)\phi(B)^{-1}\eta_t.$$

But modeling a multiple input transfer function is considerably more difficult than modeling the single input case owing to correlation between the exogenous variables. Because of this, most transfer function analysis has been concerned with only one input.

Excluding relevant variables, however, will lead to biased coefficients. From the standpoint of forecasting, this may not be as major a problem as it seems. The model would then be testing to see if the use of the exogenous series and past values of the output series lead to better forecasts than just use of past values of the endogenous series.

Furthermore, if additional variables were tested to see if they too were relevant, then the model could be expected to give better forecasts and would have more credibility. One easy way of using multiple variables is a stepwise regression procedure. However, just as in OLSQ, as long as the independent variables are not orthogonal, the estimated parameters will be biased and the order in which they are included in the model will be important. So, to have adequate confidence in the models' forecasts, it seems necessary to suffer through the difficulties of modeling the multiple inputs simultaneously. Therefore in our models, though we have in no way tested for the inclusion of all relevant variables, we have tested for the possible inclusion of a number of macro variables that we felt would be most important.

11.3.3   Feedback

The other major issue to be addressed is the notion of feedback and causality. It may be that series X influences series Y and series Y influences series X so that the transfer function procedure outlined would not be correct. Although there are numerous methods of testing for causality (Hsiao 1977), we will not report the results, for two reasons. (In fact, using two standard feedback tests [Sims 1972; Granger 1969] on a very few occasions feedback might be concluded.) First, since our left-hand side variables are small groups of banks and our inputs are macro variables, theory tells us it is doubtful that these banks can significantly influence the economy variables. Next, trying to build a complete transfer function for the banking sector or even trying to model a bank simultaneously is beyond the scope of this study. A vector ARMAX model (Hillmer and Tiao 1977) of the necessary size is really not feasible at this time. In general, however, we felt that the single input transfer function model would give adequate forecasts.

11.4   Fitting the Model

11.4.1   The Variables Defined

The methodology outlined in the preceding section was used to model 9 bank variables (see Appendix). From the twenty-two bank groups, we selected three for modeling. The banks were selected to be representative of the reporting banks and extremes for the classifications used in aggregating. Thus, group 1 banks had assets over $1 billion, a ratio of time and savings deposits to assets under 20 percent, and a ratio of total deposits to loans under 1.2. There were twenty-one banks that were averaged in this group. Group 2 banks had assets between $0.5 billion and $1 billion, a ratio of time and savings deposits to assets over 35 percent, and a deposit-to-loan ratio between 1.2 and 1.5. Twenty-three banks fell into this grouping. Group 3 banks were under $0.5 billion in size, had a ratio of time and savings deposits to assets over 35 percent and a deposit-to-loan ratio over 1.5. This group included fifty-five banks.

The bank variables were:

1	GOVS	United States Treasury Securities + Securities of Other Government Agencies and Corporations
2	OSEC	Other Securities + Federal Funds Sold
3	MUNI	Obligations of State and Political Subdivisions
4	CIL	Commercial and Industrial Loans + Farm Loans + Loans to Carry Securities + Loans to Financial Institutions + Other Loans
5	ESTATE	Real Estate Loans
6	CONSUMER	Installment Loans
7	DD	Demand Deposits − Cash Assets
8	TD	Time and Savings Deposits − Large Certificates of Deposit
9	PM	Federal Funds Purchased + Other Purchased Money + Large Certificates of Deposit

The macroeconomic variables modeled as potential inputs were:

1	TBILL	Three-Month Treasury Bill Rate
2	UNEMP	Unemployment Rate (Seasonally Adjusted)
3	PI	Personal Income (Seasonally Adjusted)
4	MONBASE	Monetary Base (Seasonally Adjusted)
5	CPPR	Commercial Paper Rate/Prime Interest Rate
6	HSFR	Housing Starts: New Private Housing Units (Seasonally Adjusted)
7	IVMT	Manufacturing and Trade Inventories (Seasonally Adjusted)
8	MU	Manufacturing Unfilled Orders (Seasonally Adjusted)

TBILL, UNEMP, PI, and MONBASE were tested as possible inputs for all bank variables. HSFR was included only in the Real Estate Loan model, and MU, IVMT, and CPPR were exogenous factors for the loan grouping entitled CIL.

The time period used for identification, estimation, and diagnostic checking was from July 1968 to September 1975 (eighty-seven observations). The remaining twelve observations were withheld to check the forecasting ability of the model.

11.4.2   The Fitting

The first step in the procedure was to get each series stationary. For the macro variables, taking logs and first differences appeared to yield stationarity for all variables except MU and IVMT, which required second differencing. For the bank variables, all required taking logs and first differencing. However, some variables (GOVS, MUNI, DD) had a twelve-month seasonal component that, because the autocorrelations at lags of multiples of twelve were large and died out very slowly, suggested the need of taking twelve-month differences in addition to the first differences.

It must be pointed out that no attempt was made in any part of the univariate or transfer function modeling process to make the models similar between variables in a single bank or between a single variable in the different bank groups. However, on the few occasions in the transfer function modeling when parameters appeared to have "wrong signs at unusual locations" we decided to view the correlations as sampling error and not try to model it.

11.5 Results

For the sake of space, and because the models were not greatly different for the different bank groupings, only the results for bank group 2 will be presented in detail. This group was chosen for more detailed discussion, since it was modeled more carefully and its behavior appeared to be most typical. The univariate models for bank group 2 are reported in table 11.1. The parameter structures are very simple, yet they do not suggest model inadequacy based upon the Box-Pierce statistics. In general, the models contain an autoregressive, usually first-order, parameter and moving average terms, which are factors of twelve, to model the seasonal factors. The ARMA models are quite similar for the different items. The models for bank groups 1 and 3 also showed this similarity across portfolio items. In addition, as noted earlier, the models for the different bank groups are not much different. An earlier indication that the groupings would be similar was that to obtain stationarity GOVS, MUNI, and DD had to have a twelve-month differencing for all three groups. The various models have much the same parameter structure, and the magnitudes of the coefficients are close. However, the differences are significant enough for both the bank variables and for the bank groupings to warrant greater disaggregation in future study.

The univariate models, prewhitening transformations, for the macro variables are in table 11.2. The transfer function models are presented in table 11.3. The exogenous and endogenous variables in the transfer functions are the original variables after being logged and differenced to achieve stationary series. One can quickly see that the inputs do not have too great an effect, because the transfer function error term structure and coefficients are almost exactly the same as that of the univariate models. Some facts are immediately obvious from these transfer function models. First, various macro variables that were hypothesized to have an effect on bank variables had no influence at all. For instance, the monetary base and personal income were never significant. In addition, not only were most macro variables insignificant, but they also had coefficients that

Table 11.1   Univariate Models for Bank Group 2

Variables	Models	Residual Standard Error	Box-Pierce Statistics of Model Adequacy	
			Q	Degrees of Freedom
GOVS	$(1-.50B)(1-B)(1-B^{12})Z_t = (1+.28B^4-.66B^{12})\varepsilon_t$ [4.71] [2.96] [6.41]	.025898	3.86 7.27 11.28	9 21 33
OSEC	$(1-B)Z_t = .0193 + (1+.23B^{12})\varepsilon_t$ [1.50] [2.00]	.10607	10.95 17.67 20.81	10 22 34
MUNI	$(1-.42B)(1-B)(1-B^{12})Z_t = (1-.85B^{12})\varepsilon_t$ [3.83] [9.58]	.014005	11.12 17.31 32.02	10 22 34
CIL	$(1-.22B)(1-B)Z_t = .0045 + (1+.24B^6+.23B^{12})\varepsilon_t$ [2.00] [2.00] [2.00]	.014303	8.14 11.29 19.52	8 20 32
ESTATE	$(1-B)Z_t = .0094 + (1+.18B)\varepsilon_t$ [6.35] [1.72]	.011661	7.59 12.00 19.75	10 22 34
CONSUMER	$(1-.38B-.21B^2)(1-B)Z_t = .0035 + (1+.29B^{12})\varepsilon_t$ [3.42] [1.97] [2.20] [2.56]	.0097055	3.96 14.35 23.56	8 20 32

Table 11.1 (continued)

Variables	Models	Residual Standard Error	Box-Pierce Statistics of Model Adequacy	
			Q	Degrees of Freedom
DD	$(1-B)(1-B^{12})Z_t = (1-.73B^{12})\varepsilon_t$ [7.64]	.020258	9.82 16.31 20.71	11 23 35
TD	$(1-.15B)(1-B)Z_t = .0074 + (1+.36B^{12})\varepsilon_t$ [1.38] [4.63] [2.65]	.01116	8.01 15.28 21.07	9 21 33
PM	$(1-B)Z_t + .014 + (1+.34B^3+.25B^{12})\varepsilon_t$ [3.15] [2.29]	.033568	5.01 11.26 14.55	9 21 33

Note: T-statistics in brackets; Z_t = log of original variable.

Table 11.2   Univariate Models for Macro Variables

Variables	Models	Residual Standard Error	Box-Pierce Statistics of Model Adequacy Q	Degrees of Freedom
TBILL	$(1-.31B)(1-B)Z_t = \varepsilon_t$ [2.00]	.04511	11.55 17.13 21.48	11 23 35
UNEMP	$(1-B)Z_t = (1+.33B+.20B^2+.27B^4)\varepsilon_t$ [3.14] [2.00] [2.70]	.020613	2.43 12.37 19.58	9 21 33
MONBASE	$(1-B)Z_t = .006 + \varepsilon_t$ [16.77]	.003305	10.65 19.32 20.83	11 23 35
PI	$(1-B)Z_t = .007 + \varepsilon_t$ [11.67]	.005641	13.96 22.96 39.81	11 23 35
HSFR	$(1+.28B)(1-B)Z_t = (1+.23B^3-.49B^{12})\varepsilon_t$ [2.60] [2.25] [4.37]	.069541	9.19 21.34 27.19	9 21

Table 11.2 (continued)

Variables	Models	Residual Standard Error	Box-Pierce Statistics of Model Adequacy	
			Q	Degrees of Freedom
CPPR	$(1 - .16B + .24B^2)\,(1 - B)\,Z_t = (1 - .15B^6 + .49B^{12})\,\varepsilon_t$ [1.44] [2.24] [1.45] [4.35]	.044575	6.27 13.18 20.18	8 20 33
IVMT	$(1 + .32B)\,(1 - B)^2 Z_t = \varepsilon_t$ [3.22]	.00350	8.13 15.87 19.91	11 23 35
MU	$(1 - B)^2 Z_t = \varepsilon_t$	.0066619	11.65 29.02 37.33	12 24 36

Note: T-statistics in brackets; Z_t = log of original variable.

Table 11.3   Transfer Function Models for Bank Group 2

Variables	Models	Residual Standard Error	Box-Pierce Statistics of Model Adequacy	
			Q	Degrees of Freedom
GOVS	$Y_t = -.0042 - .022\text{TBILL}_{t-2} + \left(\dfrac{.22}{-.74B}\right)\text{UNEMP}_{t-3}$ $+ \dfrac{(1-.19B^3-.57B^{12})}{(1-.20B)}\varepsilon_t$	.02369	2.9 5.68 9.37	8 20 32
OSEC	$Y_t = .025 - .32\text{UNEMP}_{t-1} + \dfrac{(1+.23B^{12})}{(1+.19B)}\varepsilon_t$	.10309	7.58 16.84 20.21	9 21 33
MUNI	No significant variables found			
CIL	$Y_t = .0047 + .077\text{CPPR}_t + \dfrac{(1+.31B^6+.28B^{12})}{(1-.19B)}\varepsilon_t$	.013824	10.93 14.51 23.97	8 20 32
ESTATE	$Y_t = .0094 + .048\text{TBILL}_{t-3} + \varepsilon_t$	.01151	7.42 13.66 19.88	11 23 35

Table 11.3 (continued)

Variables	Models	Residual Standard Error	Box-Pierce Statistics of Model Adequacy	
			Q	Degrees of Freedom
CONSUMER	$Y_t = .0095 + \dfrac{.046}{(1-.68B)}\,\text{TBILL}_t - .075\text{UNEMP}_t$ $+ (1+.28B^{12})\,\varepsilon_t$	.00899	7.25 17.89 28.97	10 22 34
DD	No significant variables found			
TD	$Y_t = .0090 - .046\text{TBILL}_t + (1+.42B^{12})\,\varepsilon_t$	.010665	11.31 22.82 28.36	10 22 34
PM	No significant variables found			

were of extremely small magnitude. These two factors give added confidence in excluding particular variables from the models.

In addition to those variables with no effect, others that we felt would have the greatest impact also had little or no effect. For instance, the Treasury bill rate, although significant on numerous occasions, was not that influential a driving variable. In addition, it was never a significant factor in modeling demand deposits.

The result of the unimportance of the macroeconomic variables was also apparent in the other two bank groups modeled. Basically, the variables that were found to be significant for bank group 2 were significant for the other bank groupings. However, though the lag structure of the transfer functions were similar, they were definitely different and once again indicate the need for further disaggregation.

Although the major difficulty in transform function analysis usually is determining $\omega(B)$ and $\delta(B)$ from the estimate of $V(B)$, this was not the case in these models. In general, the cross-correlations of the prewhitened inputs and outputs were very small compared with their standard errors. So the identification of $\omega(B)$ and $\delta(B)$ usually consisted of picking out the only significant, or nearly significant, lag and then trying overparameterization to see if the model could be improved. In fact, the additional factors generally did very little to improve the model and were subsequently dropped.

11.6   Forecasts

Because of the very nature of time-series modeling, there is little doubt it will yield good one-period-ahead forecasts. Therefore, a better test of the forecasting ability of the models is to forecast from a fixed origin a number of periods away. Table 11.4 displays the forecasts generated from the univariate and transfer function model for one through twelve periods away for bank group 2. (The inputs for the transfer function were the actual values.) No transfer function forecasts were generated for the models that contained no significant exogenous variables.

With few exceptions, the point forecasts are fairly accurate for the forecasts one through twelve periods ahead. The mean absolute percentage error[1] using the forecast from the transfer function when significant exogenous variables were found, and otherwise using the univariate forecast, for bank group 2 were 0.97 percent and 5.18 percent for the one- and twelve-months-ahead forecasts. The forecast errors for the one- and twelve-months-ahead forecasts for bank group 1 were 0.95 percent and 9.36 percent, and were 0.86 percent and 10.9 percent for bank group 3.

---

1. Mean absolute percentage error $= \dfrac{1}{K} \sum\limits_{i=1}^{K} \left| \hat{X}_{t+j,i} - X_{t+j,i} \right| / X_{t+j,i}$, where $\hat{X}_{t+j,i} =$ the jth period ahead forecast of the ith variable, and $X_{t+j,i} =$ the actual value of variable i at period $t+j$.

Table 11.4   Bank Group 2 Forecasts (in Thousands of Dollars)

Periods Ahead	Univariate Model Forecasts			Actual Value	Transfer Function Model Forecasts		
	95 Percent Lower Confidence Limit	Point Forecast	95 Percent Upper Confidence Limit		95 Percent Lower Confidence Limit	Point Forecast	95 Percent Upper Confidence Limit
	GOVS				GOVS		
1	0.5068443E+05	0.5330687E+05	0.5606495E+05	53150.	0.5074706E+05	0.5315701E+05	0.5568135E+05
2	0.4916806E+05	0.5385238E+05	0.5898294E+05	57621.	0.4952558E+05	0.5324235E+05	0.5723800E+05
3	0.4940005E+05	0.5608324E+05	0.6367050E+05	58916.	0.5062158E+05	0.5552074E+05	0.6089398E+05
4	0.4919756E+05	0.5764029E+05	0.6753181E+05	58955.	0.5122987E+05	0.5693568E+05	0.6327692E+05
5	0.4744304E+05	0.5760215E+05	0.6993569E+05	58897.	0.5086723E+05	0.5731649E+05	0.6458337E+05
6	0.4752411E+05	0.5972524E+05	0.7505875E+05	57124.	0.5309996E+05	0.6079365E+05	0.6960200E+05
7	0.4733996E+05	0.6142808E+05	0.7970869E+05	61343.	0.5487432E+05	0.6393366E+05	0.7448856E+05
8	0.4491569E+05	0.6002267E+05	0.8021069E+05	63922.	0.5244655E+05	0.6231486E+05	0.7403987E+05
9	0.4382023E+05	0.6016991E+05	0.8261969E+05	63487.	0.5065457E+05	0.6143992E+05	0.7452162E+05
10	0.4361910E+05	0.6142228E+05	0.8649175E+05	60714.	0.4970150E+05	0.6155522E+05	0.7623594E+05
11	0.4324491E+05	0.6234743E+05	0.8988800E+05	59361.	0.4860038E+05	0.6144642E+05	0.7768787E+05
12	0.4282082E+05	0.6312070E+05	0.9304394E+05	59066.	0.4769933E+05	0.6153339E+05	0.7937962E+05
	OSEC				OSEC		
1	0.3161670E+05	0.3892259E+05	0.4791668E+05	41650.	0.3275624E+05	0.4009055E+05	0.4906702E+05
2	0.3017991E+05	0.4049495E+05	0.5433545E+05	46737.	0.3271600E+05	0.4261159E+05	0.5550025E+05
3	0.2877111E+05	0.4124157E+05	0.5911713E+05	51523.	0.3253724E+05	0.4483742E+05	0.6178742E+05
4	0.2740093E+05	0.4152751E+05	0.6293700E+05	53822.	0.3138801E+05	0.4537979E+05	0.6560862E+05
5	0.2670347E+05	0.4250614E+05	0.6766050E+05	53504.	0.3175607E+05	0.4791690E+05	0.7230200E+05
6	0.2608369E+05	0.4340320E+05	0.7222275E+05	57240.	0.3109985E+05	0.4878055E+05	0.7651287E+05
7	0.2462327E+05	0.4267935E+05	0.7397581E+05	53301.	0.2935030E+05	0.4770884E+05	0.7755056E+05
8	0.2402454E+05	0.4325341E+05	0.7787269E+05	52601.	0.2923082E+05	0.4912063E+05	0.8254419E+05
9	0.2415475E+05	0.4506694E+05	0.8408394E+05	48795.	0.2892427E+05	0.5014781E+05	0.8694431E+05

						MUNI	
10	0.2323146E+05	0.4483147E+05	0.8651462E+05	49830.	0.2779575E+05	0.4963693E+05	0.8864025E+05
11	0.2251372E+05	0.4486308E+05	0.8939856E+05	50096.	0.2780100E+05	0.5106237E+05	0.9378669E+05
12	0.2149473E+05	0.4416607E+05	0.9074969E+05	49271.	0.2694565E+05	0.5083968E+05	0.9592162E+05

MUNI

1	0.9044650E+05	0.9296156E+05	0.9554650E+05	92091.
2	0.8886019E+05	0.9319725E+05	0.9774594E+05	91963.
3	0.8794119E+05	0.9382319E+05	0.1000986E+06	91750.
4	0.8801625E+05	0.9528469E+05	0.1031532E+06	91294.
5	0.8814231E+05	0.9664456E+05	0.1059667E+06	90753.
6	0.8898794E+05	0.9868481E+05	0.1094382E+06	90592.
7	0.8847981E+05	0.9913519E+05	0.1110737E+06	90396.
8	0.8773100E+05	0.9922944E+05	0.1122348E+06	90704.
9	0.8713481E+05	0.9942469E+05	0.1134478E+06	90270.
10	0.8660494E+05	0.9963744E+05	0.1146311E+06	88599.
11	0.8569644E+05	0.9936250E+05	0.1152077E+06	88151.
12	0.8484094E+05	0.9910062E+05	0.1157569E+06	88551.

CIL

							CIL	
1	0.1879079E+06	0.1932503E+06	0.1987446E+06	192471.	0.1871061E+06	0.1924029E+06	0.1978495E+06
2	0.1851102E+06	0.1934777E+06	0.2022231E+06	192917.	0.1839391E+06	0.1920681E+06	0.2005562E+06
3	0.1838018E+06	0.1945286E+06	0.2058811E+06	192440.	0.1828061E+06	0.1930989E+06	0.2039711E+06
4	0.1819655E+06	0.1945922E+06	0.2080949E+06	194684.	0.1796285E+06	0.1915604E+06	0.2042846E+06
5	0.1798702E+06	0.1940903E+06	0.2094344E+06	192986.	0.1780580E+06	0.1914741E+06	0.2059009E+06
6	0.1784426E+06	0.1941057E+06	0.2111434E+06	194565.	0.1766626E+06	0.1914009E+06	0.2073686E+06
7	0.1779779E+06	0.1955766E+06	0.2149152E+06	197508.	0.1753881E+06	0.1919932E+06	0.2101703E+06
8	0.1772184E+06	0.1966550E+06	0.2182231E+06	199124.	0.1753973E+06	0.1939166E+06	0.2143909E+06
9	0.1761422E+06	0.1972391E+06	0.2208626E+06	202024.	0.1740861E+06	0.1942351E+06	0.2167159E+06
10	0.1753993E+06	0.1980661E+06	0.2236617E+06	204102.	0.1720844E+06	0.1936331E+06	0.2178801E+06
11	0.1747415E+06	0.1988822E+06	0.2263577E+06	205038.	0.1713676E+06	0.1943552E+06	0.2204262E+06
12	0.1740551E+06	0.1995761E+06	0.2288389E+06	204290.	0.1705629E+06	0.1948847E+06	0.2226744E+06

Table 11.4 (continued)

	Univariate Model Forecasts				Transfer Function Model Forecasts		
Periods Ahead	95 Percent Lower Confidence Limit	Point Forecast	95 Percent Upper Confidence Limit	Actual Value	95 Percent Lower Confidence Limit	Point Forecast	95 Percent Upper Confidence Limit
		ESTATE				ESTATE	
1	0.1356043E+06	0.1367392E+06	0.1419464E+06	138278.	0.1366627E+06	0.1397807E+06	0.1429696E+06
2	0.1351799E+06	0.1400539E+06	0.1451036E+06	139147.	0.1370026E+06	0.1414437E+06	0.1460287E+06
3	0.1352175E+06	0.1413612E+06	0.1478256E+06	141808.	0.1372953E+06	0.1427659E+06	0.1484543E+06
4	0.1354694E+06	0.1427209E+06	0.1503606E+06	142558.	0.1371988E+06	0.1436072E+06	0.1503147E+06
5	0.1358531E+06	0.1440734E+06	0.1527911E+06	143577.	0.1371078E+06	0.1443866E+06	0.1520517E+06
6	0.1363292E+06	0.1454387E+06	0.1551567E+06	144176.	0.1375967E+06	0.1457067E+06	0.1542944E+06
7	0.1368756E+06	0.1468170E+06	0.1574804E+06	145134.	0.1374655E+06	0.1463093E+06	0.1557220E+06
8	0.1374779E+06	0.1482083E+06	0.1597760E+06	145651.	0.1381333E+06	0.1477137E+06	0.1579584E+06
9	0.1381267E+06	0.1496128E+06	0.1620538E+06	147187.	0.1389956E+06	0.1492912E+06	0.1603494E+06
10	0.1388153E+06	0.1510306E+06	0.1643206E+06	148213.	0.1395445E+06	0.1505035E+06	0.1623329E+06
11	0.1395385E+06	0.1524618E+06	0.1665818E+06	150113.	0.1407747E+06	0.1524282E+06	0.1650462E+06
12	0.1402928E+06	0.1539066E+06	0.1688415E+06	151798.	0.1418509E+06	0.1541696E+06	0.1675579E+06
		CONSUMER				CONSUMER	
1	0.7838487E+05	0.7989025E+05	0.8142450E+05	79781.	0.7850800E+05	0.8004694E+05	0.8161587E+05
2	0.7760156E+05	0.8015575E+05	0.8279394E+05	80019.	0.7798369E+05	0.8035937E+05	0.8280737E+05
3	0.7690812E+05	0.8054462E+05	0.8435300E+05	80482.	0.7766919E+05	0.8083650E+05	0.8413294E+05
4	0.7632881E+05	0.8098400E+05	0.8592300E+05	80432.	0.7741750E+05	0.8133987E+05	0.8546087E+05
5	0.7576306E+05	0.8137337E+05	0.8739919E+05	80013.	0.7715587E+05	0.8180756E+05	0.8673969E+05
6	0.7503631E+05	0.8151794E+05	0.8855950E+05	80462.	0.7689137E+05	0.8222762E+05	0.8793412E+05
7	0.7468031E+05	0.8200006E+05	0.9003712E+05	82141.	0.7672275E+05	0.8270800E+05	0.8916006E+05
8	0.7455037E+05	0.8267631E+05	0.9168781E+05	83638.	0.7725106E+05	0.8390662E+05	0.9113544E+05
9	0.7441331E+05	0.8329812E+05	0.9324362E+05	85132.	0.7743475E+05	0.8470350E+05	0.9265450E+05

#							
10	0.7446094E+05	0.8408669E+05	0.9495669E+05	86068.	0.7740969E+05	0.8524344E+05	0.9386987E+05
11	0.7455012E+05	0.8488881E+05	0.9666112E+05	87131.	0.7746450E+05	0.8584469E+05	0.9513144E+05
12	0.7453250E+05	0.8553894E+05	0.9817062E+05	88339.	0.7754387E+05	0.8645012E+05	0.9637919E+05
		DD				DD	
1	0.1399920E+06	0.1456624E+06	0.1515623E+06	145843.			
2	0.1405819E+06	0.1487017E+06	0.1572904E+06	150593.			
3	0.1447517E+06	0.1550569E+06	0.1660956E+06	159275.			
4	0.1421423E+06	0.1538903E+06	0.1666092E+06	152425.			
5	0.1363996E+06	0.1479707E+06	0.1617091E+06	146614.			
6	0.1328068E+06	0.1463724E+06	0.1613235E+06	150064.			
7	0.1352532E+06	0.1502350E+06	0.1668762E+06	149520.			
8	0.1323100E+06	0.1480356E+06	0.1656299E+06	152726.			
9	0.1343711E+06	0.1513693E+06	0.1705177E+06	153654.			
10	0.1322417E+06	0.1499336E+06	0.1699921E+06	153103.			
11	0.1298267E+06	0.1481004E+06	0.1689459E+06	153427.			
12	0.1302696E+06	0.1401781E+06	0.1715190E+06	149962.			
		TD				TD	
1	0.3102527E+06	0.3171117E+06	0.3241220E+06	315858.	0.3117472E+06	0.3186547E+06	0.3257150E+06
2	0.3093614E+06	0.3198437E+06	0.3306809E+06	318276.	0.3128030E+06	0.3228076E+06	0.3331317E+06
3	0.3090084E+06	0.3222769E+06	0.3361149E+06	321139.	0.3129128E+06	0.3253242E+06	0.3382274E+06
4	0.3167807E+06	0.3327827E+06	0.3495929E+06	328965.	0.3231722E+06	0.3380975E+06	0.3537117E+06
5	0.3180627E+06	0.3362441E+06	0.3554644E+06	335100.	0.3242806E+06	0.3411267E+06	0.3588477E+06
6	0.3195549E+06	0.3397397E+06	0.3611996E+06	340802.	0.3255811E+06	0.3441972E+06	0.3638773E+06
7	0.3206983E+06	0.3427268E+06	0.3662681E+06	344314.	0.3274776E+06	0.3477816E+06	0.3693440E+06
8	0.3227346E+06	0.3465644E+06	0.3721535E+06	345154.	0.3287326E+06	0.3505948E+06	0.3739106E+06
9	0.3238392E+06	0.3493199E+06	0.3768051E+06	346783.	0.3299487E+06	0.3532913E+06	0.3782849E+06
10	0.3253226E+06	0.3524317E+06	0.3817604E+06	349010.	0.3333564E+06	0.3582817E+06	0.3850703E+06
11	0.3262388E+06	0.3548347E+06	0.3859369E+06	351308.	0.3346774E+06	0.3609864E+06	0.3893631E+06
12	0.3271489E+06	0.3571968E+06	0.3900042E+06	352258.	0.3361976E+06	0.3638631E+06	0.3938048E+06

Table 11.4 (continued)

	Univariate Model Forecasts				Transfer Function Model Forecasts		
Periods Ahead	95 Percent Lower Confidence Limit	Point Forecast	95 Percent Upper Confidence Limit	Actual Value	95 Percent Lower Confidence Limit	Point Forecast	95 Percent Upper Confidence Limit
		PM					
1	0.1059557E+06	0.1131614E+06	0.1208569E+06	112300.			
2	0.1042018E+06	0.1143627E+06	0.1255142E+06	117000.			
3	0.1013063E+06	0.1135343E+06	0.1272381E+06	116200.			
4	0.9988581E+06	0.1153684E+06	0.1332509E+06	118900.			
5	0.9903731E+06	0.1172667E+06	0.1388513E+06	119800.			
6	0.9763987E+06	0.1181409E+06	0.1429462E+06	113600.			
7	0.9640512E+06	0.1198300E+06	0.1489468E+06	106600.			
8	0.9547031E+06	0.1215433E+06	0.1547367E+06	109200.			
9	0.9474987E+06	0.1232811E+06	0.1604035E+06	106600.			
10	0.9419181E+06	0.1250437E+06	0.1660009E+06	104400.			
11	0.9376206E+06	0.1268316E+06	0.1715643E+06	104200.			
12	0.9343706E+06	0.1286449E+06	0.1771192E+06	107900.			

As expected, the one-period-ahead forecasts were extremely accurate for all three bank groups. The value of time-series analysis for this type of forecasting is unquestionable. However, the twelve-month-ahead forecast errors are a bit larger than anticipated or hoped for. However, most of the error comes as a result of extremely large forecast errors for one or two variables. For most of the variables the forecasts were surprisingly accurate. The median forecasting error for the twelve-month-ahead forecasts for bank groups 1, 2, and 3 were a very acceptable 5.9 percent, 3.2 percent, and 4.0 percent.

Essentially, the average forecast errors were inflated because we were never able to develop a model for PM that forecast with reasonable (under 10 percent error) accuracy. The average forecast error would be as much as 35 percent lower if the errors for PM were not included in the calculations. The problem, though it was not obvious when one looked only at the eighty-seven modeling observations but was apparent by looking at the entire ninety-nine data points, was that PM was not stationary throughout the entire period. The series could not be made stationary either by differencing or by modeling it with various exogenous variables. Given the institutional changes in the federal funds market and its relative newness, this result is not hard to believe. Since the apparent structural changes occurred so late in the sample, we were unable to reestimate a model for PM using either intervention analysis or separate data segments.

Although we suspected that the grouping of banks would alleviate much of the problem, the issue of stability was of major concern throughout this study. During the period covered in the sample, July 1968 to September 1976, numerous shocks were felt throughout the economy. It was fairly clear from the outset of the study that the portfolio items that were subject to fewer and smaller shocks would yield better forecasts. In fact, the most stationary items, TD and DD, yielded extremely accurate forecasts. What was surprising was the relative robustness of the forecasts for the less stable series. The modeling of a bank using intervening variables, local exogenous variables, and knowledge of that particular bank would be a worthwhile effort to improve the accuracy of the forecasts. The efficiency and quality of the forecasts would also be enhanced if the bank's portfolio was estimated simultaneously using a vector valued autoregressive moving the average model.

Given the greater difficulty in modeling the transfer function, the forecast results indicate that the univariate models might well be preferred to multiple-input models. In any event, the use of more than two inputs does not seem called for. For actual forecasting the macro variables values could be generated from univariate models or obtained from other forecasting models (Pierce and Craine).

One of the conclusions that this study seems to imply, that macro variables have little, if any, influence on bank portfolios, is counter to most intuition and economic theory. However, this result was not completely unexpected given the results of other studies (Pierce 1977; Cramer and Miller 1976). Pierce's explanation of this apparent widespread independence seems applicable to our study. Basically, given the fact that the economy offers a miserable experimental design, we cannot verify or refute the relationship between macro variables and bank assets and liabilities. All I am saying is that, for the period in question, macro variables do not add greatly to the explanatory power compared with univariate models.

This chapter has shown that time-series analysis is, and can further be, an important tool for bank portfolio forecasting and analysis. By further disaggregating bank groups and portfolio items and by using information based on knowledge of the particular banks, time-series analysis can be even more valuable in bank analysis.

Appendix

The bank data used in this study are based on Weekly Reporting Bank data compiled by the Federal Reserve Board and the Federal Reserve Bank of San Francisco. Originally the data were for a cross section of 320 banks from 3 July 1968 to 1 September 1976, compiled from weekly reports submitted by large banks to the Federal Reserve describing their conditions. The data were checked for internal consistency and declared to be especially good based on typical microeconomic standards.

To get the data into a form suitable for our study, we carried out three operations. First, we transformed the data into separate time series for each bank. Banks that were not continuous throughout the period were dropped. Next, we combined the weekly data into a monthly average, on the assumption that the most important changes in a bank's balance sheet would be on a monthly basis and that the weekly changes would most likely contain a great deal of noise. Last, we aggregated banks according to three attributes, because of the confidentiality of individual bank data. The traits we aggregated were:

1. Level of assets: (*a*) over $1 billion, (*b*) from $0.5 billion to $1 billion, (*c*) under $0.5 billion).

2. Ratio of time and savings deposits to total assets: (*a*) over 35 percent, (*b*) between 20 percent and 35 percent, (*c*) under 20 percent.

3. Ratio of time and savings deposits to total loans: (*a*) over 1.5, (*b*) between 1.2 and 1.5, (*c*) under 1.2.

Thus there were twenty-seven possible groupings. However, four cells held no banks and three cells were combined with other cells because they held fewer than three banks. This left a total of twenty-two bank groups.

12   Multivariate Analysis of Interest Rate Risk

Roger N. Craine and James L. Pierce

12.1   Introduction

Much of the literature on the adequacy of bank capital is concerned with such factors as default risk and faulty management. These factors are important, but they neglect the role that purely stochastic elements can play in affecting the capital of a well-managed bank, even if it is free of default risk. Because banks raise funds by issuing liabilities with maturities different from those of the assets they acquire, changes in the interest rates paid on these liabilities relative to the interest rates on assets will affect earnings and, hence, bank capital.

As long as assets and liabilities have different maturities, there is no way to avoid the risk of unanticipated movements in the interest rate spread.[1] One role of bank capital is to provide a buffer that absorbs fluctuations in bank earnings caused by unexpected changes in the term structure of interest rates. Thus, banks are self-insuring against term structure risk through their capital account. Interest rate risk represents a claim on bank capital just as does default risk. It becomes important, therefore, to assess the size of this claim relative to the size of the capital position. This paper presents an empirical measure of the size of interest rate risk.

The efficient markets hypothesis requires that forward interest rates equal expected interest rates where these expectations incorporate all available information—that is, where the expectations are rational. This requirement, assuming linear optimal forecasts, implies that forecast

Roger N. Craine and James L. Pierce are assistant professor and professor of economics at the University of California, Berkeley.
1. In principle, it is possible to have insurance against term structure risk. Such insurance is beyond the scope of this paper.

revisions (expectations) are serially uncorrelated. The magnitude of the forecast errors, however, depends on the unspecified information set.

Most previous work applying efficient market models to interest rates uses a single equation, or a single time series, to forecast interest rates. These models imply restrictions on the dynamic structure or the information set or both. In this paper we show that by explicitly modeling the dynamic interaction between short and long rates and by including the inflation rate in the information set we can substantially reduce the variance of the forecasts, that is, interest rate risk. The information used in the more complicated model is readily available and should be incorporated in a rational expectation.

Section 12.2 presents the vector stochastic model of the determination of interest rates and shows its relation to a single-series model. Section 12.3 gives the empirical estimates, and section 12.4 presents the postsample forecasts and compares them with forecasts from a random walk specification.

12.2 The Model

12.2.1 Efficient Markets Definition

A form of the efficient markets hypothesis contends that the jth period forward interest rate $_tF_{t+j}$ should equal the expectation of the spot rate $_tr^*_{t+j}$ made at time t for period $t + j$ where the expectation incorporates all the currently available information Ω_t; that is,

$$(1) \qquad\qquad _tF_{t+j} \equiv {_tr^*_{t+j}} \equiv E(r_{t+j}|\Omega_t).$$

If the forward rate deviates from the expected future spot rate, then expected profits exist, and, except for transaction costs, the forward rate will be forced to the expected spot rate. Under these conditions it has been shown (e.g., see Samuelson 1972; Sargent 1972; or Shiller 1973) that the sequence of forward rates,

$$(2) \qquad\qquad _{t+i}F_{t+j} \equiv E(r_{t+j}|\Omega_t) = {_tF_{t+j}}, \qquad i > 0$$

satisfies the definition of a martingale; that is, the changes in the forward rate or the forecast revisions are serially uncorrelated. To give the efficient markets definition some empirical content, it is necessary, of course, to assume a probability distribution that describes the spot rate.

12.2.2 Single-Series Models

Recently, univariate time-series techniques have been used to model the determination of individual interest rates, (e.g., see Brick and Thompson 1978 and Nelson and Schwert 1977). In this part we discuss the assumptions behind single-series models and their relation to the efficient markets assumptions. We show that because single-series models empirically do not satisfy the efficient market assumption, a multivariate approach is called for.

Assume that the first difference of the one-period spot rate r_t is a stationary stochastic process with a finite variance (which by itself is a fairly weak assumption), so that it may be given the autoregressive moving average (ARMA) representation,

(3) $$a(z)r_t = b(z)u_t ,$$

where u is a mean zero, serially uncorrelated, constant variance (white noise) error. The coefficients in equation (3) are polynomials in the lag operator z,

$$a(z) \equiv \sum_{i=0} a(i)z^i$$
$$b(z) \equiv \sum_{i=0} b(i)z^i ,$$

and the lag operator z is defined as $z^i x_t \equiv x_{t-i}$. Wold has shown that the prediction $_t\hat{r}_{t+j}$ at time t of the spot rate r_{t+j} that has minimum expected variance and that is a linear function of the observable single series r_t, $r_{t-1}, \ldots$ is given by

(4) $$_t\hat{r}_{t+j} = \sum_{i=0}^{\infty} w(i+j)u_{t-i} ,$$

where

$$w(z) \equiv \frac{b(z)}{a(z)} \equiv \sum_{i=0}^{\infty} w(i) .$$

Thus, if it is assumed (a) that the available information Ω_t consists of the single time series, r, and (b) that the forecasts are linear, then the efficient markets hypothesis implies that the expectations of future spot rates should equal the forecasts from single-series ARMA models.

Brick and Thompson estimated equations for (the first difference of) seven federal and municipal interest rates of the form[2]

(5) $$a(z)r_{k_t} = b(z)u_{k_t} . \qquad k = 1, 2, \ldots 7.$$

Although the errors from the single-series models are serially uncorrelated and they contain all the information in the single-series, they may be correlated with other information that would be used in a rational expectation.

Brick and Thompson cross-correlated the residuals from the single-series models to determine if there was additional information about the lead-lag structure contained in the other interest rate series. For example, assume the errors for two series—the short-rate u_s and the long-rate u_L—have the following relationship:

---

2. They found that a random walk representation was adequate for most of the series (Brick and Thompson 1978, p. 96).

(6)
$$u_{L_t} = a_{Ls}(z)u_{s_t} + c_L(z)e_{l_t}$$

$$u_{s_t} = a_{sL}(z)u_{L_t} + c_s(z)e_{2_t} \, ,$$

where e_1 and e_2 are independent white-noise errors.[3] The cross-covariances

(7)
$$E(u_{L_t}, u_{s_{t-i}}) = \lambda_{L,s_i} \quad -\infty < i < \infty$$

will have some nonzero values and will be two-sided (i.e., $i \gtrless 0$) unless $a_{Ls}(z)$ or $a_{sL}(z)$ is identically equal zero. Brick and Thompson found significant sample cross-correlations, leading them to conclude that, "there was apparently a complex feedforward-feedback relationship [between the rates] rather than a simple leading or lagging relationship." But they contend that the relationship is not stable over time.[4]

12.2.3 A Vector Model

Brick and Thompson's results indicate that there is significant information in the other interest rate series so that expectations in an efficient market should incorporate this information. In other words, the assumption in the second section is too restrictive. If the cross-series information is stable, it can be incorporated in a more general vector ARMA representation. To derive a bivariate form of this model, substitute the definition of the errors from the single-series model, equation (5),

(8)
$$u_{k_t} = \frac{a_k(z)}{b_k(z)} r_{k_t} \, ,$$

into the equation (6), which defines the relationship between the single-series errors and gives the bivariate stochastic process

(9)
$$\frac{a_L(z) \, r_{L_t}}{b_L(z)} - \frac{a_{Ls}(z)a_s(z) \, r_{s_t}}{b_s(z)} = c_L(z)e_{L_t}$$

$$-\frac{a_{sL}(z)a_L(z) \, r_{L_t}}{b_L(z)} + \frac{a_s(z) \, r_{s_t}}{b_s(z)} = c_s(z)e_{s_t} \, .$$

Notice that both current and lagged long and short rates determine the current long rate and the current short rate.[5]

The variance of the forecasts from the bivariate model conditional on the information set that includes both series ($\Omega_t \equiv r_{L_{t-1}}, r_{L_{t-2}} \cdots ,$ $r_{s_{t-1}}, r_{s_{t-2}}, \dots$) is necessarily less than or equal to the forecast variance

---

3. The polynomial coefficients are restricted, since each series u_k is serially uncorrelated. See Granger and Newbold (1975).

4. Brick and Thompson (1978, p. 98 and pp. 101–2).

5. Sims (1972) has shown that distributed lag estimates of a single equation, for example, term structure models, from the bivariante system (2.3.2) cannot be interpreted as a causal or behavioral relation because the feedback has been ignored.

from the single-series models. The bivariate model includes the additional restriction that the cross-covariances

$$\lambda_{Ls_i} = E(e_{L_t}, e_{s_{t-i}}) = 0 \qquad -\infty < i < \infty$$

(as well as the autocovariances) are equal to zero. As a result the vector of forecast revisions,

$$[\, {}_t\hat{r}_{t+j} - {}_{t-1}\hat{r}_{t+j} \,], \qquad j \geq 0$$

where

$$\underline{r}_t \equiv \begin{bmatrix} r_{L_t} \\ r_{s_t} \end{bmatrix}$$

is serially uncorrelated.

The basic model used in this paper is a slight generalization of the bivariate model. We also included the first difference of the inflation rate, p, as an exogenous driving variable. The inflation rate was included in the information set because theory and previous empirical work suggest that it should be (see Modigliani and Shiller 1973) and because of its easy observability. The vector ARMA model is

(10) $$A(z)\underline{r}_t = B(z)p_t + C(z)\underline{e}_t,$$

where $\underline{r}$ is the two-element column vector containing the first difference of the long rate r_L and the short rate r_s and e is a corresponding two-element white-noise error vector. The coefficients are matrix polynomials in the lag operator z. The first term in the autoregressive power series is normalized to an identity,

$$A(z) = I + A(1)z + \ldots,$$

so that (10) is a reduced form, and the moving average matrix polynomial $C(z)$ is diagonal so that each equation contains a single moving average error.[6] The first difference of the inflation rate is assumed to follow the independent ARMA stationary-stochastic process,

(11) $$g(z)p_t = h(z)d_t,$$

where d is a white-noise error.

12.3 Empirical Estimates

12.3.1 Data and Preliminary Specification Tests

The data for the model estimation consist of monthly time-series observations on three variables—the long interest rate, which is Moody's BAA corporate bond rate, the short rate, which is the four- to six-month

---

6. The normalization involves no loss in generality if we allow the reduced-form error vector to be contemporaneously correlated, since it is still serially uncorrelated.

prime commercial paper rate, and the inflation rate, which is the seasonally adjusted annual growth rate of the consumer price index. The data come from the NBER data bank, and the period of observations is from 1953–3 (post-Korean War) to 1971–7 (just before the wage-price freeze).

The series were first-differenced and the first twenty-four sample autocorrelations were calculated for the entire period and for the sample split into pre- and post-1965 data. The autocorrelations tended to die out, indicating that the series were stationary. Brick and Thompson, however, found a significant (at the 95 percent confidence level) increase in the sample variance of their post-1965 data. Our series displayed a similar increase in the sample variance for the post-1965 data. In contrast to Brick and Thompson's results, however, the point estimates of all but one of the sample autocorrelations from the pre-1965 data fell within the confidence ban (two standard errors) of post-1965 estimates, and the majority were within one standard error. From this we concluded that the time structure was stationary but that the white-noise errors, u_k in equation (5), were heteroskedastic. If there was a one-time shift in the error variance, or if the model variance is bounded, and if the model can be correctly identified, then the final model parameter estimates are consistent but not asymptotically efficient.[7]

We also did a preliminary test of the causal structure specified in the vector model (10). Sims (1977)[8] suggested an exogeneity test based on the standard regression model

(12) $y = Xb + u$,

where the hypothesis that X is strictly exogenous is the hypothesis that $E(u|X) = 0$. If exogeneity holds for this model with sample size up to $T + s$, then we can add to the right-hand side of (12) the variable Z, whose t th component is the $t + s$ th component of X, to get

(13) $y = Xb + Zc + u$.

On the null hypothesis that (12) satisfies the assumptions of the Gauss-Markov theorem, (13) does also, with $c = 0$. Testing $c = 0$ by standard methods thus tests the null hypothesis of strict exogeneity of X in (12).[9]

To test the hypothesis that the inflation rate was exogenous in the long interest rate equation, we ran the autoregressive model

(14) $r_{L_t} = \sum_{i=1}^{12} b_{0i}\, r_{L_{t-i}} + \sum_{i=0}^{12} b_{1i}\, r_{s_{t-1}} + \sum_{i=0}^{12} b_{2i}\, p_{t-i}$

---

7. The vector model was estimated using a FIML technique (see Wall 1976) so that if the errors were homoskedastic the estimates would be asymptotically efficient.

8. Also see Sims (1972).

9. Sims (1977, p. 24).

$$+ \sum_{i=1}^{12} c_i \, p_{t+i} = u_t$$

and tested the null hypothesis that the coefficient vector $c = 0$. We then tested for exogeneity of the short rate in the long rate equation by replacing the led values of the (first difference of the) inflation rate with led values of the (first difference of the) short rate. Table 12.1 reports the F values for all combinations of the three variables. The critical $F_{(12,294)}$ value at the 5 percent level is approximately 1.79; the starred values are significant. The first row in table 12.1 indicates that the null hypothesis that short rates are exogenous in the long rate equation can be rejected, element $(1,2)$; but the null hypothesis that the inflation rate is exogenous cannot be rejected, element $(1,3)$. Row 2 presents a similar picture for the short rate. Row 3 indicates that we cannot reject the null hypothesis that the short interest rate is exogenous in the inflation equation, but we reject the null hypothesis that the long rate is exogenous. In short, table 12.1 supports the specification of the vector model (10) and (11). There is feedback between the two interest rates, but a unidirectional flow from the inflation rate to the long rate.

12.3.2 Estimation

Estimation of the vector model (10) is an iterative multistage procedure that is described in Granger and Newbold (1975), chapter 7. Briefly, the technique is to:

1. Fit single-series models to each endogenous variable using univariate techniques. Differencing may be necessary to obtain stationarity—for example, equation (5).

2. Calculate the cross-correlations between the single-series residuals and use them to identify the transfer functions between the residuals—for example, equation (6).

3. Identify the error structures—that is, the transfer function for the errors in the bivariate model.

4. Estimate the bivariate model—for example, equation (9).

5. Calculate the cross-covariances between the residuals from the bivariate model and the residuals from the single-series model for the

Table 12.1   **Pseudo-Sims Test F Values**

Dependent Variable	Coefficients on Future Values		
	r_L	r_s	p
r_L	—	1.92*	0.45
r_s	2.62*	—	0.99
p	6.41*	0.49	—

*Value is significant.

exogenous variable and use these to identify the transfer function on the exogenous variable.

6. Estimate the complete model.

7. Check the adequacy of the representation and, if necessary, modify and reestimate it.

Our estimates of the single-series models for the interest rates show a fairly simple time structure, but they are definitely more complicated than the random walk, accepted by Brick and Thompson:

$$(15) \qquad (1 - .31z - .20z^6 + .20z^7)r_{L_t} = (1 + .37z)u_{l_t}$$
$$\qquad\qquad (.084)\ (.067)\ \ (.075) \qquad\qquad (.084)$$

$$\hat{\sigma}^2_{u_1} = .0089$$

$$(16) \qquad (1 - .30z^3 - .14z^{12})r_{s_t} = (1 + .56z + .29z^2)u_{2_t}$$
$$\qquad\qquad (.082)\ \ (.070) \qquad\qquad (.067)\ (.082)$$

$$\hat{\sigma}^2_{u_2} = .0514$$

The autoregressive structure reflects complicated seasonal movements, and there are moving average errors whose effects persist for up to three months.

The cross-correlations of the single-series residuals given in table 12.2 indicate a significant relationship between the residuals of the short rate and the residuals of the long rate (column 1) at lags 1, 4, 8, and possibly 14; the asymptotic standard error of the cross-correlations is approximately .06. Somewhat to our surprise, however, the cross-correlations between the residuals of the long rate and the lagged residuals from the short rate showed no significant relationship. The cross-correlations in table 12.2 seem to indicate a recursive bivariate relationship in which lagged short rates and long rates plus an error process cause the short rate, but only lagged long rates plus an error process cause the long rate. Based on the Sims test and economic theory (intuition?) we decided to contradict the rule of parsimonious parameterization and allowed for feedback.

The parameter estimates for the complete model in rational distributed lag foⅰⅿat are given in equations (17) and (18), with the summary statistics—parameter estimates and standard errors, and the covariance matrix of the estimated residuals—given in table 12.3.

$$(17) \qquad a_{11}(z)r_{L_t} = \frac{a_{12}(z)r_{s_t}}{a^*_{11}(z)} + b_1(z)p_t + c_1(z)e_{1_t}$$

$$(1 + .123z^5 + .129z^7 + .208z^8)r_{L_t} = \frac{.07z}{1 - .454z - .537z^2}r_{s_t}$$

Table 12.2   **Cross-Correlation of the Single-Series Residuals**

Lag	Correlations $\hat{u}_{r_s}, \hat{u}_{r_L}(z)$	Correlations $\hat{u}_{r_L}, \hat{u}_{r_s}(z)$
1	.1424	.0827
2	−.0590	.0005
3	−.0941	.0288
4	−.1707	.0201
5	−.0957	.0187
6	−.0045	−.0123
7	−.0642	−.0099
8	−.1743	.0467
9	−.0713	−.0636
10	−.0164	.0365
11	.0282	.0608
12	.0570	.0991
13	−.0108	−.0641
14	−.1278	.0928
15	−.0888	.0154
16	.0077	.0065
17	−.0773	.0911
18	.0377	−.0228
19	.0758	−.0535
20	.0404	.0144
21	−.0100	.0066
22	−.0147	−.0958
23	−.0626	−.0347
24	.0408	.0703

$$+ (.437 + .46z)p_t + (1 + .495z)e_{1_t}$$

$$(18) \qquad a_{22}(z)r_{s_t} = \frac{a_{21}(z)}{a^*_{22}(z)}r_{L_t} + b_2(z)p_t$$

$$+ \quad c_2(z)e_{2_t}$$

$$(1 + .352^3 + .143z^7 + .149z^8)r_{st}$$

$$= \frac{.326z}{(1 - .071z + .214z^2 + .725z^3)}r_{L_t}$$

$$+ (.863 + .363z)p_t + (1 + .445z + .207z^2)e_{2_t}.$$

The final model exhibits a strong feedback relation between the interest rates, with the inflation rate exerting a driving influence on both. The more complicated vector model yields a substantial reduction in the residual variance (recall that all the series are first differences) of 12

Table 12.3   **Final Estimates**

β_{ij} (Lag)	Estimated Parameters	Standard Errors
Equation (17)		
$a_{11}(5)$	−.123172	.094460
$a_{11}(7)$	−.128601	.084685
$a_{11}(8)$	−.207969*	.094560
$a_{11}^*(1)$	−.453966*	.069506
$a_{11}^*(2)$	−.536739*	.068979
$a_{12}(1)$	.069834*	.013565
$b_1(0)$	.436824*	.092618
$b_1(1)$	.459561*	.097379
$c_1(1)$	.495315*	.093891
Equation (18)		
$a_{22}(3)$	.351979*	.086579
$a_{22}(7)$	−.143352	.087456
$a_{22}(8)$	−.148512	.094050
$a_{22}^*(1)$	−.070607	.089722
$a_{22}^*(2)$	.214318*	.086498
$a_{22}^*(3)$	.724717*	.094354
$a_{21}(1)$	.326328*	.093421
$b_2(0)$	.863319*	.099563
$b_2(1)$	.352870*	.106983
$c_2(1)$	.445171*	.089041
$c_2(2)$	.207059*	.075655

Residual Covariance Matrix

	r_L	r_s
r_L	$.5353E-02$	$.6856E-02$
r_s	$.6856E-02$	$.3065E-01$

percent for the long rate and 15 percent for the short rate from the single-series specification. It is also interesting from a theoretical point of view that the inclusion of the other rate and the inflation term makes most of the seasonal autoregressive parameters insignificant; the seasonal patterns seem to be explained by the complicated interaction of the interest rates plus the inflation term. We have not reestimated the model with the insignificant parameters deleted.

12.4   Predictions with the Model

We conducted several experiments to assess the predictive performance of the model. It was tested outside the sample period for the period August 1971 through October 1977—the last date for which we had collected data.

The test of the model is particularly severe because the postsample period contained the effects of an incredible number of large shocks to interest rates. Among these were price controls in their various phases, devaluation, and OPEC. To these shocks one must add the effects of monetary policy in 1974—probably the most restrictive monetary policy ever experienced in the United States—the deepest recession since the 1930s, and an unusually high and variable rate of inflation. It is asking a great deal of any model to predict the movements of interest rates during this six-year period.

Although the accuracy of the predictions deteriorated outside the sample period, the model performed very well over this difficult period. The mean squared error of the forecasts were calculated for one-period-ahead forecasts. The errors of the one-period forecast are plotted in figures 12.1 and 12.2 and are compared with the errors from a random

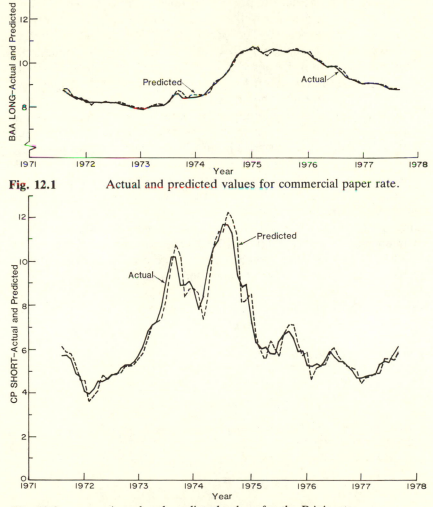

Fig. 12.1   Actual and predicted values for commercial paper rate.

Fig. 12.2   Actual and predicted values for the BAA rate.

walk specification in table 12.4. Table 12.4 contains the variance of the residuals in the sample period and the mean squared errors from the one-step-ahead model predictions and a random walk specification. Although the model errors, especially in the short rate, increase substantially for the postsample forecasts, they are still considerably better than the random walk specification.

The lower mean squared forecast errors for the vector model suggest that there is a stable time relationship among long- and short-term interest rates and the inflation rate. Including the inflation rate does not alter this conclusion, because if a random walk properly characterized the interest rate processes (the model accepted by Brick and Thompson) then the lagged inflation rates would contain no information.

Figure 12.1 plots actual and predicted values for the commercial paper rate. This figure suggests why the accuracy of prediction deteriorated outside the sample period. The period 1973–75 experienced unprecedented swings in short-term interest rates. During 1973, the commercial paper rate soared from 5.8 percent to 10.2 percent. The rate fell temporarily in 1974 before taking off for a high of 11.6 percent in August. By May of 1975 the rate was back down to 5.8 percent.

Figure 12.2 plots actual and predicted values for the BAA rate. As one would expect, the fluctuations in the long rate were much less than for short rates. The fluctuations were large by historical standards, however, and the model predicts them well.

As a final test of the model, a dynamic simulation was run over the period 1959–7 through 1977–10. For this entire period, r_s and r_L were generated endogenously, but the inflation rate was taken as its actual value in each month. The model proved to be remarkably stable over this eighteen-year period. Given the actual behavior of inflation, there was no tendency for the predicted levels of either interest rate to drift very far from their actual values. These results confirm the plausible assertion that the major problem in forecasting interest rates far into the future lies in forecasting the inflation rate. Given the inflation rate, the autoregressive processes generating interest rates appear to be highly stable.

Table 12.4   **Mean Squared Errors**

r_L	r_s	
.0053	.0307	Model, sample period
.0077	.2466	Model, postsample
.0164	.2993	Random walk, postsample

12.5   Conclusions

The interest rate risk faced by a bank depends on the distribution of the interest rate forecasts. The efficient markets criterion requires that all available information be used when forming expectations. We have shown that single-series models omit significant information that is readily available, implying that the forecast variance of these models overstates the true interest rate risk.

13 Interest Rate Risk and the Regulation of Financial Institutions

Jay B. Morrison
and David H. Pyle

13.1 Introduction

In this study we are concerned with the market value of net worth in a financial institution. The financial institution is presumed to hold assets and to issue deposits, with the difference in market values of assets and deposits being its net worth. This study considers the effects on net worth of changes in the level and structure of default-free interest rates. As net worth approaches zero, depositors have no buffer between the value of their deposits and fluctuations in asset values. Also, regulators must know the potential for a given institution's net worth falling to zero or below before the subsequent examination. This suggests that a forecast of the proportional change in net worth over a given time period is an important aspect of the examination process.

There are many sources of potential change in the net worth of a financial institution over any time period, including such important factors as default risk and the chance that the institution's employees may prove to be dishonest or incompetent. An implication of this study is that regulators' concern regarding factors such as credit risk and managerial competence may be more finely focused if the effects of interest rate risk on net worth have been quantified.

To this end, we shall begin by describing the basic model of interest rate elasticity for fixed-income securities. A discussion of the problems of adapting this model to the portfolio of a financial institution will follow. The next sections describe the results of a simulation of the interest rate elasticity model for a wholesale bank.[1] An important aspect of this

Jay B. Morrison is vice-president of the Wells Fargo Bank, and David H. Pyle is professor of business administration at the University of California, Berkeley.

1. The simulation of the wholesale bank is based on a subsector of a particular bank. The assets of this subsector are cash and commercial loans, and the liabilities are demand deposits, purchased funds (which can also be thought of as the net position in securities), and equity capital.

simulation is the attempt to account for the full cash flow effects of changes in the level and structure of default-free interest rates. For example, the effects of interest rates on cash flows owing to loan commitments are explicitly modeled. The final section contains our concluding remarks.

13.2   Interest Rate Elasticity for Bonds

It was Macaulay (1938) who first defined the concept of duration to measure the time dimension of a bond. If we let

$S_1, \ldots, S_t$ be payments received at times $1, \ldots, t$;
$P_1, \ldots, P_t$ be the present value at time 0 of those payments;

then the duration (D) of the payment stream is defined as:

$$(1) \qquad D = \frac{\sum_{i=1}^{t} P_i i}{\sum_{i=1}^{t} P_i}$$

In this view, the duration is a weighted average of the payment dates, with the weight for period i equal to the proportional contribution to the present value made by S_i.

Macaulay interpreted duration as the period of time that elapses before the average dollar of present value is received. Under this interpretation, he argued for the use of duration as a measure of how long a dollar invested in a bond remained invested, and he noted several advantages of using duration rather than maturity. Hicks (1939) defined an "average period" of a payment stream that is equivalent to Macaulay's duration. Hicks, however, interpreted and used the measure as "an elasticity [of capital value] with respect to a discount ratio." It may therefore be useful to think of duration as a measure of an investment's interest-rate elasticity which has a time dimension and interpretation.

13.2.1   A Model of Interest Rate Changes

To see that duration does have an elasticity interpretation, it is useful to specify a model for interest rate changes. First, denote the one-period interest rate expected to obtain during the period beginning at time $t - 1$ by r_t. Under the expectations hypothesis with no liquidity premium, the t-period spot rate would then be the geometric mean of the product of $1 +$ the current one-period spot rate and $1 +$ each of the $t - 1$ one-period-forward rates. If $(1 + R_t)^{-t}$ denotes the t-period discount factor, then

$$(2) \qquad 1 + R_t = \left[\sum_{i=1}^{t} (1 + r_i) \right]^{1/t}$$

To simplify the notation let $r_{Ft} = 1 + r_t$ and $R_{Ft} = (1 + R_t)^t$. Using this notation, the present value of the certain payment stream, $S_1 , \ldots , S_t ,$ can be written as:

$$(3) \qquad PV_s = \sum_{i=1}^{t} \frac{S_i}{R_{Fi}} .$$

Now, assume that shifts in interest rates can be described by some multiplicative function $f(h, t)$, such that

$$R_{Ft} = \hat{R}_{Ft} \cdot f(h, t)$$

$$\frac{\partial R_{Ft}}{\partial h} = \hat{R}_{Ft} \frac{\partial f(h, t)}{\partial h} ,$$

where $h = r_{F1} = 1$ plus the first-period spot rate. This assumption allows (3) to be rewritten as

$$(3') \qquad PV_s = \sum_{i=1}^{t} \frac{S_i}{f(h, i)\hat{R}_{Fi}} .$$

13.2.2   Interest Rate Elasticity with Equal Proportional Effects on All One-Period Rates

This formulation provides a tractable means of expressing rate changes, which allows for the possibility that some of the one-period rates change more than others. For this example, however, we will assume that all one-period rates (spot and forward) change by the same proportional amount, which can be modeled with a shift function of the form

$$(4) \qquad f(h,t) = h^t .$$

This means that when shifts in the discount function occur, they do so in such a way that the entire function is shifted up or down without distortion. Under this specification, we can study the effect of rate shifts on the present value of the stream $S_1 , \ldots , S_t$. Using (4), we can express the present value as:

$$PV_s = \sum_{i=1}^{t} S_i \delta_i ,$$

where

$$\delta_i = \frac{1}{h^i \hat{R}_{Fi}} .$$

Taking the differential, we get:

$$dPV_s = - \sum_{i=1}^{t} \frac{S_i \delta_i i}{h} \, dh ,$$

and dividing by PV gives:

$$\frac{dPV_s}{PV_s} = -\left[\frac{\sum\limits_{i=1}^{t} (S_i\delta_i)i}{\sum\limits_{i=1}^{t} S_i\delta_i} \right] \cdot \frac{dh}{h}.$$

By noting that $S_i\delta_i$ is equal to P_i, the present value of the bond payment S_i, it is clear that the term in brackets in equation (5) is, in fact, Macaulay's duration. Since dPV_s/PV_s is the percentage change in present value, and dh/h is the percentage change in the discount factor, the ratio $-\sum\limits_{i=1}^{t} (S_i\delta_i)i/\sum\limits_{i=1}^{t} S_i\delta_i$ is the interest rate elasticity of net worth. It is important to note that duration and interest rate elasticity (IRE) will be equivalent only for this particular specification of $f(h,t)$, that is, one in which unanticipated rate movements shift the entire yield curve up or down by proportionately identical amounts.

13.2.3   Interest Rate Elasticity with Decreasing Effects on Forward Rates

The relationship for interest rate elasticity established by Macaulay is simple and appealing. However, the interest rate change process that underlies it is not very realistic. Observers of the behavior of default-free interest rates suggest that a preferable model is one in which the change in rates is largest for the near term one-period rates and smaller for later one-period rates (see Hodges 1975 and Yawitz, Hempel, and Marshall 1975).

An alternative specification for the interest rate shift function is

(4') $f(h,t) = h^{t^\alpha}.$ $0 < \alpha \le 1$

With this shift function, we can derive the following relationship:

(5') $\frac{dPV_s}{PV_s} = -\left[\frac{\sum\limits_{i=1}^{t} (S_i\delta_i)i^\alpha}{\sum\limits_{i=1}^{t} S_i\delta_i} \right] \cdot \frac{dh}{h},$

where the term in brackets is the interest rate elasticity (IRE). Comparing equations (5) and (5'), it is clear that Macaulay's duration is the upper limit ($\alpha = 1$) on the interest rate elasticity of bond value for the more general shift function.

Using equation (5'), we can then generate the values of IRE as a function of α for two hypothetical three-period loans, one with equal cash flows in each period and the other a 10 percent coupon bond paying three coupons and repaying the face value. The example in table 13.1 is for a particular structure of default-free interest rates, but the qualitative effect of decreasing α would be the same for any structure of rates. The effect of a decreasing impact on forward rates becomes apparent in table

Table 13.1   **Interest Rate Elasticity (IRE) from Equation (5′) for Three-Period Debts When $\delta_1 = 0.9$, $\delta_2 = 0.8$, and $\delta_3 = 0.75$**

α	IRE Equal Payment Loan	IRE 10% Coupon Bond
1	−2.11	−2.74
.75	−1.76	−2.12
.5	−1.48	−1.64
.25	−1.26	−1.28

13.1. For example, if there is no attenuation (i.e., $\alpha = 1$), a 1 percent increase in one plus the first- , second- , and third-period default-free rates (which is a 110 basis point increase for a 10 percent spot or forward rate) would produce a 2.74 percent decrease in the value of the hypothetical 10 percent bond. For $\alpha = 0.75$, a 1 percent increase in one plus the one-period rate would result in an increase of about 0.7 percent in one plus the second-period rate, and an increase of about 0.6 percent in one plus the third-period rate. This level of attenuation in the interest rate change results in the decrease in value of the 10 percent bond being 2.12 percent. In other words, the loss of value for $\alpha = 0.75$ is about 77 percent of the loss of value for $\alpha = 1$. Similarly for the equal payment loan, the loss of value of the loan resulting from a 1 percent increase in one plus the first-period rate is about 17 percent less if $\alpha = 0.75$ rather than 1.

13.3 An Empirical Model of Interest Rate Changes

The example in the preceding section serves to illustrate the effect on IRE of interest rate changes that diminish as one considers forward rates for times ever more distant from the present. This model is purely hypothetical. For the analysis of the IRE for bonds, we need an empirically estimated model of the process by which default-free rates change.

Details of the model of interest rate changes that is used in the simulations reported later in this study may be found in Morrison (1977). Morrison developed a testable model of changes in the term structure of default-free interest rates from a stochastic model of the term structure by Vasicek (1976). Fundamental assumptions in the Vasicek model are (*a*) the spot rate follows a continuous Markov process; (*b*) the price of a discount bond maturing at time *s* is determined by the anticipated spot rate process from the present until time *s*; and (*c*) the bond market is efficient. For our purposes, the importance (and perhaps the limitation) of these assumptions is revealed by their implication that the value of the spot rate is the only state variable determining the term structure of interest rates.

For empirical estimation, Morrison used Vasicek's term structure equation to derive the effect of changes in the spot rate on yields to maturity. Furthermore, Morrison decomposed changes in the spot rate into a change in the ex ante real component of that rate and a change in the anticipated inflation component. While this decomposition is ad hoc in terms of the Vasicek model, a considerable literature exists that suggests that anticipated inflation is an important determinant of interest rates. The variability of ex ante real rates is a matter of some controversy (see Fama 1975 and Nelson and Schwert 1977). Morrison's estimating equation allows for changes in the ex ante real component of spot rates. If deviations in the real component of spot rates are considered temporary, but deviations in current inflation anticipations are correlated with changes in inflation anticipations for future periods, we would expect these two components to have different effects on forward rates. Consequently, the estimating equation permits the impact of the real and the inflationary effects of the one-period spot rate on yields to maturity to be different.

The form estimated was:

$$(6) \qquad \frac{dr_k}{R_{Fk}} = \frac{drr_1}{RR_{F1}} e^{-\gamma_0 - \gamma_1 k} + \frac{di_1}{I_1} e^{-\beta_0 - \beta_1 k},$$

where

$$r_k = \text{the risk } k\text{-period risk-free rate}$$
$$R_{Fk} = 1 + r_k$$
$$rr_1 = \text{real one-period rate}$$
$$RR_{F1} = 1 + rr_1$$
$$i_i = \text{one-period inflationary expectation}$$
$$I_i = 1 + i_1$$
$$rr_1 + i_1 = r_1 .$$

The unit time period chosen to estimate equation (7) was one month. Term structures for default-free securities were estimated for thirty months from January 1973 through July 1975 using the tax adjusted, cubic spline method developed by McCulloch (1975a). The data used were Salomon Brothers quotations for the last trading day of each month. This provided fifteen independent sets of adjacent term structures to be used in computing proportional rate changes for different maturities. Thirty maturities, ranging from two months to ten years, were used for each term structure, for a total of 450 pooled observations.[2]

The nominal spot rate obtained for each of the term structures was decomposed into an ex ante real component and an inflationary anticipations component. Inflationary expectations were estimated by using the method in the Nelson and Schwert (1977) article.

---

2. Because of the estimation technique employed, a few periods that displayed no spot rate changes could not be used.

Equation (6) was estimated by a two-step process. First, the coefficients of the real component (γ_0 and γ_1) were estimated by ignoring the inflation term, performing a log transform, and using linear regression. The estimated coefficients were then used to form a set of residuals (dr_k/R_{Fk} unexplained by drr_1/RR_{F1}). These residuals were then used to estimate the inflationary coefficients (β_0, β_1), again using linear regression on a log transform, this time ignoring the real term. The results are shown in table 13.2. As the table shows, coefficients on each term have the correct sign and are statistically significant. As a check, the procedure was repeated with the coefficients estimated in the reverse order. Although the results were not identical, the sign and general magnitude of each coefficient remained unchanged. More important, the general pattern of transmission discussed below remains the same with the alternative specification. This, combined with some preliminary results by other researchers indicating that the IRE estimates are fairly insensitive to the transmission process, indicated that the results as shown in table 13.2 should be sufficient for use in the analysis that follows. The resulting empirical model of interest rate changes is

$$(7) \qquad \frac{dr_k}{RF_k} = \frac{drr_1}{RR_{F1}} e^{-.148k} + \frac{di_1}{I_1} e^{-(.41+09k)}$$

13.3.1   Interest Rate Elasticity Based on an Empirical Model of Interest Rates

With the interest rate process described by equation (7), the expression for the proportional change in the present value of a bond may be written as

Table 13.2   **Regression of Nominal Rate Changes on Real Rate Changes and Changes in Inflationary Expectations**

$$\frac{\Delta r_k}{R_{Fk}} = \frac{\Delta rr_1}{R_{F1}} e^{-\gamma_0\gamma_1 k} + \frac{\Delta i_1}{I_1} e^{-\beta_0-\beta_1 k}$$

γ_0	γ_1	β_0	β_1	$\hat{\sigma}_e$	R_2
.41	.14			1.04	.13
(.58)	(7.5)				
	.148			1.04	.12
	(10.7)				
		.41	.09	1.3	.04
		(4.6)	(3.9)		

(8)
$$\frac{dPV_s}{PV_s} = -\frac{\sum\limits_{i=1}^{t} (S_i \delta_i)\left[\left(\frac{drr_1}{RR_{Fl}}\right)e^{-.148i} + \left(\frac{di_1}{I_1}\right)e^{-.41-.09i}\right]\cdot i}{\sum\limits_{i=1}^{t} S_i \delta_i}.$$

A given proportional change in one plus the spot rate will be distributed between the proportional change in the real component and the proportional change in the inflationary component. By examining equation (8), we can see that the estimated IRE of a bond for a given spot rate change will be a weighted average of one, the IRE due to the real component, and two, the IRE due to the inflationary component, with the weights being the respective contributions of those components to the proportional change in the spot rate. These two IRE relationships are:

(9)
$$\text{IRE (real)} = \frac{-\sum\limits_{i=1}^{t}(S_i\delta_i)\cdot i\cdot e^{-.148i}}{\sum\limits_{i=1}^{t}(S_i\delta_i)}$$

(9')
$$\text{IRE (inflation)} = \frac{-\sum\limits_{i=1}^{t}(S_i\delta_i)\cdot i\cdot e^{-.41-.09i}}{\sum\limits_{i=1}^{t}(S_i\delta_i)}.$$

In table 13.3 we have reported some interest rate elasticities (proportional change in value per 1 percent change in the spot rate) based on equations (9) and (9'). Two of the loans considered in table 13.3 are directly comparable to the loans reported in table 13.1. The more rapid fall-off in the effects of changes in the real component of spot rates is apparent from the lower IRE values for this case. The IRE was also calculated for a conventional 10 percent coupon, ten-year bond using a flat (10 percent) term structure and also using the estimated term structure for May 1975. In the least extreme case for this longer-term bond

Table 13.3   **Interest Rate Elasticities (IRE) from Equations (9) and (9')**

Change	Flat Term Structure			May 1975 Term Structure
	IRE Equal Payment Loan	IRE 10% Coupon, 3-Year Bond	IRE 10% Coupon, 10-Year Bond	IRE 10% Coupon, 10-Year Bond
Change in real rate only	−1.61	−2.08	−2.43	−2.40
Change in inflationary anticipations only	−1.73	−2.31	−3.55	−3.53

(change in inflationary expectations only), the IRE based on the empirical model of interest rate changes is 3.53, which is just over 50 percent of the IRE of 6.76, obtained using Macaulay's duration.

The method used to obtain the interest rate elasticities in table 13.3 is directly applicable to the estimation of interest rate elasticities for the securities in a financial institution's investment portfolio. As we noted earlier, this measure of the proportional change in net worth incorporates only the effects of change in the level and structure of default-free interest rates. For a security that is not issued by the federal government, for example, state and local government securities, there will be other sources of change in the security's value. To the extent that these other sources of change can be incorporated into a model of interest rate changes that can be estimated, the approach discussed here may be broadened to provide a measure of the proportional change in security value as a function of a vector of determinants of that change.

Whether one uses the somewhat restrictive default-free interest rate elasticity or a more comprehensive measure of the potential change in investment portfolio value, the estimate of the price sensitivity of the investment portfolio should be useful information for the regulators of financial institutions. In the case of the IRE estimates given by equations (9) and (9′), this information is relatively easy to obtain. A program exists for estimating the default-free term structure from United States government bond data (see McCulloch 1975a). A periodic, perhaps weekly, estimation of the term structure could be used to provide examiners with timely estimates of the discount function (i.e., the δ_i values). Equations (9) and (9′) may be programmed on a hand-held programmable calculator. By taking an appropriately designed sample of the securities in an investment portfolio, estimating their interest rate elasticities, and then taking a weighted average of the sample elasticities using known portfolio weights, the examiner could obtain an estimate of the sensitivity of that investment portfolio to changes in the short-term, default-free interest rate.

There remain a number of open questions regarding the application of interest rate elasticities (i.e., generalized duration concepts) in the prediction of expected security price changes. In terms of the model used by Morrison, one such question concerns the assumption that interest rate changes are independent of the level of interest rates. Intuition and observation suggest that tax effects are likely to be related to the extent to which securities are selling above or below par, and hence that the current level of rates (relative to past levels) should be important. Furthermore, there is evidence (see Nadauld 1977) that the model used by Morrison tends to underpredict changes in longer-term rates. Perhaps more important, recent research by Lanstein and Sharpe (1978) has shown that very strong assumptions about the correlation of nonsystematic changes in interest rates are necessary to theoretically justify the use of (generalized) duration as a determinant of the ex ante interest rate risk of a security. However, they also give evidence that even a crude measure of duration (i.e., Macaulay's definition) is significantly related to components of security risk.

13.3.2   Interest Rate Elasticity of Financial Institutions

Samuelson (1945) used duration to study the effects of interest rate changes on financial institutions. To derive his result, let:

PV_A = present value of the stream of payments deriving from asset holdings;

PV_L = present value (cost) of the payments required for liability holdings, presumably negative;

Q_A = duration of the asset holdings;

Q_L = duration of the liability holdings.

Assuming that:

1. spot and forward rates on all liabilities and all assets change by the same amount; and
2. the amount of each asset and liability held by the bank remains unchanged when rates change,

the above result can be applied directly to the asset and liability portfolios of a bank, giving

$$\frac{dPV_A}{PV_A} = -Q_A \frac{dh}{h}$$

for the asset portfolio and

$$\frac{dPV_L}{PV_L} = -Q_L \frac{dh}{h}$$

for the liabilities. Note that these assumptions imply that the asset portfolio is essentially a fixed-payment, fixed-maturity bond that the bank has purchased, with the liability portfolio equivalent to a bond with fixed payments and fixed maturity that the bank has issued.

Defining the capital or net worth of the bank by $PV_T = PV_A + PV_L$, the Samuelson result is:

(10)
$$\frac{dPV_T}{PV_T} = -\frac{(Q_A PV_A + Q_L PV_L)}{PV_A + PV_L} \cdot \frac{dh}{h} = -Q_T \frac{dh}{h};$$

$$PV_T > 0.$$

Equation (10) says that the percentage change in capital is proportional to the percentage change in interest rates, with the constant of proportionality, $-Q_T$, being the negative of the duration of the bank as a whole. The bank's duration is, in turn, a weighted average of the durations of the asset and liability holdings, with the weights being the fractional contributions to total present value.

A major implication of (10) is that a necessary (but not sufficient) condition for a bank to be made better off by a rate increase is that its liabilities be of longer duration than its assets—that is, that $Q_L > Q_A$. Since the prevailing opinion appears to be that banks' borrowings are of shorter term than their lendings, it seems more likely that $Q_A > Q_L$, from which it follows that a bank would be made worse off by a rate increase. The result, of course, is both intuitive and a result of the simplifying assumptions on which the analysis is based. The "bank" is in fact equivalent to an investor who simultaneously purchases a bond with a duration of, say, ten years and issues a bond of equal value with a duration of two years. If rates subsequently rise, he must either finance the remaining eight years of his investment at a higher cost or sell his investment at a discount from his purchase price, both of which entail losses relative to the earlier situation.

As we have seen from our discussion of the interest rate elasticity of bonds, an assumption implicit in the conventional duration formulation is that forward rates change in the same proportion as spot rates. Empirically this assumption does not appear to be warranted. Clearly, we can proceed as we did in the case of bonds, using an empirically estimated model of interest rate changes to formulate a generalized duration for a financial institution. For financial institutions with assets that are longer-lived than liabilities, the interest rate elasticities of net worth will tend to be smaller when based on the interest rate process summarized in equations (9) and (9') than if these net worth elasticities were based on the conventional duration calculation.

Adopting a generalized duration formulation does not solve all the problems encountered in calculating an interest rate elasticity for the net worth of financial institutions. The major difficulties that remain are:

1. Not all of a bank's assets and liabilities have fixed payment streams and a well-defined maturity. Therefore a method of estimating the cash flows associated with these assets and liabilities must be developed.

2. Many of a bank's assets and liabilities are not market instruments and do not have an observable market value. To study the sensitivity of the bank's net present value, these market values must be imputed from the anticipated cash flows.

3. The cash flows are neither single-period nor risk-free, which complicates the discounting technique.

In the analysis that follows, we have attempted to deal with most of these problems. The approach taken is a simulation based on an analysis of the effect of macroeconomic variables on bank cash flows using data normally available to bank regulatory agencies. The selected subsector of the bank is intended to reflect the most important characteristics of a wholesale bank (i.e., a bank dealing mainly in corporate and commercial lending supported by corporate and commercial demand and time deposits). The asset categories modeled are commercial loans and cash. The liabilities are demand deposits, purchased funds (negotiable certificates of deposit, NCDs), and equity capital.[3]

13.4 Modeling Bank Cash Flows

The bank to be considered has only one type of earning asset (commercial loans) and one interest-bearing liability, negotiable certificates of deposit (NCDs). In addition, the bank obtains some of its funding from demand deposit balances held by business firms. Demand deposit balances and NCDs outstanding imply cash balances in the form of required and excess reserves. In the simulations described here, it is assumed that the ratio of total book assets to book equity (capital ratio) is held constant through time, and this assumption completes the specification of the bank's balance sheet.

To estimate the interest rate elasticity of the bank's net worth, we must estimate the payout stream to the bank's owners and the response of that stream to changes in the level and structure of interest rates. The payout stream consists of net income for each future time period, less the change in equity capital implied by the constant capital ratio assumption. Models of these cash flows are described in detail in Morrison (1977). In summary, the structure of system estimated by Morrison is:

1. A model of future commercial loan commitments was developed.

2. A model of future commercial loan volume (in part dependent on commitments) was developed.

3. Future demand deposit balances (in part dependent on loan volume and loan commitments) were modeled and used to project the cash assets for the bank.

4. The period by period estimates of future total assets (loan volume plus cash assets) times the assumed capital ratio provided an estimate of equity capital and total assets less demand deposits and equity capital provided an estimate of the future volume of purchased funds.

5. Models of the future yields on loans and the future NCD rates were estimated.

3. These asset/liability categories are few even for a money center, wholesale bank, with the main omissions being real estate loans and the investment portfolio. The contribution of the latter to net worth elasticity is a straightforward application of the method discussed in the previous section of this paper. An application of generalized duration estimation for a real estate portfolio is contained in Nadauld (1977).

6. The periodic future net income was obtained by multiplying the estimated loan volumes by estimated loan yields and subtracting the estimated volume of purchased funds times the estimated NCD rates.

7. The periodic payout to bank owners was obtained by subtracting the estimated change in equity capital for each period from the estimated net income for that period.

13.4.1   Commercial Loan Commitments

Morrison's model of commercial loan commitments is based on a disequilibrium credit market. Firms are assumed to face uncertainty regarding the timing of future transactions. Each firm chooses between fixed-maturity borrowing and loan commitments by comparing the minimum expected cost of a loan with the expected cost of a commitment. Given this description of the loan choice problem, it can be shown that the relative demand for commitments (*a*) decreases as the rate charged for funds borrowed on commitments increases; (*b*) increases as the uncertainty associated with future transaction dates increases; (*c*) decreases as the loan size increases (absolute commitment demand may increase); and (*d*) increases as the rate on fixed-maturity borrowing increases.

The bank is assumed to set the commitment fee, the loan rate, and the maximum commitment it is willing to make to any customer. The actual commitment size is then the minimum of the firm's demand and the maximum supply. For the bank to set rationally both the rate and a quantity maximum, thereby introducing the possibility of nonprice rationing, it must be that the bank can increase the expected value of the loan by decreasing the loan size below the amount demanded at the rate that is optimal for the bank. Briefly, this could be true for two reasons:

1. Banks potentially have some degree of monopoly power over at least some customers, but the degree of collusion necessary to maximize joint profits would be socially and legally unacceptable. An alternative is to classify customers into groups based on riskiness, tie the rate for each class to the least risky rate, and engage in price-leadership behavior by making that rate (and changes in that rate) widely publicized. To the extent that riskier customers also have lower price elasticities of demand, this process can be successful in achieving some degree of price discrimination.

2. Since it is probably not operationally feasible to have a great number of risk classes (traditionally, spreads over prime are quoted in half-percent intervals), and the number of customers will exceed the number of classes, it will be necessary to charge similar but not identical customers the same rate. In such a situation it may be optimal to ration the amount of credit extended to the riskiest customers in each class. The existence of usury ceilings strengthens this effect.

In summary, the existence and rationality of nonprice credit rationing derives from both competitive and institutional factors.

We assume that the loan officer of the bank is trying to maximize expected profit on the commitment relative to an uncertain opportunity cost over a single-period horizon. This optimization process leads to a supply of commitments that is a function of a pair of loan rate parameters (among other things). If the bank were able to set these parameters differently for each borrower having a different riskiness, there would be no rationing. However, if—as is assumed here—the bank charges the same rate for a group of borrowers who are heterogeneous in terms of risk, the commitment demand for the riskiest borrowers in the group may be greater than the optimum commitment supply. Therefore, actual commitments will be the smaller of two numbers: the borrower's optimum commitment demand or the bank's maximum supply.

Given this description of the bank's optimization problem, it can be shown that the supply schedule displays certain properties: (*a*) the maximum commitment supplied approaches zero as the loan rate or the commitment fee gets arbitrarily large; (*b*) the maximum commitment supplied decreases as the bank's opportunity cost increases; (*c*) under reasonable conditions, the maximum supply decreases with increases in the uncertainty of the opportunity rate; and (*d*) an increase in the loan rate increases the maximum commitment supply.

13.4.2   Estimation of Commercial Loan Commitments

The major problem in estimating disequilibrium models is that the observed quantity may not satisfy both the supply and the demand schedules. The practical importance of the problem is demonstrated in recent studies of the market for housing starts by Fair and Jaffee (1972) and of the watermelon market by Goldfeld and Quandt (1975). In estimating the loan commitment model, Morrison followed the so-called quantitative method described by Fair and Jaffee. Using this approach, the model derived earlier for commitment supply and demand may be written as:

$$D_t = \alpha_0 + \alpha_1 I_t + \alpha_2 \, Std(T_t) + \alpha_3 P_t + \alpha_4 CP_t + \varepsilon_t^d$$

(11)
$$S_t = \beta_0 + \beta_1 I_t + \beta_2 Std(I_t) + \beta_3 P_t + \beta_4 LEV_t + \varepsilon_t^s$$

$$Q_t^* = \text{Min}(S_t, D_t) \, ,$$

where

I_t = opportunity rate during month t (secondary three-month CD rate)

$Std(T_t)$ = measure of economic uncertainty (twelve-

month moving standard deviation of
gross business sales)

P_t = prime rate

CP_t = commercial paper volume during month t (a
measure of external liquidity)

$Std(I_t)$ = measure of rate uncertainty (twelve-month
moving standard deviation of I_t)

LEV_t = leverage at t, defined as total assets/capital;
capital includes capital notes

Q_t^* = desired volume of commitments.

In estimating the disequilibrium equations, the following equation for
excess demand was used:

(12) $$D_t - S_t = \frac{1}{\gamma} X_t ,$$

where X_t is a measure of the bank's willingness to make loans.[4]

The final specification is a lag adjustment in the actual volume of
commitments. This specification is justified on the basis of prenegotiated
contracts and other institutional factors that prevent immediate adjustment to desired levels of commitments. Assuming that a stock-
adjustment process is appropriate, we have:

$$\Delta Q_t = \lambda(Q_t^* - Q_{t-1}) ,$$

where

Q_t = actual commitments outstanding during
month t

λ = coefficient measuring the speed of adjustment.

Using monthly microeconomic data from a major bank and monthly
macroeconomic data from an aggregate macroeconomic model, the loan
commitment model was estimated over the period January 1974–May
1976.[5] The resulting equations for forecasting loan commitments are
given in table 13.4.[6]

---

4. The bank involved participates in the Federal Reserve's Quarterly Survey of Bank
Lending Practices, a survey intended to measure the nonprice lending practices of commercial banks. X_t is set equal to the first principal component of the survey responses in month t.

5. A major problem in doing empirical research at the bank level is the lack of consistent
data for the microeconomic variables. The data used by Morrison were created by a
management information system that began operating in January 1974.

6. The terms in parentheses below the coefficient estimates are t-statistics for the
coefficient. The mean value of the dependent variable was 129. A two-stage regression with
the prime rate and rationing proxy as endogenous variables was used.

Table 13.4   **Forecasting Equations in Loan Commitments**

Commitment Demand

$$Q_t = \lambda[\alpha_0 + \alpha_1 I_t + \alpha_2 \text{Std}(S_t) + \alpha_3 \hat{P}_t + \alpha_4 CP_t - \frac{1}{\gamma}\hat{X1}_t] - \lambda Q_{t-1}$$

$\lambda\alpha_0$	$\lambda\alpha_1$	$\lambda\alpha_2$	$\lambda\alpha_3$	$\lambda\alpha_4$	$-\lambda/\gamma$	λ
1584	−24	2.2	21	.016	39	.51
(1.9)	(−1)	(2.1)	(.6)	(1.1)	(.7)	(2.2)

Durbin-Watson = 1.7; standard error = 64; N = 27.

Commitment Supply

$$\Delta Q_t = \lambda[\beta_0 + \beta_1 I_t + \beta_2 \text{Std}(I_t) + \beta_3 \hat{P}_t + \beta_4 LEV_{t-1} - \frac{1}{\gamma}\hat{X2}_t] - \lambda Q_{t-1}$$

$\lambda\beta_0$	$\lambda\beta_1$	$\lambda\beta_2$	$\lambda\beta_3$	$\lambda\beta_4$	$-\lambda/\gamma$	λ
3216	−69	−70	74	−41	−73	.59
(3.2)	(−2.5)	(−.25)	(2.6)	(−2.1)	(−1.5)	(2)

Durbin-Watson = 2.4; standard error = 59; N = 26.

Note: I_t, CP_t, $\text{Std}(S_t)$, $\text{Std}(I_t)$, and LEV_t are as defined earlier. $\hat{X1}_t$ is the first-stage regression estimate of the credit rationing proxy for periods of excess demand, $\hat{X2}_t$ is the estimated credit rationing proxy for periods of excess supply, and $\hat{P}_t$ is the first-stage regression estimate of the prime rate. A discussion of the estimation of the credit rationing proxies and of the prime rate follows.

13.4.3   Loan Volume

The loan volume for the bank is determined by the credit needs of its customers, the rate differentials between loans and other sources of credit, and the severity of commitment rationing. Essentially, once a commitment is made, the bank's only influence over whether the line is used is through variations in the prime rate. A model of loan demand becomes a model of loans outstanding, except for periods of rationing.

Building on previous studies (Goldfeld 1966 and Jaffee 1971), Morrison modeled loan demand as a function of borrowers' asset stocks, with the choice of loan financing instead of direct financing being influenced by the spread between the rate paid on loans and the rates paid on direct forms of financing. In the absence of nonprice rationing, the specific form of the loan volume equation would be:

(13)
$$L_t = b_0 + b_1 K_t + b_2 T_t + b_3 Z_t + b_4[(r_{CP} - P)_t T_t]$$

$$+ b_5[(r_{AAA} - P)_t T_t] - b_6 K_{t-1} - b_7 T_{t-1} - b_8 z_{t-1}$$

$$+ (1 - \lambda)L_{t-1},$$

where

$K_t =$ the fixed investment of borrowers
$T_t =$ gross business sales (a proxy for transactions assets)

$$Z_t = \text{inventory stocks held by borrowers}$$
$$r_{CP} = \text{the commercial paper rate}$$
$$P = \text{the prime rate}$$
$$r_{AAA} = \text{the } AAA \text{ corporate bond rate}$$
$$L_t = \text{loan demand.}$$

In the presence of rationing, the observed quantity of loans may differ from the quantity demanded. A bank cannot ration loans directly except in the case of a line of credit that is completely used. However, the rationing of new commitments may cause customers with unused commitments to seek financing elsewhere or to defer expenditures rather than use up existing commitments. For either case, the loan demand function will overstate actual demand when commitments are being rationed. Letting R_t be the reduction in loan demand due to commitment rationing, the observed quantity of loans outstanding becomes:

$$L_t^r = \begin{cases} L_t & \text{if there is no rationing} \\ L_t - R_t & \text{if there is rationing} \end{cases}$$

It is assumed that R_t is proportional to XI_t (the positive values of the first principal component of the Federal Reserve Board loan survey responses) and ΔCP_t (the change in the volume of commercial paper outstanding). The constant of proportionality is assumed to depend on U_{t-1} (the lagged ratio of commitment usage). Making these substitutions, the equation to be estimated for loan volume prediction becomes:

(14)
$$L_t^r = \begin{cases} L_t & \text{if } X_t \leqq 0 \\ L_t - (a_0 + a_1 U_{t-1})(b_0 X_t + b_1 \Delta CP_t) & \text{if } X_t > 0 \end{cases}$$

13.4.4 Estimation of Loan Volume

The desired specification of the loan volume equation calls for data on the assets (fixed investment, inventory, and transactions assets) of the bank's actual and potential customers. Since these data are not available, it was assumed that the values for the bank's customers were proportional to the aggregate figures. Furthermore, since consistent aggregate series are not available for all variables in the loan volume equation, the equation was estimated in first difference form. An examination of the results for the full model suggested that the lagged dependent variables and the lagged customer asset variables were not contributing to the explanation of loan volume in a significant manner. Consequently, for the estimate that was used in subsequent simulations these terms and the insignificant term for current fixed investment were dropped and the equation was estimated using the Hildreth-Lu (1960) transformation. The resulting equation for forecasting loan volume for the bank is given in table 13.5.

Table 13.5   Forecasting Equation for Loan Volume

$$L_t^r = b_0 + b_2 T_t + b_3 Z_t + b_4[(r_{CP} - \hat{P})_t K_t] + b_5[(r_{AAA} - \hat{P})_t K_t]$$
$$- c_0 X\hat{1}_t - c_1 X\hat{1}_t U_{t-1} - c_2 \Delta CP_t U_{t-1}$$

b_0	b_2	b_3	b_4	b_5	$-c_0$	$-c_1$	$-c_2$
−17.8	1.24	2.74	−.41	−.30	548	−1807	−.12
(−1.2)	(2.6)	(3.1)	(−2.8)	(−1.1)	(5.2)	(−5.2)	(−3.9)

Durbin-Watson = 2.2; standard error = 30; N = 26; ρ = −.67.

13.4.5 The Rationing Variable

Since the first principal component of the response to the Federal Reserve Board loan activity survey is a determinant of loan commitments and loan volumes at the bank, we must forecast this factor to carry out the simulation of the bank's net worth elasticity. The specification used for estimating a predicting equation is

(15) $$\Delta X_t = \lambda[\delta_0 + \delta_1(S_t - Q_{t-1}) - X_{t-1}] ,$$

where

S_t = the supply of commitments during month t
Q_t = the quality of commitments outstanding
during month t.

After substituting for S_t , the resulting forecasting equation for the change in the rationing proxy is as shown in table 13.6.

13.4.6 Loan Interest Rates

The forecasting equations for loan commitments, loan volume, and the rationing variable require a forecast of the prime rate. Furthermore, to calculate the income from the loan portfolio, we need a period-by-period forecast of the yield on the loan portfolio.

In the model we used, the change in the prime rate is determined by a rate of adjustment factor times the difference between the desired prime rate in the current period and the prime rate for the period just prior. The desired prime rate is taken to be a function of the federal funds rate (r_{ft}),

Table 13.6   Forecasting Equation for the Change in the Rationing Proxy

$$\Delta X_t = \lambda[d_0 + d_1 I_t + d_2 \text{Std}(I_t) + d_3(\hat{P}_t - I_t) + d_4 \text{LEV}_t - d_5 Q_{t-1} - X_{t-1}]$$

λd_0	λd_1	λd_2	λd_3	λd_4	$-\lambda d_5$	$-\lambda$	R^2	D-W
−4.85	.15	.63	−1.81	.80	−.004	−.67	.44	1.72
(−.76)	(.40)	(.41)	(−1.9)	(.85)	(−.9)	(−1.5)		

the bank's loan/deposit ratio ($LNDP_t$), and the bank's leverage ratio (LEV_t). The speed of adjustment is assumed to be determined by lagged values of changes in the opportunity rate of interest for the bank (ΔI_t). The resulting forecasting equation for the prime rate is given in table 13.7.[7]

The loan yield will differ from the prime rate because (a) much of the loan portfolio consists of nonprime borrowers; (b) only about half of the loan portfolio floats with the prime rate, and (c) the composition of the portfolio (maturity, percentage of floating loans, etc.) may vary systematically with the level of interest rates. In Morrison (1977) it is shown that under a particular set of assumptions the steady-state relationship for the loan yield may be written as a linear function of lagged values of the prime rate. The estimation was based on this model with control variables added to allow for a different relationship during periods of rising rates. Additionally, the coefficients of the estimated equation were constrained to reflect a priori knowledge regarding the proportion of term loans in the portfolio. The estimation procedure used the Hildreth-Lu transformation for serial correlation.

The equation used for the loan yield forecasts is given in table 13.8.[8]

Table 13.7   **Forecasting Equation for the Prime Rate**

$$\Delta P_t = \lambda[e_0 + e_1 r_{ft} + e_2 LNDP_t + e_3 LEV_t + e_4(r_{ft}\Delta I_t)$$
$$+ e_5(r_{ft}\Delta I_{t-1}) + e_6(r_{ft}\Delta I_{t-2}) - P_{t-1}]$$

λe_0	λe_1	λe_2	λe_3	λe_4	λe_5	λe_6	$-\lambda$	R^2	D-W
.037	.26	−.60	.025	.006	.021	.0005	−.27	.84	1.77
(.19)	(5.64)	(−.57)	(1.13)	(.88)	(3.62)	(.1)	(−5.7)		

Table 13.8   **Forecasting Equation for Loan Yield**

$$Y_t = g_0 + g_1 P_t + g_2 P_{t-1} + g_3 P_{t-2} + g_4 P_{t-3} + g_5(F_t P_t)$$
$$+ g_6(F_t P_{t-1}) + g_7(F_t P_{t-2}) + g_8(F_t P_{t-3})$$

g_0	g_1	g_2	g_3	g_4	g_5	g_6	g_7	g_8
1.48	.43	.29	.08	.1	−.011	.002	.013	−.004
(12.3)	(9.3)	(5.3)	(1.4)		(−1.4)	(.3)	(1.6)	

$R_2 = .89$; Durbin-Watson = 2.3; $\rho = .85$.

7. The estimation was by two-stage least squares because of the presumed simultaneity between the prime rate and other micro variables for the bank. For the subsequent simulations it was necessary to forecast the federal funds rate. A linear regression of the federal funds rate on the three-month risk-free rate was used for these forecasts.

8. Because of the a priori constraints, independent t-statistics are not obtained for g_4 and g_8. F_t is a control variable that is 1 during periods of increasing rates and 0 otherwise.

13.4.7 Demand Deposit Volume

There are three major determinants of demand deposit volume:

1. Compensating balances, usually some percentage of commitments plus some percentage of outstandings (loans).

2. Active balances, for use in meeting a firm's required disbursements (payroll, taxes, etc.).

3. Service balances, used to cover the activity charges associated with determinant 2.

If the different types of deposits were recorded separately, different models could be developed for each type. Compensating balances could be estimated as a function of loans and commitments, with active and service balances depending on transactions volume and the level of interest rates. Unfortunately, no distinction is made on the balance sheet among the different deposit types, so one model will have to suffice for all three. The model we estimated assumes that demand deposit volume is a linear function of commitment volume (Q_t) and loan volume (L_t) with the coefficients of these two factors being dependent on the current prime rate.

The demand deposit forecasting equation is given in table 13.9.

13.4.8 NCD Rate

The final factor that must be forecast for the net worth simulations is the rate paid on purchased funds which in this study was taken as the three-month rate on negotiable certificates of deposit (NCDs). Since the basic rates driving the simulation are the risk-free rates, an attempt was made to find a stable relationship between the three-month risk-free rate and the three-month NCD rate. Owing to serial correlation in the residual of least-squares estimates, the Hildreth-Lu transformation was used. The resulting equation for forecasting the spread between the three-month NCD rate and the three-month risk-free rate $(SPRD_t)$ is given in table 13.10.[9]

13.5 A Model of Net Worth and Net Worth Elasticity

In addition to the problem of predicting future cash flows to the bank's owners, one must also specify a method for calculating the current value

Table 13.9   **Forecasting Equation for Demand Deposit Volume**

$$D_t = h_1 Q_t + h_2 (Q_t P_t) + h_3 L_t + h_4 (L_t P_t)$$

h_1	h_2	h_3	h_4	R^2	D-W
$-.8$	.11	.4	$-.05$	.53	2.2
(-1.9)	(2.0)	(3.2)	(-2.2)		

9. r_t is the three-month risk-free rate.

Table 13.10   **Forecasting Equation for the NCD Rate**

$$\text{SPRD}_t = j_0 + j_1 r_t + j_2 r_t$$

j_0	j_1	j_2	R^2	D-W	ρ
−2.57	.03	.55	.37	1.6	.75
(−2.6)	(.8)	(4.5)			

of those cash flows and for predicting the effects of changes in interest rates on that value. The approach we have taken is based on the following valuation model developed by Rubinstein (1975):[10]

(16)
$$PV = \sum_{t=1}^{\infty} \frac{E(X_t) - [COV(X_t - R_{mt}^{-b})/E(R_{mt}^{-b})]}{R_{Ft}} ,$$

where

PV = the present value of the cash flow stream X_t

R_{Ft} = one plus the future value at time t of \$1 invested today in risk-free bonds

R_{mt} = one plus the future value of \$1 invested today for t periods in the market portfolio

E = the expected value operator

COV = the covariance operator

b = the level of proportional risk aversion.

By making some simplifying assumptions, (16) can be used to derive an interest rate elasticity framework. First, suppose the (t-period spot rate + 1) on risk-free bonds, $R_{Ft}^{1/t}$, is a function of both time and the short rate, that is, $R_{Ft}^{1/t} = R_F(t, r_0)$. One interpretation of this is that the major determinants of shifts in interest rates is the release of new data containing information that affects relative returns. This assumption is consistent with much of existing term-structure theory, which attempts to explain the shape of the yield curve but takes the level (the value of the short rate, for example) as exogenous (see Kane 1975). Next, we will assume that the probability distribution of the random cash flows is a function of time and the t-period 1 + spot rate, that is:

$$\tilde{X}_t = \tilde{X}_1(t, R_F(t, r_0)) = \tilde{X}(t, r_0) .$$

10. The assumptions underlying Rubinstein's valuation equation are: (a) if two securities have the same payoff in all future states, they will have the same current price; (b) investors maximize the expected utility of compensation over their lifetimes, and their utility functions are concave, additive in consumption at each date, and never evidence satiation; (c) financial markets are perfect, competitive, and Pareto-efficient; and (d) there is weak aggregation, and investors evidence constant proportional risk aversion. While these assumptions are restrictive, they lead to a simple, closed-form equation for valuing arbitrary cash flow streams in a multiperiod setting.

Similarly, assume that the compound return on the market (+ 1) is a function of time and the compound return (+ 1) on risky bonds, or

$$E(R_{mt}) = R_1(t, R_{Ft}) = R_2(t, R_F (t, r_0)^t) = E(R_m(t, r_0)).$$

Finally, assume that the covariance between the cash flows generated by the project or security in question and the compound return (+ 1) on the market portfolio raised to the $- b$ power, $COV(X_t, - R_{Mt}^{-b})$, is not a function of interest rates for any t.[11] With these assumptions, we can then rewrite (16) as:

(17)
$$PV = \sum_{i=1}^{\infty} \frac{E(X(t, r_0)) - \dfrac{COV(X_t, - R_{mt}^{-b})}{E(R_m(t, r_0))^{-b}}}{R_F(t, r_0)^t}$$

$$= \sum_{i=1}^{\infty} \frac{N_t}{R_F(t, r_0)^t} .$$

Differentiating with respect to r_0 and dividing by PV to obtain the proportional change gives:

(18)

$$\frac{\dfrac{dPV}{dr_0}}{PV} = \frac{\displaystyle\sum_{t=1}^{\infty} R_F(t, r_0)^{-t} \frac{dN_t}{dr_0} - \sum_{t=1}^{\infty} t \frac{N_t}{R_F(t, r_0)^t} \cdot \frac{\partial R_F(t, r_0)}{\partial r_0} \cdot \frac{1}{R_F(t, r_0')}}{\displaystyle\sum_{t=1}^{\infty} \frac{N_t}{R_F(t, r_0)^t}}$$

where

$$\frac{dN_t}{dr_0} = \frac{d}{dr_0} \left[E(X(t, r_0)) - \frac{COV(X_t, - R_{mt}^{-b})}{E(R_m(t, r_0))^{-b}} \right]$$

(19)
$$\frac{dN_t}{dr_0} = \frac{\partial E(X(t, r_0)}{\partial r_0} + \frac{COV(X_t, - R_{mt}^{-b}) \dfrac{\partial E(R_m(t, r_0)^{-b}}{\partial r_0}}{E(R_{mt}^{-b})^2} .$$

Equation (18) is an analog to the generalized duration measured obtained for bonds. Note, however, that it has not been converted into elasticity terms, but rather gives the proportional change in net worth for a given

---

11. This assumption restricts our analysis to the pure interest rate elasticity of net worth, since it precludes any changes in the riskiness of cash flows that are correlated with changes in the spot rate.

absolute change in the spot rate. The values calculated using equation (18) may be interpreted as the percentage change in net worth for the bank per 100 basis point change in the spot rate. Another difference from the generalized duration measure for bonds is that the proportional change in net worth for the bank accounts for the effects of changes in interest rates on the future cash flows received by the bank's owners.

Given the forecasts of the periodic payout to the bank's owners that may be obtained using the cash flow forecasting equations given in tables 13.4 through 13.10 and a term structure of risk-free rates, one has the basic data for estimating the current net worth of the bank, using equation (17).

13.5.1 Risk Adjustment Estimation

For our estimates the proportional risk aversion factor, b, was taken to be 1 (which implies logarithmic utility). The excess return on the market was estimated as a linear function of the one month risk-free rate. The resulting forecasting equation, based on monthly observations[12] from 1965 to 1975, is given in table 13.11. Finally, to estimate the covariance between the bank's cash flows and the compound market return, it was assumed that (*a*) market returns are serially uncorrelated; (*b*) bank cash flows are uncorrelated with lagged market returns; (*c*) the variability of net interest income is a reasonable proxy for the variability in the net cash flows to the bank's owners; (*d*) the correlation between the net cash flows and the market return is not a function of time or interest rates; and (*e*) the variance of the market return is constant. With these simplifying assumptions, the sample correlation between the bank's net interest income and the inverse of the monthly market returns was estimated for the period 1969–75. The results were:

$$Std(1/r_m) = .06$$

$$Std(X) = 1.96 \text{ million} \qquad N = 69 \text{ months}$$

$$\rho(X, r_m^{-1}) = -.22.$$

Table 13.11   **Excess Market Return (EX_t) vs. the Risk-Free Rate (r_t)**

$$EX_t = a + br_t$$

a	b	N	D-W	Std Error
$-.043$	13	119	1.81	.037
(-2.14)	(2.6)			

---

12. Both excess market return and the risk-free rate are expressed as one-month returns, that is, without conversion to an annually compounded equivalent.

With $Std(X_t)$ and $E(r_{mt})$ permitted to depend on the funding strategy employed and on interest rates, the entire risk adjustment term becomes:

(20)
$$\frac{COV(X_t, -R_m^{-1}{}_t)}{E(R_m^{-1}{}_t)} = \frac{E(R_m^{-1}{}_{t-1}).22(.06)Std(X_t)}{E(R_m^{-1}{}_t)}$$

$$= .0132 \; Std(X_t) \frac{E(R_{m,t-1}^{-1})}{E(R_{m,t}^{-1})} \; .$$

13.5.2 Estimation of Future Spot Rates

McCulloch (1971) described a procedure for estimating the discount function (i.e., the value today of a certain promise to pay $1 at time t for all values of t) from observed prices. With the additions contained in his later article (McCulloch 1975a), this method was adapted for term structure estimation in this study. Once the discount function is obtained by McCulloch's procedure, estimated forward rates for all future periods may be calculated along with the current spot rate.

The estimated forward rates will differ from estimated future spot rates to the extent that the current term structure includes liquidity premiums. A number of studies of the liquidity premium have been made, and, though many of these studies agree that premiums exist, there is considerable disagreement on the details of the liquidity premium structure. Again we have adopted results obtained by McCulloch (1975a) to obtain the mean liquidity premium as a function of the time period for which each premium applies. The resulting estimates of liquidity premiums were subtracted from the forward rate estimates to obtain the estimates of future spot rates period by period.

The procedures just described provide two of the three characteristics of risk-free interest rates needed for the simulations of proportional changes in net worth. The estimated function is used directly in calculating the estimated present value of net worth, as shown in equation (17). The estimated future spot rates are a major determinant of the estimates of future cash flows for the bank. The third aspect of risk-free interest rates needed for the simulations is the response of future spot rates and the discount function to changes in the spot rate. This is obtained from the empirical model of interest rate changes discussed earlier and summarized in equation (7).

13.5.3 Simulation of the Interest Rate Elasticities of Bank Net Worth

The calculation of net worth elasticities for the hypothetical wholesale bank examined in this study begins with the selection of a time at which the present value of net worth and its interest rate sensitivity are to be calculated. A basic interest rate forecast is obtained by the methods pioneered by McCulloch and discussed earlier. The term structure is estimated for the base period, forward rates are calculated, and a liquidity premium estimate is subtracted from each to give estimates of future one-month rates. The future spot rates are used to forecast prime rates, NCD rates, and expected returns on market portfolio. Prime rates are used to calculate the loan yield series.

Macroeconomic variable forecasts are taken from publications of the producer of one of the aggregate macroeconomic forecasting services, again as of the base period.[13] The macro variable forecasts, along with the interest rate forecasts, allow monthly loan volume and commitments to be estimated. With loan volume and commitments forecasts, one can forecast monthly deposit balances. When combined with an assumption about the bank's capital structure, these various forecasts are sufficient to generate cash flow forecasts for the payout stream to the owners of the bank's equity. As noted earlier, the procedure used in this study is to assume that the ratio of total book assets to book equity (capital ratio) is held constant through time.[14] Recalling that the balance sheet of the simplified model of a wholesale bank includes loans and cash as assets and demand deposits, purchased funds, and equity capital liabilities, the forecasts of demand deposit volume are used to forecast cash balances. These cash balances plus the estimated loan volume provide a total asset forecast that, when multiplied by the inverse of the assumed capital ratio, gives an estimate of book equity. Purchased fund balances are then obtained as the difference between book total assets and the sum of demand deposits plus book equity.

In addition to the expected cash flow forecasts for each future time period, the valuation method we have employed requires estimates of the standard deviation of these cash flows. These estimates were obtained by assuming that the growth rate in the cash flow is from a stationary distribution and is serially uncorrelated. The mean growth rate and the variance of the growth rate needed for these estimates are derived from historical patterns in the bank's net interest income. Since those patterns resulted from a capital ratio of about 22, an adjustment is made when other capital ratios are assumed.[15]

The final problem to be solved before making the calculations is choosing a horizon. A horizon of ten years is assumed largely because it

---

13. If no forecasts were published during the base period, the most recent forecasts are assumed to remain in effect. Linear approximations are used if forecasts were other than monthly. When forecasts end before the horizon, the rest of the values are generated by using an average growth rate based on the forecasts that are provided.

14. This assumption has the advantage of centering attention on a major regulatory measure of capital adequacy, but otherwise it is arbitrary and used for computation convenience.

15. Using this approach $Std(X_t)$ increases with t and decreased with the capital ratio. Morrison (1977) also made estimates for $Std(X_t)$ was assumed constant for all t. The differences in results were slight, and only the results using the growth rate assumption are used here.

appears to be an upper limit for accurate forecasts of forward rates. The end-point problem is solved by assuming that the risk-adjusted book equity at the end of ten years is invested in one-month Treasury bills forever.

There is an added complication in calculating the interest-rate sensitivity of net worth, since one is required to calculate the derivative of expected cash flows with respect to the spot rate. This derivative is evaluated by numerical analysis, specifically by the technique of extrapolation to the limit.[16]

13.5.4   Simulation Results

Simulations of the market value of net worth for the hypothetical bank and of the interest rate elasticity of the market net worth are reported for three basis periods, January 1973, January 1974, and May 1975. The estimated yield curves for these three dates are given in table 13.12. The January 1973 curve can be described as mildly upward sloping (173 basis points from $t = 0$ to $t = 10$ years), while the May 1975 curve is sharply upward sloping (330 basis points from $t = 0$ to $t = 10$ years). In contrast, the January 1974 curve has a "hump" that peaks at $t = 5$ months and is slightly downward sloping over most of the rest of its span. These three curves encompass the main term structure shapes that existed during the period for which the bank data are available.

The estimates of market net worth and the interest rate elasticities of net worth for various book capital ratios are given in table 13.13. The market net worth values are the solutions to equation (17) given the previously discussed estimates of the variables in that equation. Clearly, as the ratio of total assets to book equity decreases, the quantity of purchased funds decreases, and the market value accruing to the owners of the equity increases.

Four estimates of the interest rate elasticities (IRE) are given. Since the empirical model of interest rate changes in equation (7) shows the response of future spot rates to changes in the current spot rate to be different for spot rate changes due to changes in the real component as compared with changes in the inflation rate, it is possible to estimate the percentage change in the market value of net worth for a 100 basis point change in the real rate and for a 100 basis point change in the inflation rate. $\overline{IRE}_1$ and $\overline{IRE}_2$ are based on a 100 basis point change in the real component of spot rates and $\overline{IRE}_3$ and $\overline{IRE}_4$ on a 100 basis point change in the inflation rate. For a change in the nominal spot rate that is partly due to real effects and partly due to inflation, a weighted average of the real and inflationary $\overline{IRE}$s would be calculated.[17]

16. The method is explained in detail in most elementary numerical analysis texts (see, for example, Conte 1965, pp. 114–20).

17. We have placed the bar over the symbol for the percentage change in bank net worth per 100 basis point change in interest rates to distinguish this concept from the interest rate elasticities for bonds that were expressed as percentage changes in value for a 1 percent change in one plus the spot interest rate.

Table 13.12		Tax-Adjusted Yield Curve on 1/73, 1/74, and 5/75	
Maturity	1/73	1/74	5/75
0	4.77 ± .16	7.21 ± .23	4.86 ± .58
1 mo	4.89 ± .05	7.23 ± .07	5.10 ± .17
2 mo	5.03 ± .03	7.36 ± .05	5.34 ± .08
3 mo	5.19 ± .02	7.53 ± .03	5.57 ± .06
4 mo	5.32 ± .02	7.62 ± .03	5.80 ± .09
5 mo	5.43 ± .02	7.63 ± .03	6.02 ± .07
6 mo	5.49 ± .02	7.60 ± .03	6.22 ± .07
7 mo	5.53 ± .02	7.54 ± .03	6.39 ± .07
8 mo	5.55 ± .02	7.47 ± .04	6.54 ± .07
9 mo	5.56 ± .03	7.40 ± .04	6.68 ± .06
10 mo	5.58 ± .03	7.34 ± .05	6.80 ± .05
11 mo	5.61 ± .03	7.27 ± .05	6.91 ± .05
12 mo	5.63 ± .03	7.21 ± .05	7.01 ± .05
13 mo	5.66 ± .03	7.16 ± .05	7.10 ± .05
14 mo	5.70 ± .03	7.11 ± .04	7.19 ± .05
15 mo	5.73 ± .03	7.07 ± .04	7.27 ± .05
16 mo	5.76 ± .03	7.03 ± .04	7.35 ± .05
17 mo	5.79 ± .03	6.99 ± .04	7.42 ± .04
18 mo	5.82 ± .03	6.96 ± .04	7.48 ± .04
21 mo	5.91 ± .03	6.89 ± .04	7.65 ± .03
2 yrs	5.97 ± .03	6.86 ± .04	7.78 ± .04
30 mo	6.07 ± .02	6.85 ± .02	7.96 ± .04
3 yrs	6.13 ± .02	6.85 ± .03	8.07 ± .05
4 yrs	6.18 ± .02	6.82 ± .03	8.17 ± .05
5 yrs	6.21 ± .02	6.77 ± .02	8.17 ± .04
6 yrs	6.27 ± .02	6.74 ± .02	8.15 ± .04
7 yrs	6.34 ± .02	6.74 ± .02	8.14 ± .06
8 yrs	6.42 ± .02	6.77 ± .02	8.14 ± .07
9 yrs	6.47 ± .02	6.82 ± .03	8.15 ± .07
10 yrs	6.50 ± .02	6.88 ± .03	8.16 ± .07

Note: All yields are annual internally compounded rates of return. Numbers following the ± signs are standard errors.

The second distinction in $\overline{\text{IRE}}$ estimates involves the separation of income and wealth effects in the equation for the proportional change in net worth (equation 18). The wealth effect results from the existing cash flows being priced by a new discount factor. The income effect involves the pricing of the changes in future cash flows resulting from changes in future spot rates. It has been suggested that in an efficient market, with all the components of risk adjustment correctly specified and measured, there would be no income effect.[18] $\overline{\text{IRE}}_1$ and $\overline{\text{IRE}}_3$ are estimates of the percentage change in net worth including the full income effect, while $\overline{\text{IRE}}_2$ and $\overline{\text{IRE}}_4$ include only the wealth effect. Thus, since the income effect is positive, $\overline{\text{IRE}}_1$ and $\overline{\text{IRE}}_3$ are lower limits on the estimates of the percentage change in net worth, and $\overline{\text{IRE}}_2$ and $\overline{\text{IRE}}_4$ are upper limits on these estimates.

18. This point was first brought to our attention by William Sharpe.

An examination of table 13.13 shows that the estimates of the sensitivity of bank net worth to spot rate changes are all negative. Banks of the sort modeled in this study are made worse off by interest rate increases. However, the magnitude of the estimated net worth losses is quite small, especially in comparison with the elasticity estimates for bonds reported in table 13.3. For example, according to table 13.3 a 100 basis point increase in the May 1975 spot rate would have resulted in a decrease in the net worth of a 10 percent, ten-year coupon bond of between 2.3 and 3.4 percent. From the final section of table 13.13, we can see that the same spot rate change is estimated (at most) to result in a change in the net worth of the hypothetical bank of less than 0.5 percent.

Another point of interest from the table is that the $\overline{IRE}$ estimates for the bank are rather insensitive to whether the source of the spot rate change is real rates or inflation. Again we can contrast this result with the almost 50 percent greater sensitivity to inflation displayed by ten-year bonds in table 13.3.

Table 13.13   Market Values and Interest Rate Elasticities

Book Capital Ratio	Estimated Market Value of Bank Net Worth	IRE Estimates			
		$\overline{IRE}_1$	$\overline{IRE}_2$	$\overline{IRE}_3$	$\overline{IRE}_4$
		January 1973			
30	447.9	−.40	−.44	−.38	−.41
20	468.2	−.40	−.44	−.38	−.42
10	528.9	−.40	−.45	−.40	−.44
2	1,014.8	−.40	−.47	−.44	−.50
		January 1974			
30	464.4	−.23	−.26	−.22	−.25
20	489.5	−.23	−.26	−.22	−.25
10	564.9	−.23	−.27	−.23	−.26
2	1,168.0	−.23	−.28	−.24	−.28
		May 1975			
30	516.9	−.29	−.39	−.29	−.37
20	546.1	−.29	−.39	−.29	−.37
10	633.7	−.30	−.40	−.31	−.39
2	1,134.8	−.32	−.45	−.35	−.45

Note: $\overline{IRE}_1$ ($\overline{IRE}_3$) is the percentage change in bank net worth for a 100 basis point change in the real spot rate (one-month inflation rate) assuming both an income effect and a wealth effect.
$\overline{IRE}_2$ ($\overline{IRE}_4$) is the percentage change in bank net worth for a 100 basis point change in the real spot rate (one-month inflation rate) assuming there is no income effect.
Market values are in units of $1 million.

Both the small magnitude of the estimated net worth elasticities for bank net worth and their insensitivity to the source of spot rate changes can be attributed to the model bank's loan mix, which is predominantly floating rate loans and short-term notes. Even though loan renewals and loan commitments tend to make the effective maturity of loan portfolios longer than their nominal maturities, that they are largely floating rate loans (or equivalently renegotiable on renewal) and are supported to a significant degree by interest-sensitive borrowed funds means that the hypothetical bank is very close to being immunized from nominal interest rate changes.

These conclusions should be tempered somewhat by the realization that the market value estimates are biased upward. The major reason for this bias is that the estimated cash flows do not include noninterest expenses for the hypothetical bank. Including noninterest expenses would have involved arbitrary allocation of actual expense for the bank to the asset and liability categories that were modeled in the hypothetical bank, and we did not attempt this. However, it is clear that including such expenses would have reduced the measured income effect (assuming that noninterest cash flows would tend to increase as spot rates increase) and reduced the market value of the bank's net worth. Both effects would tend to increase the sensitivity of the hypothetical bank's net worth to interest rate changes, but perhaps not much beyond the estimates that assume no income effects (i.e., $\overline{IRE}_2$ and $\overline{IRE}_4$).

Another notable result of the simulations is the insensitivity of the $\overline{IRE}$ estimates to the book capital ratio. As we decrease the book capital ratio, equity capital is substituted for purchased funds to support the bank's assets. Since the asset structure is unchanged in the process, this appears to imply that the absolute values of $\overline{IRE}$ should fall as the book capital ratio decreases. This line of reasoning ignores the effects of reducing the amount of interest-sensitive purchased funds. As rates increase, future income flows are reduced owing to increases in the rates paid on purchased funds, and as the amount of purchased funds decreases this negative income effect on the $\overline{IRE}$ estimates is weakened. However, the relative insensitivity of $\overline{IRE}_2$ and $\overline{IRE}_4$ (i.e., the estimates that do not include income effects) to changes in the assumed book capital ratio suggests that this income effect is not important; on the whole, purchased funds are being purchased at market prices. On the other hand, rate increases result in decreases in the market value of outstanding liabilities and, of course, decreases in the market value of purchased funds result in increases in the bank's net worth. As purchased funds become a less important source of funds for the bank, this positive wealth effect on $\overline{IRE}$ as the book capital ratio decreases completely offsets the associated increase in the market value of the equity.

The level and structure of interest rates is seen to have some effect on $\overline{IRE}$ estimates. For the two upward sloping term structures (January 1973 and May 1975), the difference in the $\overline{IRE}$ estimates is small, especially when we consider only wealth effects. However, the $\overline{IRE}$ estimates for the humped curve of January 1974 are consistently smaller than their counterparts for the other two term structures. This suggests that the level of interest rate risk for banks of the sort described here is smaller when interest rates are anticipated to be at or near a peak than it is when rates are expected to rise. Given the importance of wealth effects in determining the $\overline{IRE}$ estimates, this is a reasonable result.

13.6   Conclusions

In this study we have demonstrated a method for estimating the market value of net worth and the sensitivity of that net worth to changes in interest rates for a hypothetical wholesale bank. The major conclusion reached from our simulations is that interest rate risk is not a very significant proposition for a bank similar to the bank in our model (or for the loan portfolio of a more complex bank with a similar loan mix, where it is assumed that loans are supported by demand deposits and purchased funds). Decreasing the ratio of total assets to book capital was shown to have little effect on the interest rate sensitivity in percentage terms, though of course the smaller asset/capital ratio implies a larger buffer for depositors in absolute terms.

While the results of this study suggest that there is little need for regulatory attention to interest rate risk for loan portfolios of the sort modeled here, it does not follow that the approach discussed here is useless in other aspects of risk evaluation for banks. The results in table 13.3 suggest that the interest rate for municipal bond portfolios may well be an important source of risk for banks. Application of generalized duration concepts to bond portfolios is relatively simple and could readily be incorporated into the examination process. Furthermore, except in money center banks, loan portfolios may be less well immunized from interest rate changes than was true for the simplified bank examined here.

This is clearly the case for real estate portfolios. A companion study to the one reported here was made by Nadauld (1977). He attempted to measure market values of net worth and interest rate elasticities of net worth for savings and loan associations. The results in the Nadauld study suggest that net worth losses from 36 percent to 71 percent (depending on the association considered) are feasible for interest rate changes similar to those that have occurred in the past. Clearly, the real estate portfolio of commercial banks is another potential area where examiners might apply the principles discussed in this study.

14 Calculating the Present Value of an Asset's Uncertain Future Cash Flows

Stephen D. Nadauld

14.1 Introduction

This chapter explains the application of a multiperiod uncertainty model whose theory has been discussed in previous chapters. The model makes it possible to calculate the present value of uncertain future cash flows generated by any asset. The approach may be applied to a wide variety of asset classes. However, this paper uses as an example an actual computer program designed to calculate the present value of a mortgage portfolio and comments on how such a program could be modified and applied to other types of assets.

For illustration, the approach is applied to mortgage portfolio data obtained from the Federal Home Loan Bank Board for eighteen savings and loan associations in the San Francisco standard metropolitan statistical area (SMSA).

The usefulness of this approach to multiperiod valuation under uncertainty stems from its similarity to the common certainty formulation, which may be written as

$$(1) \qquad PV = \frac{x_1}{(1+r)^1} + \frac{x_2}{(1+r)^2} + \dots + \frac{x_T}{(1+r)^T}$$

$$= \sum_{t=1}^{T} \frac{x_t}{(1+r)^t},$$

where

PV = present value of the income stream
x_t = *certain* cash flow received in period t
t = the risk-free interest rate

Stephen D. Nadauld is associate professor and director of the MBA program at Brigham Young University.

315

The equation (1) approach of discounting *certain* future cash flows by a rate that is the same for each period in the future should be familiar to the reader.

A similar simple closed form equation for discounting *uncertain* future cash flows is as follows:

(2)
$$PV = \sum_{t=1}^{\infty} \frac{E(X_t) - \dfrac{COV(X_t, -R_{mt}^{-b})}{E(R_{mt}^{-b})}}{R_{Ft}},$$

where

PV = present value of the income stream
X_t = the uncertain cash flow in period t
R_{mt} = the future value of \$1 invested for t periods in the market portfolio
R_{Ft} = the future value of \$1 invested for t periods in risk-free bonds
b = level of proportional risk aversion which will be assumed equal to one.

Since the theoretical development behind this model has been discussed in previous chapters, attention in this chapter will focus on application of equation (2).

To understand the application, it is important to note both the similarities and the differences of equations (1) and (2). The two formulations are similar in that both have cash inflows in the numerator, and both discount the cash flows for time value in the denominator. However, there are three important differences between the two equations. First, equation (2) uses expected cash inflows in the numerator ($E(X_t)$) instead of the single-point certainty cash flows of equation (1). Second, equation (2) has a term in the numerator that adjusts the expected cash flows for uncertainty. While this term appears complex, it may be thought of as simply a dollar amount that, when subtracted from the expected cash flows, supplies a certainty equivalent in place of the expected value. Third, the denominator in equation (2) employs a full specification of the term structure in place of the single level rate assumption of equation (1).

As suggested by the differences between equations (1) and (2), equation (2) is the conceptual basis for a much richer approach to the valuation of financial instruments. In addition to the obvious allowance for uncertainty, equation (2) allows for the cash flow in each period to be discounted by the risk-free discount factor appropriate to that period and thus uses all the information available in the term structure. Also, the approach is extremely useful in dealing with the question of interest sensitivity, since equation (2) makes provision for specifying differences in the response of short and long rates and allows computation of the resulting effect on valuation.

Because the approach affords important insights into the impact of interest rate changes on valuation, it is important at the outset to specify how interest rate changes must be incorporated in the analysis. Interest rate changes have three separate effects. First, they may affect the expected future cash flows. In the mortgage application, for example, the effect of rate changes on future prepayments and defaults may considerably alter the expected cash flows. Second, a change in interest rates obviously changes the discount factors in the denominator. Third, and potentially the most troublesome, is the effect of interest rate change on the risk premium. The risk premium may be affected because of changes in aggregate risk tolerance or through changes in the systematic riskiness of the asset that reflect a change in the joint distribution of asset cash flows and market returns. To make maximum use of the model, specific equations linking each of these three areas to interest rate change need to be incorporated into the analysis.

The process of applying equation (2) consists of four steps for any type of asset:

1. Determination of the expected cash flows for the asset. This may be easy or more difficult depending on the nature of the instrument and the distribution of the cash flows. Mortgages, for example, require specification of future contract payments and future prepayments, and some estimate of defaults. In addition, time-series or cross-sectional data are necessary to give some insight into the distribution.

2. Specification of the risk-free term structure. There are several ways to determine the necessary term structures: (*a*) present or past term structures may be calculated from risk-free government securities; (*b*) future term structures may be obtained from macro models such as the Penn-MIT model, from systematic adjustments of forward rates obtained from present term structures, or from arbitrary specifications.

3. Calculation of the uncertainty adjustment term. To calculate the uncertainty term, it is necessary to make assumptions that allow the computations to be done in the form

$$U_t = COR(X_t, \frac{1}{r_m}) \; Std(\frac{1}{r_m}) \; Std(X_t) \; E(r_{mt}) \; ,$$

where

$$U_t = \text{uncertainty adjustment for period } t$$
$$COR = \text{coefficient of correlation}$$
$$Std = \text{standard deviation}$$
$$E = \text{expectation operator}$$
$$r_m = \text{the one-period return on the market.}$$

The correlation, standard deviations, and expectation must be calculated from time-series or cross-sectional data obtained for asset cash flows and market returns.

4. Computation of the present value. The respective elements of equation (2) are combined by the computer program into the calculated present value.

The rest of the chapter will be divided into two sections. Section 14.2 will explain the basic calculations in steps 1 through 4 and apply them to the question of valuing a mortgage portfolio, and section 14.3 will demonstrate the computer program operations and give sample inputs and outputs.

14.2 Basic Calculations and Applications

14.2.1 Step 1: Determining the Expected Cash Flows

The cash flows from a mortgage portfolio are made up of regular mortgage payments (including principal plus interest) and of mortgage prepayments. For the typical mortgage, the contract rate and maturity are fixed at the time of origination. The combination of rate and maturity specifies a fixed-payment cash inflow that the mortgage promises to generate at each point in the future. The payment is made up of principal plus interest and follows a prescribed amortization schedule depending on the rate and maturity. Because in the typical situation the promised individual mortgage payments are fixed, the promised portfolio cash inflow is fixed. Therefore in general the value of the portfolio varies inversely with fluctuating market rates.

The difficulty that financial institutions have with fixed-rate instruments is well known, and some mortgage-granting institutions have recently attempted to solve the problem by issuing variable-rate mortgages. A variable-rate mortgage allows the institution to raise (or lower) the mortgage contract rate according to the rise or fall of an index of appropriately constructed market rates. This kind of mortgage has some advantages to the institution, especially in times of rising interest rates. Variable-rate mortgages have become popular with selected institutions and are increasingly being issued, especially by California institutions. However, the trend toward variable-rate mortgages is relatively recent. Since the data gathered for this application are from portfolios formed in 1975 or before, they are made up almost wholly of fixed-rate mortgages; for this reason, the analysis in this paper will concentrate on their behavior.

Two factors substantially complicate the cash inflows generated by a mortgage portfolio. The first of these is the prepayment option. Although the contract payments are spoken of as fixed, the mortgagee has the option to prepay part or all of the principal in conjunction with the refinancing or sale of the mortgaged property. Because of the mobility of many homeowners, the option to prepay is often exercised, and the resulting prepayment cash flows are a substantial factor in analyzing the total cash flows from the mortgage portfolio. The second factor concerns mortgage defaults. The payments spoken of as fixed are fixed only in the sense that they are promises to pay. In the case of default, these promised payments are not realized by the mortgage-granting institution.

Fixed Payments

The basic element of mortgage portfolio cash flows is derived from the fixed mortgage payment. The standard parameters of the fixed-payment, self-amortizing mortgage, are straightforward. The regular monthly payment is determined as a function of the amount of the principal, contract rate, and term to maturity and may be computed by applying the following simple payment algorithm:

$$\text{payment} = \frac{\text{Principal}}{1 - \dfrac{1}{(1 + r)^t}},$$

where

$r =$ contract rate on monthly basis

$t =$ term to maturity in months.

These fixed payment amounts must be adjusted in each period to take into account foreclosures or prepayments that occurred in prior periods. The effect of the foreclosure or prepayment is to eliminate loans from the portfolio and therefore reduce the fixed payment portion of the cash flow.

Prepayments

Since mortgage holders have the option to pay down their mortgage by amounts in excess of the scheduled amortization, mortgage portfolios have cash flows that may in any period substantially exceed the prescribed fixed payments for the period. It is important to consider these prepayments, since their timing may greatly affect the value of the mortgage portfolio. There are several ways to include prepayments in the analysis. It is possible, for example, to use an arbitrary set of prepayment data in the form of annual mortgage termination rates. Termination rates are defined as a fraction of the portfolio balance that would be paid off in any year. The rates may be stated as a fraction of the original portfolio amount (fixed basis) or as a fraction of the remaining portfolio amount (current basis). Typical termination patterns are available from Federal Housing Administration (FHA) data.

Another more interesting alternative is available for dealing with prepayments and illustrates the concept of linking cash flows to interest rate changes. The approach is based on a model developed by Curley and Guttentag (1974). The model explains mortgage termination rates as a function of policy year, maturity, the relationship between the current mortgage contract rate and original contract rate, and the discount points charged in the specified year. Their results are contained in a single equation of the following form:[1]

$$\log TR_t = -.56178 + .90249 \log(P/M) - .10580$$
$$(-32.67) \quad (56.29) \qquad\qquad (15.61)$$
$$(C_t - C) - .02179D_t \, ,$$
$$(5.97)$$

where

$$R^2 = .867$$
TR_t = annual termination rate in year
    t (current basis)
P = policy year
M = maturity
C_t = mortgage rate in year t
D_t = discount in year t
C = original contract rate.

The termination rate in year t (TR_t) is defined as a function of the portfolio balance that will be paid off in that year. The prepayment equation estimates current basis termination rates, but these may easily be converted to fixed basis rates if desired. The prepayment equation was estimated using FHA annual data covering the period 1951–67 for twenty-, twenty-five-, and thirty-year mortgages. The absolute level of both long- and short-term interest rates was generally lower during this period than during subsequent periods to which the equation may be applied. However, the variables in the prepayment equation that would be affected, namely the original contract rate and the mortgage rate in year t, enter the equation in the form of a yield differential. Since relative

---

1. The numerator of the valuation equation requires expected cash flows. The prepayment cash flows are determined by finding the prepayment function (TR) which is the analog of the log TR_t equation. It is clear that $E(x) \neq \exp[E(ln(x))]$; but it can be shown that the difference is small. One approach is to suppose the generalized function $g(x) = a + bx + cx^2 + dx^3 + \ldots$. Both $ln(x)$ and e^x meet this criterion. Expanding $g(x_0 + \varepsilon)$ and taking the expectation ($E[g(x_0 + \varepsilon)]$) gives $x_0 + E(\varepsilon)$ plus the expectation of higher-order term of ε^2, i.e., $E[0(\varepsilon)^2]$. In the same fashion, $g[E(x)] = g[x_0 + E(\varepsilon)] + x_0 + E(\varepsilon)$ plus higher-order terms of the square of the expectation, i.e., $0[E(\varepsilon)]^2$. If ε is small, ε^2 is very small, so $E[0(\varepsilon)^2] \cong 0$; and $E[\varepsilon]$ is small, so $0(E[\varepsilon])^2$ is also $\cong 0$. This leaves the constant and first-order terms the same; and with only small differences in the second-order terms, it appears safe to use the analog of the log TR_t equation in place of the expectation.

differentials or spreads have approximately the same range in subsequent periods as in the estimation period, the prepayment equation should retain its usefulness when applied to more recent data.

The prepayment equation makes it possible to calculate prepayments and add them to the fixed mortgage payments for each period in the future. However, because the equation uses projected future mortgage rates, it is necessary to supply these rates in some fashion. This may be done arbitrarily or, since other numerator and denominator changes are driven by changes in short-term rates, it may be done by attempting to link future mortgage rates to future short-term interest rates.

Mortgage Rates

As an illustration of an attempt to determine the nature of the relationship between mortgage rates and short-term rates, a monthly mortgage rate series from December of 1969 through December of 1975 was analyzed in conjunction with three-month Treasury bill rates over the same period. The most notable feature of these two series is the extremely high level of serial correlation that exists in each. For example, a regression of the spread between the mortgage rate and the Treasury bill rate against the Treasury bill rate yields the following equation:

$$MRT - TBRT = 6.11 - 0.579 \ TBRT + e$$

$$\bar{R}^2 = 0.60 \qquad (.34) \qquad (.056) \qquad D\text{-}W = 0.1398$$

$$N = 73,$$

where

> MRT = mortgage rate,
> TBRT = Treasury bill rate,
> $D\text{-}W$ = Durbin-Watson statistic,
> and the figures in parentheses are standard errors. The resulting t-statistics are significant at the 99 percent level.

The Durbin-Watson statistic of 0.1398 shows the high level of serial correlation in the residuals. This could be anticipated, since the mechanism described by several practitioners for mortgage rate determination is to set the current period mortgage rate equal to the previous period's rate and adjust slightly upward or downward, depending on short-term rate movements. The autocorrelation is strong enough to require second-order autocorrelation correction, which yields the following results:

$$MRT - TBRT = 8.77 - 1.03\,TBRT + 1.65\,RHO1$$
$$(.45)\quad (.03)\qquad\qquad (.085)$$
$$- 0.69\,RHO2$$
$$(0.087)$$
$$D = W = 1.83$$
$$\bar{R}^2 = 0.98$$
$$N = 73.$$

The resulting t-statistics are again significant at the 99 percent level. However, there is a difficulty involved in using the equation above to predict future mortgage rates in the current setting. The prepayment algorithm requires a pattern of future mortgage rates over a thirty-year period in order to compute a thirty-year pattern of prepayments and the resulting pattern of cash flows. When the equation is used to predict beyond five to ten periods, the predicted mortgage rates diverge rapidly from the average relationship that has existed in the past between mortgage rates and short-term Treasury bill rates. This average spread was computed for 1961 through 1975 and was found to be approximately 210 basis points. Using the 210 basis point average spread to predict future mortgage rates was found to produce more reasonable prepayment patterns than those developed from the autocorrelation-corrected equation.

Defaults

While it is possible to relate the question of prepayments and interest rate changes in a fashion sympathetic to the overall approach, the problem of defaults is not so easily handled. The numerator-related concern is essentially a question of how the expected value of cash flows are affected by defaults. Since it is reasonable to assume that short-term interest rates, either directly or as a proxy, may have some influence on default, it should be possible in principle to link rate changes through defaults to the expected cash flows. However, because default data were not available for the portfolios in the data sample, it was not possible to examine the linkage between rate changes and defaults. Nevertheless, the computer program written to do the calculation allows for the possibility of arbitrarily varying the default rates by year for each association. For example, the first year foreclosure rate could be determined as 2 percent, meaning that 2 percent of the book value of the portfolio would be eliminated for all subsequent periods. However, the program allows the user to specify an average percentage of the foreclosed amount to be recovered, and the recovered amount is added to the normal payment and prepayment cash flows for the period. The foreclosed mortgages are subtracted from the portfolio, and future cash flows from both regular payments and prepayments are appropriately reduced.

14.2.2   Step 2: Specification of the Risk-Free Term Structure

As suggested previously, there are several ways to obtain the necessary risk-free interest rates that make up the denominator of equation (2). To examine the question of how changes in rates affect the resulting present values, it is useful to have both present and projected future term structures that can be used to discount the projected cash flows.

Current estimates of the term structure may be obtained from an estimation of the discount function accomplished by a computer program developed by J. Huston McCulloch (1975a). The basic concept is to fit a discount function to the observed prices of United States government Treasury obligations. The program uses as inputs the bid and ask prices of bill, note, and bond quotes for a given date and applies an instrumental variables technique to fit the discount function to a cubic spline (a flexible curve much like a polynomial). An example of the program's output is the point yield for 2 January 1976, which appears in table 14.1. These data are used directly as inputs to the present value calculation. The calculations are done in continuous time so that the denominator at any quarter t

Table 14.1   **"2 January 1976," "Shifted," and "Arbitrary" Term Structures, Quarterly for Five Years**
$$\left(\begin{array}{ll} \text{Shift Parameter Values: RR} = .015 & \text{RR-HAT} = .015 \\ \text{II} = .0377 & \text{II-HAT} = .1477 \end{array}\right)$$

Month/Year	2 January 1976 Term Structure	Shifted Term Structure	Arbitrary Term Structure
3/76	5.27	10.92	11.40
6/76	5.62	9.95	10.70
9/76	5.89	9.20	10.00
12/76	6.13	8.67	9.80
3/77	6.35	8.29	9.50
6/77	6.54	8.02	9.25
9/77	6.69	7.82	9.10
12/77	6.81	7.68	9.00
3/78	6.92	7.58	8.91
6/78	7.02	7.53	8.84
9/78	7.10	7.49	8.78
12/78	7.17	7.47	8.73
3/79	7.24	7.47	8.68
6/79	7.29	7.46	8.63
9/79	7.35	7.48	8.59
12/79	7.39	7.49	8.55
3/80	7.44	7.52	8.52
6/80	7.48	7.54	8.50
9/80	7.52	7.56	8.50
12/80	7.55	7.58	8.50

is $DNOM_t = EXP(K_t * t/4)$, where K_t is the point yield for period t determined as in table 14.1.

The current term structure may be used as a basis for obtaining future term structures through a technique developed by Morrison and described in chapter 13. The function used to shift the term structure takes the following form:

$$(3) \qquad \frac{\Delta r_k}{R_{Fk}} = \frac{\Delta rr_1}{R_{F1}} e^{-.41 - .14k} + \frac{\Delta i_1}{I_1} e^{-.14 - .09k},$$

where

rr_1 = real one-period rate
R_{Fk} = 1 + the k-period risk-free nominal compound rate
i_1 = one-period inflationary expectation
$I_1 = 1 + i_1$
$r_1 = rr_1 + i_1$
Δ = difference operator
k = time period in months.

As an example of how the function works, suppose:

$r_1 = .06$
$rr_1 = .03$
$i_1 = .03$
$\Delta rr_1 = .01$
$\Delta i_1 = .03.$

Since $\Delta r_k = r_k^* - r_k$, it is possible to find a new value of the k-period rate from $r_k^* = (1 + r_k) \frac{.01}{1.06} e^{-.41 - .14k} + \frac{.03}{1.03} e^{-.41 - .09k} - r_k.$

For $k + 4$ and $r_k = .07$,

$$r_k^* = (1.07) \frac{.01}{1.06} e^{-.97} + \frac{.03}{1.03} e^{-.77} + .07$$

$$= .0883.$$

The rate of each period making up the term structure may be shifted in the same manner.

Table 14.1 contains an example of a shifted term structure that has been computed using equation (3) and the shift parameters shown in the table. As an alternative, it is possible to choose arbitrary term structures and employ them as the denominator of equation (2). An example of such an arbitrary designated term structure is also shown in the table. Figure 14.1 shows the shapes of the 2 January 1976, revised, and arbitrary term structures. Each of these three-term structures will subsequently be used to discount mortgage portfolio cash flows. Of course, the method

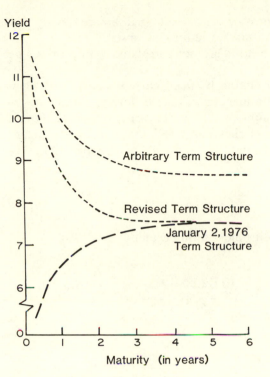

Fig. 14.1   Shapes of the "2 January 1976," "revised," and "arbitrary" term structures.

used for determining the term structure will restrict what may or may not be said concerning the resulting present values.

14.2.3   Step 3: Calculation of the Uncertainty Adjustment Term

As will be recalled from equation (2), the uncertainty adjustment term takes the form:

$$U = - \frac{COV\,(X_t\,,\, -R_{mt}^{-b})}{E(R_{mt}^{-b})},$$

where

$$R_{mt} = \text{the one plus compound return on the}$$
$$\text{market portfolio in period } t$$
$$X_t = \text{cash flow in period } t$$
$$b = \text{the level of proportional risk aversion.}$$

To calculate a value for the term, it is necessary to make the following assumptions:

  1. The level of proportional risk aversion (b) is set equal to one.

2. The returns on the market portfolio are serially uncorrelated, and the variance of market returns is constant.

3. The cash flows are not correlated with previous period's market returns.

4. The correlation between current period cash flows and market returns is not a function of time or interest rates.

These assumptions allow the covariance between the cash flow (X_t) and the product of market returns (R_{mt}) to be factored into the expectation of a product term and the covariance of a simpler term that can be calculated. Thus

$$- COV\,(X_t,\, -R_{mt}^{\,-1}) = E\!\left(\frac{1}{R_{mt-1}}\right) COV\,\left(X_t,\,\frac{1}{r_{mt}}\right).$$

The whole adjustment term becomes

$$\frac{- COV(X_t,\, -R_{mt}^{\,-1})}{E(R_{mt}^{-1})} = \frac{E\!\left(\dfrac{1}{R_{mt-1}}\right) COV\,\left(X_t,\,\dfrac{1}{r_{mt}}\right)}{E\!\left(\dfrac{1}{R_{mt}}\right)}$$

$$= \frac{COV\!\left(X_t,\,\dfrac{1}{r_{mt}}\right)}{E\!\left(\dfrac{1}{r_{mt}}\right)}$$

$$\text{(4)} \qquad = E(r_{mt})\, COR\,\left(X_t,\,\frac{1}{r_{mt}}\right) Std\,(X_t)\, Std\!\left(\frac{1}{r_{mt}}\right).$$

As suggested previously, the risk premium may be affected either through changes in aggregate risk tolerance or through changes in the joint distribution of mortgage cash flows and market returns. Setting $b = -1$ is theoretically justified (see Hakansson 1971c, Rubinstein 1973b), and in this context it essentially means that interest rate changes are assumed not to affect the risk premium through any influence on aggregate risk tolerance.

The second effect, namely the impact of interest rate change on the joint distribution of portfolio cash flows and market returns, can be seen quite clearly from equation (4). Equation (4) contains terms for the mean and standard deviation of the reciprocal of market returns, the standard deviation of cash flows, and the correlation between the cash flows and the reciprocal of market returns. Fortunately, it is possible to say something about how expected market returns vary with short-term interest rates, as will be shown subsequently.

It is also possible that interest rate changes affect the correlation of cash flows with market returns or the standard deviation of cash flows. For example, in the case where investor expectations concerning interest rates influence the distribution of cash flows through defaults, both the correlation and the standard deviation of cash flows would be affected. To measure the effect requires cross-sectional data, including a number of observations of portfolio cash flows at each of several interest rates. Because these data are not available, and since it is still useful to calculate the correlation coefficient, it is necessary to assume that the correlation is not a function of interest rates, and it can then be calculated from the available time-series observations. For the same reason, the standard deviations of both the cash flows ($Std[X_t]$) and the reciprocal of market returns ($Std\left[\dfrac{1}{r_{mt}}\right]$) are assumed to be invariant with respect to time and interest rates. It is useful to note that the data used to calculate both the correlations and standard deviations of cash flows are actual savings and loan mortgage portfolio data, which include the effect of defaults, and therefore the correlations and standard deviations may be thought of as including average default characteristics.

Thus, under the stated assumptions, interest rate changes do influence the risk premium, but only through an effect on the expected market return. It is difficult to estimate the size or nature of the bias that may be introduced by the assumptions above. When risk premiums are stated in terms of yield differentials, the suspicion is that they exhibit sizable changes. For example, the yield spread between long-term government bonds and mortgage rates ranged from 145 to 375 basis points over the time period studied. However, it is important to note that a "yield" calculation assumes that interest rates are level through time and that contract rates or coupon rates represent certain cash flows. Therefore, any adjustments in expected cash flows, in the term structure, or in strict risk premium changes are thrown together into the reported "yield." Since the analysis above does incorporate interest rate changes into the term structure, the expected cash flows, and the risk premium, it is difficult to estimate how much of the difference in observed yield spreads may be unaccounted for.

To incorporate the uncertainty adjustment term in the analysis, we must estimate values for each of the four terms of equation (4). Consider first the term $E(r_{mt})$, which is the expected one plus return on the market portfolio. In this application the return is assumed to be a function of the level of risk-free interest rates. Since the uncertainty adjustment is done quarterly, the appropriate relationship is between the quarterly return on the market and the three-month Treasury bill yield. This relationship was estimated for the twenty-five quarters from 1969-IV to 1975-IV. Table 14.2 gives the results:

Table 14.2   Excess Market Return (r_x) versus the Risk-Free Rate (r_t)

$$r_x = .140 - 3.19\, r_t \quad \text{Durbin-Watson} = 1.83$$
$$(1.99)\ (2.79) \qquad \text{Standard error} = .084$$
$$\text{N} = 25$$

Figures in parentheses are t-statistics.

Since $r_x = r_m - r_t$, the return on the market portfolio in any period can be determined from the risk-free rate for the period in the form:

$$\hat{r}_{mt} = .14 - 2.19\hat{r}_{ft}\ .$$

One way of obtaining a series of future three-month spot rates needed as the independent variable is to obtain from the term structure the liquidity-adjusted three-month-forward rates. (Assuming that the liquidity-adjusted three-month-forward rates are unbiased projection of future three-month spot rates.) These forward rates can be computed from the term structure by using the relationship

$$_e(r_t)(1/4)_e{}^{(k_t)(1/4)} \qquad = \qquad \frac{_e(k_{t+1})(t+1)}{4}\ ,$$

which, when solved for r_t, gives

$$r_t = 4\ \ln^e \frac{(k_t+1)\left(\dfrac{t+1}{4}\right)}{_e(k_t)(t/4)}\ ,$$

where

$$r_t = \text{rate on three-month loan to begin at time } t$$
$$k_t = \text{point yield on a risk-free security of maturity } t.$$

Before the calculated forward rate (r_t) can be used as a spot rate projection, it must be adjusted by subtracting off a liquidity premium. The three-month liquidity premiums estimated by McCulloch (1975b) are shown in table 14.3.

Calculation of the correlation coefficient, $COR\left(x, \dfrac{1}{r_m}\right)$, requires cash flow data from the mortgage portfolio and a corresponding series of market returns. For this application, the data employed were six years of quarterly cash flows from a savings and loan association mortgage portfolio and market return data for the same period from the Center for Research in Security Prices (CRSP) tapes. Since the mortgage portfolio cash flows were separated into interest and principal payments, three separate correlation coefficients were calculated: ρ_1 is the correlation between the interest payments and the reciprocal of market returns, ρ_2 is

Table 14.3   **Estimates of Mean Liquidity Premium $p(m_1, m_2)$**
                       (Standard Errors in Parentheses)

m_1	$m_2 = 3$ Months	m_1	$m_2 = 3$ Months
1 month	0.09 (0.01)	2 years	0.22 (0.06)
2 months	0.14 (0.02)	3 years	0.22 (0.06)
3 months	0.17 (0.03)	5 years	0.22 (0.06)
6 months	0.21 (0.05)	10 years	0.22 (0.06)
9 months	0.22 (0.06)	20 years	0.22 (0.06)
1 year	0.22 (0.06)	30 years	0.22 (0.06)

Source: J. Huston McCulloch, "An Estimate of the Liquidity Premium" (dissertation submitted to Department of Economics, University of Chicago, June 1973), p. 57.
Note: Table 14.3 gives the premium on an m_2 maturity loan entered into m_1 years into the future.

the correlation between principal payments and the reciprocal of market returns, and ρ_3 is the correlation between the combined cash flows and the reciprocal of market returns. Table 14.4 shows the results of the calculations for a typical savings association's mortgage portfolio.

When examining the results, one should note that the sign of the uncertainty adjustment term in equation (4) is positive. This may seem counterintuitive, since the usual notion is to subtract from the expected cash flow a term that reflects the undesirability of highly correlated cash flows. However, because the correlation calculated here is between a cash flow and the reciprocal of the market return, the signs will be opposite those normally expected. Since the sign of the correlation may be either positive or negative, the sign of the whole adjustment term may be either positive or negative. Thus the sign of the correlation coefficient determines whether the mortgage portfolio's value is increased or decreased when held in a portfolio with other assets. For the example above, the combined cash flows have a positive correlation with the reciprocal of market returns (meaning the correlation between cash flows and regular market returns would be negative), and therefore the value of the mortgages is increased when held in conjunction with the market portfolio.

Table 14.4   **Correlations between the Reciprocal of Market Returns**
                       and Mortgage Portfolio Cash Flows

ρ_1	ρ_2	ρ_3
$-.22$	.52	.45

Correlation coefficients greater than 0.36 are significant

at the 90 percent level for $\dfrac{\rho^2}{k-1} \cdot \dfrac{n-k}{1-\rho^2} \sim F(1,20)$.

To complete the risk adjustment term, it is necessary to calculate the standard deviation of both the reciprocal of market returns and the portfolio cash flows. From the CRSP data, the standard deviation of the reciprocal of the one-plus market return was computed to be 0.0882 for the sample time period. For the portfolio cash flows, the quarterly standard deviation was calculated to be $1,708.

It should be noted that for cash flows that are serially uncorrelated and have a growth rate with a stationary mean, the standard deviation can be computed as:

$$Std(X_t) = X_0 \left[(\sigma_g^2 + \mu_y^2)^t \right]^{\frac{1}{2}},$$

where

X_t = cash flow at time t
g = 1 + rate of growth of cash flows
σ = standard deviation of the growth rate
μ = mean of the growth rate.

However, the cash flows from a mortgage portfolio do not fit this pattern because they do not grow over time. Since regular payments are fixed, any variation in the cash flows results from variation in the prepayment or foreclosure rates. It is generally assumed that, as a portfolio ages, the absolute number of foreclosures and prepayments decreases. Consequently, the standard deviation of cash flows also ought to decrease with time. However, because analysis of how the standard deviation of cash flows behaves as a function of foreclosure rates, prepayments, and time was not possible, the program assumes for this application that the standard deviation is constant over time.

14.2.4   Step 4: Calculation of the Present Value

Calculation of the present value requires that each of the previously described steps can be combined in the appropriate relationship according to equation (2). The computer program developed to do the calculations performs essentially five operations; four operations are related to the numerator, and one is related to the denominator. These operations are discussed relative to the mortgage portfolio application and may need to be altered slightly for use in other contexts. They are essentially a review of steps 1 through 3.

Certainty Equivalences

With respect to the numerator, the program first takes the individual mortgage data for each mortgage in the portfolio and calculates the future fixed monthly payments. Second, it calculates a series of future mortgage rates based on a specified term structure and uses them in conjunction with the prepayment algorithm to calculate the dollar amount of prepayments in each period. The program then applies an arbitrarily determined set of foreclosure rates to the portfolio. The foreclosure rates can be varied at will but are not included as a function of any other endogenous or exogenous parameters. At this point the program combines the fixed payments, prepayments, and foreclosures for each loan into a specified quarterly cash flow for the entire portfolio. As a fourth step, the parameters of the uncertainty adjustment term are computed and added to or subtracted from the expected cash flow for each period.

Discounts

The denominator calculation consists of taking the series of forward rates describing the term structure and forming the appropriate discount factor for each period. The discounted, uncertainty-adjusted cash flows are summed over the total number of periods, and the sum is the resulting present value.

Tables 14.5 and 14.6 show the results of applying the approach to eighteen San Francisco SMSA savings and loan association portfolios. The results in table 14.5 have been calculated assuming uncertainty, no

Table 14.5   **Value of Mortgage Portfolios under Uncertainty: No Foreclosures–Revised Term Structure**

Asso-ciation	Book Value	Present Value 2 January 1976 Term Structure	% Present Value Exceeds Book Value	Present Value Revised Term Structure	% Change in Present Value
1	$ 759,921	$ 800,833	5.4	$ 795,506	−0.67
2	129,936	135,400	4.2	134,493	−0.67
3	685,939	720,440	5.0	715,673	−0.66
4	155,617	164,576	5.8	163,483	−0.66
5	424,979	443,282	4.3	440,346	−0.66
6	1,213,133	1,282,471	5.7	1,274,043	−0.66
7	333,094	354,720	6.5	352,385	−0.66
8	109,255	115,396	5.6	114,635	−0.66
9	457,858	483,613	5.6	480,400	−0.66
10	80,478	85,171	5.8	84,602	−0.67
11	155,200	163,823	5.6	162,731	−0.67
12	133,800	140,774	5.2	139,841	−0.66
13	50,124	53,656	7.0	53,302	−0.66
14	1,237,126	1,296,441	4.8	1,287,847	−0.66
15	26,851	27,674	3.1	27,488	−0.67
16	26,215	27,768	5.9	27,583	−0.66
17	38,210	40,253	5.3	39,985	−0.67
18	24,139	25,698	6.5	25,526	−0.67

foreclosures, and the term structure and revision discussed in step 2. Note that the portfolio values as of 2 January 1976 exceeded the book values in every case. This is because the rates represented by the 2 January 1976 term structure were lower than the average mortgage portfolio contract rates. Note also that, even when the portfolio cash flows were valued using the revised downward sloping term structure, the present values remained above book value. This occurred because the portfolio cash flows are received over a very long period of time; and, even though the term structure was shifted upward, the nature of the shift was such as to leave long-term rates relatively unchanged.

Table 14.6 shows the effect of discounting the expected mortgage cash flows by the arbitrarily designated term structure described previously. As seen most clearly from figure 14.1, the main difference between the revised and arbitrary term structures is that the arbitrary term structure exhibits higher long-term rates. Discounting by this term structure decreases the mortgage portfolio values by more than 6 percent in every case.

14.3   Program Operation and Sample Inputs and Outputs

This section contains more specific information and description concerning the computer program discussed previously. The first part of the section describes the real time program requests and the nature of the inputs requested. The second part contains a sample of the program output.

The program is currently set to run on a Dec 10 computer system; however, only slight modifications of certain control statements would be required to make it compatible with similar time-shared systems. The input steps correspond with the previous discussion on projecting cash flows, adjusting for uncertainty, and so forth. Table 14.7 contains a sample of the program statements and inputs and should be referred to in conjunction with the description of program steps.

After logging in and receiving the prompt character, the user types RUN FLO, and the computer responds with the first input requested.

14.3.1   Projecting Cash Flows

Items 1–12 allow for the calculation of cash flows for a savings and loan mortgage portfolio. These items could be modified to accept coupon bond data or any other data representing cash flows from financial instruments.

1. ENTER THE SAVINGS & LOAN DOCKET NO. AND THE NUMBER OF LOANS
The user must input two numbers separated by a comma. The first number is simply a number that identifies the run. This number will appear in the heading of the output. The second number indicates how

Table 14.6   **Value of Mortgage Portfolios under Uncertainty: No Foreclosures–Arbitrary Term Structure**

Asso- ciation	Book Value	Present Value 2 January 1976 Term Structure	Present Value Arbitrary Term Structure	% Change in Present Value
1	$ 759,921	$ 800,833	$ 749,391	−6.42
2	129,936	135,400	126,777	−6.37
3	685,939	720,440	673,916	−6.46
4	155,617	164,576	154,015	−6.42
5	424,979	443,282	414,687	−6.45
6	1,213,133	1,282,471	1,199,008	−6.51
7	333,094	354,700	331,642	−6.51
8	109,255	115,396	107,923	−6.48
9	457,858	483,613	452,558	−6.42
10	80,478	85,171	79,738	−6.38
11	155,200	163,823	153,388	−6.37
12	133,800	140,774	131,672	−6.47
13	50,124	53,656	50,178	−6.48
14	1,237,136	1,296,441	1,213,063	−6.43
15	26,851	27,674	25,917	−6.35
16	26,215	27,768	25,986	−6.42
17	38,209	40,253	37,685	−6.38
18	24,139	25,698	24,060	−6.37

many separate loans will be entered for analysis. After the second number, the user enters a carriage return that tells the computer to go to the next step.

2. WHEN DO YOU WANT THE CASH FLOWS TO START PRINTING?
User enters a two-digit number (e.g., 76) that specifies the first year the output will begin to appear.

3. ARE THE LOAN DATA ON DISK?
If the user inputs "Y," meaning yes, the computer responds with statement 4. If the user inputs "N," the computer responds with statement 3A.

3A. WHAT WOULD YOU LIKE TO CALL THE FILE?
The user inputs a file name to which the loan data will be assigned.

3B. ENTER 1—THE LOAN AMOUNT
           2—THE YEAR LOAN HAD THAT AMOUNT
           3—THE CONTRACT RATE
           4—THE NUMBER OF MONTHS LEFT TO MATURITY
           5—THE AGE (IN MONTHS) OF LOAN

4. WHAT FILE ARE THEY IN?
The response to this statement must be the name of a data file in which the loan data have previously been put. Loan data must include for each loan the four items described in 3B.

Table 14.7   Sample Program Statements and Inputs

.RUN FLO

ENTER THE SAVINGS & LOAN DOCKET NO. AND THE # OF LOANS
2.6

WHEN DO YOU WANT THE CASH FLOWS TO START PRINTING?
76

ARE THE LOAN DATA ON DISK?
Y

WHAT FILE ARE THEY IN?
LOAN.A2

ARE THE PREPAYMENT DATA ON "DISK", TO BE "HAND" ENTERED, OR TO BE "CALCULATED"?
C

DO YOU WANT THEM CALCULATED FROM "ARBITRARY" MORTGAGE RATES, OR THE "TERM" STRUCTURE DETERMINED MORTGAGE RATES?
T

YOU NEED 5. PAST MORTGAGE RATES AND DISCOUNT POINTS. WHAT FILE ARE THEY IN?
MORT.PST

WHAT FILE ARE THE LIQUIDITY PREMIUMS IN?
L.DT

WHAT SPREAD DO YOU PROJECT FOR THE MORTGAGE RATE OVER THE TREASURY BILL RATE? (I.E.
0.021)
.021

WHERE ARE THE EXPECTED FORECLOSURE RATES FOUND?
FORC.RAT

WHAT PERCENTAGE OF FORECLOSURES DO YOU EXPECT TO RECOVER?
100

HOW MANY MONTHS INTEREST WILL BE CHARGED FOR THE PREPAYMENT PENALTY (ENTER 100 FOR THE FHLMC METHOD)?
0

WHERE ARE THE K'S FOUND?
K.DT

DO YOU WANT TO ARBITRARILY SHIFT THE TERM STRUCTURE?
N

ENTER RR, RR-HAT, II, AND II-HAT
.015,.015,.0377,.1477

DO YOU WISH TO ADJUST FOR UNCERTAINTY?
Y

ENTER 1—THE CORRELATION BETWEEN CASH FLOWS AND RETURN ON THE MARKET,
        2—THE MEAN OF (1+ THE GROWTH RATE OF THE CASH FLOWS),
        3—THE STANDARD DEVIATION
.5,0,2000

DO YOU WANT THE MONTHLY CASH FLOWS PRINTED OUT?
N

DO YOU WANT DETAILED PREPAYMENTS, ETC.?
N

STOP

END OF EXECUTION
CPU TIME: 7.86 ELAPSED TIME: 1:28.45
EXIT

---

5. ARE THE PREPAYMENT DATA ON "DISK" TO BE "HAND" ENTERED OR TO BE "CALCULATED"?

The user may respond with "D," "H," or "C."

A "D" response means that the user has previously placed in a disk file the fraction of mortgages in the specified year that will be terminated. A typical data file would contain thirty decimal fractions similar to those that appear on the output for each loan under "has the following prepayment experience."

An "H" response means the user is prepared to input the decimal fractions at the terminal one at a time separated by commas.

A "C" response means the user wishes the computer to calculate the prepayment fractions based on the algorithm described in the text. The calculated fractions are printed out for each loan on the output. A "C" response involves statement 6.

6. DO YOU WANT THEM CALCULATED FROM "ARBITRARY MORTGAGE RATES" OR THE TERM STRUCTURE DETERMINED MORTGAGE RATES?

The user may respond with an "A" or a "T." The "A" response means the user wants to specify a set of future annual mortgage rates that will be used in the prepayment algorithm to calculate the prepayment fractions. This allows the user to uncouple the prepayment fractions from the term structure and have them calculated from arbitrarily determined future mortgage rates. After an "A" response, the computer will come back and ask for a file name in which the future mortgage rates have been stored. The "T" response instructs the computer to calculate the forward rates from the term structure and use the forward rates to calculate the future mortgage rates that are to be used to determine the prepayment fractions.

7. YOU NEED X PAST MORTGAGE RATES AND DISCOUNT POINTS. WHAT FILE ARE THEY IN?

The program has been written so that prepayment fractions would be applied to loans that were closed in previous years. To calculate the prepayment experience, the computer uses the prepayment algorithm and requires as inputs the past mortgage rates and discount points. These need to be placed in a data file.

8. WHAT FILE ARE THE LIQUIDITY PREMIUMS IN?

The user responds with the file name. The file may specify the McColloch liquidity premium or any arbitrarily chosen set.

9. WHAT SPREAD DO YOU PROJECT FOR THE MORTGAGE RATE OVER THE TREASURY BILL RATE? (I.E. 0.021)

The user enters a decimal fraction. For example, the 0.021 adds 2.1 percent to an 8.0 percent forward rate to give a 10.1 percent mortgage rate.

10. WHERE ARE THE EXPECTED FORECLOSURE RATES FOUND?

The user enters a file name. See, for example, FORC.RAT.

11. WHAT PERCENTAGE OF FORECLOSURES DO YOU EXPECT TO RECOVER?
The user enters a number such as 50 (50 percent) or 100 (100 percent), that specifies the percentage of the value of foreclosed property that will be realized.

12. HOW MANY MONTHS INTEREST WILL BE CHARGED FOR THE PREPAYMENT PENALTY (ENTER 100 FOR THE FHLMC METHOD)?
User enters a number like 6 (6 months) or 0 (no months interest penalty).

14.3.2   Specification of the Risk-Free Term Structure

Items 13–15 relate to the development of discount factors that make up the denominator of equation (2).

13. WHERE ARE THE K'S FOUND?
User enters a file name. See for example K.DT. The Ks are the quarterly rates (on annual basis) obtained from the McColloch program that specify the term structure.

14. DO YOU WANT TO ARBITRARILY SHIFT THE TERM STRUCTURE?
User responds with "Y" or "N." A "Y" response means the user does not wish to have the term structure shifted by using the computational algorithm but prefers to arbitrarily designate a new shifted term structure. The computer requests the file name of the shifted term structure.

An "N" response means the user wishes to use the algorithm for shifting the term structure, and the computer responds with statement 15.

15. ENTER RR, RR-HAT, II, AND II-HAT
The user enters four decimals separated by commas. RR and II are respectively the real rate and rate of inflation components that make up the nominal short term (three-month)rate. RR-HAT and II-HAT are the real and inflationary rate components that are projected to make up the short-term nominal rate in the shifted term structure.

14.3.3   The Uncertainty-Adjustment Term

Items 16 and 17 allow for the computation of the uncertainty-adjustment term as previously described.

16. DO YOU WISH TO ADJUST FOR UNCERTAINTY?
User enters "Y" or "N." An "N" response sets the uncertainty-adjustment term at zero. If the user responds in the affirmative, the computer proceeds to statement 17.

17. ENTER 1—THE CORRELATION BETWEEN CASH FLOWS AND RETURN ON THE MARKET
   2—THE MEAN OF (1 + THE GROWTH RATE OF THE CASH FLOWS)
   3—THE STANDARD DEVIATION
Two separate versions of the uncertainty-adjustment term are available in the program. Both use the correlation coefficient, which is entered as the first input. The first version for uncertainty adjustment uses the mean and standard deviation of the 1 + growth rates of cash flows. These data

would be entered, for example, as $\mu = 1.05$, $\sigma = .06$. The second version of uncertainty adjustment uses only the standard deviation of the cash flows themselves, in which case the mean is entered as zero and the standard deviation is entered as a whole number.

14.3.4   Calculation of the Present Value

In addition to the present value, which is automatically provided by the program, it is possible to specify more detailed output such as that described by items 18 and 19.

18. DO YOU WANT THE MONTHLY CASH FLOWS PRINTED OUT?

This option allows the user to obtain cash flow figures by month for the whole portfolio for interest, principal, principal repayments, and total cash flow.

19. DO YOU WANT DETAILED PREPAYMENTS, ETC?

An affirmative response for this option gives the user a detailed printout of cash flows by month for each individual loan in the portfolio.

14.3.5   Sample Output

An example of the abbreviated program output appears as table 14.8. The more detailed outputs are much longer, and therefore examples have not been included. The output first lists the assumptions that have been used in the particular run called for. Since many of the data files are extensive, only the file names are referred to in the assumptions. The output then details each of the loans in the portfolio and prints the termination fractions that are assumed for the loan prepayments. The program then prints a present value and book value based on the initially specified term structure. The output then presents a second present value calculation, both of which are based on the revised or arbitrary term structure as specified. The percentage change in present value is calculated as the concluding data item.

**Table 14.8   Sample Output: Cash Flows for Savings and Loan Docket
Number 2**

THESE CASH FLOWS ASSUME:

1— 0.00% LATE PAYMENTS
2—100.0% RECOVERY OF FORECLOSURES
3— 0 MONTHS PREPAYMENT PENALTY
4—THE FOLLOWING FORECLOSURE EXPERIENCE

0.0200	0.0200	0.0200	0.0200	0.0200	0.0200	0.0200	0.0200	0.0200	0.0200
0.0200	0.0200	0.0200	0.0200	0.0200	0.0200	0.0200	0.0200	0.0200	0.0200
0.0200	0.0200	0.0200	0.0200	0.0200	0.0200	0.0200	0.0200	0.0200	0.0200
0.0200	0.0200	0.0200	0.0200	0.0200	0.0200	0.0200	0.0200	0.0200	0.0200

5—PREPAYMENTS WERE TERM STRUCTURE DETERMINED USING
FILE MORT.PST FOR PAST MORTGAGE RATES,
FILE L.DT FOR LIQUIDITY PREMIUMS,
AND A SPREAD OF 0.0210

6—TERM STRUCTURE SPECIFIED FROM FILE K.DT

7—SHIFTED TERM STRUCTURE USING PARAMETERS
RR = 0.0150 RR-HAT = 0.0150 II = 0.0377 II-HAT = 0.1477

8—UNCERTAINTY ADJUSTMENT ASSUMING
RHO = 0.500 MU = 0.000 SIGMA = 2000.000

LOAN # 1, AS OF '71 HAS A BALANCE OF 12898. AT A RATE OF .088
IT HAS 360 MONTHS LEFT, AND HAS BEEN ON THE BOOKS 0 MONTHS
AND HAS THE FOLLOWING PREPAYMENT EXPERIENCE

0.0128	0.0239	0.0344	0.0444	0.0544	0.0643	0.0737	0.0830	0.0923	0.1015
0.1107	0.1198	0.1288	0.1377	0.1465	0.1553	0.1640	0.1727	0.1814	0.1899
0.1985	0.2070	0.2155	0.2239	0.2323	0.2407	0.2490	0.2573	0.2656	0.2739

LOAN # 2, AS OF '72 HAS A BALANCE OF 28722. AT A RATE OF .077
IT HAS 360 MONTHS LEFT, AND HAS BEEN ON THE BOOKS 0 MONTHS
AND HAS THE FOLLOWING PREPAYMENT EXPERIENCE

0.0127	0.0238	0.0342	0.0443	0.0544	0.0639	0.0734	0.0828	0.0920	0.1013
0.1104	0.1194	0.1284	0.1373	0.1461	0.1549	0.1636	0.1722	0.1808	0.1894
0.1979	0.2064	0.2149	0.2233	0.2317	0.2400	0.2483	0.2566	0.2649	0.2731

LOAN # 3, AS OF '73 HAS A BALANCE OF 26850. AT A RATE OF .074
IT HAS 360 MONTHS LEFT, AND HAS BEEN ON THE BOOKS 0 MONTHS
AND HAS THE FOLLOWING PREPAYMENT EXPERIENCE

0.0127	0.0237	0.0342	0.0444	0.0542	0.0638	0.0733	0.0827	0.0920	0.1013
0.1104	0.1194	0.1283	0.1372	0.1460	0.1548	0.1635	0.1721	0.1807	0.1893
0.1978	0.2063	0.2147	0.2231	0.2315	0.2399	0.2482	0.2564	0.2647	0.2729

LOAN # 4, AS OF '74 HAS A BALANCE OF 18275. AT A RATE OF .081
IT HAS 360 MONTHS LEFT, AND HAS BEEN ON THE BOOKS 0 MONTHS
AND HAS THE FOLLOWING PREPAYMENT EXPERIENCE

0.0127	0.0237	0.0343	0.0444	0.0542	0.0639	0.0734	0.0829	0.0922	0.1014
0.1105	0.1196	0.1285	0.1374	0.1462	0.1550	0.1637	0.1724	0.1810	0.1896
0.1981	0.2066	0.2151	0.2235	0.2319	0.2402	0.2486	0.2569	0.2651	0.2734

LOAN # 5, AS OF '75 HAS A BALANCE OF 20806. AT A RATE OF .094
IT HAS 360 MONTHS LEFT, AND HAS BEEN ON THE BOOKS 0 MONTHS
AND HAS THE FOLLOWING PREPAYMENT EXPERIENCE

0.0127	0.0239	0.0343	0.0445	0.0544	0.0641	0.0737	0.0832	0.0925	0.1018
0.1109	0.1200	0.1290	0.1379	0.1467	0.1555	0.1643	0.1730	0.1816	0.1902
0.1988	0.2073	0.2158	0.2242	0.2327	0.2410	0.2494	0.2577	0.2660	0.2743

Table 14.8 (continued)

LOAN # 6, AS OF '76 HAS A BALANCE OF 31368. AT A RATE OF .095
IT HAS 360 MONTHS LEFT, AND HAS BEEN ON THE BOOKS 0 MONTHS
AND HAS THE FOLLOWING PREPAYMENT EXPERIENCE

0.0128	0.0238	0.0343	0.0445	0.0544	0.0641	0.0738	0.0832	0.0925	0.1018
0.1109	0.1200	0.1290	0.1379	0.1467	0.1556	0.1643	0.1730	0.1816	0.1903
0.1988	0.2073	0.2158	0.2243	0.2327	0.2411	0.2494	0.2578	0.2661	0.2743

PRESENT VALUE AS OF '76 =   133730.570
BOOK VALUE AS OF '76 =   122949.230

LOAN # 1, AS OF '71 HAS A BALANCE OF 12898. AT A RATE OF .088
IT HAS 360 MONTHS LEFT, AND HAS BEEN ON THE BOOKS 0 MONTHS
AND HAS THE FOLLOWING PREPAYMENT EXPERIENCE

0.0128	0.0239	0.0344	0.0444	0.0544	0.0639	0.0738	0.0832	0.0924	0.1015
0.1107	0.1198	0.1288	0.1377	0.1465	0.1553	0.1640	0.1727	0.1814	0.1899
0.1985	0.2070	0.2155	0.2239	0.2323	0.2407	0.2490	0.2573	0.2656	0.2739

LOAN # 2, AS OF '72 HAS A BALANCE OF 28722. AT A RATE OF .077
IT HAS 360 MONTHS LEFT, AND HAS BEEN ON THE BOOKS 0 MONTHS
AND HAS THE FOLLOWING PREPAYMENT EXPERIENCE

0.0127	0.0238	0.0342	0.0443	0.0541	0.0640	0.0735	0.0828	0.0921	0.1013
0.1104	0.1194	0.1284	0.1373	0.1461	0.1549	0.1636	0.1722	0.1808	0.1894
0.1979	0.2064	0.2149	0.2233	0.2317	0.2400	0.2483	0.2566	0.2649	0.2731

LOAN # 3, AS OF '73 HAS A BALANCE OF 26850. AT A RATE OF .074
IT HAS 360 MONTHS LEFT, AND HAS BEEN ON THE BOOKS 0 MONTHS
AND HAS THE FOLLOWING PREPAYMENT EXPERIENCE

0.0127	0.0237	0.0342	0.0442	0.0543	0.0639	0.0734	0.0827	0.0920	0.1013
0.1104	0.1194	0.1283	0.1372	0.1460	0.1548	0.1635	0.1721	0.1807	0.1893
0.1978	0.2063	0.2147	0.2231	0.2315	0.2399	0.2482	0.2564	0.2647	0.2729

LOAN # 4, AS OF '74 HAS A BALANCE OF 18275. AT A RATE OF .081
IT HAS 360 MONTHS LEFT, AND HAS BEEN ON THE BOOKS 0 MONTHS
AND HAS THE FOLLOWING PREPAYMENT EXPERIENCE

0.0127	0.0237	0.0541	0.0445	0.0543	0.0640	0.0734	0.0829	0.0922	0.1014
0.1105	0.1196	0.1285	0.1374	0.1462	0.1550	0.1637	0.1724	0.1810	0.1896
0.1901	0.2066	0.2151	0.2235	0.2319	0.2402	0.2486	0.2569	0.2651	0.2734

LOAN # 5, AS OF '75 HAS A BALANCE OF 20806. AT A RATE OF .094
IT HAS 360 MONTHS LEFT, AND HAS BEEN ON THE BOOKS 0 MONTHS
AND HAS THE FOLLOWING PREPAYMENT EXPERIENCE

0.0127	0.0237	0.0344	0.0446	0.0544	0.0641	0.0737	0.0832	0.0925	0.1018
0.1109	0.1200	0.1290	0.1379	0.1467	0.1555	0.1643	0.1730	0.1816	0.1902
0.1988	0.2073	0.2158	0.2242	0.2327	0.2410	0.2494	0.2577	0.2660	0.2743

LOAN # 6, AS OF '76 HAS A BALANCE OF 31368. AT A RATE OF .095
IT HAS 360 MONTHS LEFT, AND HAS BEEN ON THE BOOKS 0 MONTHS
AND HAS THE FOLLOWING PREPAYMENT EXPERIENCE

0.0127	0.0239	0.0344	0.0445	0.0544	0.0642	0.0738	0.0832	0.0925	0.1018
0.1109	0.1200	0.1290	0.1379	0.1467	0.1556	0.1643	0.1730	0.1816	0.1903
0.1988	0.2073	0.2158	0.2243	0.2327	0.2411	0.2494	0.2578	0.2661	0.2743

PRESENT VALUE AS OF '76 =   132722.710
BOOK VALUE AS OF '76 =   122949.230
PERCENT CHANGE IN PV =   −0.754

15 Some Simulation-Based Estimates of Commercial Bank Deposit Insurance Premiums

David Lane and Lawrence Golen

15.1 Introduction

Much of the empirical work in this volume is directed to a single question: What is the amount of risk in an insured financial intermediary? The chapter by Sharpe (chap. 8) shows that a useful way to view this question is in terms of the fair deposit insurance premium for an institution with a given initial asset and liability structure and capital position. The probability that an insurer will have to make a payout, and hence the size of the fair premium, varies with initial capital and depends upon a number of other factors. Among these are the value of operating earnings and expenses during the examination period; the extent of interest rate risk occasioned by imperfect alignment between time flows on assets and those on liabilities; the amount of undiversified default risk; and the covariances between these factors. Risk factors within an intermediary are not independent. Thus, for example, high interest rates tend to be associated with large default premiums. Both of these may have adverse effects on the value of a currently held portfolio.

To calculate fair insurance premiums, joint probability distributions of returns from each of the institution's activities must be specified. Given such distributions and the initial level of capital, the insurance premiums are determined by evaluating the expected end-period value of capital given that capital is negative and weighting this expected value by the probability that end-of-period capital is negative.

The problems of determining fair insurance premiums involve modeling all aspects of financial intermediaries and are difficult. It should come as no surprise, then, that none of the approaches in this volume is able to

David Lane is assistant professor at California State University, Northridge. Lawrence Golen is a graduate student in the Department of Business Administration at the University of California, Berkeley.

determine fair premiums based on all elements of risk contained within an institution. Each of them deals with certain aspects of financial intermediary risk and in so doing ignores other aspects. The value of employing multiple approaches is that each approach possesses some advantage for dealing with a particular aspect of the insurance problem.

The simulation approach utilized in this chapter involves sampling repeated end-of-period net values for a stylized intermediary operating in a simulated environment. For some of the sampled values net worth will be negative, and the deposit insurer will face payouts. The average amount of these payouts over all the drawings is the simulated fair insurance premium.

The steps in a simulation to determine fair insurance premiums are straightforward:

1. Utilizing an appropriate discounting technique, determine the current net market value of the institution. This is the institution's current capital.

2. Using a macroeconometric model, specify a joint probability distribution over all the variables exogenous to the intermediary that may affect the intermediary. We may call these environmental variables. These variables are of two types. The first are macro variables affecting the current or future levels of the intermediary's activities (asset or liability flows, operating earnings, etc.), and the second are discount variables affecting interest factors to be utilized in valuing these activities.

3. Specify quantitative relationships between the exogenous environmental variables and the levels of intermediary activities. This amounts to forming a micro model of the bank.

4. From the macroeconometric model obtain a drawing on the value of the relevant environmental variables.

5. Use the drawing to obtain a net market value of the intermediary. This is done by applying discount factors to the determined levels of the intermediary's activities.

6. Repeat steps (4) and (5) to obtain a frequency distribution of the intermediary's net market value.

7. Use this frequency distribution to calculate fair deposit insurance premiums for the institution, given its portfolio composition and initial capital. These premiums are equal to the summation of all negative simulated values of net worth divided by the number of simulations.

Fair insurance premiums appropriate to a particular institution can be calculated by using steps 1 through 7 above, based on the portfolio composition and capital value of the institution. By repeating the process for a variety of portfolio/capital assumptions, one can determine premiums appropriate for many different institutions.

Although the simulation procedure is conceptually clear, application is difficult for several reasons.

First, given our present state of knowledge, it is not possible with macroeconometric models or other techniques to adequately specify joint probability distributions over all the elements of the economic environment that might affect the levels or values of the intermediary's activities. Such distributions would have to provide accurate joint probability information on all major macroeconomic variables as well as on many regional and local variables. They would also have to specify relationships between measures of economic activity and a host of discount rates. Although such complete distributions could not be specified for this paper, the distributions utilized below do account for stochastic interrelationships between many government, municipal, and mortgage rates. No attempt is made, however, to deal with correlation between rates and other macro variables. Thus the interest rate distributions used below are not conditioned on the values of relevant macro variables, and these distributions have larger variance than would distributions correctly conditioned on appropriate macro variables.

The second major problem with the simulation approach is that comprehensive empirical models of financial intermediaries are not available. Thus in many cases it is not even possible to specify the relationship between the external economic environment and the level of bank activities. This problem is dealt with below principally by assuming nominal levels of portfolio items remaining fixed throughout the examination period.

The results obtained in this paper represent the fruits of a limited application of the simulation technique. In what follows, the simulation technique is applied only to simple, stylized financial intermediaries. It is assumed that such institutions hold fixed asset portfolios containing specified amounts of government securities, municipal securities, and mortgages. These assets are financed by capital and Treasury bill rate borrowing. For ease of exposition the technique is initially developed for government securities alone, then subsequently extended to more complex portfolios.

15.2   Insurance Premiums for Portfolios of Government Assets

In this section empirical estimates of fair insurance premiums are calculated for financial intermediaries holding only government assets. The approach is one of simulating term structures of interest rates and valuing hypothetical portfolios under the simulated structures. Through repeated simulation, distributions of portfolio values can be obtained and fair insurance premiums determined.

Future term structures are simulated by utilizing implicit rates contained in current structures, adjusting for systematic relationship between adjacent term structures, and adding noise. The noise is introduced to reflect the fact that forecasts of future rates based on implicit rates often show substantial deviation from realizations.

Techniques for dealing with shifting term structures often assume that changes in intermediate and long rates are determined exclusively by changes in short rates. The technique developed here allows for substantial variation of the former rates independent of the latter. However, to account for the tendency of adjacent forward rates to move together, much of the simulation is done in terms of the principal components of interest rate changes rather than the raw changes themselves.

Each simulation drawing consists of a sequence of 24 consecutive monthly observations, where each observation is composed of a one-period spot rate and 149 one-period forward rates. The program generates 700 such drawings. As noted, each consecutive observation on a structure in a sequence is derived from the previous one by adjusting term premiums and adding noise. Simulated observations from two different sequences on the term structure corresponding to the same date may differ owing to differences in current random drawings in the noise terms and owing to differences in the term premium adjustment. The premium adjustments differ because they are based in part on earlier noise drawings that differ across sequences.

The capital valuation element of the technique generally assumes that for the entire insurance period the financial intermediary holds a fixed portfolio of assets with known cash flows. The portfolio is financed by capital and borrowing at six-month intervals at the then-existing simulated six-month Treasury bill rate. For each drawing an observation on the value of the portfolio at the end of a specified insurance period is obtained by applying simulated six-month Treasury bill rates at semiannual intervals to flows received within the period and by evaluating anticipated flows remaining at the end end of the period by the simulated end of insurance period term structure.

For each simulation drawing the value of a portfolio may change owing to changes in borrowing costs or owing to changes in end-period asset values. The evaluation process is repeated for each of 700 simulation drawings, and an end-of-period frequency distribution of the intermediary's net worth is obtained. From such a distribution fair insurance premiums may be calculated given the initial characteristics of the intermediary. For each of four hypothetical insurance periods—six, twelve, eighteen, and twenty-four months—distributions are calculated for assumptions regarding asset holdings and initial capitalization, and corresponding insurance premiums are obtained. Some asset maturities are less than twenty-four months long. For these the simulated term structures that correspond to dates after the end of the period are not used.

Insurance premiums are specified as the expected value of the deposit insurer's liability per dollar of assets. This is calculated as the average amount by which end-of-period value of capital is negative, given that it is negative, times the probability that end-of-period capital is negative. For given portfolio and capital assumptions, this is simply the average amount per dollar of assets paid out by the deposit insurer per simulation drawing.

Since capital acts as a buffer against insolvency, the fair insurance premium will increase as the initial level of capital decreases. The premium will also increase with the length of time between inspections.

15.2.1   Simulating the Riskless Term Structure

Techniques for evaluating term structure changes are not new (see Bradley and Crane 1975 and chapters 13 and 14 above); however, many of these techniques share the characteristic that changes in intermediate and long-term rates bear a deterministic relationship to changes in spot rates. Often sensitivity of portfolios to interest rate changes is evaluated under the assumption that longer rates change by the same absolute amount as short rates.

This approach is at odds with the observed tendency of long rates to vary less than shorts and may lead to unduly pessimistic views of the riskiness of long-term assets. Chapter 13 drops the assumption of equal absolute changes but continues to assume a fixed deterministic relationship between changes in short and long rates. Morrison finds, however, that changes in the current one-period spot rate account for very little of the variability of current long rates. The simulation technique developed in this paper allows for changes in short rates to be correlated with changes in intermediate and long rates; however, it also allows for substantial variability of intermediate and long rates independent of short rates.

A simulated observation on a term structure for a particular period is produced by utilizing the implicit rates from the immediately preceding period's term structure, adjusting for forecast changes in term premiums, and adding noise terms. The noise terms are necessary because forecasts based on implicit rates generally exhibit substantial deviation from subsequent realizations.

Before proceeding further, it is useful to define terms:

$F_t(j)$ — is the forward rate at the start of period t for a one-period loan to begin $j - 1$ periods after the start of t.

$r_t = F_t(1)$ — is the spot rate for a one-period loan to begin at the start of t.

$P_t(j)$ — is the term premium at the start of t for a one-period loan to begin $j - 1$ periods later.

Under a wide variety of term-structure hypotheses:

$$F_t(j) = E_t(r_{t+j-1}) + P_t(j) \qquad j = 2 \text{ to } M.$$

Simple manipulations yield:

(1)
$$F_t(j) - F_{t+1}(j-1) = E_t(r_{t+j-1}) - E_{t+1}(r_{t+j-1})$$
$$+ P_t(j) - P_{t+1}(j-1) , \qquad j = 2, \dots, M$$

or

(2)
$$F_t(j) - F_{t+1}(j-1) = \Delta P_{t+1}(j-1) + \mu_{t+1}(j-1) ,$$

where

$$\Delta P_{t+1}(j-1) = P_t(j) - P_{t+1}(j-1)$$

and

$$\mu_{t+1}(j-1) = E_t(r_{t+j-1}) - E_{t+1}(r_{t+j-1}).$$

Rewriting (2), we obtain:

(3)
$$\Delta F_{t+1}(j-1) = \Delta P_{t+1}(j-1) + \mu_{t+1}(j-1).$$

If the market is efficient, $\mu_{t+1}(j-1)$ has zero mean, since if one had systematic information that the future expectation would differ from the current expectation, that information would be incorporated into E_t, bringing it into line with E_{t+1} (cf. Roll 1970).

Equation (2) suggests an approach to simulating the term structure. Rearranging the equation and using double tildes for simulated values and "hats" for forecast values we obtain:

(4)
$$\widetilde{F_{\tau+1}(j-1)} = F_\tau(j) - \widehat{\Delta P_{\tau+1}(j-1)} - \widetilde{\mu_{\tau+1}(j-1)}.$$

If the premiums vary over time in some systematic manner, an estimation technique is needed to capture this variation. Structural modeling on equation (3) would be appropriate; however, to facilitate forecasting and simulation, Box-Jenkins methods of time-series analysis are used below.

If, as is often assumed, term premiums are constant, and past ΔF contain no information about future ΔF, then simulation can be accomplished by merely drawing on the error term (after adjusting for its mean).

Simulations based on both these approaches are presented in this paper. The first of these approaches is considered immediately below, and the second is considered subsequently.

15.2.2   Simulation Based on Box-Jenkins Analysis of the Systematic Element of the ΔF

Box-Jenkins techniques could have been applied individually to each forward rate in equation (3). However, this approach would have ignored the tendency of adjacent forward rates to move together. To capture this tendency, we first calculated the principal components of the standardized ΔF, then applied time-series techniques to these components, which formed the basis of subsequent analysis. These components were simulated and their simulated values combined to simulate the individual ΔF. For ease of exposition, the discussion below refers to ΔF; the reader should keep in mind that analysis was done on the standardized rather than the raw ΔF.

By the nature of principal component analysis, each of the ΔF can be written as:

$$(5) \qquad \Delta F_t(j) = \sum_{i=1}^{N} \alpha_i(j)\, C_{it} + \eta_{jt}, \qquad j = 2, \ldots, M-1$$

where

C_{it} is the ith principal component at time t,
N is the number of components selected for analysis,
$\alpha_i(j)$ is the loading of the jth ΔF on component i, and
η_{jt} is the portion of ΔF that is left unexplained
by the N principal components.

In what follows we ignore the η_{jt}.

The principal components simply linear combinations of the ΔF.

$$(6) \qquad C_{it} = \sum_{j=2}^{M-1} \beta_{ij}\Delta F_t(j), \qquad i = 1, \ldots, N$$

where β_{ij} is the weight of $\Delta F_t(j)$ in component i.

By substitution from (3):

$$(7) \qquad C_{it} = \sum_{j=2}^{M-1} \beta_{ij}[\Delta P_t(j) + \mu_t(j)].$$

Rewriting and separating terms:

$$(8) \qquad C_{it} = \sum_{j=2}^{M-1} \beta_{ij}\, \Delta P_t(j) + \sum_{j=2}^{M-1} \beta_{ij}\mu_t(j).$$

The last term is the sum of error terms, which by the assumption of efficiency have zero mean and are serially independent. Hence this term must have these same properties.

Equation (8), like equation (3), is in a form appropriate for time-series analysis. However, inspection of either of these equations shows that ΔP is measured (as ΔF) with considerable error. Thus, if one were interested in premiums alone, these errors in measurement would probably impair the optimal forecast properties of the Box-Jenkins technique. However, the underlying purpose in the instant paper is to capture the systematic element of the ΔF and then utilize this element in subsequently simulating the ΔF. For this purpose time-series analysis should retain its optimal properties. From the time-series analysis, one can obtain forecasts of the systematic portion of each of the principal components:

$$(9) \qquad \sum_{j=2}^{M-1} \beta_{ij}\, \Delta P_{\tau+1}(j) \,. \qquad i = 1, \ldots, N$$

Adding a random drawing on a serially independent error term, one can obtain a simulated value for each component:

$$(10) \qquad C_{i\tau+1} = \sum_{j=2}^{M-1} \beta_{ij}\, \Delta P_{\tau+1}(j) + \varepsilon_{i\tau+1}\,, \qquad i = 1, \ldots, N$$

where $\varepsilon_{i\tau+1}$ is the drawing on the error term. For all simulations in this paper error terms are drawn from normal distributions.

Substituting $\tilde{C}$ for C in equation (5) yields

$$(11) \qquad \Delta F_{\tau+1}(j) = \sum_{i=1}^{N} \alpha_i(j)\, C_{i\tau+1} \,. \qquad j = 2, \ldots, M-1$$

Equation (11) yields the simulated changes from one term structure to the immediately following term structure in terms of the simulated changes in the principal components.

Using the definition of ΔF in equation (3) and substituting into equation (4) yields:

$$(12) \qquad F_{\tau+1}(j-1) = F_{\tau}(j) + \Delta F_{\tau+1}(j-1) \,. \qquad j = 2, \ldots, M$$

Equation (12) provides one complete simulated observation on the term structure at time $\tau + 1$. Equation (12), like equation (4), suggests that a simulated term structure can be obtained by "aging" the implicit forecasts contained in the previous period's term structure through adjustment for premium changes and then adding the error term.

A simulated term structure for period $\tau + 2$, dependent on the structure for $\tau + 1$, can be obtained by repeating the process above. $F_{\tau}(j)$ in equation (12) is replaced by $F_{\tau+1}(j)$ and a simulated value of $\Delta F_{t+2}(j-1)$ obtained from equation (11) is added to yield $F_{t+2}(j-1)$. This technique is repeated until the desired number of related consecutive simulated monthly structures is obtained. The entire sequence of such related monthly structures is referred to here as a simulation drawing.

There is no condition imposed on the simulation that satisfies the efficient markets equilibrium condition of ex ante portfolio equilibrium. Thus, for example, securities with large simulated price variance may yield lower returns than those with small variance. In fact, since such behavior is characteristic of the sample period, it is also likely to be characteristic of the simulation.

15.2.3   Results of Estimation and Term Structure Simulation

Term structure data were supplied by J. Huston McCulloch. They were derived by applying a cubic spline term structure fitting technique to mean monthly bid-ask prices for specified government securities. The estimation period is from 1 January 1960 to 1 June 1975. Each observed term structure contains 150 rates; the current one-month spot rate plus 149 one-month forward rates (McCulloch 1971).

As noted above, the first step in the simulation process was to compute the principal components of the correlation matrix of the ΔF. The component analysis indicates that most of the historical variation of the 149 ΔF can be accounted for by relatively few factors. The first principal component accounts for roughly half the variation of ΔF. The first seven components account for 99 percent of the variation. The contributions of the principal components to the variation of the ΔF are summarized in table 15.1. For purposes of time-series analysis and subsequent simulation, we used only the first seven components. This cut-off corresponds to a widely used convention of retaining only those components that account for a portion of the variance larger than one over the number of raw variables (Kaiser 1960). The individual factors did not correspond in any obvious ways to particular identifiable variables or to particular interest rates.

As we had expected, the components were less closely associated with the $\Delta F(j)$ for the first three or four values of j than they were for higher values of j. The first seven components accounted for 99 percent of the variance of most ΔF, but for only 80 to 85 percent of the variance of the

Table 15.1	Contribution of Principal Components to Total Variation of 149 ΔF	
Component	Contribution	Cumulative Contribution
1	.418	.418
2	.291	.709
3	.128	.837
4	.084	.921
5	.039	.960
6	.015	.975
7	.011	.986

first three or four ΔF. Thus some of the variation in very short rates is not shared by other rates.

Table 15.2 presents the results of the Box-Jenkins analysis on the standardized components. In all cases the time-series analysis yielded at least one autoregressive term. For components four, five, and six there were also moving average terms.

While the time-series analysis did not produce a constant term, this does not imply that the ΔF do not have a constant element; the constant element of the ΔF is suppressed because the principal components are standardized.

For most of the principal components, tests for white noise yielded the result that at roughly the 10 percent level we could not accept the hypothesis that the residuals were nonwhite.

For simulation purposes, we drew error terms for each component from normal distributions. There is considerable interest and controversy in the literature as to the proper distribution of the error terms for financial assets. Some observers (chap. 9) have suggested using stable Paretian distributions for financial models. Compared with normal distributions, such distributions have more of their mass in the tails and less near the mean. Because of this characteristic, use of such distributions would yield larger values for fair insurance premiums than those presented below.

Graphic presentations of term structures are presented in figure 15.1, which shows simulated structures for June 1976 that produce quartile values for an average bank portfolio of government securities. The median June 1976 structure reflects forward rates implicit in the June 1975 structure as well as changes in term premiums. Seven hundred simulated sequences of term structures were produced. Each sequence consisted of observations for twenty-four consecutive months on the spot rate and 149 forward rates.

Table 15.2   Time-Series Analysis on Standardized Principal Components

Component	First-Order Autoregressive Coefficient	Second-Order Autoregressive Coefficient	First-Order Moving Average Coefficient	Second-Order Moving Average Coefficient	Probability That Residuals Are White Noise
1	−.3897				.9105
2	−.2900				.2270
3	−.2240				.0774
4	.1162		.4814	.1998	.0989
5	−.3925	−.3845	−.2459	−.0877	.0578
6	−.0359		.2309	.1002	.0649
7	−.2669				.1038

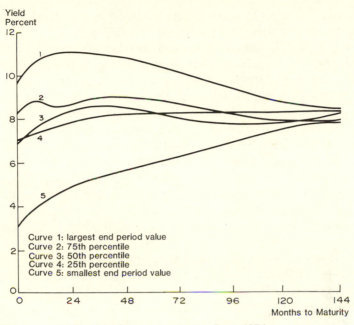

Fig. 15.1   Simulated term structures, June 1976.

15.2.4   Insurance Premiums and Portfolio Values

Using the simulated riskless term structures, we evaluated simple balance sheets of government assets at the end of hypothetical examination periods ranging in six-month intervals from six months to two years. We considered simple financial intermediaries whose assets consisted entirely of hypothetical par coupon bonds.

For these intermediaries, we calculated for each hypothetical examination period the average end-of-period value of capital and the fair insurance premiums.

For these calculations we assumed that assets were financed by six-month Treasury bill rate borrowing plus various amounts of equity. Net cash inflows, whether from coupons or principal, that were received during the examination period were applied to reduce borrowing; any surpluses were then invested at the six-month Treasury bill rate. For assets of maturity shorter than the examination period, this assumption means that principal repayments are reinvested at the six-month Treasury bill rate.

Changes in the value of capital derive either from changes in borrowing costs or from changes in asset values brought about by unexpected changes in discount rates. For assets of maturity shorter than the examination period the latter factor is not operative, since the par value of the asset will be received during the examination period. The simulation allows capital changes to accumulate by prohibiting dividend payments and capital contributions during the examination period.

We assume that the same instrument or instruments are held at the end of the period that were held at the beginning. Thus the maturity of the portfolio shortens by the length of the examination period.

Results are presented for intermediaries holding bonds of a single maturity and also for an intermediary holding an average portfolio of governments. The former intermediaries may be viewed as being composed of two activities. The first activity is lending in a specified maturity range, and the second is borrowing at the six-month Treasury bill rate. The latter intermediary may be viewed as engaging in many activities— lending in various maturity ranges and borrowing at the six-month bill rate. The average government portfolio weights, displayed in table 15.3, were obtained from May 1975 commercial bank holdings of government securities as published in the *Treasury Bulletin*.

Table 15.4 shows the end-of-examination-period value of equity for combinations of initial capital, portfolio composition, for a one-year examination period ending June 1976. (Similar tables for different examination periods are available from the authors.) Although only par bond portfolios are displayed, the technique used in generating the tables is capable of dealing with government portfolios of mixed maturities and with discount instruments. The mean values shown are based on the initial capital, on the earnings of that capital at the simulated interest rates during the year, on the difference between the yield on the portfolio of a particular maturity and the cost of funds at the six-month Treasury

Table 15.3   Weights in Average Government Portfolio

Par Bond Maturity in Years	Weight
1	.35
2	.26
3	.12
4	.10
5	.05
6	.04
7	.04
8	.01
9	.01
10	.01
11	.005
12	.005

Source: Bulletin of the U.S. Treasury Department, June 1975.
Note: Weights are calculated from reported par values, not market values.

Table 15.4   **Mean Value at End of Twelve-Month Examination Period of Government Par Bond Portfolio with Stated Maturity (700 ARIMA Simulations)**

Percentage Capital	Average Government Portfolio	Maturity in Years						
		1	2	3	5	7	10	12
0	.11	.04	.22	.33	−.12	−.18	.30	.52
1	1.17	1.10	1.28	1.39	.94	.88	1.36	1.58
3	3.30	3.23	3.41	3.52	3.07	3.00	3.49	3.71
5	5.42	5.35	5.54	5.65	5.45	5.13	5.62	5.83
7	7.55	7.48	7.66	7.77	7.57	7.26	7.74	7.96
10	10.74	10.67	10.85	10.96	10.76	10.45	10.93	10.09

bill rate, and on any simulated changes in end-of-period capital values for securities one year shorter than held initially.

Since the simulation drawings were for a period of positive capital gains and an upward sloping term structure, most entries show positive expected increases in capital for the simulated year. The pattern of earnings in the tables is consistent with habitat or segmentation theories of the term structure. The pattern is probably not consistent with a capital asset pricing model concept of ex ante portfolio equilibrium, since long-term securities (which generally evidence greater price variability) show smaller returns than short-term securities.

The low return–high total variance pattern implicit in our results might be consistent with capital asset pricing models if the market correlation of long-term securities were smaller than that of the short securities. However, an attempt to test this hypothesis showed that correlation with the market was generally an increasing function of maturity. Because of a narrow stock market definition of the market, these results might be viewed as inconclusive. Nevertheless, our model seems more akin to segmentation than to capital asset theories of term structure. An observer with a high degree of prior confidence in the appropriateness of the capital asset pricing model as a description of the government debt market would construct a term structure simulation technique that embodied this model in its assumptions. We made no attempt to construct such a simulation technique for this paper.

Fair insurance premiums for a twelve-month examination period are given in table 15.5. The examination period begins in June 1975. The insurance premiums are calculated:

$$\text{Fair premium}_t = E_t\,(\text{capital}_{t+\alpha}\,|\,\text{capital}_{t+\alpha} < 0) \cdot \text{Probability}\,(\text{capital}_{t+\alpha} < 0),$$

where the examination period runs from t to $t + \alpha$. The premiums are small. With 3 percent capital, the premium on the average portfolio is

Table 15.5   **Insurance Cost for Twelve-Month Examination Period of Government Par Bond Portfolio with Stated Maturity (700 ARIMA Simulations) (Cost per Year as a Percentage of Assets)**

Percentage Capital	Average Government Portfolio	Maturity in Years						
		1	2	3	5	7	10	12
0	.49433	.15423	.40068	.60045	1.17292	1.41348	1.42786	1.48770
1	.15528	.00034	.09795	.26428	.70098	.92067	.96955	1.03696
3	.00489	.00000	.00088	.02724	.20236	.31950	.36348	.41962
5	.00000	.00000	.00000	.01483	.04300	.09502	.12003	.13470
7	.00000	.00000	.00000	.00109	.00501	.01989	.02798	.02997
10	.00000	.00000	.00000	.00000	.00000	.00000	.00120	.00275

.005, or one-half cent on one hundred dollars of securities. This small premium reflects directly the information contained in table 15.4 and the fact already noted that the assumptions underlying that table lead to fairly sizable increases in capital for most simulations. The probabilities of failure depend on both the initial capital and these assumed earnings.

The table shows, as one would expect, that fair premiums increase with increases in maturity and in examination period and decrease with increases in capital.

The insurance premiums in this section are derived on the assumption of an autoregressive integrated moving average (ARIMA) structure in past rates. In the following section premiums are derived on the assumption that past rates contain no useful information about changes in future rates.

15.2.5   Insurance Premiums When Adjacent Term Structures Differ Only by Noise

The term structure simulation technique described above adjusts for the estimated correlation of the ΔF across time. Under some notions of the term structure, this correlation may be viewed as stemming from changes in term premiums. This view seems consistent with market efficiency in Roll's sense (Roll 1970), in that simulated expected future spot rates are a martingale; however, some notions of market efficiency hold that there is no exploitable regularity in interest rate movements (cf. Phillips and Pippenger 1976). The results presented in this section assume that there is no correlation of the ΔF over time and thus are consistent with the no-exploitable-regularity view of market efficiency.

Successive term structures are simulated by "aging" the previous period's structure one period, adjusting for a constant term premium, and adding noise. As before, this is done in terms of principal components to account for the tendency of adjacent forward rates to fluctuate together over time.

For this section we calculated the principal components as in the previous section. However, no time-series analysis was done on these components. Rather, each component was assumed to come from independent standard normal distributions. Drawings on these independent distributions yielded simulated values for each component. Simulated values of ΔF were obtained by combining the simulated components utilizing the loadings, α_i, as weights. Each consecutive term structure in a sequence was then formed by "aging" the prior term structure, adjusting for a constant term premium and adding the simulated ΔF.

Each simulation drawing consists of a sequence of twenty-four consecutive monthly observations on the term structure; each observation consists of a one-period spot rate and 149 one-period forward rates. The program generates 700 such drawings. Simulated observations from two different sequences on the term structure corresponding to the same data may differ owing to differences in current and previous drawings on the principal components.

For ease of reference the insurance premiums of the previous section are referred to as ARIMA-based estimates, while the insurance premiums of the instant section are referred to as noise-based estimates.

As in the ARIMA case, the noise-based insurance premium analysis was done with seven principal components.

More formally, the simulated principal components:

$$(13) \qquad \tilde{C}_{i\tau + 1} \qquad i = 1, \ldots, 7$$

were drawn from independent normal distributions. The single tilde indicates noise-based simulation. The ΔF were derived in a manner similar to equation (11) above by:

$$(14) \qquad \overline{\Delta F_{\tau + 1}(j)} = \sum_{i = 1}^{F} \alpha_i(j)\, \tilde{C}_{i\tau + 1} \cdot \qquad j = 2, \ldots, M - 1$$

By analogy to equation (12):

$$(15) \qquad \overline{F_{\tau + 1}(j - 1)} = F_\tau(j) + \overline{\Delta F_{\tau + 1}(j -)} \cdot \qquad j = 2, \ldots, M$$

Equation (15) provides one complete simulated observation on the term structure at time $\tau + 1$.

The balance of the noise-based procedure for the derivation of the 700 sequences of twenty-four consecutive monthly term structures is identical to that used for the ARIMA simulations.

Mean portfolio values and insurance premiums derived from the noise-based term structure sequences were calculated and are presented in tables 15.6 and 15.7. The formats of these tables are identical to those of the previous tables. All examination periods begin in June 1975.

Inspection of table 15.6 reveals that average end-of-period value peaks for maturities of about two or three years and then generally declines.

Table 15.6   Mean Value at End of Twelve-Month Examination Period of
                        Government Par Bond Portfolio with Stated Maturity (700 Noise
                        Simulations)

Percentage Capital	Maturity in Years						
	1	2	3	5	7	10	12
0	.18	.45	.52	.38	.23	.00	−.16
1	1.24	1.51	1.58	1.44	1.29	1.06	.90
3	3.37	3.63	3.71	3.56	3.41	3.19	3.03
5	5.49	5.76	5.83	5.68	5.53	5.31	5.15
7	7.61	7.88	7.95	7.81	7.66	7.43	7.27
10	10.80	11.07	11.14	10.99	10.77	10.62	10.46

Table 15.7   Insurance Cost for Twelve-Month Examination Period of
                        Government Par Bond Portfolio with Stated Maturity (700 Noise
                        Simulations) (Cost per Year as a Percentage of Assets)

Percentage Capital	Maturity in Years						
	1	2	3	5	7	10	12
0	.14520	.49827	.84887	1.39974	1.75911	2.23395	2.55016
1	.00250	.19410	.47361	.97340	1.30236	1.73904	2.02352
3	.00000	.01433	.12071	.40557	.64739	.9960	1.21309
5	.00000	.00056	.01798	.14631	.29668	.52976	.67879
7	.00000	.00000	.00054	.04379	.11788	.26544	.35584
10	.00000	.00000	.00000	.00231	.01560	.06854	.11190

This pattern primarily reflects the magnitude of term premiums. Casual comparison of sample period mean term premiums with differences across maturities of portfolio end-of-period values showed high correspondence. In other words, in the sample period ex post holding period returns were often lower for long-term securities than for short-term securities. The simulation results, based on the sample period, simply reflect this fact.

The noise-based insurance premiums are generally larger than those derived using the ARIMA techniques. Nevertheless, the premiums are still relatively small. With 3 percent capital, the premium on a three-year par bond is 12 basis points. This is about four times larger than the corresponding ARIMA-based premium.

For some maturity-capital combinations the noise-based insurance premiums are greater than the ARIMA-based premiums even though the mean portfolio values are greater for the former than for the latter. This is because the μ_{t+1}, the change between t and $t+1$ in the expected spot rate corresponding to a fixed future date, is larger for the noise estimates than for the ARIMA. Thus, while in some cases the noise estimates have larger means than the ARIMA, they also generally have larger variance around these means. It is this larger variance that produces the larger insurance premiums.

Wealth effect risk is likely to be greater for municipal and mortgage elements of portfolios than for governments, since these elements typically have longer duration than governments.

The following sections address the problems of calculating insurance premiums on municipal and mortgage portfolios.

15.3   Insurance Premiums for Portfolios of Municipal Assets

This section presents a simulation model of the municipal term structure and uses this model to estimate insurance premiums for portfolios of municipal bonds. The simulated municipal term structure runs off the ARIMA-based simulated government structure; however, adjustments are made for certain systematic tendencies of municipal and government rates to behave differently.

Equations determining municipal rates for specified maturities are estimated by regressing municipal rate relatives on roughly corresponding government rate relatives. Values for municipal rates between those specified are interpolated. This procedure yields the municipal term structure as a function of the current level and recent history of the government term structure. Drawings from the government term structure simulator are then used to provide a simulated history necessary to generate a simulated observation on the municipal term structure. Repeated drawings on the government term structure provide repeated simulated observations on the municipal term structure.

Using the simulated municipal term structures with procedures similar to those described above for government term structures, frequency distributions of portfolio end-of-period value are generated, and fair insurance premiums against pure interest rate risk are calculated for intermediaries with specified municipal portfolios and initial capital positions.

Finally, through a simple extension of the techniques of the previous section, mixed portfolios of government and municipal securities are evaluated and fair insurance premiums calculated.

15.3.1   Some General Characteristics of the
Municipal Securities Market

Before we consider the details of the municipal simulation model, some general comments about the characteristics of the municipal securities market are in order. Any adequate simulation model of this market must attempt to deal with these characteristics.

Differences in behavior of municipal interest rates and other rates primarily reflect differences in tax treatment. Coupon payments on most securities are subject to federal income taxes, while those on municipals are not. The differential tax treatment means that yields on municipals are generally substantially lower than those on corresponding taxable securities. However, the term structure for municipals tends to be steeper than that for taxable securities, and in high interest rate periods, yield differentials between these two classes of securities tend to close.

Although this converging effect takes place throughout most of the maturity structure, it is most pronounced for the longer maturities. Thus long municipal rates tend to display more variability than corresponding government rates. Finally, the shorter municipal rates tend to be less responsive to changes in the one-month government rate than do corresponding government rates.

The factors determining the municipal rate behavior described are not clearly understood, but explanations resting on institutional factors are common. It is argued that, because of the short maturities of their liabilities, banks wish to hold short-maturity municipals. Owing to their size, banks dominate this sector of the market, and yields on short-term municipal issues tend to average about 52 percent of those on corresponding government issues. This ratio results in rough equality in bank after-tax earnings on municipal and government securities. However, banks resist getting heavily into longer-term municipal instruments; hence this sector is left to lower-bracket taxpayers who drive up long-term rates, since they require a higher ratio of municipal risk-free yields to equate after-tax earnings. The tendency of municipal rates to rise more than other rates in high interest rate periods probably reflects the banking community's attitude that maintaining customer relationships by assuring availability of credit is of primary importance in maximizing long-run earnings. Thus, in high rate periods banks tend to unload municipals to finance commercial lending. This scenario seems to be an accurate description of events in the high rate days of 1966 and 1969, when banks sold substantial volumes of municipals and rates on tax-exempts soared.

15.3.2 Municipal Term Structure Simulation and Insurance Premiums

We simulated the municipal term structure by relating three municipal rates to roughly corresponding government rates and interpolating to obtain the entire term structure for the remaining municipal rates.

We ran regressions explaining the 12- , 60- , and 360-month municipal rate by the 12- , 60- , and 120-month government rates, respectively. We used the 120-month government rate because 360-month government data were not available. The municipal rate data were taken from Salomon Brothers (1974) quarterly "good" grade municipal yield series. The government data were the McCulloch data described above. The sample period was mid-1965 to mid-1975.

The regression equations were:

(16)   and

$$\left[\frac{MN_t(m)}{MN_{t-1}(m)} - 1\right] = \alpha_m + \beta_m\left[\frac{G_t(m)}{G_{t-1}(m)} - 1\right] \qquad m = 12, 60$$

$$\left[\frac{MN_t(360)}{MN_{t-1}(360)} - 1\right] = \alpha_{360} + \beta_{360}\left[\frac{G_t(120)}{G_{t-1}(120)} - 1\right] \quad ,$$

where

$MN_t(m)$ is the m month municipal yield at time t, and
$G_t(m)$ is the m month government yield at time t.

The regression results are presented in table 15.8. All the estimated parameters are significant at the 5 percent level. About half of the variation in the municipal relatives is explained by variation in the government relatives. The presence of a significant constant indicates that during the sample period there was a slight tendency for municipal rates to increase relative to government rates. The magnitude of the coefficients of determination indicates that factors other than changes in government rates play an important role in explaining municipal rates. We attempted to increase the explanatory power of the equations by adding variables representing government rate levels. The coefficients these attempts yielded were generally not significant, and hence we used the simple form of equation (16).

Using the results in the table, we obtained 12- , 60- , and 360-month municipal yields by plugging simulated government rates into the equations and solving. In this way it was possible, for each term structure in a simulated sequence of government term structures, to obtain three simulated municipal rates that were dependent on the associated government structure. However, this technique did not provide a complete municipal term structure. To obtain such a term structure, we needed some interpolation technique. We selected a technique used by Bradley and Crane (1975) for interpolating municipal yield curves. The yield curve is assumed to follow a function of the form:

(17) $MN(m) = am^b e^{cm}$,

where $MN(m)$ is the yield to maturity of an m period municipal bond and a, b, and c are parameters. Given three yields on a particular yield curve, it is possible to treat (17) as three equations in these unknowns and solve for these parameters; the remaining yields along the given curve can then

Table 15.8   **Regressions of Municipal Rates on Government Rates**

Dependent Variable	Independent Variable	α (Standard Error)	ß (Standard Error)	R^2
MN(12)	G(12)	.00167 (.00036)	.69381 (.05557)	.63
MN(60)	G(60)	.00138 (.00038)	.68436 (.07315)	.49
MN(360)	G(120)	.00148 (.00027)	.57761 (.05917)	.15

be solved for using these parameters. New parameter values must, of course, be obtained for each set of three municipal yields belonging to a single given yield curve.

Using equation (16) and a given simulated ARIMA government term structure, we obtained simulated 12- , 60- , and 360-month municipal rates along a single municipal yield curve. We then used these three simulated municipal yields with equation (17) to obtain the complete yield curve corresponding to the three simulated yields. For each successive set of three simulated municipal yields (generated from equation 16 and successive simulated government term structures), we repeated this procedure to obtain a complete simulated municipal yield curve.

The final result is similar to that obtained for governments. Seven hundred simulated municipal term structure sequences were generated. Each sequence consists of eight consecutive simulated quarterly observations on a municipal term structure composed of the one-month municipal spot rate and 359 one-month forward rates.

The simulated sequences of municipal rates were used in the same fashion as the simulated risk-free rates to generate estimates of mean portfolio values and of fair insurance premiums. The results are presented in tables 15.10 and 15.11. The weights used for the average municipal portfolio, obtained from the *1976 Annual Report of the Federal Deposit Insurance Corporation*, are displayed in table 15.9. The insurance premiums for municipals are generally from 35 to 60 percent of the premiums on corresponding government bonds. Often they are far smaller than this. These small premiums reflect the relatively low coefficients of determination of table 15.8. Government rates explain only about half the variation in municipal rates. Thus the simulated municipal rates, dependent as they are only on government rates, display less variability than do actual municipal rates. That the simulated municipal term structures have low variability does not render the insurance premiums derived from them useless. However, care must be taken in interpreting these premiums. The premiums in table 15.11 must be interpreted as fair insurance premiums against pure government interest rate variability risk only. These premiums do not account for all sources of variability in municipal rates; they are appropriate insurance premiums on municipals owing to variations in government rates alone.

Table 15.9   **Weights in Average Municipal Portfolio**

Par Bond Maturity in Years	Weight
1	.17
3	.15
5	.14
7	.14
10	.14
15	.10
20	.08
25	.05
30	.03

Source: Annual Report of the Federal Deposit Insurance Corporation, 1975.
Note: Weights are calculated from reported par values, not market values.

Table 15.10   **Mean Value at End of Twelve-Month Examination Period of Municipal Bond Portfolio with Stated Maturity (700 Simulations)**

Percentage Capital	Average Municipal Portfolio	Maturity in Years								
		1	3	5	7	10	15	20	25	30
0	.27	.04	.07	.07	.16	.34	.60	.72	.69	.59
1	1.31	1.08	1.11	1.11	1.20	1.38	1.65	1.76	1.74	1.63
3	3.39	3.16	3.19	3.20	3.28	3.47	3.73	3.84	3.82	3.71
5	5.47	5.25	5.28	5.28	5.37	5.55	5.81	5.92	5.90	5.80
7	7.56	7.33	7.36	7.36	7.45	7.63	7.89	8.01	7.98	7.88
10	10.68	10.45	10.48	10.49	10.57	10.76	11.02	11.13	11.11	11.00

Table 15.11   **Insurance Cost for Twelve-Month Examination Period for Municipal Bond Portfolio with Stated Maturity (700 Simulations) (Cost per Year as a Percentage of Assets)**

Percentage Capital	Average Municipal Portfolio	Maturity in Years								
		1	3	5	7	10	15	20	25	30
0	.50813	.06882	.30736	.47354	.59920	.68616	.80772	.90854	1.01365	1.12029
1	.17575	.00000	.03785	.13366	.22164	.32263	.44340	.53175	.61233	.70008
3	.00975	.00000	.00000	.00337	.01671	.05185	.10644	.14648	.18477	.22205
5	.00000	.00000	.00000	.00000	.00000	.00239	.01349	.02497	.03624	.04756
7	.00000	.00000	.00000	.00000	.00000	.00000	.00042	.00188	.00282	.00516
10	.00000	.00000	.00000	.00000	.00000	.00000	.00000	.00000	.00000	.00000

While the long maturity of municipal securities apparently does not require large premiums to cover risk of variation in default-free rates, the same need not be true of other long-maturity instruments. The following section provides rough estimates of premiums on commercial bank mortgage portfolios.

15.4   Insurance Premiums on a Commercial Bank Mortgage Portfolio

Because of their relatively long nominal maturities, real estate mortgages might be expected to be a source of considerable interest rate risk. The interest rate sensitivity of the commercial bank mortgage portfolio is carefully dealt with in the chapter by Nadauld (chap. 14). However, some rough calculations are done in this section to get a notion of the magnitude of fair insurance premiums on commercial bank mortgage portfolios.

We calculate the insurance premiums using the technique developed above for government securities. Rather than simulating appropriate discount rates for mortgages, we discount the flows off the mortgage portfolio by the previously derived ARIMA-based simulated government term structure sequences. While mortgage portfolios generally include little default loss, the appropriateness of discounting by government rates is open to question.

Since the simulated government term structures extend only to maturities of twelve years, it was necessary to specify values for rates from twelve to thirty years. We did this by assuming that the thirty-year yield was 50 basis points greater than the twelve-year yield and linearly interpolating to obtain rates between these two rates. The 50 basis point spread is one that has prevailed at times in the past. While this assumption too is open to question, it should not cause substantial error in the premium estimates, since most of the value of a mortgage portfolio derives from flows within the first twelve years.

A commercial bank mortgage portfolio that appeared to be representative was selected for analysis. The portfolio was composed of new and seasoned mortgages. We calculated expected flows off the portfolio by correcting the scheduled nominal flows for average experiences with prepayments and defaults. The method is described in detail in Nadauld's chapter.

Mean end-of-period mortgage portfolio values and corresponding insurance premiums are reported in table 15.12. Examination periods begin in June 1975. Once again the premiums are small. With 5 percent capital, the fair premium on an average mortgage portfolio is only 5 basis points. The small premiums reflect the short actual duration of mortgages. Prepayments and amortization bring the duration of most residential mortgages to below ten years.

Table 15.12   Mean Value at End of Twelve-Month Examination Period and Insurance Cost for an Average Mortgage Portfolio (700 ARIMA Simulations)

Percentage Capital	Mean Value	Insurance Cost per Year as Percentage of Assets
0	.28	1.16002
1	1.35	.71988
3	3.47	.20903
5	5.60	.04344
7	7.73	.00459
10	10.92	.00166

15.5   Insurance Premiums on a Mixed Portfolio of Governments, Municipals, and Mortgages

The previous sections have presented fair insurance premiums for portfolios composed of single classes of assets—government securities, municipal securities, or mortgages. Commercial banks often hold all these assets simultaneously. This section presents estimates of fair insurance premiums on what might be considered an average commercial bank portfolio composed of all three of these assets.

The average portfolio was formed by using the average government, municipal, and mortgage portfolios considered above and weighting these portfolios by the weights displayed in table 15.13.

Insurance premiums were derived by combining techniques used in earlier sections. First, we obtained a simulation drawing on a sequence of consecutive ARIMA-based government term structures, and we applied the procedure outlined in the section on governments to the government element of the average portfolio to obtain a single observation on this element's end-of-period value. Second, we determined the municipal term structure sequence associated with the given government sequence and applied the procedure outlined in the section on municipals to the municipal element of the average portfolio to obtain an observation on this element's end-of-period value. Finally, we extrapolated the term structures in the given government sequence to thirty years and applied the procedure outlined in the section on mortgages to the mortgage element of the average portfolio to obtain an observation on its end-of-period value.

The end-of-period values of each of the three elements of the average portfolio were summed to obtain a single end-of-period observation on the value of the entire portfolio. This observation is associated with a single given government term structure sequence. For each examination period we repeated this entire procedure 700 times to obtain a frequency

Table 15.13   **Weights of Component Portfolios in Average Bank Portfolio**

Portfolio	Weight
Average government portfolio	.26
Average municipal portfolio	.31
Representative mortgage portfolio	.43

Source: Annual Report of the Federal Deposit Insurance Corporation, 1976.

distribution of end-of-period values of the average portfolio. From this distribution we calculated insurance premiums.

The mean end-of-period values and the associated insurance premiums are reported in table 15.14. All simulated examination periods begin in June 1975. Once again the premiums are small.

15.6   Conclusion

This chapter demonstrates a method for simulating sequences of government term structures and associated sequences of municipal term structures. We used the simulated term structure sequences to obtain frequency distributions of net end-of-period values of relatively simple hypothetical portfolios. From these distributions we calculated fair insurance premiums as the average loss (per dollar of assets) paid out by a deposit insurer. Insurance premiums were calculated for individual government, municipal, and mortgage securities as well as for combinations of these assets roughly corresponding to average commercial bank portfolios.

The insurance premiums depend upon the expected end-of-period net worth and its probability distribution. In these simulations expected income from assets depends upon initial capital, upon the distribution of the asset portfolio by type of asset and maturity, by past relationship of returns to the risk-free rate, and by movements in the risk-free interest

Table 15.14   **Mean Value at End of Twelve-Month Examination Period and Insurance Cost for an "Average" Bank Portfolio (700 Simulations)**

Percentage Capital	Mean Value	Insurance Cost per Year as Percentage of Assets
0	.23	.76407
1	1.29	.36742
3	3.40	.05262
5	5.52	.00236
7	7.63	.00000
10	10.80	.00000

rates across the term structure. The cost of liabilities is assumed to be equal to the six-month Treasury bill rate.

We use two methods of simulating movements in the term structure. In the first (ARIMA) method, the implicit forecasts of future rates contained in the previous period's term structure are "aged" by adjusting for expected movements. The movements are projected from a time-series analysis of the principal components of past interest rate changes and by an added error term. An entire 150-month term structure is aged, with a separate estimate for each interest rate in the structures for each of the following twelve months. (Six and twenty-four month simulations were also available.) Each of these processes or simulation drawings is repeated 700 times to obtain a distribution of term structures for the end of the period as shown in figure 15.1. In the second technique, successive term structures are aged by adjusting for the constant term premiums (cf. chap. 9 and table 14.3) and by drawing from a normal distribution fitted to month-to-month interest movements in the period 1 January 1960 to 1 June 1975.

The expected value of each specific portfolio at the end of the period is calculated for each of 700 term structure simulations. The value for a portfolio under a drawing depends upon: (*a*) the initial capital; (*b*) the June 1975 level and term structure of interest rates; (*c*) the content of the portfolio by type of asset and maturity; (*d*) the assumption that all liabilities carry the six-month simulated bill rate; (*e*) that all receipts from principal are used to reduce the size of the portfolio, while all receipts from income are reinvested at the six-month bill rate; (*f*) that no earnings are paid out; and, most important (*g*), that remaining assets are revalued at the term structure projected for the end of the period.

Fair insurance premiums are calculated by examining all the drawings with negative values among the 700 simulations for a specific portfolio, estimating the expected loss for each of these, and summing costs by applying to each negative value its proportion of the total simulations. Required insurance premiums increase with the maturity of a portfolio and fall as the capital/asset ratio rises.

The insurance premiums under these particular assumptions are low. For example, existing FDIC rates, according to table 15.14, would cover the simulated interest rate risk for this portfolio in a bank with 3 percent capital. This is a far lower risk than estimated in chapter 9, and somewhat less than estimated in chapter 4. Major differences arise from the assumptions concerning the shape of the variance distribution and from the expected net worths around which the variances are measured. Clearly these tables cannot be applied directly in their present form. They must be adjusted to the time of evaluation, to the specific portfolio, and for other risks.

16 The Fundamental Determinants of Risk in Banking

Barr Rosenberg and Philip R. Perry

16.1 Introduction

A complete model of the joint probability distribution of prices and volumes of bank assets and liabilities, incorporating those aspects of management and financial structure which influence bank success, would predict banking risk as a function of regulatory parameters. From the model, optimal regulatory strategy could be derived. However, many of the data necessary to estimate the joint distribution are not available, and, even where data are available, sample size is often inadequate. An appealing alternative is to seek an empirical relationship between the probability distribution of outcomes and available "descriptors" of banking activity. The descriptors can be chosen, insofar as possible, to approximate the variables that would enter into a complete and correctly specified model—at the same time, they can be constructed to minimize the effects of measurement error in available data and to provide surrogates for unreported items.

Three topics relating to banking risk can be distinguished: First, What is the magnitude of each bank's risk relative to the industry norm, and what fundamental determinants of individual bank risk can be identified? Second, What is the industry risk level and what causes this to fluctuate? Third, What common factors influence groups of banks differentially from others and how much risk is attached to each factor? We have planned three studies, one with reference to each topic. The first study is contained in this chapter.

Barr Rosenberg is professor at the Berkeley Business School, University of California, Berkeley. Philip R. Perry is assistant professor at the School of Management, State University of New York at Buffalo.

We gratefully acknowledge the comments of Sherman Maisel, Vinay Marathe, David Pyle, and William Sharpe, and the Management Sciences Department of Wells Fargo Bank. Responsibility for errors is, of course, our own.

Cross-sectional time-series data for a panel of banks, derived largely from the COMPUSTAT data base, are used in all studies. Individual bank data are required for the first and third studies, which focus on differences between banks. The estimated relationships, when aggregated across the industry, predict the industry risk level. This indirect prediction is potentially the most powerful approach to the second topic, for the greater variability of explanatory variables across disaggregated data allows more accurate parameter estimation than can be obtained from time-series variation in industry data alone. However, this indirect approach involves extrapolation of a relationship across banks at one point in time to predict the effects of changes over time in the industry norm, a method that must be scrutinized carefully and adopted cautiously.

The risks to the bank's depositors, creditors, insurers, and owners all hinge upon the present value of the bank. As long as the present value as an ongoing enterprise is positive, some form of reorganization can presumably be found that fully satisfies the claims of those who hold the bank's liabilities and that returns the net present value to the stockholders. When net present value drops below zero, claim holders will suffer to varying degrees, but net present value is still the single most important determinant of the magnitude of their losses. Thus the essential target for any study of banking risk is the probability distribution of present value.

Two measures of changes in present value are available: reported earnings—the accountant's measure—and change in the market value of the bank's capital—the economist's measure. We have elected to work with changes in market value. Market values of senior liabilities (bonded debt and preferred stock) are difficult to obtain for most of the historical sample. Since senior liabilities are generally a small portion of bank capital, and since proportional variability in their value is small in comparison with proportional variability of common stock (unless the bank is in severe trouble), senior liabilities can be neglected, with the proportional change in common stock value serving as a surrogate for the whole. The proportional change in value of the common stock, which is the investment return to the common stockholder, becomes the variable for which risk must be predicted.

When investment return is compared with earnings as an indicator of unpredictable outcomes, the advantages of investment return are frequency and timeliness, serial independence, and lack of bias. Investment returns provide frequent and timely observations of unpredictable events, since an event that influences the bank is incorporated into its stock price as soon as the event is recognized and its value appraised. Thus, if twelve monthly returns are observed, each return is likely to reflect the unanticipated events in that month. Such events would not be reflected in accounting earnings until quarterly or annual statements were prepared, and they are often deferred to later fiscal years. (For example, a gain or loss owing to fluctuation in the dollar value of an international debt when the exchange rate changes is sometimes amortized over the life of the debt.)

Investment returns tend to lack serial correlation, because, as each forthcoming trend in bank earnings is discerned, its estimated discounted value is immediately reflected in stock price. By contrast, the effects of the trend may show up as a smooth, serially correlated disturbance in earnings extending over many years. Moreover, accounting procedures allow earnings to be "smoothed" from quarter to quarter and year to year, so that even when the true events are serially independent their effects can be flattened into smooth and serially correlated perturbations in reported earnings.

Finally, the current value of the bank's common stock is not intrinsically biased, when viewed as an estimator of true present value. Both positive and negative errors permit profit to traders aware of the discrepancy and are therefore self-destroying. Accounting principles, on the other hand, often deliberately ignore a component of earnings that is difficult to evaluate, with the result that reported earnings are a valid estimate of total earnings exclusive of that component but a biased estimate of the total. For example, the unrealized inflation-caused increase in the market value of a bank's real property is excluded from reported earnings.

These defects of reported earnings force the use of investment returns as a means of studying unpredictable events. A ten-year history of investment returns provides 120 largely independent observations on variance per unit time, whereas a ten-year history of reported earnings may provide the equivalent of fewer than ten biased observations, after problems of timeliness and serial dependence have been dealt with. Reported earnings can at best serve to capture the impact of cataclysmic and enduring events, whereas investment returns not only capture these but are also a window on smaller transitory outcomes that are no less important in a cumulative sense.

The advantages of accounting earnings are traditional visibility and precision. Some professionals in banking distrust the market value of bank common stock, believing it to be a product of market whims. Earnings, though subject to the arbitrariness of accounting conventions, are preferred because those conventions are familiar, but the analytical process resulting in market value is obscure and decentralized. In response to this objection, one can cite negative evidence, in that studies of stock market prices have failed to find gross inefficiencies, and also positive evidence: if one believes that market valuation is ill informed, one has the opportunity for speculative profit. The act of speculative trading moves price toward correct present value—for instance, if price is below present value, the speculator buys the stock, thereby increasing demand and raising price. It is precisely this opportunity for all those possessed of information to profit from a discrepancy between market value and present value that encourages confidence in market price as a value measure.

The study reported here, "The Fundamental Determinants of Risk in Banking," is concerned with prediction of the two essential aspects of risk: exposure to systematic risk, or "beta," and the magnitude of residual risk, the "residual standard deviation." Systematic risk dominates in an investor's diversified portfolio and is therefore the aspect of risk that is compensated by excess return in the theory of capital markets. Hence beta is the crucial determinant of the cost of equity capital to the bank. Residual risk, also called diversifiable risk, is the remaining element of risk, independent of systematic risk. Residual standard deviation is the magnitude of the independent variability of the bank's present value and hence expresses the likelihood of problems arising for the bank independently of problems for the economy as a whole.

Seventy-eight descriptors of bank activity are formulated, grouped into categories relating to asset mix, liability mix, other asset/liability characteristics, operating characteristics, earnings success, growth, size, (stock) market price variability, descriptors of many kinds dependent on the market valuation of common stock, and regional variables. The usefulness of the descriptors as indicators of troubled situations is touched upon. Then the predictive power of the descriptors, both singly and in multiple regressions, is reported for beta and for residual risk. The fundamental descriptors as a group capture a large proportion of risk variations between banks. The relationship does not importantly change between the first and second halves of the twelve-year history. Thus the fitted prediction rules provide an appealing risk-forecasting tool.

A study under way, "Changing Risk in Banking," compares two approaches to risk analysis for the industry aggregate. One approach applies stochastic parameter regression to infer industry risk fluctuations from the history of price variability in the Standard and Poor's banking indexes. Here no fundamental concomitants are used. The analysis does show large, statistically significant changes in industry risk over the fifty-year history. However, the standard error of estimate at any one point in time is moderately large, so that the approach cannot be used with confidence to identify year-to-year changes in risk from monthly index returns. Possibly the use of more frequent weekly or daily returns would help in this regard. The second approach aggregates individual bank risk predictions to predict industry risk. The standard error of prediction is smaller in this case, but potential differences between the cross-bank relationship and the relationship over time must be considered.

A third study, "Common Factors in Banking," attempts to decompose residual risk into two components: the outcome of common factors influencing groups of banks and the remaining risk, specific to individual banks and independent across banks. The distinction is important for regulatory purposes, since a common factor might cause difficulties for many banks at once, whereas specific events will tend to be distributed more randomly and regularly over time. As a by-product of this more sophisticated model of residual risk, the systematic risk model of the first study will be reestimated. The estimated coefficients will probably not change significantly, but the standard errors of the estimates may increase.

16.2 Overview

The operating risk in a bank can be precisely defined as the unpredictable variability of the present value of the bank. Risk is most commonly studied by observing changes in the earnings or worth of the firm. Such measures of risk, based as they are upon the bank's accounting practices, accurately capture some aspects of risk but overlook others. For example, changes in the market value of the bank's assets are imperfectly captured. Accounting measures of earnings also tend to smooth the time path of earnings and, in so doing, tend to obscure the fluctuations that can be used to establish the level of risk.

The market value of the bank's liabilities, at any point in time, is an estimate of the present value of the bank. The common stock is a large portion of the long-term capital of most banks, and it is that part with the greatest exposure to changes in the bank's present value. Since accurate measures of the market value of other bank liabilities are lacking, a study of the month-to-month variability in the outstanding value of the bank's common stock becomes a natural approach to measuring bank risk.

Two aspects of the risk of common stock are studied below. The first is the systematic risk as measured by beta. The second is the residual variability, measured by the variance of the stock's residual or unsystematic return. A number of "descriptors" of the bank's operating characteristics are used as predictors for these two risk measures.

Data on more than 100 banks for about 100 months are available; there are 11,219 data points in all. Predictive models for systematic and residual risk are fitted to this pooled cross-sectional time series.

The empirical results are satisfying. The estimated coefficients are generally consistent with our a priori expectations concerning the effects of a bank's operations upon its risk. The coefficients are estimated with fair precision, and a large number of the effects are statistically significant.

One important measure of the success of the prediction rule is the degree to which fundamental descriptors (descriptors of the operating characteristics of the bank) can substitute for historical risk measures as predictors of future risk. If all operating determinants of risk were perfectly captured, the historical risk measure would become redundant and would make an insignificant contribution to future prediction. Conversely, if the fundamental descriptors were inadequate, the historical risk measure would remain as an important predictor of future risk. In this study the historical risk measures are only marginally significant and add very little to the explanatory power of the fundamental prediction rules.

Two other satisfying aspects of the estimated prediction rules are insensitivity to the time period selected and insensitivity to the inclusion or deletion of various descriptors. We have estimated the models over several time periods and found little change in estimated coefficients. Indeed, "Chow" tests of changed coefficients only weakly reject changes in the structure of the model. Also, deleting insignificant variables or groups of variables of different types generally does not change the signs of the remaining coefficients. This makes it seem less likely that the coefficients of included variables are importantly influenced by surrogate effects for other variables that may have been excluded.

The results of the study may be useful in a number of ways. First, they provide prediction rules for investment risk that have potential usefulness in regulatory practice. Second, the information content of various descriptors is tested: some commonly used descriptors of operating characteristics are found to be important predictors of investment risk and others are not. Third, the risk coefficients for various asset and liability categories are a natural measure of the capital costs that should be associated with them.

The plan of the paper is as follows. Section 16.3 defines the components of risk. Section 16.4 explains the procedure used to fit prediction rules for systematic and residual risk. The exact formulas are given in the Appendix to the paper. Section 16.5 discusses the descriptors that have been employed. Section 16.6 explains the sample. Section 16.7 reports the empirical results, and section 16.8 provides a conclusion.

16.3   The Components of Risk

The single-factor, market-index model of security returns has received widespread attention. It has the advantage of simplicity, and it exploits the fact that a large part of the covariance among security returns can be explained by a single factor analogous to a market index. Yet, in a pioneering study, King (1966) concluded that there are important covariances among security returns beyond those attributable to an overall market factor. His conclusions are consistent with the beliefs of professional portfolio managers and security analysts, who generally agree that there are important components of security returns associated with the economic and financial characteristics of the firm. These components of return influence all (or almost all) firms having the associated characteristics and thereby induce correlations among the returns of different firms possessing such characteristics.

In a recent paper, Rosenberg (1974) developed a multiple-factor model of security returns. This model implies a single-factor, market-index model of the usual form, which, however, possesses two additional interesting properties: (*a*) there exists a set of residual factors that contribute additional, or "extramarket," components of covariance among security returns; (*b*) the familiar beta coefficient (a measure of systematic risk) is a function of the parameters of the underlying multiple-factor model. With the additional assumption that both the specific risk and the factor loadings of the firm are linear functions of known characteristics of the firm, which can be represented by "descriptors" derived from accounting data and stock market price behavior, Rosenberg showed that it is possible to construct a set of transformed factors with loadings identical to the descriptors. These transformed factors may be directly estimated by ordinary regression. This approach—which is the one utilized in this paper—has the advantage of statistical simplicity, and it exploits such information as is available concerning the economic character of the factor loadings.

The single-index model of security returns provides a relationship between returns and two aspects of risk, systematic and specific; the multiple-factor model includes a third type of risk, extramarket covariance. To make this terminology a bit clearer, consider the following explanations of the three types of risk that contribute to security returns—systematic risk, specific risk, and extramarket covariance.

1. *Systematic risk* arises from the tendency of the asset price to move along with the market index. The amount of systematic risk of any asset is sometimes called its "volatility." The measure of systematic risk is widely known as "beta." If beta is 1, then the asset price tends to fall in the same proportion that the market falls, other things being equal, and to rise by the same proportion that the market rises. If beta is 1.5, the asset price tends to fall (or rise) proportionally by one and one-half times as much as the market falls (or rises).

2. *Specific risk* is the uncertainty in the return of an asset that arises from events that are specific to that firm. It is that part of risk that is due to events in the firm that are unrelated—or, at most, distantly related—to events that influence other firms. A leading example of this kind of risk was provided by the sudden announcement of Franklin National Bank's

troubles. The news had a disastrous effect on the prices of its common stock and other liabilities. Of course the announcement also conveyed, by implication, some fresh news about the state of the economy and banking in general. The interrelationship was negligibly small in comparison to the changed values of Franklin's own liabilities. This aspect of risk has been called the "unique" risk or "independent" risk of the company.

3. *Extramarket covariance* is the remaining component of risk. It is manifested as a tendency for the prices of related assets to move together in a way that is independent of the market as a whole. An illustration is the tendency for money-center banks to rise and fall together as the prospects of the group change, at times when the market may be moving in the other direction. The term "covariance" refers to the tendency of the stock prices to move together, or to "covary." The adjective "extra-market" rules out that part of the tendency of assets to move together that is related to the market as a whole. Covariance within an industry group is intermediate between systematic and specific risk: systematic risk affects all firms in some way, specific risk affects only one firm, and industry-group covariance affects a group of firms. Other forms of extra-market covariance may affect a very large number of firms; for example, a contractional monetary policy may reduce the values of firms that have assumed much financial risk, at the same time that the market as a whole is rising because of favorable economic news. In this example, a large group of firms, which cuts across industries, will be exposed to the change in monetary policy and will covary.

Residual return is the sum of specific return and return due to extra-market factors. It is called the "residual" return because, in a regression model to explain the security return as a function of the market return, it is the residual from the market return (the difference between the actual security return and the predicted value).

The rest of this paper deals with the prediction of systematic and residual risk for banks. The decomposition of residual risk will be reported in a later paper.

16.4   Evaluating and Fitting Prediction Rules for Systematic and Residual Risk

With respect to systematic risk, we will consider the prediction of beta, the response coefficient that determines relative exposure to market risk. To predict beta successfully, it is necessary to discriminate between stocks that will tend to move substantially when the market moves and stocks that will move little. Figure 16.1 shows an instance of relatively successful beta prediction. On the horizontal axis are plotted the betas published by Merrill Lynch for roughly 700 companies with largest capitalization on 31 December 1972. Hereafter the beta computed by this

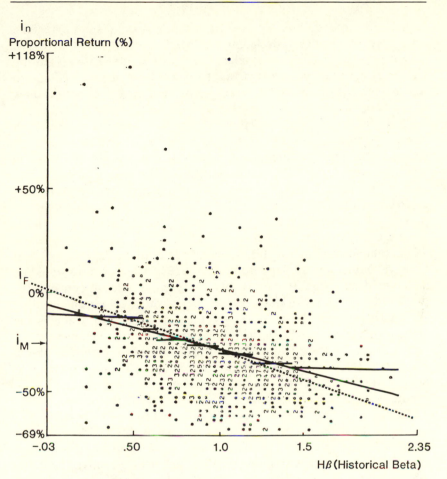

Fig. 16.1   Common stock returns 1 January 1973 to 20 June 1973 for 700 large United States companies plotted against 30 December 1972 historical beta. Regression line $r = b_0 + b_1 (H\beta r_M)$, and average returns by beta deciles are shown as solid lines. The dashed line shows the expected relationship, under the basic capital asset pricing model, if $H\beta$ were a perfect predictor of ß.

formula on any date will be called the "historical beta" as of that date and will be denoted by the two-letter symbol $H\beta$. On the vertical axis are plotted the returns to these common stocks in the next six months. This was a period when the market declined substantially, so that if the historical betas were correctly predictive, stocks with high $H\beta$ should have declined more than stocks with low $H\beta$.

The figure clearly shows that this has occurred. (The strength of this tendency is apparent when it is noticed that tightly clustered points are represented by integers [e.g., 7 indicates 7 cases].) The regression line through the data shows a pronounced downward slope, and the average returns for ten deciles of $H\beta$ (shown as ten horizontal steps extending across the decile ranges) decline in an orderly fashion as $H\beta$ increases. When the market falls, the results appear as in figure 16.1. When the market rises, the results appear as if reflected about the axis of zero return: high $H\beta$ stocks show greater positive returns; low $H\beta$ stocks show smaller positive returns.

The criterion for a successful prediction rule for beta is that it accurately arranges stocks in proportion to the response to the market. The closer the fit of the predicted market response for the security to the actual security return, the better is the prediction. Each interval of market movement provides an opportunity to test the accuracy of predictions available at the start of the interval. A succession of monthly intervals provides a long history of evaluations and hence an extensive examination of a prediction rule.

The solid line in figure 16.1 is the line of best fit to the data. However, if we were actually predicting returns using $H\beta$, our predictions would lie along the dashed line. In the case of a stock with predicted beta of zero, predicted return is the riskless rate, which was roughly 4 percent over that six-month period. For other stocks, the predicted return equals the riskless rate plus beta times the market excess return. The measure of success is the degree to which the return predictions for individual stocks lying along the dashed line fit the actual returns. The measure of goodness of fit is the coefficient of determination, or R^2.

Although the regression line achieves a good fit, there remain large errors about the line. These errors are the manifestation of residual risk, or the residual returns of the stocks. Of course, the residuals are influenced by the predicted betas. If a better rule were used to predict betas, residuals would be typically smaller. Nevertheless, all the improvements that appear to be possible in beta prediction achieve only a small reduction in the magnitude of the typical residual return. Further, we know from a multitude of studies that little of the variance of residual returns can be accounted for by security analysis predictions of mean returns. Hence these residual returns are largely unpredictable elements of return. The problem of predicting residual risk is equivalent to the problem of predicting the expected magnitude (absolute value) of the residual return on a stock. If this expected magnitude is small, the residual risk is small—and conversely.

Figure 16.2 illustrates the prediction of residual risk. On the horizontal axis, the residual risk prediction, defined as the predicted standard deviation of residual return, or $\hat{\sigma}$, is plotted. Stocks with higher levels of risk appear to the right. The vertical axis represents the absolute residual return for the stock. At several points, the expected frequency distribution of residual returns for stocks at that level of residual risk is drawn. Since the absolute value of residual return is under analysis, it will always

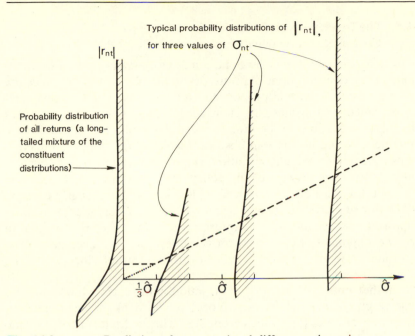

Fig. 16.2   Prediction of cross-sectional differences in variance.

be positive. The shape of the curve is that of half a bell-shaped curve. Even for stocks with very high levels of risk, as in the probability distribution at the right, the most likely residual return lies at the bottom of the bell-shaped half-curve, a residual return of zero. However, for high-residual-risk stocks, there is a possibility of very large residual returns, and so the distribution extends upward to the top of the page. For low-residual-risk stocks, with small $\hat{\sigma}$, we expect a tightly bunched distribution of returns, as in the drawings nearer the vertical axis. The dashed line drawn in the figure plots the predicted mean absolute residual return. This is a constant proportion of the standard deviation (76 percent in the model that will be developed below). The small kink in the straight line near zero is explained in the Appendix.

There is a natural statistical procedure to evaluate a prediction rule for residual risk. The dependent variable is the observed absolute residual return for the stock. The independent variables are predictions for the amount of residual risk. If the prediction is successful, then those stocks with high levels of predicted residual risk will show frequent large absolute residual returns, as in the distribution at the extreme right. Conversely, stocks having low levels of predicted risk will exhibit a tight distribution of residual returns, as in the distributions farther to the left. A suitably defined measure of goodness of fit for the regression, analogous to an R^2, summarizes the success of the prediction rule. This approach is explained in section 16.7.

16.5   The Descriptors: Information Sources
Used in Risk Prediction

In an attempt to predict risk, one can draw on many kinds of information. There are indications of future risk in the *current balance sheet and income statement*, such as proportions in various asset and liability categories, and operating margins. There are indications of the normal risk of the firm's operations in the *historical variability* of items in the income statement. When fluctuations obscure a policy of the firm, as in fluctuations over time in the payout ratio owing to transitory earnings fluctuations, a *historical average* of the policy, such as a five-year cumulative payout ratio, is useful. *Trends* in variables measure the changing position of the firm and provide some indication of growth orientation. Variables capturing *market judgment*, expressed as ratios of market values to income-statement or balance-sheet variables, such as "leverage at market value," are often powerful indicators of the market's forecasts of the firm's prospects.

Another important item of information is the regional location and type (e.g., money center, New York) of the bank; we use indicator (dummy) variables for six such groupings. The final category of information is the behavior of the market price of the common stock. Table 16.1 lists the descriptors we have used, along with a brief definition of each; detailed definitions are provided in Rosenberg and Perry (1978). Summary statistics for these descriptors are in table 16.2.

The reader may complain that we are going too far afield in amassing information from so many distinct sources. Why not restrict oneself to a historical measure of the aspect of risk in question? One justification is that it is important to ascertain the fundamental determinants of risk. And the second justification will be found in predictive performance.

A number of principles were observed in constructing the descriptors.

1. No descriptor was employed unless there were compelling a priori grounds to believe it might be predictive of subsequent risk. Such descriptors were found in three categories:

   a) Historical statistics on past risk for the bank's stockholders: these may be viewed as estimates (subject to measurement error) of past underlying aspects of risk. As such, they are useful in predicting an aspect of subsequent risk to the degree that both the following conditions are satisfied:

   i) the historical estimate is an accurate estimator of the underlying aspect of past risk, not obscured by measurement error;

   ii) the historical aspect of risk is correlated with the future aspect of risk that is to be predicted.

   b) Fundamental descriptors of the bank's operations and balance sheet, which economic theory leads us to believe are determinants of risk or correlated with risk. These may be subdivided into those that

Table 16.1   **The Descriptors**

A. Descriptors of Asset Mix

1 NCMLDA — THE RATIO OF NET COMMERCIAL LENDING TO ASSETS
2 COMLNA — THE RATIO OF COMMERCIAL LOANS TO ASSETS
3 NCNLDA — THE RATIO OF NET CONSUMER LENDING TO ASSETS
4 CONLNA — THE RATIO OF CONSUMER LOANS TO ASSETS
5 MUNIBA — THE RATIO OF TAX-EXEMPT BONDS TO ASSETS
6 RELNSA — THE RATIO OF REAL ESTATE LOANS TO ASSETS
7 ISECTA — THE RATIO OF ALL INVESTMENT SECURITIES TO ASSETS
8 TRDASA — THE RATIO OF TRADING ACCOUNT SECURITIES TO ASSETS

B. Descriptors of Liability Mix

9 CONTDA — THE RATIO OF CONSUMER TIME DEPOSITS TO ASSETS
10 DEMNDA — THE RATIO OF DEMAND DEPOSITS TO ASSETS
11 NFFBA — THE RATIO OF (NET) FEDERAL FUNDS BORROWED TO ASSETS
12 FORDPA — THE RATIO OF FOREIGN DEPOSITS TO ASSETS
13 SAVEDA — THE RATIO OF SAVINGS DEPOSITS TO ASSETS
14 TBORA — THE RATIO OF TOTAL BORROWINGS TO ASSETS
15 TCAPA — THE RATIO OF TOTAL CAPITAL TO ASSETS
16 TIMEDA — THE RATIO OF TIME DEPOSITS (OTHER THAN SAVINGS) TO ASSETS

C. Descriptors of Asset/Liability Characteristics

17 ATOLB — THE RATIO OF ASSETS TO LONG-TERM LIABILITIES (BOOK VALUE OF EQUITY, PLUS LONG-TERM DEBT)
18 BLEV — LEVERAGE, AT BOOK VALUE: THE RATIO OF THE BOOK VALUE OF (EQUITY PLUS DEBT) TO THE BOOK VALUE OF EQUITY
19 DILU — POTENTIAL DILUTION: THE RATIO OF NET INCOME PER SHARE FULLY DILUTED TO NET INCOME PER SHARE
20 DTOA — THE RATIO OF TOTAL DEBT TO ASSETS
21 KMTMN — AVERAGE MATURITY OF TAX-EXEMPT BOND PORTFOLIO, IN MONTHS
22 KMTUS — AVERAGE MATURITY OF TAXABLE BOND PORTFOLIO, IN MONTHS
23 KPDEP — THE PERCENTAGE DEPRECIATION IN THE BOND PORTFOLIO: THE RATIO OF THE DIFFERENCE BETWEEN BOND PORTFOLIO MARKET AND BOOK VALUES TO BOND PORTFOLIO BOOK VALUE
24 RLTLTL — THE RATIO OF "RISKY" LIABILITIES TO LONG-TERM LIABILITIES

D. Descriptors of Operating Characteristics

25 ATAX — THE RATIO OF INCOME TAXES TO PRETAX INCOME, PAST FIVE YEARS
26 FFMKT — FEDERAL FUNDS MARKET-MAKING ACTIVITY: THE RATIO OF THE MINIMUM OF (FEDERAL FUNDS PURCHASED, FEDERAL FUNDS SOLD) TO ASSETS
27 FLO1 — THE RATIO OF AVERAGE CASH FLOW TO CURRENT LIABILITIES
28 FRGNO — THE RATIO OF FOREIGN OFFICES TO TOTAL OFFICES
29 PAY1 — PAYOUT: THE RATIO OF COMMON DIVIDENDS TO EARNINGS AVAILABLE FOR COMMON THE PRIOR YEAR, PAST FIVE YEARS
30 PNCV — THE ESTIMATED PROBABILITY OF NONCOVERAGE OF FIXED CHARGES USING A TRENDED VALUE FOR CURRENT OPERATING INCOME
31 SALTOR — THE RATIO OF SALARIES AND RELATED EXPENSES TO CURRENT OPERATING REVENUE
32 TRDVRA — THE RATIO OF (THE VARIABILITY [STANDARD DEVIATION] OF TRADING ACCOUNT INCOME $\times$ 100) TO ASSETS
33 VCAP — THE VARIABILITY OF CAPITAL STRUCTURE: THE RATIO OF THE SUM OF THE ABSOLUTE VALUES OF CHANGES IN THE BOOK VALUES OF EQUITY AND LONG-TERM DEBT TO THE SUM OF THE BOOK VALUES OF EQUITY AND LONG-TERM DEBT
34 VERN — THE VARIABILITY OF EARNINGS: THE RATIO OF THE STANDARD DEVIATION OF EARNINGS TO THE ABSOLUTE VALUE OF AVERAGE EARNINGS
35 VFLO — THE VARIABILITY OF CASH FLOW: THE RATIO OF THE STANDARD DEVIATION OF CASH FLOW TO THE AVERAGE ABSOLUTE CASH FLOW
36 ABET — AN ACCOUNTING BETA, EQUAL TO THE "COEFFICIENT OF EXPLAINED VARIATION" OF THE FIRM'S EARNINGS WITH RESPECT TO ECONOMYWIDE EARNINGS

Table 16.1 (continued)

E. Descriptors of Earnings Success

37 CUTD — THE AVERAGE PROPORTIONAL CUT IN DIVIDENDS, PAST FIVE YEARS
38 DELE — THE PROPORTIONAL CHANGE IN EARNINGS PER SHARE
39 DMNE — A DUMMY VARIABLE INDICATING NEGLIGIBLE EARNINGS
40 MRGIN — THE RATIO OF NET INCOME TO CURRENT OPERATING REVENUE
41 REVENA — THE RATIO OF CURRENT OPERATING REVENUE TO ASSETS
42 ROEQ — RETURN ON EQUITY: THE RATIO OF NET INCOME TO BOOK VALUE OF EQUITY, PAST FIVE YEARS

F. Descriptors of Growth

43 AGRO — ASSET GROWTH RATE, EQUAL TO THE RATIO OF THE ANNUAL TREND IN ASSETS TO THE AVERAGE VALUE
44 DMS5 — A DUMMY VARIABLE INDICATING THE AVAILABILITY OF A FIVE-YEAR HISTORY OF EARNINGS INFORMATION
45 EGRO — EARNINGS GROWTH RATE, EQUAL TO THE RATIO OF THE ANNUAL TREND IN EARNINGS TO THE ABSOLUTE VALUE OF THE AVERAGE
46 OFFEX — DOMESTIC OFFICE EXPANSION RATE, EQUAL TO THE RATIO OF THE ANNUAL TREND IN THE NUMBER OF DOMESTIC OFFICES TO THE AVERAGE VALUE
47 RSKLGO — GROWTH RATE OF RISKY LIABILITIES, EQUAL TO THE RATIO OF THE ANNUAL TREND IN RISKY LIABILITIES TO THE AVERAGE VALUE

G. Descriptors of Size

48 ASSI — THE (NATURAL) LOGARITHM OF AVERAGE (PAST FIVE YEARS) TOTAL ASSETS (IN MILLIONS)
49 MKTS — CURRENT OPERATING REVENUE (IN MILLIONS)

H. Descriptors of (Stock) Market Price Variability

50 HBET — HISTORICAL BETA, THE REGRESSION COEFFICIENT TAKEN FROM THE REGRESSION OF MONTHLY COMMON STOCK RETURNS ON MONTHLY RETURNS FOR THE MARKET
51 BTSQ — THE SQUARE OF HBET, DEFINED ABOVE
52 HSIG — HISTORICAL SIGMA, THE STANDARD DEVIATION OF RESIDUAL RETURNS FROM THE REGRESSION FOR HBET, DEFINED ABOVE
53 SGSQ — THE SQUARE OF HSIG, DEFINED ABOVE
54 BS — THE SQUARE ROOT OF THE PRODUCT OF HBET AND HSIG, AS DEFINED ABOVE
55 BADJ — THE BAYESIAN ADJUSTMENT TO HBET, DEFINED ABOVE, UNDER THE (ERRONEOUS) ASSUMPTION THAT THE UNDERLYING VALUES OF BETA AND SIGMA ARE INDEPENDENT
56 LPRI — THE (NATURAL) LOGARITHM OF THE STOCK PRICE
57 RSTR — THE LOGARITHMIC RATE OF RETURN OVER THE PAST YEAR
58 TREC — A MEASURE OF COMMON STOCK TRADING RECENCY, EQUAL TO THE RECIPROCAL OF THE NUMBER OF PRIOR YEARS OF AVAILABLE MONTHLY STOCK PRICES

I. Descriptors Dependent upon the Market Valuation of Common Stock

59 ATOLM — THE RATIO OF ASSETS TO LONG-TERM LIABILITIES (MARKET VALUE OF EQUITY, PLUS LONG-TERM DEBT)
60 BBET — "BEAVER" BETA: THE REGRESSION COEFFICIENT TAKEN FROM THE REGRESSION OF THE NORMALIZED EARNINGS/PRICE RATIO OF THE FIRM ON THE NORMALIZED EARNINGS/PRICE RATIO OF THE ECONOMY
61 BTOP — THE RATIO OF BOOK VALUE TO MARKET VALUE OF EQUITY
62 CAPT — THE (NATURAL) LOGARITHM OF THE MARKET VALUE OF EQUITY (IN MILLIONS)
63 DMYL — A DUMMY VARIABLE INDICATING EXTREMELY LOW DIVIDEND YIELD
64 ENTP — THE NORMALIZED EARNINGS/PRICE RATIO
65 ETOP — THE RATIO OF EARNINGS TO PRICE
66 ETP5 — THE "TYPICAL" EARNINGS/PRICE RATIO, PAST FIVE YEARS
67 LIQU — A MEASURE OF LIQUIDITY, EQUAL TO THE RATIO OF (CASH PLUS RECEIVABLES LESS CURRENT LIABILITIES) TO THE MARKET VALUE OF EQUITY

Table 16.1 (continued)

68 MLEV	—	LEVERAGE, AT MARKET VALUE: THE RATIO OF (MARKET VALUE OF EQUITY PLUS BOOK VALUE OF DEBT) TO THE MARKET VALUE OF EQUITY
69 ECAP	—	THE MARKET VALUE OF EQUITY (IN MILLIONS)
70 PTEQ	—	THE RATIO OF PLANT (FIXED ASSETS) TO THE MARKET VALUE OF EQUITY
71 YILD	—	THE RATIO OF DIVIDENDS PAID TO THE MARKET VALUE OF EQUITY
72 YLD5	—	THE "NORMAL" VALUE OF DIVIDEND YIELD (OVER FIVE YEARS)

J. Descriptors of Bank Type/Location

73 DRMNY	—	A DUMMY VARIABLE INDICATING A NEW YORK MONEY-CENTER BANK
74 DRMON	—	A DUMMY VARIABLE INDICATING A MONEY-CENTER BANK OUTSIDE NEW YORK
75 DRSE	—	A DUMMY VARIABLE INDICATING A SOUTHEASTERN BANK
76 DRMW	—	A DUMMY VARIABLE INDICATING A MIDWESTERN BANK
77 DRSW	—	A DUMMY VARIABLE INDICATING A SOUTHWESTERN BANK
78 DRWC	—	A DUMMY VARIABLE INDICATING A WEST COAST BANK

Note: Detailed descriptor definitions are available in NBER Working Paper no. 265.

relate exclusively to business risk, those that relate exclusively to financial leverage, and those that measure the interaction of both.

c) Indicators of the judgment of investors concerning the firm, which provide indirect measures of the bank's risk. Foremost among these are valuation ratios such as book/price and earnings/price (indicative of investors' expectations concerning the bank's future growth and success).

2. The second principle concerns the problem of multicollinearity. When a number of descriptors are included in the analysis, correlation among them will inevitably arise, and it will therefore be more difficult to discriminate among their effects. There is a remarkably widespread misunderstanding of the effects of multicollinearity in a multiple regression: many people believe that the presence of multicollinearity results in bias in estimated coefficients, or estimated standard errors, or both. This is not true. The regression provides an unbiased indication of the coefficients for (partial derivatives with respect to) the descriptors and of the degree to which these are accurately estimated in spite of the correlation with other descriptors. The *t*-statistics for the estimated coefficients provide a reliable test of the wisdom with which descriptors were constructed. With this in mind, we were not excessively afraid of multicollinearity.

On the other hand, when two descriptors are highly correlated, it becomes difficult to distinguish their effects; consequently, every effort was made to anticipate correlations in advance and to construct well-differentiated descriptors that would exhibit significant variation relative to one another. For instance, instead of employing a multitude of financial ratios, we designed one or two that we believed were the best measures of that aspect of financial condition. When we employed two measures of the same conceptual variable, it was always for one of two

Table 16.2 Summary Statistics of the Descriptors for the June 1977 Cross Section

Descriptor	Minimum Value	Equal-Weighted Mean	Maximum Value	Capitalization-Weighted Mean	Standard Deviation
1 NCMLDA	−.1475	.1460	.4120	.1239	.0844
2 COMLNA	.1057	.2333	.3837	.2298	.0557
3 NCNLDA	−.6350	−.2385	.1193	−.3405	.1259
4 CONLNA	.0089	.1130	.2454	.0744	.0535
5 MUNIBA	.0156	.0891	.2267	.0691	.0446
6 RELNSA	.0061	.1249	.4460	.0883	.0701
7 ISECTA	.0537	.2017	.3648	.1576	.0727
8 TRDASA	0	.0073	.0495	.0102	.0102
9 CONTDA	0	.1456	.5266	.0960	.1435
10 DEMNDA	0	.3023	.4522	.2603	.0695
11 NFFBA	−.1106	.0227	.1874	.0338	.0518
12 FORDPA	0	.0747	.4860	.2007	.1054
13 SAVEDA	0	.1357	.4891	.0899	.1295
14 TBORA	.0011	.1131	.3119	.1220	.0610
15 TCAPA	.0441	.0785	.1543	.0698	.0170
16 TIMEDA	0	.3513	.6782	.4322	.1329
17 ATOLB	8.5768	16.8619	29.1167	19.4978	4.0698
18 BLEV	1.0000	1.1357	3.5593	1.0957	.2510
19 DILU	.7135	.9803	1.0000	.9813	.0432
20 DTOA	0	.0533	.2001	.0663	.0451
21 KMTMN	18.00	129.45	199.00	109.35	34.71
22 KMTUS	7.00	25.84	50.00	26.40	8.83
23 KPDEP	−.0530	−.0044	.0424	−.0071	.0165
24 RLTLTL	.2305	6.9374	18.3476	10.2528	3.5803
25 ATAX	0	.1945	.4367	.2767	.1113
26 FFMKT	0	.0425	.1811	.0359	.0391
27 FLO1	−.0503	.5694	2.6196	.5017	.6807
28 FRGNO	0	.0009	.0390	.0071	.0048
29 PAY1	.1453	.4405	.6564	.4245	.0925
30 PNCV	0	.0667	.8997	.0205	.1745
31 SALTOR	.0950	.2063	.3644	.1723	.0456
32 TRDVRA	0	.0295	.3160	.0313	.0485
33 VCAP	.0284	.1029	.2146	.1052	.0357
34 VERN	.0550	.3014	2.4219	.2114	.4270
35 VFLO	.0076	.2274	.8744	.2863	.1062
36 ABET	0	.0468	.4109	.0200	.0874
37 CUTD	0	.0271	.4870	.0055	.0932
38 DELE	−2.0000	.0753	2.0000	.0356	.5295
39 DMNE	0	.0407	1.0	.0048	.1983
40 MRGIN	−.0390	.0817	.1733	.0830	.0404
41 REVENA	.0321	.0699	.0942	.0680	.0076
42 ROEQ	−.0732	.1192	.2201	.1378	.0377

Table 16.2 (continued)

Descriptor	Minimum Value	Equal-Weighted Mean	Maximum Value	Capitalization-Weighted Mean	Standard Deviation
43 AGRO	−.0544	.0760	.3186	.1031	.0537
44 DMS5	0	.9593	1.0	.9849	.1983
45 EGRO	−.3415	−.0068	.2059	.0643	.1336
46 OFFEX	−.8224	.0880	.9950	.0890	.3342
47 RSKLGO	−.2488	.0084	.2658	.0275	.0889
48 ASSI	6.5201	7.8866	10.9728	9.1057	.9347
49 MKTS	59.05	392.32	4844.75	1494.70	723.91
50 HBET	.1684	.9593	1.9306	1.0873	.3133
51 BTSQ	.0284	1.0129	3.1565	1.2484	.6166
52 HSIG	.0252	.0709	.1247	.0684	.0185
53 SGSQ	.0006	.0053	.0135	.0048	.0027
54 BS	.0796	.2573	.4235	.2705	.0633
55 BADJ	−.1787	−.0073	.2523	.0186	.0773
56 LPRI	1.3218	3.0758	4.0254	3.3659	.5323
57 RSTR	−.5275	.0231	.3881	−.0371	.1612
58 TREC	0	.0644	.2927	.0253	.0744
59 ATOLM	9.5411	21.7743	47.3130	19.1801	9.1119
60 BBET	−.3395	.1704	.2769	.1584	.0671
61 BTOP	.5498	1.3745	4.2768	1.0333	.5760
62 CAPT	14.3343	18.6962	22.2060	20.1191	1.0909
63 DMYL	0	.0163	1.0	.0009	.1270
64 ENTP	−3.3691	.0818	.2043	.1125	.3214
65 ETOP	−.1867	.1126	.2090	.1109	.0618
66 ETP5	−.0088	.1215	.2023	.1099	.0367
67 LIQU	−3.4624	1.5571	11.7263	1.9314	2.0686
68 MLEV	1.0000	1.2283	8.7087	1.1119	.7082
69 ECAP	1.68	247.27	2577.91	927.15	411.69
70 PTEQ	.0566	.4358	1.3210	.2711	.2861
71 YILD	0	.0531	.0893	.0444	.0185
72 YLD5	0	.0533	.0995	.0447	.0188

Descriptor		
73 DRMNY	9	
74 DRMON	8	
75 DRSE	29	Number of banks in each group
76 DRMW	31	
77 DRSW	13	
78 DRWC	11	

reasons: sometimes both measures were subject to independent measurement errors, so that a weighted average of the two would be a more accurate estimator of the underlying concept than either separately; sometimes we were uncertain a priori which would be the better descriptor, recognizing that the two definitions were clearly substitutes for one another, and so we relied on the regression to discriminate between the two. The latter was the case for four descriptors (NCMLDA, NCNLDA, FLO1, PAY1). We used two definitions of each in the early stages and chose the best for the subsequent analysis.

3. The third principle was the requirement that each descriptor be valid across the entire cross section of banks. We were careful to operationalize our concepts through formulas that would be applicable to all cases. This aspect of our approach is best explained by illustrating its violation. In many studies, the chosen measure of earnings growth was useless when earnings were negative, with the result that all banks that had had negative earnings had to be excluded from the sample; in contrast, we never deleted an observation because a computational formula failed. As another instance of this principle, we employed only descriptors for which data were available for the majority of our sample.

4. A fourth principle was the search for robust formulas—in other words, for formulas that yielded reasonable descriptors for the conceptual variable regardless of the peculiar historical circumstances of the bank. This principle led in many cases to the use of five-year averages, to smoothed values, or to the need for a truncation rule that wiped out otherwise extreme values. In general, the goal was a formula that would always produce a value that seemed reasonable when the raw data were examined.

5. A fifth principle was a variant of Occam's razor: When alternative formulas for a conceptual variable were available, and the difference in their validity was expected to be small, we chose the formula that was more familiar to professionals in the field of finance.

6. A sixth principle was that the descriptors were transformed to obtain a model that was linear. We attempted to transform descriptors and to draw in extreme outliers, so that the relationship between risk and the descriptors would be linear. In all cases, histograms of the descriptors were constructed to verify that the descriptor's range was appropriate and that a linear relationship would make sense. Only in the cases of historical beta, historical sigma, and capitalization (descriptors that have important predictive content for risk, and for which the relationship is clearly nonlinear) did we include several functions of the variables as descriptors in order to obtain a nonlinear relationship.

7. A seventh and final principle was that we relied on a priori judgment wherever possible. In other words, we attempted to select the descriptors on the basis of economic theory and in conformity with the above-

mentioned principles. Then we computed the values of each descriptor and examined them across a sample population to check for robustness and reasonableness. We examined the correlation matrix among descriptors and redefined them in a few cases where extreme correlations showed up. Only after this was done were the descriptors introduced into a regression where any aspect of risk was the dependent variable.

Another important issue concerns the treatment of extreme or outlying values of the descriptors. No matter how robust a formula is, a few extraordinarily low or high values for banks in peculiar circumstances may be generated. Sometimes the formula is so constructed that these values represent equally extreme states of the underlying characteristic. In this case the descriptor should be left as it is. But in other cases the extreme values exaggerate the differences between the bank and the population of banks with ordinary values. In this case it is appropriate to "pull in" the extreme value toward a more ordinary one. The reasoning behind this is that the bank really does not differ much from the group of banks at the boundary of the commonly observed region for the descriptor, so that the descriptor for this bank should be set equal to the value at the boundary.

This can be done by defining a lower and upper bound for the descriptor and redefining all values that fall outside the bounds to equal the bounds. Any value that falls below the lower bound is transformed to equal the lower bound; any value that is above the upper bound is transformed to equal the upper bound. This process may be called "Windsorizing" or, to use a more familiar but less specific term, truncation. For the majority of descriptors, the truncation criteria have been expressed in terms of multiples of the cross-sectional standard deviation among all banks. This means that values falling more than some number (five, for example) of cross-sectional standard deviations above the capitalization-weighted mean will be set equal to that upper bound.

The outcome of all this is that the descriptors seem to be fairly satisfactory. First, they appear to be meaningful in comparison across the full range of normal banks; this applies both within a cross section and in comparisons of the same bank over time. Second, the outlying cases have tended to coincide with a difficult period for the bank in question. Thus the descriptors have proved to be accurate indicators of extreme risk.

Some descriptors that may indicate banks with potential or clear-cut problems are listed in table 16.3, and the banks so indicated (as of June 1977) are listed in table 16.4. In general, these outliers are quite far from the mean—the values for ROEQ, ENTP, ETOP, and MLEV are, for example, ten standard deviations. Two variables, DMNE and DMYL, are dummy variables; the outliers here are values of one. It is interesting to note that, of all twelve descriptors, five are calculated from only accounting data (BLEV, PNCV, VERN, DMNE, ROEQ), one is a descriptor of market price

Table 16.3   Descriptor Outliers from the June 1977 Cross Section

Descriptor	Outlier Direction	Outlying Banks[a]
18 BLEV — leverage at book	High	72
30 PNCV — probability of noncoverage	High	28, 66, 72, 99
34 VERN — variance of earnings	High	28, 57, 66
39 DMNE — dummy, negligible earnings	High[b]	24, 57, 66, 72, 87
42 ROEQ — income/equity	Low	72
52 HSIG — historical sigma	High	72
61 BTOP — book/price	High	72
63 DMYL — dummy, low yield	High[b]	72, 99
64 ENTP — normalized earnings/price	Low	72
65 ETOP — earnings/price	Low	72
66 ETP5 — earnings/price, five years	Low	66, 72
68 MLEV — leverage at market	High	72

[a]See table 16.4 for bank identification.
[b]A value of one.

variability (HSIG), and the remaining six utilize both accounting data and the market valuations of common stock. We feel that these findings are potentially important and deserve further study.

16.6 Procedure

Our primary data source is the COMPUSTAT bank tapes, which contain data on 124 large United States banks. Both the annual and the quarterly tapes were used, although the only information taken from the latter was the monthly closing price of the common stock. A few additional items were drawn from the Keefe Bank Manuals. Because of the pattern of data availability, the present study begins in March 1969 and continues through June 1977; this gives us a total of 11,219 data points, each being a monthly observation of a bank.

The first step is to compute, for each of the thirty-four quarters, the value of each descriptor for each bank in the sample, as it could have been computed at the beginning of that quarter. It is important to note that

Table 16.4   Bank Identification

Number	Region	Name
24	Eastern	First Empire State Corporation
28	Eastern	Hartford National Corporation
57	Southeastern	Flagship Banks
66	Southeastern	Union Planters Corporation
72	Midwestern	Bank of Commonwealth, Detroit
87	Midwestern	Indiana National Corporation
99	Midwestern	Union Commerce Corporation

data are used for any quarter only if they would have been available at the start of that quarter. Data related to the stock market are presumed to be published immediately. Annual accounting data are not presumed to become available until four months after the end of the fiscal year; this allows for the ninety-day reporting delay and thirty more days for the data to be assembled into machine-readable form. This procedure ensures that an observer could actually have computed these descriptors at the start of each quarter.

The sample of banks for any quarter is made up of all banks; any descriptor that is unavailable for a particular bank is assumed to be equal to the average value of that descriptor for that cross section. For each of the three months in the quarter, the monthly subsample is made up of all banks for which stock price returns in that month are available. These stock price returns are analyzed in relation to the descriptors computed as of the beginning of the quarter. Thus, three monthly samples are predicted with each set of descriptors, in conformity with a prediction rule that is revised quarterly and is based upon previously published information.

The model and the estimation procedure used are described in detail in the Appendix. Several interesting points that should be noted are:

1. The estimation approach is iterative, in that the prediction rule for beta is estimated first; this is then used to define the dependent variable for the sigma prediction rule regression.

2. Generalized least squares is used to account for heteroskedasticity. The resulting prediction rules are more statistically efficient.

3. The prediction rules are estimated simultaneously for all individual banks in all time periods, through a pooled time-series, cross-sectional regression.

4. The beta prediction rule is conditional upon the market return (the CRSP RETV index), and the sigma prediction rule is conditional upon the typical cross-sectional standard deviation of residual return in any given month.

The study adhered strictly to the principles of experimental design. All procedures were specified in advance of examining the returns to be predicted. This was done to ensure that the study would be self-validating. Otherwise there would be no assurance that the results were likely to persist into the future.

16.7   Empirical Results

As a preliminary to the multiple-regression results, table 16.5 reports the simple regressions of investment risk on each of the descriptors. The predictive content of each descriptor, taken separately, is given for beta and for sigma. Since the multiple regression is not used, the predictive

Table 16.5   **Individual Descriptors as Predictors of Systematic and Residual Risk**

	Prediction of Beta			Prediction of Sigma		
Descriptor	Coef-ficient[a]	t-Sta-tistic[b]	Order of Impor-tance[c]	Coef-ficient[a]	t-Sta-tistic[b]	Order of Impor-tance[c]
1 NCMLDA	−.441	−2.92	41	−.029	−.31	71
2 COMLNA	−.211	−1.14	60	−.228	−1.97	50
3 NCNLDA	−.221	−2.02	50	.122	1.75	51
4 CONLNA	−.211	−.88	64	.626	4.15	28
5 MUNIBA	−1.187	−3.77	32	−.726	−3.64	32
6 RELNSA	−.422	−2.02	49	.223	1.68	53
7 ISECTA	−1.569	−7.45	12	−.351	−2.63	44
8 TRDASA	.406	.63	71	−1.090	−2.65	43
9 CONTDA	.185	1.67	53	−.063	−.90	63
10 DEMNDA	−.905	−7.47	11	−.294	−3.73	31
11 NFFBA	1.512	.5.17	26	−.0051	−.03	78
12 FORDPA	1.139	7.18	14	−.030	−.30	72
13 SAVEDA	.121	1.04	62	−.087	−1.19	59
14 TBORA	1.093	4.86	28	−.011	−.07	77
15 TCAPA	−4.689	−5.59	21	−1.898	−3.61	33
16 TIMEDA	.207	2.20	45	.162	2.67	42
17 ATOLB	.026	8.12	9*	.014	6.47	19
18 BLEV	.208	3.75	33	.302	7.84	8*
19 DILU	−.739	−1.99	51	.719	3.14	40
20 DTOA	1.583	5.22	25	.179	.90	64
21 KMTMN	−.00037	−.81	65	.00031	1.06	62
22 KMTUS	−.0058	−3.74	34	−.00043	−.42	69
23 KPDEP	.483	1.22	57	−.475	−2.04	48
24 RLTLTL	.022	5.72	20	.0097	3.85	30
25 ATAX	−.185	−1.24	56	−.325	−3.59	34
26 FFMKT	−.039	−.10	78	−.468	−2.00	49
27 FLO1	−.038	−2.63	44	−.046	−5.08	26
28 FRGNO	6.401	3.17	37	−2.407	−2.17	46
29 PAY1	−.214	−1.40	55	.0077	.08	76
30 PNCV	−.303	−.69	66	1.282	6.44	20
31 SALTOR	.040	.16	77	.522	3.35	36
32 TRDVRA	.139	.28	75	−.421	−1.49	54
33 VCAP	1.443	4.80	29	.737	3.89	29
34 VERN	.134	1.06	61	.958	13.21	3*
35 VFLO	.542	3.48	36	.657	6.87	17
36 ABET	−.520	−1.14	59	2.006	8.03	7*
37 CUTD	1.293	2.05	48	2.076	5.60	25
38 DELE	.204	2.98	40	−.116	−3.18	39
39 DMNE	−.147	−.90	63	.589	6.02	23
40 MRGIN	−1.789	−5.79	19	−1.454	−7.57	11
41 REVENA	.274	.26	76	2.232	3.37	35
42 ROEQ	2.445	4.05	31	−.095	−.24	73

Table 16.5 (continued)

Descriptor	Prediction of Beta			Prediction of Sigma		
	Coefficient[a]	t-Statistic[b]	Order of Importance[c]	Coefficient[a]	t-Statistic[b]	Order of Importance[c]
43 AGRO	2.162	8.33	8*	1.305	7.49	13
44 DMS5	.174	4.99	27	−.031	−1.34	56
45 EGRO	.145	.66	67	−.285	−2.15	47
46 OFFEX	.019	.44	74	−.014	−.48	68
47 RSKLGO	.148	2.09	47	.028	.58	67
48 ASSI	.125	9.29	3*	−.020	−2.39	45
49 MKTS	.00020	6.43	16	−.000014	−.77	65
50 HBET	.444	9.97	1*	.217	7.64	10*
51 BTSQ	.269	9.05	4*	.134	7.33	14
52 HSIG	6.778	6.72	15	8.844	14.44	1*
53 SGSQ	48.575	5.87	18	68.098	13.84	2*
54 BS	2.325	9.96	2*	1.594	11.00	4*
55 BADJ	1.015	5.48	23	.151	1.22	58
56 LPRI	−.068	−2.84	42	−.161	−10.12	5*
57 RSTR	−.411	−8.85	5*	−.039	−1.13	61
58 TREC	−.382	−7.23	13	.025	.74	66
59 ATOLM	.0046	3.15	38	.0033	3.26	37
60 BBET	−1.874	−5.92	17	−.921	−4.46	27
61 BTOP	−.013	−.49	73	.0059	.32	70
62 CAPT	.112	8.45	7*	−.027	−3.21	38
63 DMYL	.332	1.58	54	1.068	7.55	12
64 ENTP	.141	.61	72	−1.059	−6.89	16
65 ETOP	.292	1.18	58	−1.159	−6.92	15
66 ETP5	−4.230	−7.96	10*	−2.418	−7.81	9*
67 LIQU	.013	1.77	52	−.0059	−1.18	60
68 MLEV	.131	2.80	43	.268	8.65	6*
69 ECAP	.00019	5.51	22	−.000032	−1.46	55
70 PTEQ	.120	2.17	46	.245	6.63	18
71 YILD	−.346	−.63	70	−.077	−.21	75
72 YLD5	−9.248	−8.58	6*	−3.741	−5.91	24
73 DRMNY	.200	4.30	30	−.050	−1.68	52
74 DRMON	.030	.65	68	−.0064	−.21	74
75 DRSE	.097	3.00	39	.129	6.22	22
76 DRMW	−.152	−5.41	24	−.112	−6.28	21
77 DRSW	−.027	−.64	69	.033	1.26	57
78 DRWC	.175	3.73	35	.092	3.02	41

[a]For beta, the coefficient gives the adjustment to predicted beta for a unit change in the descriptor. For sigma, the coefficient gives the adjustment to the relative value of sigma (i.e., sigma ÷ cross-sectional average sigma) for a unit change in the descriptor. For purposes of interpretation, it is also useful to know the change in the dependent variable implied by a one-standard-deviation shift in the descriptor, i.e., the coefficient with respect to a normalized descriptor. This adjusted coefficient is obtained by multiplying the reported coefficient by the descriptor's standard deviation, which is given in column 5 of table 16.2.

content of each descriptor includes its role as a surrogate for all other descriptors as well as its own intrinsic relevance.

The *t*-statistics for the relationships and the relative order of importance of the descriptors are interesting. For beta, the single most powerful predictor is HBET, the historical estimate of beta. The second- and fourth-best predictors are BS, the geometric average of the historical estimates of beta and sigma, and BTSQ, the square of HBET. The third most effective is ASSI, which measures the total assets of the bank: the larger the bank, the greater its beta. The fifth most important is the "relative strength" (RSTR) of the bank in the preceding year: the better the past market performance of the common stock, the lower the expected beta. Sixth is YLD5, the "normal" dividend yield. Seventh is total equity (market) capitalization (CAPT). Eighth is AGRO, the asset growth rate: the higher this growth rate, the higher the bank's beta. Next is a measure of leverage, the ratio of total assets to long-term liabilities or capital, valued at book (ATOLB). Tenth is ETP5, the bank's "typical" earnings/price ratio: the higher this ratio (or the lower the price/earnings ratio), the lower the bank's beta.

For residual standard deviation, or sigma, the two most important descriptors are measures related to historical sigma (HSIG, SGSQ). The third is the historical variability of earnings (VERN), while the fourth is related to historical sigma and beta (BS). Fifth is the logarithm of the price of the common stock (LPRI): the higher the price, the lower is sigma. Two different measures of leverage in the capital structure (MLEV and BLEV) are sixth and eighth in importance: the greater the leverage—whether calculated using book or market value of equity—the greater the residual variance. Seventh is a measure of "accounting beta" (ABET), and ninth is ETP5: the higher this ratio, the lower is sigma. Finally, historical beta (HBET) is tenth.

It is significant that those descriptors with the highest predictive content for beta are not the same as those for sigma; only three (HBET, ETP5, BS) are among the top ten for both beta and sigma. Thus, not only are systematic risk and residual risk fundamentally different aspects of the overall risk of a bank, but they are, in addition, determined by different aspects of the bank's operational characteristics.

Table 16.6 reports the results of regressions for beta, using descriptors of assets and liabilities. Using the simplest model of the investment risk of

---

[b]This is the *t*-statistic for the simple GLS regression in which the descriptor is the only information used to predict risk, with 11,217 degrees of freedom. The critical point for the 99 percent confidence level is 2.58. The larger the absolute value of the *t*-statistic, the larger is the predictive content of this descriptor when used alone. The R^2 (coefficient of determination) achieved by each descriptor alone is proportional to the squared *t*-statistic.
[c]This is the rank of the descriptor, among all descriptors, in terms of explanatory power, with 1 being the highest. The asterisks denote the top ten.

a portfolio of assets and liabilities, the systematic risk of the net portfolio (excluding capital accounts) is a linear function of the proportions in asset and liability categories, with coefficients that reflect the systematic risks of the various categories. The systematic risk of the shareholders' equity

Table 16.6   **Asset/Liability Descriptor Regressions for Beta**

Descriptor	Assets Only	Liabil- ities Only	All Asset/ Liability Descriptors	With Net Asset/ Liability Descriptors
Constant	.278 (.182)	.658 (.239)	1.013 (.285)	.731 (.213)
1 NCMLDA				.185 (.187)
2 COMLNA	−.381 (.218)		−.355 (.251)	
3 NCNLDA				.302 (.135)
4 CONLNA	.612 (.292)		.278 (.308)	
5 MUNIBA	1.764 (.514)		1.724 (.537)	1.698 (.528)
6 RELNSA	−.367 (.239)		−.737 (.295)	
7 ISECTA	−1.900 (.364)		−1.955 (.412)	−1.708 (.400)
8 TRDASA	−.983 (.671)		−1.538 (.711)	−1.378 (.703)
9 CONTDA		1.505 (.579)	1.394 (.585)	
10 DEMNDA		−.658 (.176)	−.645 (.179)	−.670 (.146)
11 NFFBA		.606 (.327)	.849 (.337)	.850 (.348)
12 FORDPA		.092 (.237)	−.442 (.295)	−.081 (.263)
13 SAVEDA		−.145 (.624)	.0010 (.638)	
14 TBORA		.078 (.285)	−.342 (.343)	.010 (.307)
15 TCAPA		−1.949 (1.009)	−1.953 (1.052)	−1.400 (.984)
16 TIMEDA		−.324 (.170)	−.111 (.187)	
48 ASSI	.109 (.016)	.086 (.020)	.085 (.021)	.083 (.020)

Note: The standard error of each coefficient is given in parentheses.

is then obtained by multiplying portfolio systematic risk by the leverage ratio and is consequently a nonlinear (inverse) function of the proportion of long-term capital. However, for simplicity, we first estimated a model for beta as a linear function of asset and liability proportions. (The coefficient of the equity proportion in this equation can be interpreted as the first-order term in a Taylor expansion and is therefore expected to be negative.)

Relationships including asset and liability proportions as descriptors were estimated first alone, then with one added descriptor of the size of the institutions: ASSI, the logarithm of total assets. The total asset variable is highly significant: the coefficient is positive for beta and negative for sigma. The coefficients of asset and liability proportions generally change very little as ASSI is brought into the regressions. The major exception is in the coefficient of foreign deposits (FORDPA), which is positive for beta and negative for sigma when ASSI is excluded and reverses sign in both cases when ASSI is brought into the regression. Clearly, the proportion of foreign deposits is a surrogate for bank size. The general insensitivity of other coefficients to inclusion of ASSI is a sign that multicollinearity is absent. To save space, the results are reported for only one set of regressions, those including ASSI.

The regressions for beta in table 16.6 are of the form predicted $\beta = \text{constant} + b_{ASSI} (\ln [\text{total assets}])$

$$+ \sum_{j=1}^{J} b_j \left(\frac{\text{dollars in asset/liability category } j}{\text{total assets}} \right)$$

The regressions for sigma in table 16.7 are of the form $\dfrac{\text{predicted sigma}}{\text{average sigma}}$ $= \text{constant} + s_{ASSI} (\ln [\text{total assets}])$

$$+ \sum_{j=1}^{J} s_j \left(\frac{\text{dollars in asset/liability category } j}{\text{total assets}} \right)$$

The asset categories and liability categories are mutually exclusive but not exhaustive. The coefficients b_j (or s_j) are not the beta (or sigma) *levels* for the categories, but rather are adjustments to the otherwise normal beta (or sigma) for a bank owing to the category. The essential content of the results lies in the differences between any pair of coefficients b_i and b_j (or s_i and s_j). If funds are moved from category i to category j, the difference in coefficients gives the expected effect on risk. For example, if one-tenth of a bank's liabilities are shifted from net federal funds borrowed (NFFBA) to demand deposits (DEMNDA), the effect on risk can be found by comparing the coefficients for these two categories. For beta, $b_{NFFBA} = .849$ and $b_{DEMNDA} = -.645$. The difference in beta is $(-.645) - (.845) = -1.494$. A shift of one-tenth of liabilities from

NFFBA to DEMNDA would cause one-tenth of this change, or a reduction in beta by 0.1494. For sigma, the difference is $^1/_{10}$ $((-.563) - (.239)) = -.080$. This is interpreted as a reduction in residual standard deviation (sigma) equal to 0.080 (8.0 percent) of average sigma. Of course these computed values are only estimates, but the relatively small standard errors for the coefficients allow us to place some confidence in the results, as being representative of the sample period in which the model was estimated.

The first regression in table 16.6 predicts beta based upon asset proportions. Tax-exempt bonds (MUNIBA) and to a lesser degree consumer loans (CONLNA) are found to be high-beta categories, while investment securities other than tax-exempts (ISECTA) and the trading account (TRDASA) are found to be very low beta, and real estate loans (RELNSA) and commercial loans (COMLNA) are moderately low beta. The standard errors of the estimated coefficients are typically small relative to the estimated magnitudes.

The second regression includes liabilities only. Consumer time deposits other than passbook savings (CONTDA) is a high-beta category, and net federal funds borrowed (NFFBA, the excess of borrowing over lending on the federal funds market) is moderately high beta. Demand deposits (DEMNDA) are relatively low beta. Shareholders' equity (TCAPA) greatly reduces beta, as is to be expected.

The third regression brings in both assets and liabilities. When compared with the two previous regressions, there are no changes in sign among the assets and several changes in sign involving insignificant magnitudes in the liabilities. The stability of coefficients suggests that each group of variables is not an important surrogate for the opposite category.

The final regression uses alternative measures of the portfolio, which rely on net differences between asset and liability groups rather than the separate amounts in the categories. Net consumer lending (NCNLDA), for example, equals consumer lending (CONLNA) plus real estate loans (RELNSA) less passbook savings (SAVEDA) and consumer time (CONTDA). The original reasoning behind the definition of these net activities was that interest rate and liquidity risks of the paired asset and liability categories were similar, so that the net would be a parsimonious measure of exposure. As expected, the loss in explanatory power owing to replacement of asset/liability categories by the nets is relatively small (table 16.10 below). For consumer lending, the net category is bound to be overly simplistic, for it lumps together real estate loans, a very low-beta category, with consumer lending, a relatively high-beta category. It probably would have been better to net consumer lending (CONLNA) against consumer time deposits other than passbook (CONTDA) and to net real estate lending against passbook deposits.

Table 16.7 reports the regressions for sigma. It is interesting to compare these regressions with the beta regressions. The sigma regressions are estimated with substantially greater accuracy: the typical standard error is about one-half as great as for beta. This generally occurs when the same data base is used to estimate systematic risk and residual risk,

Table 16.7   Asset/Liability Descriptor Regressions for Sigma

Descriptor	Assets Only	Liabilities Only	All Asset/ Liability Descriptors	With Net Asset/ Liability Descriptors
Constant	1.399 (.118)	2.043 (.156)	2.163 (.184)	2.104 (.139)
1 NCMLDA				.035 (.116)
2 COMLNA	−.166 (.135)		−.152 (.157)	
3 NCNLDA				.176 (.086)
4 CONLNA	.579 (.181)		.502 (.190)	
5 MUNIBA	−.904 (.323)		−.657 (.334)	−.729 (.329)
6 RELNSA	−.015 (.152)		−.243 (.191)	
7 ISECTA	−.368 (.229)		−.459 (.258)	−.306 (.247)
8 TRDASA	−1.280 (.424)		−1.362 (.449)	−1.356 (.445)
9 CONTDA		.176 (.344)	−.059 (.349)	
10 DEMNDA		−.572 (.117)	−.562 (.118)	−.547 (.094)
11 NFFBA		−.033 (.216)	.239 (.225)	.185 (.225)
12 FORDPA		.121 (.152)	−.115 (.190)	.034 (.168)
13 SAVEDA		−.246 (.377)	−.217 (.388)	
14 TBORA		−.350 (.189)	−.540 (.227)	−.318 (.201)
15 TCAPA		−3.367 (.632)	−2.665 (.661)	−2.439 (.617)
16 TIMEDA		−.150 (.114)	−.116 (.127)	
48 ASSI	−.032 (.010)	−.065 (.013)	−.061 (.014)	−.069 (.013)

Note: The standard error of each coefficient is given in parentheses.

because the data are more informative concerning residual risk (a variance) than concerning systematic risk (a covariance).

Comparison of the asset/liability regressions for the two aspects of risk is also instructive. Equity capital and demand deposits are in both cases the two most risk-reducing liabilities. Conversely, net federal funds borrowing is a major risk-enhancing liability in both. However, two liability categories differently affect beta and sigma: consumer time deposits (CONTDA) and foreign deposits (FORDPA) negligibly affect sigma, but each variable has a substantial estimated effect on beta. Foreign deposits are estimated as reducing beta, as is natural, since the covariance of their profitability with the economy might be expected to be low. Consumer time deposits are the highest-beta liability.

On the asset side, consumer lending (CONLNA) is a high-risk category in both cases; the trading account and investment securities (TRDASA, ISECTA) are the lowest and second or third lowest in risk in the two cases. The risk contributions of municipal bonds (MUNIBA) are opposite in the two cases: municipal bonds are a far higher risk as regards beta and a far lower risk as regards sigma.

The coefficient of asset size (ASSI) remains to be discussed. It is negative and virtually constant in all regressions for sigma and positive and virtually constant in all regressions for beta. The coefficient for beta is quite similar to the simple regression coefficient, but the coefficient for sigma is larger in magnitude than the simple.

Table 16.8 reports regressions including all fundamentals. In addition to those relating to asset and liability proportions and total assets, descriptors of asset ratios and of the operating characteristics and income statement of the bank are added. The coefficients of the first sixteen descriptors are directly comparable with the estimates in tables 16.6 and 16.7. The sign of an estimated effect that is significant in one or the other table never changes as a result of including the other fundamentals. The insensitivity of signs and magnitudes of estimated effects to the added fundamentals is another encouraging indication of low multicollinearity.

A number of descriptors of operating characteristics are significant in the prediction of residual risk, but only one is significant in the prediction of beta. Among the significant descriptors in prediction of residual risk, most signs are plausible: the higher the effective tax rate (ATAX), the lower the residual risk; the greater the ratio of average cash flow to liabilities (FLO1), the lower the residual risk; the greater the payout ratio (PAY1), the lower the residual risk; the greater the earnings variability (VERN), the higher the residual risk; and the greater covariability of earnings with economywide earnings (ABET), the higher the residual risk. However, one effect is puzzling: the greater the apparent probability that fixed charges will not be covered (PNCV), the lower is the predicted residual risk. Obviously, the reverse sign is the one to be expected. The simple regression coefficient was positive and highly significant.

Table 16.8 **Regressions with All Fundamentals, Including Descriptors Dependent upon the Market Valuation of Common Stock**

	Regressions for Beta		Regressions for Sigma	
Descriptor	Selected	All	Selected	All
Constant	−.868	−2.890*	−.915	−1.737*
1 NCMLDA		.0055		−.111
2 COMLNA	−.776**	−.869**		−.381
3 NCNLDA		.123		−.0048
4 CONLNA		−.658		.041
5 MUNIBA		.421	−.810**	−.915*
6 RELNSA	−.382	−.529		−.278
7 ISECTA	−1.080***	−1.426**		−.447
8 TRDASA	−1.234	−1.384	−1.351**	−1.331*
9 CONTDA	.069	.611	−.267*	−.085
10 DEMNDA	−.988***	−.957***	−.229	−.242
11 NFFBA	.963*	1.011*		.227
12 FORDPA		.301	.200	.298
13 SAVEDA		.203		−.285
14 TBORA		1.094		−.105
15 TCAPA		−.258		.333
16 TIMEDA		.799*		.110
17 ATOLB	.012	.025	.028***	.024*
18 BLEV	.159*	.346*	.036	.103
19 DILU	−.600	−.528	.869***	.873***
20 DTOA		−1.101		−.822
21 KMTMN		−.00029		−.00067
22 KMTUS	−.0041*	−.0035		−.00056
23 KPDEP	−.537	−.715	−.472	−.737*
24 RLTLTL	−.021	−.058**	−.0025**	−.023
25 ATAX		.114	−.338*	−.325*
26 FFMKT	−.097	−1.164	−1.031***	−1.157*
27 FLO1	−.028	−.030	−.027**	−.024*
28 FRGNO		2.831		−1.187
29 PAY1	−.499*	−.575	−.340*	−.275
30 PNCV		.183		−.964**
31 SALTOR	.807*	1.160**		.346
32 TRDVRA		−.407		−.171
33 VCAP		.196	−.722**	−.762**
34 VERN		−.140	.383***	.497***
35 VFLO		.068		.132
36 ABET		.280	1.030***	1.173***
37 CUTD	1.592*	1.637*	1.426***	1.318**
38 DELE		.170		.00038
39 DMNE		.097		−.239
40 MRGIN	−.590	−.780	−1.125**	−.858
41 REVENA	−9.233***	−11.011***		−.664
42 ROEQ	1.858*	1.968		.458

Table 16.8 (continued)

	Regressions for Beta		Regressions for Sigma	
Descriptor	Selected	All	Selected	All
43 AGRO		−.241	.367	.090
44 DMS5	.0075*	.088*		−.0070
45 EGRO		.230		.370
46 OFFEX		−.087		−.030
47 RSKLGO		.084		−.015
48 ASSI		−.146	−.177***	−.182***
49 MKTS		.000060	−.000044	−.000036
59 ATOLM		.0055		.0050
60 BBET		−.468		.187
61 BTOP		.047		.073
62 CAPT	.208***	.352***	.138***	.188***
63 DMYL		.250	.554***	.589***
64 ENTP		.061		−.602
65 ETOP	1.464**	.673	−.290	−.846
66 ETP5	−5.359***	−3.769*	−1.056	−1.259
67 LIQU		−.026*	−.012	−.034***
68 MLEV		−.115	.138*	.112
69 ECAP	−.00040***	−.00048***		−.00011
70 PTEQ		.034		.071
71 YILD	3.120**	5.432**	3.089***	3.768**
72 YLD5	−4.941	−6.286*	−2.333	−1.892

Note: Significance levels, as derived from the appropriate F-statistic, are denoted as follows: * 95 percent; ** 99 percent; *** 99.9 percent.

Apparently this variable is interacting with other measures of leverage. Also, the degree of variability in capital structure (VCAP) was expected to be predictive of higher residual risk but, in fact, has a significant negative coefficient. Finally, one significant effect was not clearly predictable from our a priori expectations: the extent of federal funds market making activity (FFMKT) is found to be predictive of lower residual risk. This suggests that an active market-maker can better control its destiny. The reverse sign would have suggested that market-making leads to increased uncertainty, owing to speculative risk from unpredictable short-term movements in the federal funds market.

In prediction for beta, only one of these descriptors of operating characteristics achieves significance. Signs of the effects are typically the same, with the exception of PNCV and VCAP, where the expected positive signs occur, and VERN, where the expected positive sign is contradicted by a small negative coefficient.

Turning next to measures of earning success, the indicator for previous dividend cuts (CUTD) is a highly significant predictor of both higher systematic risk and higher residual risk. Operating margin (MRGIN) is predictive of lower systematic and residual risk. The ratio of operating revenue to total assets (REVENA) is likewise predictive of lower residual and systematic risk. Return on equity (ROEQ) is predictive of higher risk.

No measures of earnings growth are consistently important, though the indicator for an available earnings history is marginally predictive of higher systematic risk with a negligible effect on sigma. Of the two measures of size, only ASSI (asset size) achieves significance. The coefficients are somewhat greater in magnitude than they were in the previous regressions with asset/liability characteristics only, probably because of an interaction with the size of market capitalization descriptor (CAPT), to be discussed below. The coefficient for asset size (ASSI) in prediction of beta has changed sign and lost significance. Again, this is probably the result of interaction with the coefficient for market capitalization.

Finally, we come to measures of financial ratios and other characteristics that are dependent on the market valuation of common stock, taken in conjunction with income-statement and balance-sheet data. Here the nature of the effects must be interpreted with some care. First, the dummy variable for negligible yield (DMYL) is predictive of greater risk, as is to be expected. However, current yield is significantly predictive of higher risk. When this is contrasted with the negative coefficient for the five-year normal yield and for the payout ratio, it may be interpreted as a surrogate for a recent decline in the bank's circumstances. Current yield is defined as the ratio of the previous year's dividends to current price. This ratio is often high relative to the payout ratio, because of a recent pessimistic adjustment in the future prospects of the bank, which causes a reduction in the denominator (price) but is not yet reflected in the numerator (last year's dividends). Thus a high value of current yield, relative to past yield, often indicates that the circumstances of the bank have recently declined and is thus predictive of greater risk.

The same pattern of signs is seen in the earnings/price ratio. The normal earnings/price ratio (ETP5) is predictive of lower risk or, equivalently, a high price/earnings ratio is predictive of higher risk. This is consistent with a general property of growth-oriented firms, which is that the longer the apparent duration of the promised stream of future dividends, the greater is investment risk. The sign of the current earnings/price ratio (ETOP) is also negative for sigma, but it is positive for beta. This last effect can possibly be understood again as indicating that the decline in the present price is reflective of a downward adjustment in future prospects, relative to recent earnings.

Greater liquidity (LIQU) is predictive of lower residual risk and has a smaller effect upon systematic risk. Finally, greater market capitalization (CAPT) is predictive of higher risk. It is important to note here that (*a*) there is a substantial positive correlation (approximately .72 in our sample) between CAPT, the logarithm of market capitalization, and ASSI, the logarithm of total assets; and (*b*) their difference (ASSI − CAPT) is the logarithm of "the market valuation of each dollar of assets." This difference is thus a measure of the manner in which the bank is operated. Consequently, a positive coefficient for CAPT, in conjunction with a negative coefficient for ASSI, suggests that greater expected profitability with a given asset base results in higher risk.

Finally, table 16.9 reports the regression coefficients for the six dummy variables that bring in the regional characteristics of the banks. The regressions show that the typical New York money-center bank is much higher in systematic risk than the norm, but a little bit below normal in residual risk. West Coast banks are next highest in systematic risk and also a little above the norm in residual risk. The southeastern banks are significantly above normal in both the risk measures. All of the earlier regressions, reported in tables 16.6–9, were also run in an alternative mode with regional dummy variables included. Happily, when the fundamental characteristics of banks are included, the regional dummies lose significance: the group as a whole generally lacked statistical significance (by the *F*-test), and when the regional variables were considered singly, only the dummy variable for the southeastern region was usually significant, with a small positive coefficient. Thus most of the regional differences in systematic and residual risk can be attributed to various fundamental characteristics of the banks.

Table 16.10 reports the overall adjusted R^2 statistics for the regressions in the earlier tables. In addition, adjusted R^2s are reported for certain regressions of special interest which incorporate historical risk measures, as well as fundamental descriptors. The first row of the table relates to the assumption that all banks have identical risk levels in each period. R^2 in the predictive regression for beta is .2594, indicating that this proportion of the variance of monthly bank common stock returns can be attributed to a common and identical dependence on the overall market return. R^2

Table 16.9   **Regressions with Only the Regional-Type Dummy Variables**

Descriptor	Beta Prediction Rule	Sigma Prediction Rule
73 DRMNY	.239***	−.035
74 DRMON	.083	.0048
75 DRSE	.135***	.116***
76 DRMW	−.055	−.070**
77 DRSW	.031	.041
78 DRWC	.217***	.095**

Note: Significance levels, as derived from the appropriate *F*-statistic, are denoted as follows: * 95 percent; ** 99 percent; *** 99.9 percent.

Table 16.10   Summary of Adjusted R^2 Statistics

	Regression	
Independent Variables	Beta	Sigma
Constant	.2594	.0887
Historical estimate	.2659	.1052
Historical estimate for beta and Bayesian adjustment thereto	.2675	—
All market price variability descriptors	.2755	.1096
Asset proportions and asset size	.2671	.0929
Liability proportions and asset size	.2673	.0933
All asset/liability proportions and asset size	.2690	.0959
Net asset/liability proportions and asset size	.2685	.0954
Selected fundamentals (including market valuation descriptors)	.2830	.1222
All fundamentals (including market valuation descriptors)	.2829	.1235
All descriptors	.2852	.1321

for the corresponding assumption for the prediction of sigma is .0887, indicating that this proportion of the variance in the average absolute residuals in the pooled cross-section time series can be attributed to month-to-month differences in cross-sectional average residual variability.

The second row refers to the attained R^2 when the only descriptor is the historical estimate of the risk measure (beta and sigma, respectively). Next is the R^2 achieved in prediction of beta, where a Bayesian adjustment term for measurement error in historical beta is included along with the historical beta. The fourth row of the table gives results when all market-price-variability descriptors are incorporated.

The second section of the table gives R^2 for the various regressions including asset/liability descriptors and asset size. The third section reports the regressions including all fundamental variables. The final row reports the regressions including all descriptors.

It is encouraging that the regressions including all fundamentals but no others (i.e., market-price-variability descriptors are omitted) achieve nearly the same R^2 as the regressions that include the market-price-variability descriptors as well. The increase in R^2 from use of all descriptors is .0258 (.2852 − .2594) for beta, and .0434 (.1321 − .0887) for sigma. The prediction rule for beta based on all fundamentals attains 90 percent of this increase, while the prediction rule for sigma attains 80 percent. Thus the measures of the behavior of the stock price in the market add little to our ability to predict its subsequent variability in the market. Moreover, the fundamentals taken alone do substantially better than the market-price-variability descriptors taken alone. Since the market-price-variability descriptors include the natural Bayesian predictions from historical data, this result suggests that the explanatory power of the fundamental descriptors is fairly complete. Otherwise the historical descriptors would serve as surrogates for the omitted fundamental variables and would achieve substantial importance in the prediction of systematic and residual risk. Because of the small significance of the market-price variability descriptors, we chose to save space by omitting the tables referring to these regressions. It is sufficient to note that, in general, inclusion of the market-price-variability descriptors did not importantly affect the signs or significance of the fundamental variables.

The regressions reported thus far are related to the period from March 1969 through June 1977: thirty-three quarters and one partial quarter, or one hundred months. We also had available to us less complete data on a smaller sample of banks for a longer history (forty-five quarters). We divided this longer history into two intervals and fitted separate regressions to each interval to investigate the stability of the coefficients. Tests for significant changes in the structure of coefficients were either insignificant or barely exceeded the 99 percent critical level. This was encouraging in indicating that the structure of the risk relationships has not substantially changed in the recent past.

16.8 Conclusions and Implications

The central conclusion of the study is that systematic and residual risk in banks can be predicted from predetermined fundamental data. Prediction rules estimated in this way can serve a useful function in monitoring bank risk. The predictive significance of fundamental descriptors serves as a measure of the appropriateness of the descriptor as an indicator of risk, and hence as a target for regulation. For example, alternative formulas for capital adequacy can be validated and compared in terms of their predictive content.

The descriptors used in this study were restricted to the limited coverage of the COMPUSTAT data base and Keefe manual. It was not possible to test the various capital-adequacy formulas that are now used, since some data were missing. However, a number of natural descriptors of balance sheet, income statement, and operating variance could be computed. Some of these were found to be indicative of serious bank difficulties, in the sense that they produce substantial outliers when bank circumstances were aberrant. Perhaps more important, after the effect of the outliers was diminished by truncation of extreme values, the transformed descriptors were predictive of differences in risk across the full continuum of banks in the sample.

The fundamental descriptors were rather successful in predicting differences in risk. A large number of descriptors were statistically significant. The historical measures of market-price variability added little to the explanatory power of the fundamentals. The fundamental information, taken as a group, explains more than the market-price-variability data.

Interestingly, the predictors of systematic and residual risk differ importantly. Only three of the ten best simple predictors of beta are also included among the ten best simple predictors of residual risk, and two of these are historical measures of market variability. Among the important simple fundamental predictors of beta are descriptors of size, dividend yield, equity capitalization, and the asset/long-term liability ratio. The most important simple predictors of residual risk are earnings variability, leverage in the capital structure (with common stock valued at book and market), and a measure of accounting beta. In the multiple-regression models, the signs of descriptors are generally the same for prediction of beta and residual risk, but the relative magnitudes are often significantly different.

Several aspects of the results are suggestive. For example, size (best measured by total assets or, alternatively, measured by market share or total value of common stock) is a good single predictor of beta: the larger the size of the bank, the higher the expected systematic risk. However, in the multiple regression models, size is only one among a number of important descriptors and loses its dominant role. Thus, the larger banks are clearly more exposed to systematic risk in the economy, but most causes for this exposure are captured by other descriptors in the model.

It is interesting that net federal funds borrowed (NFFBA) is a predictor of increased risk in regressions for both beta and sigma (statistically significant for beta), but that federal funds market-making activity (FEMKT)—defined as the volume of offsetting borrowing and lending—is predictive of lower risk (significant for sigma). This suggests that measures of risk based on the gross amount of federal funds borrowed are incorrect. Instead, net borrowing, being predictive of higher risk, should be used as an indication of increased leverage.

It is also interesting that the ratio of long-term debt to total assets is predictive of lower risk, confirming that long-term debt is a stabilizing influence that can be regarded as an element of capital. However, from the point of view of variability of the common stock price, senior liabilities constitute a leveraging device that increases investment risk, and it is not surprising that leverage due to senior long-term liabilities, whether measured in terms of the book value of capital (BLEV) or the market value of capital (MLEV), is a good simple predictor of increased risk. In the multiple regressions, BLEV is the more important descriptor. The two measures of leverage that are the best simple predictors of beta are the ratio of total assets to long-term liabilities (ATOLB) and the ratio of risk liabilities to long-term liabilities (RLTLTL). These are also effective simple predictors of residual risk. However, in the multiple regressions, with a number of other highly correlated leverage descriptors present, ATOLB is less significant, and the coefficient of RLTLTL changes sign.

No single descriptor in the model fully captures the profitability of the bank. One can think of profitability as the product of two ingredients: revenue per dollar of assets (REVENA) and operating profit per dollar of revenue (MRGIN). The former is a simple predictor of increased risk, but the sign changes in the multiple regressions for beta and sigma. Operating margin (MRGIN) is consistently a predictor of reduced risk, presumably because the bank's assets are being managed more effectively. The extent of prior dividend cuts (CUTD) is another strong and consistent predictor of increased risk, which amplifies the effect of operating margin.

It is natural, from the point of view of capital asset theory, to assign capital costs for assets and liabilities in relation to the contribution of the item to systematic risk. For this purpose, the adjustments for systematic risk obtained from table 16.6 are the appropriate estimates. For example, the beta coefficients for municipal bonds and for real estate loans differ by $(1.724 - (-.737)) = 2.461$. In a typical bank, after correction for the leverage in the capital structure, the beta of municipal bonds is estimated to be 2.461 greater than for real estate loans. Since the contribution to beta per dollar of assets in municipals significantly exceeds the contribution to beta from real estate loans, the capital cost assessed per dollar of municipal investment should be correspondingly greater. Investment securities other than municipals and trading account securities show up as other low-beta assets. On the liability side, capital accounts, demand deposits, and foreign deposits show as low-beta liabilities, and consumer time deposits and net federal funds borrowed show as high-beta liabilities.

A number of measures of aggressiveness in the bank's growth policy show up as predictive of higher risk, particularly in regard to residual risk. These include the normal payout ratio and normal yield (both indicators of lower retention rates and hence of lower growth), which are predictive of lower risk, and the growth rate of total assets, predictive of higher residual risk.

Having discussed the prediction of differences in risk, we should mention the absolute risk levels in our sample of banks. Natural measures of risk are averages of beta, computed relative to the CRSP RETV index over a sixty-month history, and the average residual standard deviation (sigma) in these regressions. The sample average beta, with each bank weighted by the market value of outstanding common stock (market capitalization), was .71 for the sixty-month period ending in January 1969, and was 1.10 for the sixty-month period ending in January 1977. The equal-weighted average increased similarly, from .63 to .96. For residual risk, defined as the standard deviation of monthly residual returns, the capitalization-weighted average increased from .051 in the early period to .072 in the latter, while the equal-weighted average increased from .054 to .068. These increases signal increased difficulty in bank regulation. Increased systematic risk in the banking system raises the probability of widespread disaster, however small the probability may be, since the aggregate net worth of all banks is more unstable. Increased residual risk is associated with more frequent difficulties for individual banks, independent of the economy as a whole. The prevention of failure has become more difficult, and the insurance liability has grown because of the higher probability that extreme returns will occur as a result of the intrinsic uncertainty in the bank's operations.

Appendix: The Model Used

The Model and Definitions

The following definitions will be used:

$t = 1, \, , T$	the month, varying from 1 to T
$n = 1, \, , N$	the index of the individual bank, varying from 1 to N
$j = 1, \, , J$	the index of an individual descriptor, with J descriptors
$(1 + i_{Ft})$	the riskless return in month t, defined as the four- to six-month prime commercial paper rate at the start of that month
$(1 + i_{Mt})$	the market return in month t. We use the CRSP RETV (value-weighted returns, including dividends)
$(1 + i_{nt})$	the return on security n in that month
r_{Mt}	$= \ln(1 + i_{Mt}) - \ln(1 + i_{Ft})$ the logarithmic excess return for the market index, closely similar to the arithmetic excess return $i_{Mt} - i_{Ft}$.
r_{nt}	$= \ln(1 + i_{nt}) - \ln(1 + i_{Ft})$ the logarithmic excess return relative on security n
x_{jnt}	the value of the jth descriptor for bank n in month t.

In each month t, let the probability distribution of logarithmic return relatives be determined by the model:

$$r_{nt} = \alpha + \beta_{nt} r_{Mt} + e_{nt}, \qquad n = 1, \ldots, N_t$$

with
$$\alpha = \text{overall average excess return, approximately zero}$$
$$\beta_{nt} = \text{systematic risk coefficient of bank } n \text{ in month } t$$
$$e_{nt} = \text{residual return of bank } n \text{ in month } t$$
$$N_t = \text{number of banks in month } t.$$

Let the model for β_{nt} be:

$$\beta_{nt} = b_0 + b_1 x_{1nt} + \ldots + b_J x_{Jnt} ,$$

for all time periods t and banks n, where $b_0, \ldots, b_J$ are the coefficients of the prediction rule for systematic risk. Let

$$E(e_{nt}) = 0, \quad COV(e_{nt}, r_{Mt}) = 0 \text{ for all } t,$$

and let σ_{nt}^2 be the residual variance of e_{nt}. The model for the standard deviation is:

$$\sigma_{nt} = \bar{s}_t \left(s_0 + s_1 x_{1nt} + \ldots + s_J x_{Jnt} \right) ,$$

where $\bar{s}_t$ is the typical cross-sectional standard deviation in month t and $s_0, \ldots, s_J$ are the coefficients of the prediction rule for residual risk.
Define:

$$\delta_{nt} = E(|e_{nt}|), \text{ the mean absolute residual return for security } n \text{ in month } t$$
$$\gamma = \sigma_{nt}/\delta_{nt} . \text{ It may be shown that}$$

$$\gamma = \sqrt{1 + c^2(|x|)} \text{ when } E(x) = 0, \text{ where } c(|x|) \text{ is the coefficient of variation of } |x|.$$

Then the model for residual risk can be rewritten as:

$$\delta_{nt} = \bar{\delta}_t (s_0 + s_1 x_{1nt} + \ldots + s_J x_{Jnt}) ,$$

where $\bar{\delta}_t = \frac{1}{\gamma}(\bar{s}_t)$ is the typical mean absolute residual in month t.

The Estimation Approach

Each regression is run over the pooled sample of all data points n in all months t. The estimation proceeds in two passes: Each pass consists of two forms of regression. The first is a "market-conditional" regression for beta. In pass 1, it takes the form:

(1) $$r_{nt} = \alpha + b_0(r_{Mt}) + b_1(x_{1nt} r_{Mt}) + b_2(x_{2nt} r_{Mt})$$

$$+ \ldots + b_J(x_{Jnt} r_{Mt}) + e_{nt} . \quad n = 1, \ldots, N_t$$

$$t = 1, \ldots, T$$

This regression provides preliminary estimates of the prediction rule for beta, with coefficients $\hat{b}_0, \hat{b}_1, \ldots, \hat{b}_J$. Then, for each bank in each month, a preliminary prediction of beta is computed as:

(2) $$\hat{\beta}_{nt} = \hat{b}_0 + \hat{b}_1 x_{1nt} + \ldots + \hat{b}_J x_{Jnt} .$$

These preliminary predictions for beta are substituted to obtain predictions of residual returns defined as:

(3) $$\hat{e}_{nt} = r_{nt} - \hat{\beta}_{nt} r_{Mt} .$$

The next regression is fitted to estimate residual risk. It takes the form:

(4) $$\frac{|\hat{e}_{nt}|}{\bar{\delta}_t} = s_0 + s_1(x_{1nt}) + s_2(x_{2nt}) + \ldots + s_J(x_{Jnt}) + \varepsilon_{nt} ,$$

(5) where: $$\bar{\delta}_t = \frac{\sum\limits_{n=1}^{N_t} w_{Mnt} |\hat{e}_{nt}|}{\sum\limits_{n=1}^{N_t} w_{Mnt}} ,$$

where w_{Mnt} is the capitalization weight for bank n at time t, equal to the proportion of the market value of all equity in that bank. Thus, $\bar{\delta}_t$ is the capitalization-weighted, cross-sectional average of absolute residual returns. This regression obtains the preliminary prediction rule for relative specific risk, with estimated coefficients $\hat{s}_0, \ldots, \hat{s}_J$.

Pass 2 involves repetition of each of these equations using generalized least squares. To accomplish generalized least squares, each observation is weighted inversely to its disturbance variance. In this model, the disturbance variance is proportional to the variance of the bank's residual return in both regressions! Therefore we compute for each bank n in each month t a prediction of residual risk provided by:

(6) $$\hat{\sigma}_{nt} = \gamma \bar{\delta}_t(\hat{s}_0 + \hat{s}_1 x_{1nt} + \ldots + \hat{s}_J x_{Jnt}) .$$

To avoid extremely small predicted variances, $\hat{\sigma}_{nt}$ is set equal to $(\frac{1}{3})\gamma\bar{\delta}_t$ if the prediction for relative standard deviation is less than $(\frac{1}{3})$; hence the kink in figure 16.2. Then the market-conditional regression for beta is repeated, with observations divided by their predicted residual risk.

Type B Regression

(7) $$\frac{r_{nt}}{\hat{\sigma}_{nt}} = \alpha\left(\frac{1}{\hat{\sigma}_{nt}}\right) + b_0\left(\frac{r_{Mt}}{\hat{\sigma}_{nt}}\right) + \ldots + b_J\left(\frac{x_{Jnt} r_{Mt}}{\hat{\sigma}_{nt}}\right) + e'_{nt} .$$

These weights obtain estimates that are efficient in the statistical sense of maximal accuracy. The intuitive meaning of the weights is best understood by noting that banks with low residual risk are given greater weights than banks with high residual risk, with the weights in proportion to $1/\hat{\sigma}_{nt}^2$. Also, the weights vary over time periods owing to fluctuations in $\bar{\delta}_t$: A cross section with the highest level of residual variance is given about one-sixth the weight of a cross section with a very low level of residual variance. Predictions for systematic risk in tables 16.5, 16.6, 16.8 and 16.9 were obtained from type B regressions.

The fitted betas from the type B regression are used to recompute the estimates of residual returns e_{nt}. With these modified residual returns, the next step is to carry out the second-pass regression for residual risk.

Type R Regression

$$(8) \qquad \frac{|\hat{e}_{nt}|}{\hat{\sigma}_{nt}\hat{\delta}_t} = s_0\left(\frac{1}{\hat{\sigma}_{nt}}\right) + s_1\left(\frac{x_{1nt}}{\hat{\sigma}_{nt}}\right) + \ldots + s_J\left(\frac{x_{Jnt}}{\hat{\sigma}_{nt}}\right) + \varepsilon'_{nt}.$$

Notice that the same weights are used here as in the prediction rule for beta. Predictions for residual risk in tables 16.5, 16.7, 16.8, and 16.9 were obtained from type R regressions.

The rationale behind this estimation approach is derived in detail in Rosenberg and Marathe (1979). The only changes in the present approach, relative to the approach set forth in that paper, are (a) the ignoring of extramarket covariance in the second-pass generalized least-squares regression for beta, and (b) the use of a regression for absolute residual returns rather than for squared residual returns in the type R regressions for residual risk. The first change simplified the computational procedure and will be reconsidered if time permits. The second change was taken in part because, in the presence of the slightly long-tailed distributions of security returns that we find, the use of absolute residual returns should slightly improve statistical efficiency.

References

Aigner, D. J., and Bryan, W. R. 1971. A model of short-run bank behavior. *Quarterly Journal of Economics* 85(1):97–118.

Altman, E. I. 1968. Financial ratios, discriminant analysis, and the prediction of corporate bankruptcy. *Journal of Finance* 23(4):589–609.

———. 1971. *Corporate bankruptcy in America*. Lexington, Mass.: Heath Lexington.

Altman, E. I.; Haldeman, R. G.; and Narayanan, P. 1977. ZETA™ Analysis. *Journal of Banking and Finance* 1(1):24–54.

Anderson, L. C., and Burger, A. E. 1969. Asset management and commercial bank portfolio behavior: Theory and practice. *Journal of Finance* 24(2):207–22.

Anderson, P. E., and Knight, R. E. 1967. Bank loan losses, past and present. *New England Business Review*, May, pp. 2–7.

Arrow, K. J. 1964. The role of securities in the optimal allocation of risk-bearing. *Review of Economic Studies* 31(2):91–96.

Baltensperger, E. 1973. Optimal bank portfolios: The liability side. *Jahrbücher für Nationalökonomie und Statistik* 187(2):147–60.

BANK COMPUSTAT, published June 1977 by Investors Management Sciences, Inc. (a subsidiary of Standard and Poor's Corp.), 7400 South Alton Court, Englewood, Colorado 80110.

Barnett, R. E. 1976a. Deposit insurance. Address before the 82d Annual Convention, Kentucky Bankers Association, Galt House, Louisville, Kentucky, 13 September 1976. Reprinted in *FDIC Annual Report*, 1976, pp. 159–67.

———. 1976b. Six alternatives to the present deposit insurance system. Address before the Nebraska Correspondence Bank Conference, Lincoln, Nebraska, 24 September 1976, Reprinted in *FDIC Annual Report*, 1978, pp. 168–75.

Barnett, R. E.; Horvitz, P. M.; and Silverberg, S. C. 1977. Deposit insurance: The present system and some alternatives. *Banking Law Journal* 45(4): 304–32.

Baumol, W., and Malkiel, B. G. 1967. The firm's optimal debt-equity combination and the cost of capital. *Quarterly Journal of Economics* 81:547–78.

Beaver, W. 1966. Financing ratios and predictors of failure. In *Empirical research in accounting*, pp. 71–111. Chicago: University of Chicago, Institute of Professional Accounting.

———. 1968. Market prices, financial ratios and prediction of failure. *Journal of Accounting Research*. 6(2):179–92.

Beaver, W.; Kettler, P.; and Scholes, M. 1970. The association between market determined and accounting determined risk measures. *Accounting Review* 45:654–82.

Benston, G. J. 1973. Bank examination. *Bulletin of the Graduate School of Business Administration* (New York University), no. 89–90 (May), pp. 3–73.

Benston, G. J., and Marlin, J. T. 1974. Bank examiners' evaluation of credit: An analysis of the usefulness of substandard loan data. *Journal of Money, Credit, and Banking* 6(1):23–44.

Bicksler, J. L., and Samuelson, P. A., eds. 1974. *Investment portfolio decision-making*. Lexington, Mass.: Lexington Books.

Black, F. 1972. Capital market equilibrium with restricted borrowing. *Journal of Business* 44(3):444–55.

Black, F.; Jensen, M.; and Scholes, M. 1972. The capital asset pricing model: Some empirical tests. In *Studies in the theory of capital markets*, ed. M. Jensen. New York: Praeger.

Black, F.; Miller, M. H.; and Posner, R. A. 1978. An approach to the regulation of bank holding companies. *Journal of Business* 51(3):379–412.

Black, F., and Scholes, M. 1973. The pricing of options and corporate liabilities. *Journal of Political Economy* 81(2):637–54.

Blume, M. E. 1971. On the assessment of risk. *Journal of Finance* 26(1):1–10.

Board of Governors of the Federal Reserve System, Press Release, 11 May 1978.

Boquist, J. A.; Racette, G. A.; and Schlarbaum, G. G. 1975. Duration and risk assessment for bonds and common stocks. *Journal of Finance* 30(5): 1360–65.

Bosworth, B., and Duesenberry, J. 1973. A flow of funds model and its implications. *Issues in Federal Debt Management*, Federal Reserve Bank of Boston. no. 10, pp. 39–149.

Bosworth, B., and Duesenberry, J. S. 1975. *Capital needs in the seventies*. Washington, D.C.: Brookings Institution.

Box, G. E. P., and Jenkins, G. M. 1976. *Time series analysis, forecasting and control.* San Francisco: Holden Day.

Bradley, S., and Crane, D. 1975. *Management of bank portfolios.* New York: John Wiley.

Brennan, M. J. 1971. Capital market equilibrium with divergent borrowing and lending rates. *Journal of Financial and Quantitative Analysis* 6(5):1197–1205.

Brick, J. R., and Thompson, H. E. 1978. Time-series analysis of interest rates; Some additional evidence. *Journal of Finance* 33(1):93–103.

Cass, D., and Stiglitz, J. E. 1970. The structure of investor preferences and asset returns, and separability in portfolio allocation: A contribution to the pure theory of mutual funds. *Journal of Economic Theory* 2:122–60.

Chase, S. B., and Mingo, J. J. 1975. The regulation of bank holding companies. *Journal of Finance* 30(2):281–93.

Chipman, J. S. 1973. The ordering of portfolios in terms of mean and variance. *Review of Economic Studies* 40(122):167–90.

Clarke, R. C. 1976. The soundness of financial intermediaries. *Yale Law Journal* 86(1):1–102.

Cohen, K. J. 1970. Improving the capital adequacy formula. *Journal of Bank Research* 1(1):13–16.

Cohen, K. J., and Elton, E. J. 1967. Inter-temporal portfolio analysis based on simulation of joint returns. *Management Science* (Theory) 14(1):5–18.

Cohen, K. J., and Hammer, F. S., eds. 1966. *Analytical methods in banking.* Homewood, Ill.: Irwin.

———. 1967. Linear programming and optimal bank asset management decisions. *Journal of Finance* 22(2):147–68.

Cohen, K. J., and Pogue, J. A. 1967. An empirical evaluation of alternative portfolio selection models. *Journal of Business* 40:166–93.

Cohen, K. J., and Rotenberg, D. P. 1971. Toward a comprehensive framework for bank financial planning. *Journal of Bank Research* 1(4):41–57.

Cohen, K. J. and Thore, S. 1970. Programming bank portfolios under uncertainty. *Journal of Bank Research* 1(1):42–61.

Conte, S. D. 1965. *Elementary numerical analysis.* New York: McGraw Hill.

Cootner, P. 1969. The liquidity of the savings and loan industry. In *Study of the savings and loan industry*, ed. I. Friend. Washington, D.C.: Federal Home Loan Bank Board.

Cootner, P., and Holland, D. 1970. Rate of return and business risk. *Bell Journal of Economics and Management Science* 1(2):211–26.

Cotter, R. V. 1966. Capital ratios and capital adequacy. *National Banking Review* 3(3):333–46.

Cox, J. C.; Ross, G. A.; and Rubenstein, M. 1979. Option pricing: A simplified approach. *Journal of Financial Economics* 7:229–63.

Cramer, R., and Miller, R. 1976. Dynamic modeling of multivariate time series for use in bank analysis. *Journal of Money, Credit and Banking* 8(1):85–96.

Crane, D. B. 1971. A stochastic programming model for commercial bank bond portfolio management. *Journal of Financial and Quantitative Analysis* 6(3):955–76.

Curley, A. J., and Guttentag, J. M. 1974. The yield on insured residential mortgages. *Explorations in Economic Research* (National Bureau of Economic Research) 1(3):114–61.

Daellenbach, H. G., and Archer, S. H. 1969. The optimal bank liquidity: A multiperiod stochastic model. *Journal of Financial and Quantitative Analysis* 4(3):329–43.

Dince, R. R., and Fortson, J. C. 1972. The use of discriminant analysis to predict capital adequacy of commercial banks. *Journal of Bank Research* 3(1): 54–62.

Donaldson, G. 1961. *Corporate debt capacity*. Boston: Harvard University Press.

Dothan, U., and Williams, J. 1980. Banks, bankruptcy and public regulations. *Journal of Banking and Finance* 4(1):65–87.

Durand, D. 1957. *Bank stock prices and the bank capital problem*. Occasional Paper no. 54. New York: National Bureau of Economic Research.

Edmister, R. O. 1972. An empirical test of financial ratio analysis for small business prediction. *Journal of Financial and Quantitative Analysis* 7(2):1477–94.

Edwards, F. R., and Scott, J. H. 1977. Regulating the solvency of depository institutions: A perspective for change. Working Paper, Graduate School of Business, Columbia University.

————. 1979. Regulating the solvency of depository institutions: A perspective for deregulation. In *Issues in financial regulation*, ed. F. R. Edwards. New York: McGraw-Hill.

Fair, R. C., and Jaffee, D. M. 1972. Methods of estimation for markets in disequilibrium. *Econometrica* 42(2):497–514.

Fama, E. 1970. Efficient capital markets: A review of theory and empirical work. *Journal of Finance* 25:383–423.

————. 1971. Risk, return, and equilibrium. *Journal of Political Economy* 79(1):30–55.

————. 1975. Short-term interest rates as predictors of inflation. *American Economic Review* 65(3):269–82.

Fama, E., and Laffer, A. B. 1971. Information and capital markets. *Journal of Business* 44(3):289–98.

Fama, E., and Miller, M. H. 1972. *The theory of finance*. New York: Holt, Rhinehart and Winston.

Fama, E., and Roll, R. 1968. Some properties of symmetric stable distributions. *Journal of the American Statistical Association* 63:817–36.

————. 1971. Parameter estimates for symmetric stable distributions. *Journal of the American Statistical Association* 66(335):331–38.

Farrar, D. E. 1962. *The investment decision under uncertainty*. Englewood Cliffs, N.J.: Prentice-Hall.

Federal Deposit Insurance Corporation. 1976. *Annual Report*.

Federal Deposit Insurance Corporation. 1977. *Annual Report*.

Federal Financial Institutions Examination Council. 1980. Staff study: Capital trends in federally regulated financial institutions.

Federal Reserve Bulletin. Various issues.

Feldstein, M. S. 1969. Mean-variance analysis in the theory of liquidity preference and portfolio selection. *Review of Economic Studies* 36:5–12.

Fisher, L., and Lorie, J. H. 1964. Rates of return on investments in common stocks. *Journal of Business* 37(11):1–21.

Fisher, L., and Weil, R. L. 1971. Coping with the risk of interest rate fluctuations: Returns to bondholders from optimal strategies. *Journal of Business* 44(4):111–18.

Flannery, M. J., and Guttentag, J. M. 1979. Identifying problem banks. *Bank Structure and Competition* (Federal Reserve Bank of Chicago), 3–4 May.

Fraser, D. R., and Rose, P. S. 1973. Short-run bank portfolio behavior: An examination of selected liquid assets. *Journal of Finance* 28(2):531–37.

Fried, J. S. 1970. Bank portfolio selection. *Journal of Financial and Quantitative Analysis* 5(2):203–27.

Friend, I., and Blume, M. 1970. Measurement of portfolio performance under uncertainty. *American Economic Review* 60:561–75.

Gable, L. C. 1974. Bank capital: We are being misled. *Journal of Commercial Bank Lending* 57(4):2–14.

Gibson, W. E. 1971. Deposit insurance in the U.S.: Evaluation and reform. Working Paper no. 71–14. Federal Deposit Insurance Corporation.

Goldfeld, S. M. 1966. *Commercial bank behavior and economic activity*. Amsterdam: North-Holland.

Goldfeld, S. M., and Quandt, R. E. 1965. Some tests for homoscedasticity. *Journal of the American Statistical Association* 60:539–54.

————. 1975. Estimation in a disequilibrium market and the value of information. *Journal of Econometrics* 3(3):325–48.

Goodman, L., and Sharpe, W. 1978. Perspective on bank capital adequacy: A time series analysis. Working Paper 247, National Bureau of Economic Research.

Graham, D. R., and Humphrey, D. B. 1976. Predicting net loan losses using disclosed and undisclosed bank data: A comparison. In *Conference on Bank Structure and Competition*. Chicago, Ill.: Federal Reserve Bank of Chicago.

Granger, C. W. S. 1969. Investigating causal relations by econometric models and cross-spectral methods. *Econometrica* 37(3):424–38.

Granger, C. W. S., and Newbold, P. 1977. *Forecasting economic time series*. New York: Academic Press.

Greenbaum, S. I. 1975. Economic instability and commercial banking. In *Compendium of major issues in bank regulation* ed. Committee on Banking, Housing and Urban Affairs, U.S. Senate, 94th Congr. 1st sess. pp. 281–309.

Grove, M. A. 1974. On "duration" and the optimal maturity structure of the balance sheet. *Bell Journal of Economics and Management Science* 5(2):696–709.

Hakansson, N. H. 1971a. Capital growth and the mean-variance approach to portfolio selection. *Journal of Financial and Quantitative Analysis* 6:517–57.

———. 1971b. Multiperiod mean-variance analysis: Toward a general theory of portfolio choice. *Journal of Finance* 26(4):857–84.

———. 1971c. Optimal entrepreneurial decisions in a completely stochastic environment. *Management Science*, March, pp. 427–49.

Haugen, R. A., and Pappas, J. L. 1971. Equilibrium in the pricing of capital assets, risk-bearing debt instruments, and the question of optimal capital structure. *Journal of Financial and Quantitative Analysis* 6(3):943–53.

Haugh, L. D. 1972. The identification of time series interrelationships with special reference to dynamic regression. Ph.D. diss., University of Wisconsin.

Henderschott, P. H., and Winder, J. P. 1979. Commercial bank asset portfolio behavior in the United States. *Journal of Banking and Finance* 3(2):113–32.

Hester, D., and Pierce, J. 1975. *Bank management and portfolio behavior*. New Haven: Yale University Press.

Hester, D., and Zoellner, J. 1966. The relationship between bank portfolios and earnings: An econometric analysis. *Review of Economics and Statistics* 48(4):372–86.

Hicks, J. R. 1939. *Value and Capital*. London: Oxford University Press.

Hildreth, G., and Lu, J. Y. 1960. Demand relations with autocorrelated disturbances. Technical Bulletin 276. Michigan State University Agricultural Experiment Station.

Hillier, F. S. 1969. The evaluation of risky interrelated investments. In *Studies in mathematical and managerial economics*, vol. 9, ed. H. Theil. Amsterdam: North-Holland.

Hillmer, S. C., and Tiao, G. C. 1977. Likelihood function of stationary multiple autoregressive moving average models. Technical Report. Department of Statistics, University of Wisconsin, Madison.

Hirshleifer, J. 1970. *Investment, interest and capital*. Englewood Cliffs, N.J.: Prentice-Hall.

Hodges, S. 1975. Some thoughts on the pricing of default-free bonds. Working Paper, Research Program in Finance, Institute of Economic Research, University of California, Berkeley.

Hoenig, T., and Spong, K. Examiner loan classifications and their relationship to bank loan charge-offs and economic conditions. Working Paper, Federal Reserve Bank of Kansas City.

Hopewell, M. H., and Kaufman, G. G. 1973. Bond price volatility and term to maturity: a generalized respecification. *American Economic Review* 63(4):749–53.

Horvitz, P. J. 1975. Failures of large banks: Implications for banking supervision and deposit insurance. *Journal of Financial and Quantitative Analysis* 10(4):589–601.

Hsiao, Cheng. 1977. Money and income causality detection. Working Paper 167, National Bureau of Economic Research.

Hunt, L. H. 1976. *Dynamics of forecasting financial cycles*. Greenwich, Conn.: JAI Press.

Jaffee, D. M. 1971. *Credit rationing and the commercial loan market*. New York: John Wiley.

Jensen, M. C. 1969. Risk, the pricing of capital assets, and the evaluation of investment portfolios. *Journal of Business* 42:167–247.

———. 1972. Capital markets: Theory and evidence. *Bell Journal of Economics and Management Science* 2:357–98.

———, ed. 1972. *Studies in the theory of capital markets*. New York: Praeger.

Johnson, C. G. 1970. Ratio analysis and the prediction of firm failure. *Journal of Finance* 25(5):1166–68.

Kaiser, H. F. 1960. The application of electronic computers to factor analysis. *Educational and Psychological Measurement* 20:141–51.

Kane, E. J. 1975. Direct cross-section tests of alternative term-structure theories. Working Paper, College of Administrative Science, Ohio State University.

———. 1978. The three faces of commercial bank liability management. Working Paper Series 78-66, College of Administrative Science, Ohio State University.

Karaken, J. H., and Wallace, N. 1977. Deposit insurance and bank regulation: A partial equilibrium exposition. Staff Report no. 15, Research Department, Federal Reserve Bank of Minneapolis.

Kaufman, G. 1975. Preventing bank failures. In *Compendium on major issues in bank regulation*, ed. Committee on Banking, Housing, and Urban Affairs, U.S. Senate 94th Congr., 1st sess.

Keefe Bank Stock Manual. 1970–75. New York: Keefe, Bruyette and Woods.

Kessel, R. 1965. *The cyclical behavior of the term structure of interest rates.* Occasional Paper no. 91. New York: National Bureau of Economic Research.

King, B. F. 1966. Market and industry factors in stock price behavior. *Journal of Business* 39:139–91.

Klein, M. A. 1970. Imperfect asset elasticity and portfolio theory. *American Economic Review* 60(3):491–94.

———. 1971. A theory of the banking firm. *Journal of Money, Credit, and Banking* 3(2):205–18.

Kraus, A., and Litzenberger, R. H. 1973. A state-preference model of optimal and financial leverage. *Journal of Finance* 28(4):911–22.

Kreps, C. H., and Wacht, R. F. 1971. A more constructive role for deposit insurance. *Journal of Finance* 26(2):605–14.

Lanstein, R., and Sharpe, W. F. 1978. Duration and security risk. Research Paper no. 451, Graduate School of Business, Stanford University.

Lemke, K. W. 1970. The evaluation of liquidity: An analytical study. *Journal of Accounting Research* 8(1):47–77.

Lintner, J. 1965a. Security prices, risks, and maximal gains from diversification. *Journal of Finance* 20:587–615.

———. 1965b. The valuation of risk assets and the selection of risky investments in stock portfolios and capital budgets. *Review of Economics and Statistics* 47:13–37.

———. 1975. Presidential address. Inflation and security returns. *Journal of Finance* 30(2):259–80.

Macaulay, F. R. 1938. *Some theoretical problems suggested by the movements of interest rates, bond yields, and stock prices in the United States since 1856.* National Bureau of Economic Research, General Series no. 33. New York: Columbia University Press.

McCulloch, J. H. 1971. Measuring the term structure of interest rates. *Journal of Business* 44(1):19–31.

———. 1975a. The tax-adjusted yield curve. *Journal of Finance* 30(3):811–30.

———. 1975b. An estimate of the liquidity premium. *Journal of Political Economy* 83(1):95–119.

———. 1978a. Continuous time processes with stable increments. *Journal of Business* 51(4):601–19.

———. 1978b. The pricing of short-lived options when price uncertainty is log-symmetric stable. Working Paper no. 264, National Bureau of Economic Research.

————. 1980. The ban on indexed bonds, 1933–77. *American Economic Review* 70:1018–21.

Maisel, S. J. 1973. *Managing the dollar*. New York: W. W. Norton.

Mandelbrot, B. 1963. The variation of certain speculative prices. *Journal of Business* 36(4):394–419.

Markowitz, H. M. 1971. *Portfolio selection: Efficient diversification of investments*. New York: Wiley (1st ed. 1959).

Martin, D. 1977. Early warning of bank failure: A logit regression approach. *Journal of Banking and Finance* 1:249–76.

Mayer, T. 1965. A graduated deposit insurance plan. *Review of Economics and statistics* 47(1):114–16.

————. 1975. Preventing the failure of large banks. In *Compendium on major issues in bank regulation, 1975*, ed. Committee on Banking, Housing, and Urban Affairs, U.S. Senate, 94th Congr., 1st Sess.

Mayne, L. S. 1972. Supervisory influence on bank capital. *Journal of Finance* 27(3):637–51.

————. 1973. The deposit reserve requirement recommendations of the Commission on Financial Structure and Regulation: An analysis and critique. *Journal of Bank Research* 4(1):41–51.

Mehta, D. R.; Eisemann, P. C.; Moses, E. A; and Deschamps, B. 1979. Capital structure and capital adequacy of bank holding companies. *Journal of Banking and Finance.* 3(1):5–22.

Meltzer, A. H. 1967. Major issues in the regulation of financial institutions. *Journal of Political Economy* 75(4):482–500.

Merton, R. C. 1971. Optimum consumption and portfolio rules in a continuous-time model. *Journal of Economic Theory* 3:373–413.

————. 1973. An intertemporal capital asset pricing model. *Econometrica* 41(5):867–87.

————. 1974. On the pricing of corporate debt: The risk structure of interest rates. *Journal of Finance* 29(2):449–70.

————. 1977a. An analytic derivation of the cost of deposit insurance and loan guarantees: An application of modern option pricing theory. *Journal of Banking and Finance* 1(1):3–11.

————. 1977b. *On the cost of deposit insurance when there are surveillance costs.* Working Paper, Massachusetts Institute of Technology.

————. 1979. Discussion. In *The regulation of financial institutions*. Boston: Federal Reserve Bank of Boston.

Meyer, P. A., and Pifer, H. W. 1970. Prediction of bank failures. *Journal of Finance* 25(4):853–68.

Modigliani, F., and Miller, M. H. 1958. The cost of capital, corporation finance, and the theory of investment. *American Economic Review* 48:261–97.

Modigliani, F., and Shiller, R. J. 1973. Inflation, rational expectations and the term structure of interest rates. *Economica* 40(157):12–43.

Morrison, G. R. 1967. *Liquidity preferences of commercial banks*. Chicago: University of Chicago Press.

Morrison, J. 1977. Interest rate risk in commercial banking: Some implications for capital adequacy. Dissertation, Graduate Division, University of California, Berkeley.

Mossin, J. 1966. Equilibrium in a capital asset market. *Econometrica* 34:768–83.

———. 1969. Security pricing and investment criteria in competitive markets. *American Economic Review* 59(5):749–56.

Murphy, N. B., and Weintrob, H. 1970. Evaluating liquidity under conditions of uncertainty in mutual savings banks. *Journal of Financial and Quantitative Analysis* 4(5):559–68.

Nadauld, S. 1977. The interest rate elasticity of networth in savings institutions. Ph.D. diss., University of California, Berkeley.

Nelson, C. R. 1972. *The term structure of interest rates*. New York: Basic Books.

Nelson, C. R., and Schwert, G. W. 1977. On testing the hypothesis that the real rate of interest is constant. *American Economic Review* 67(3):478–86.

Orgler, Y. E., and Wolkowitz, B. 1976. *Bank Capital*. New York: Van Nostrand Reinhold.

Peltzman, S. 1968. Bank stock prices and the effects of regulation of the banking structure. *Journal of Business* 41(4):413–30.

———. 1970. Capital investment in commercial banking and its relationship to portfolio regulation. *Journal of Political Economy* 78(1):1–26.

———. 1972. The costs of competition: An appraisal of the Hunt Commission report. *Journal of Money, Credit, and Banking* 4:1001–4.

Pendyck, R., and Rubinfeld, D. 1976. *Econometric models and economic forecasts*. New York: McGraw-Hill.

Phillips, L., and Pippenger, J. 1976. Preferred habitat vs. efficient market: A test of alternative hypotheses. *Federal Reserve Bank of St. Louis Review* 58 (May):11–19.

Pierce, D. A. 1977. Relationships—and the lack thereof—between economic time series, with special reference to money, reserves, and interest rates. *Journal of the American Statistical Association* 72(357):11–26.

Pierce, J. L. 1967. An empirical model of commercial bank portfolio management. In *Studies in portfolio behavior*, ed. D. D. Hester and J. Tobin. New York: Wiley.

Pogue, C. A. 1970. An extension of the Markowitz portfolio selection model to include variable transactions' costs, short sales, leverage policies, and taxes. *Journal of Finance* 25(5):1005–28.

Pogue, T. F., and Soldofsky, R. M. 1969/70. What's in a bond rating? *Journal of Financial and Quantitative Analysis* 4:201–28.

Pringle, J. J. 1974*a*. The capital decision in commercial banks. *Journal of Finance* 29(3):779–95.

———. 1974*b*. The imperfect-markets model of commercial bank financial management. *Journal of Financial and Quantitative Analysis* 9(1):131–36.

Pyle, D. H. 1968. On the theory of financial intermediation. Ph.D. diss., Massachusetts Institute of Technology.

———. 1971. On the theory of financial intermediation. *Journal of Finance* 26(3):737–49.

Ramaswamy, K. 1978. The loan operations of financial intermediaries and the valuation of secondary financial claims. Ph.D. diss., Stanford University.

Robinson, R. I., and Pettway, R. H. 1967. *Policies for optimum bank capital: A study prepared for the trustees of the banking research fund.* Chicago: Association of Reserve City Banks.

Robinson, R. S. 1973. BANKMOD: An interactive simulation aid for bank financial planning. *Journal of Bank Research* 4(3):212–24.

Roll, R. 1970. *The behavior of interest rates: Application of the efficient market model to United States Treasury bill rates.* New York: Basic Books.

———. 1971. Investment diversification and bond maturity. *Journal of Finance* 26(1):51–66.

Rosenberg, B. 1974. Extra-market components of covariance among security prices—I. *Journal of Financial and Quantitative Analysis* 9:263–74.

Rosenberg, B., and Guy, J. 1975. The prediction of systematic risk, Research Program in Finance, no. 33, Graduate School of Business Administration, University of California, Berkeley.

Rosenberg, B.; Houglet, M.; Marathe, V.; and McKibben, W. 1973. Extra-market components of convariance among security prices—II. Presented at the Western Finance Association Meetings, August. (Under revision.)

Rosenberg, B., and McKibben, W. 1973. The prediction of systematic and specific risk in common stocks. *Journal of Financial and Quantitative Analysis* 8:317–33.

Rosenberg, B., and Marathe, V. 1975. The prediction of investment risk: Systematic and residual risk. In *Proceedings of the Seminar on the Analysis of Security Prices*, pp. 85–225. Chicago: University of Chicago.

———. 1979. Tests of capital asset pricing hypotheses. In *Research in finance*, ed. Haim Levy, 1:115–223. Greenwich, Conn.: JAI Press.

Rosenberg, B., and Perry, P. R. 1978. The fundamental determinants of risk in banking. Working Paper no. 265, National Bureau of Economic Research.

Ross, S. A. 1977. The determination of financial structure: The incentive-signalling approach. *Bell Journal of Economics* 8(1):23–40.

Rothschild, M., and Stiglitz, J. E. 1970. Increasing risk: 1. A definition. *Journal of Economic Theory* 2(3):225–43.

Rubinstein, M. E. 1973*a*. A mean-variance synthesis of corporate financial theory. *Journal of Finance* 28(1):167–82.

———. 1973*b*. Corporate financial policy in segmented securities markets. *Journal of Financial and Quantitative Analysis* 8(5):749–61.

———. 1975. The valuation of uncertain income streams and the pricing of options. Research Program in Finance, Working Paper no. 37, Berkeley Institute of Business and Economic Research, University of California.

Russell, W. R. 1964. Commercial bank portfolio adjustments. *American Economic Review* 54(2):544–53.

Salomon Brothers. 1974. *An analytical record of yields and yield spreads*. New York: Salomon Brothers.

Samuelson, P. A. 1945. The effect of interest rate increases on the banking system. *American Economic Review* 35(1):16–27.

———. 1970. The fundamental approximation theorem of portfolio analysis in terms of means, variances, and higher moments. *Review of Economic Studies* 37:537–42.

———. 1972. Proof that properly anticipated prices fluctuate randomly. In *Collected scientific papers of Paul A. Samuelson*, ed. R. C. Merton. Cambridge: MIT Press.

Samuelson, P. A., and Merton, R. C. 1974. Generalized mean-variance tradeoffs for best perturbation corrections to approximate portfolio decisions. *Journal of Finance* 29(1):27–40.

Santomero, A. M., and Watson, R. D. 1977. Determining an optimal capital standard for the banking industry. *Journal of Finance* 32(4):1267–81.

Sargent, T. J. 1972. Rational expectations and the term structure of interest rates. *Journal of Money, Credit and Banking* 4(1), part 1:74–97.

———. 1978. A note on maximum likelihood estimation of the rational expectations model of the term structure. Working Paper, University of Minnesota.

Scott, K. E., and Mayer, T. 1971. Risk and regulation in banking: Some proposals for FDIC reform. *Stanford Law Review* 23:857–902.

Sharpe, W. F. 1963. A simplified model for portfolio analysis. *Management Science* 9:277–93.

————. 1964. Capital asset prices: A theory of market equilibrium under conditions of risk. *Journal of Finance* 19(3):325–442.

————. 1966. Mutual fund performance. *Journal of Business* 39(2):119–38.

————. 1970. *Portfolio theory and capital markets*. New York: McGraw-Hill.

————. 1977. Bank capital adequacy, deposit insurance and security values (part I). Working Paper no. 209, National Bureau of Economic Research.

Sherman, L. F. 1977. Measurement of banking risk and capital adequacy: A linear structural relations approach. M.S. thesis, University of Illinois at Urbana-Champaign.

Shiller, R. J. 1973. Rational expectations and the term structure of interest rates. *Journal of Money, Credit and Banking* 5(3):856–60.

Shoven, J. B., and Bulow, J. I. 1978. The bankruptcy decision. Discussion Paper no. 16, Inflation Workshop, Department of Economics, Stanford University.

Silverberg, S. C. 1973. Deposit costs and bank portfolio policy. *Journal of Finance* 28(4):881–96.

Sims, C. A. 1972. Money, income and causality. *American Economic Review* 62(4):540–52.

————. 1977. Exogeneity and causal ordering in macroeconomic models. In *New methods in business cycle research: Proceedings from a conference*, ed. C. A. Sims. Minneapolis: Federal Reserve Bank of Minneapolis.

Sinkey, J. F. 1975. A multivariate statistical analysis of the characteristics of problem banks. *Journal of Finance* 30(1):21–36.

————. 1981. A comparative analysis of the portfolio and performance operations of problem commercial banks. FDIC Working Paper, forthcoming.

Skelton, J. 1978. A model of tax effects in coupon bonds. Mimeographed. Graduate School of Business, University of Chicago.

Smith, J. E. 1974. Assessing the capital needs of banking. *Journal of Commercial Bank Lending* 56(5):14–21.

Smith, K. V. 1968. Alternative procedures for revising investment portfolios. *Journal of Financial and Quantitative Analysis* 3:371–403.

Smith, K. V., and Tito, D. A. 1969. Risk-return measures of ex post portfolio performance. *Journal of Financial and Quantitative Analysis* 4:449–70.

Spong, K., and Hoenig, T. 1978. Bank examiner classifications and loan risk. Working Paper, Federal Reserve Bank of Kansas City.

Stiglitz, J. E. 1970. A consumption-oriented theory of the demand for financial assets and the term structure of interest rates. *Review of Economic Studies* 37:321–51.

————. 1974. On the irrelevance of corporate financial policy. *American Economic Review* 64(6):851–66.

Tinsley, P. A. 1970. Capital structure, precautionary balance, and the valuation of the firm: The problem of financial risk. *Journal of Financial and Quantitative Analysis* 5(1):33–62.

Tobin, J. 1958. Liquidity preference as behavior towards risk. *Review of Economic Studies* 25:65–86.

Treynor, J. L. 1965. How to rate management of investment funds. *Harvard Business Review* 43 January/February: 63–75.

Treynor, J. L., and Black, F. 1973. How to use security analysis to improve portfolio selection. *Journal of Business* 46(1):66–86.

Tussing, A. D. 1967. The case for bank failure. *Journal of Law and Economics* 10:129–47.

————. 1970. Meaningful bank failure: A proposal. *Journal of Industrial Economics* 18(3):242–54.

Tuttle, D. L., and Litzenberger, R. H. 1968. Leverage, diversification and capital market effects on a risk-adjusted capital budgeting framework. *Journal of Finance* 23(3):427–43.

United States Code, Title Twelve.

United States House of Representatives. 1975. *Hearings before the Subcommittee on Financial Institutions Supervision, Regulation and Insurance of the Committee on Banking, Currency and Housing on H.R. 8024 Part 2*, 94th Congr., 1st Sess., Washington, D.C.: U.S. Government Printing Office.

United States Senate Committee on Banking, Housing and Urban Affairs. 1975. *Compendium of Major Issues in Bank Regulation.* 94th Congr. 1st Sess., Washington, D.C.: U.S. Government Printing Office.

United States Treasury. *Bulletin.* various issues.

Van Horne, J. J. 1977. *Fundamentals of financial management.* 3d ed. Englewood Cliffs, N.J.: Prentice-Hall.

Vasicek, O. A. 1973. A note on using cross-sectional information in Bayesian estimation of security betas. *Journal of Finance* 28:1233–39.

————. 1976. The term structure of interest rates. Working Paper. Wells Fargo Bank, San Francisco.

————. 1977. Liquidity premia and market implicit forecasts. Mimeographed. Wells Fargo Bank.

Vojta, G. J. 1973. *Bank capital adequacy.* New York: First National City Bank.

Wall, K. D. 1976. FIML estimation of rational distributed lag structural form models. *Annals of Social and Economic Measurement* 5(1):53–63.

Wallich, H. C. 1975. The foundations of lasting recovery. Federal Reserve press release, 6 May.

Weaver, A. S., and Herzig-Marx, Chayim. 1978. A comparative study of the effect of leverage on risk premiums for debt issues of banks and bank holding companies. Staff Memoranda, Federal Reserve Bank of Chicago, Research Paper no. 78–1.

Weil, R. L. 1973. Macauley's duration: An appreciation. *Journal of Business* 46(4):589–92.

White, J. J. 1976a. *Teaching materials on banking law*. St. Paul, Minn.: West Publishing Company, pp. 715–911.

————.1976b. *Statutory supplement to teaching materials on banking law*. St. Paul, Minn.: West Publishing Company.

Wold, H. 1948. On prediction in stationary time series. *Annals of Mathematical Statistics* 19:558–67.

Woodworth, G. W. 1967. *The management of cyclical liquidity of commercial banks*. Boston: Bankers Publishing.

Wu, H.-K. 1972. Bank examiner criticism, bank loan defaults, and bank loan quality. *Journal of Finance* 25(4):637–51.

————. 1977. Effectiveness of bank examiners' loan criticism: Some new evidence. Comptroller of the Currency Research Paper no. 77-5.

Yawitz. J. W.; Hempel, G. H.; and Marshall, W. J. 1975. Average maturity as a risk proxy in investment decisions. *Journal of Finance* 30(2):325–33.

Zellner, A. 1962. An efficient method of estimating seemingly unrelated regressions and tests for aggregation bias. *Journal of the American Statistical Association* 5:348–68.

Contributors

Roger Craine
Department of Economics
275 Barrows Hall
University of California at Berkeley
Berkeley, California 94720

Lawrence P. Golen
P.O. Box 4412
Berkeley, California 94704

Laurie Goodman
Federal Reserve Bank of New York
Nassau and Maiden Lane
New York, New York 10045

Robert Jacobson
Federal Reserve Bank of San
   Francisco
400 Sansome Street
San Francisco, California 94111

David Lane
School of Business Administration
   and Economics
California State University at
   Northridge
Northridge, California 91330

Sherman Maisel
School of Business Administration
350 Barrows Hall
University of California at Berkeley
Berkeley, California 94720

J. Huston McCulloch
Department of Economics
Ohio State University
Columbus, Ohio 43210

Jay Morrison
Wells Fargo Bank
464 California Street
San Francisco, California 94104

Stephen Nadauld
School of Management
Brigham Young University
Provo, Utah 84602

Phillip Perry
School of Management
State University of New York at
   Buffalo
Buffalo, New York 14214

James Pierce
Department of Economics
275 Barrows Hall
University of California at Berkeley
Berkeley, California 94720

David Pyle
School of Business Administration
350 Barrows Hall
University of California at Berkeley
Berkeley, California 94720

Barr Rosenberg
School of Business Administration
350 Barrows Hall
University of California at Berkeley
Berkeley, California 94720

William Sharpe
Graduate School of Business
Stanford University
Stanford, California 94305

Author Index

Subject Index

ABC form, Federal Reserve, 150, 177
Acceptances, and net earnings assets, 106
Accord, Federal Reserve–Treasury, 230, 232
Activities: breakdown, in capital adequacy measurement, 42–43; value of, 27–28
Agressiveness, and risk, 403
American Bank and Trust of Orangeburg, South Carolina, 159
Amortized loans, price movements, 229–41
Arbitrage: and leverage, 44, 104, 110, 111; and simplifying assumptions of risk models, 66, 67, 68
Assets: and bank size, 72, 78, 168; depreciation, and interest rates, 170; descriptors for, 390–401; economic value, 37–38; First Pennsylvania Bank, 128, fixed, investment in, 113–14, 116; foreign, 4, 106–7; growth rate, descriptor for, 390; liquidation value, 156; loan losses as percentage, 88; mergers, value in, 156; net earnings, defined, 106; operating expenses as percentage, 87–88; revenue per dollar, descriptor for, 403; size, coefficient of, descriptor for, 390, 392, 395, 398, 399, 402; total, 106; total, ratio to long-term liabilities, descriptor for, 390; variations among banks, and interest rate risk, 78, 81–82. See also Capital/asset ratios
Assets, return on: book values, and costs, 204–13; distributions, 24, 27–29; excess, 70–71; total, 213–17, 219–20; and value-preserving spreads, 200–201

Autoregressive integrated moving average (ARIMA), 354, 355, 356–57, 365
Autoregressive moving average (ARMA), 251; forecasts, 263–70; models, 256, 257–70; single-series models, 273; vector model, 274

Balance sheet, current, and risk descriptors, 378
Bank examinations, 92, 116, 138, 143, 173, 174, 175; and bank size, 168–69; and capital/asset ratios, 108; early warning systems, 150–51; efficacy of, 144–51; and insurance terms, 176; rating system, 146–47; and stable distributions of asset values, 228; and unexpected events, 26, 48–49, 145, 168–69; value of, 76. See also Regulation
Bank failures, 3, 140, 141, 246; and capital adequacy, 236–37; Federal Reserve predictions, 151; and mergers, 155; and uninsured depositors, 36. See also Insolvency
Bank holding companies, 3, 4, 107, 150
Bank of the Commonwealth of Detroit, 159, 160
Bank Operating Statistics (Federal Reserve System), 221
Bank runs, 6, 157, 169
Bankruptcy: costs, 23, 66, 68, 110–11; delay in declaring, 22, 23, 152, 158–59, 169, 176. See also Deposit payoffs; Insolvency; Mergers